Exam 70-549: *Designing and Developing Enterprise Applications Using the Microsoft .NET Framework*

Objective	Location in Book
Envisioning and Designing an Application	
Evaluate the technical feasibility of an application.	
■ Evaluate the proof of concept.	Chapter 1, Lesson 1
■ Recommend the best technologies for the features and goals of the application. Considerations include Message Queuing, Web services, .NET Framework remoting, and so on.	Chapter 1, Lesson 1
■ Weigh implementation considerations.	Chapter 1, Lesson 2
■ Investigate existing solutions for similar business problems.	Chapter 1, Lesson 2
Evaluate the technical specifications for an application to ensure that the business requirements are met.	
■ Translate the functional specification into developer terminology, such as pseudo code and UML diagrams.	Chapter 2, Lessons 1, 2
■ Suggest component type and layer.	Chapter 2, Lesson 1
Evaluate the design of a database.	
■ Recommend a database schema.	Chapter 4, Lesson 1
■ Identify the stored procedures that are required for an application.	Chapter 4, Lesson 1
Evaluate the logical design of an application.	
■ Evaluate the logical design for performance.	Chapter 3, Lesson 1
■ Evaluate the logical design for maintainability.	Chapter 3, Lesson 1
■ Evaluate the logical design for extensibility.	Chapter 3, Lesson 1
■ Evaluate the logical design for scalability.	Chapter 3, Lesson 1
■ Evaluate the logical design for availability.	Chapter 3, Lesson 1
■ Evaluate the logical design for security.	Chapter 3, Lesson 1
■ Evaluate the logical design against use cases.	Chapter 3, Lesson 1
■ Evaluate the logical design for recoverability.	Chapter 3, Lesson 1
■ Evaluate the logical design for data integrity.	Chapter 3, Lesson 1
Evaluate the physical design of an application. Considerations include the design of the project structure, the number of files, the number of assemblies, and the location of these resources on the server.	
■ Evaluate the physical design for performance.	Chapter 3, Lesson 2
■ Evaluate the physical design for maintainability.	Chapter 3, Lesson 2
■ Evaluate how the physical location of files affects the extensibility of the application.	Chapter 3, Lesson 2
■ Evaluate the physical design for scalability.	Chapter 3, Lesson 2
■ Evaluate the physical design for availability.	Chapter 3, Lesson 2
■ Evaluate the physical design for security.	Chapter 3, Lesson 2
■ Evaluate the physical design for recoverability.	Chapter 3, Lesson 2
■ Evaluate the physical design for data integrity.	Chapter 3, Lesson 2

Objective	Location in Book
Designing and Developing a Component	
Establish the required characteristics of a component.	
■ Decide when to create a single component or multiple components.	Chapter 4, Lesson 1
■ Decide in which tier of the application a component should be located.	Chapter 4, Lesson 1
■ Decide which type of object to build.	Chapter 4, Lesson 1
Create the high-level design of a component.	
■ Establish the life cycle of a component.	Chapter 4, Lesson 1
■ Decide whether to use established design patterns for the component.	Chapter 4, Lesson 1
■ Decide whether to create a prototype for the component.	Chapter 4, Lesson 1
■ Document the design of a component by using pseudo code, class diagrams, sequence diagrams, activity diagrams, and state diagrams.	Chapter 4, Lesson 1
■ Evaluate tradeoff decisions. Considerations include security vs. performance, performance vs. maintainability, and so on.	Chapter 4, Lesson 1
Develop the public API of the component.	
■ Decide the types of clients that can consume a component.	Chapter 4, Lesson 2
■ Establish the required component interfaces.	Chapter 4, Lesson 2
■ Decide whether to require constructor input.	Chapter 4, Lesson 2
Develop the features of a component.	
■ Decide whether existing functionality can be implemented or inherited.	Chapter 5, Lesson 1
■ Decide how to handle unmanaged and managed resources.	Chapter 5, Lesson 1
■ Decide which extensibility features are required.	Chapter 5, Lesson 1
■ Decide whether a component must be stateful or stateless.	Chapter 5, Lesson 1
■ Decide whether a component must be multithreaded.	Chapter 5, Lesson 1
■ Decide which functions to implement in the base class, abstract class, or sealed class.	Chapter 5, Lesson 1
Develop a component feedback mechanism.	
■ Develop a component status feedback technique.	Chapter 5, Lesson 1
■ Develop an exception handling mechanism.	Chapter 5, Lesson 1
Develop the data access and data handling features of a component.	
■ Analyze data relationships.	Chapter 5, Lesson 2
■ Analyze the data handling requirements of a component.	Chapter 5, Lesson 2
Develop a component to include profiling requirements.	
■ Identify potential issues, such as resource leaks and performance gaps, by profiling a component.	Chapter 5, Lesson 1

Objective	Location in Book
■ Decide when to stop profiling on a component.	Chapter 5, Lesson 1
■ Decide whether to redesign a component after analyzing the profiling results.	Chapter 5, Lesson 1

Choose an appropriate mechanism to deliver multimedia data across distributed applications by using Web services and Message Queuing.

Objective	Location in Book
■ Evaluate available multimedia delivery mechanisms. Considerations include bandwidth problems, file formats, and sending large attachments.	Chapter 6, Lesson 2
■ Design a multimedia delivery mechanism.	Chapter 6, Lesson 1

Designing and Developing an Application Framework

Consume a reusable software component.

Objective	Location in Book
■ Identify a reusable software component from available components to meet the requirements.	Chapter 7, Lesson 1
■ Identify whether the reusable software component needs to be extended.	Chapter 7, Lesson 2
■ Identify whether the reusable software component needs to be wrapped.	Chapter 7, Lesson 2
■ Identify whether any existing functionality needs to be hidden.	Chapter 7, Lesson 2
■ Test the identified component based on the requirements.	Chapter 7, Lessons 1, 2

Choose an appropriate implementation approach for the application design logic.

Objective	Location in Book
■ Choose an appropriate data storage mechanism.	Chapter 8, Lesson 3
■ Choose an appropriate data flow structure.	Chapter 8, Lesson 2
■ Choose an appropriate decision flow structure.	Chapter 8, Lesson 3
■ Choose an appropriate state management technique.	Chapter 8, Lesson 4
■ Choose an appropriate security implementation.	Chapter 8, Lesson 6

Choose an appropriate event logging method for the application.

Objective	Location in Book
■ Decide whether to log data. Considerations include policies, security, requirements, and debugging.	Chapter 9, Lesson 1
■ Choose a storage mechanism for logged events. For example, database, flat file, event log, or XML file.	Chapter 9, Lesson 1
■ Choose a systemwide event logging method. For example, centralized logging, distributed logging, and so on.	Chapter 9, Lesson 1
■ Decide logging levels based upon severity and priority.	Chapter 9, Lesson 1

Monitor specific characteristics or aspects of an application.

Objective	Location in Book
■ Decide whether to monitor data. Considerations include administration, auditing, and application support.	Chapter 9, Lesson 2
■ Decide which characteristics to monitor. For example, application performance, memory consumption, security auditing, usability metrics, and possible bugs.	Chapter 9, Lesson 2
■ Choose event monitoring mechanisms, such as System Monitor and logs.	Chapter 9, Lesson 2
■ Decide monitoring levels based on requirements.	Chapter 9, Lesson 2

Objective	Location in Book
■ Choose a systemwide monitoring method from the available monitoring mechanisms.	Chapter 9, Lesson 2

Testing and Stabilizing an Application

Perform a code review.

Evaluate the testing strategy.

Objective	Location in Book
■ Create the unit testing strategy.	Chapter 10, Lesson 1
■ Evaluate the integration testing strategy.	Chapter 10, Lesson 2
■ Evaluate the stress testing strategy.	Chapter 10, Lesson 2
■ Evaluate the performance testing strategy.	Chapter 10, Lesson 2
■ Evaluate the test environment specification.	Chapter 10, Lesson 3

Design a unit test.

Objective	Location in Book
■ Describe the testing scenarios.	Chapter 11, Lesson 1
■ Decide coverage requirements.	Chapter 11, Lesson 2
■ Evaluate when to use boundary condition testing.	Chapter 11, Lesson 2
■ Decide the type of assertion tests to conduct.	Chapter 11, Lesson 2

Perform integration testing.

Objective	Location in Book
■ Determine if the component works as intended in the target environment.	Chapter 12, Lesson 2
■ Identify component interactions and dependencies.	Chapter 12, Lesson 2
■ Verify results.	Chapter 12, Lesson 2

Resolve a bug.

Objective	Location in Book
■ Investigate a reported bug.	Chapter 12, Lesson 2
■ Reproduce a bug.	Chapter 12, Lesson 2
■ Evaluate the impact of the bug and the associated cost and timeline for fixing the bug.	Chapter 12, Lesson 2
■ Fix a bug.	Chapter 12, Lesson 2

Deploying and Supporting an Application

Evaluate the performance of an application based on the performance analysis strategy.

Objective	Location in Book
■ Identify performance spikes.	Chapter 13, Lesson 1
■ Analyze performance trends.	Chapter 13, Lesson 1

Analyze the data received when monitoring an application.

Objective	Location in Book
■ Monitor and analyze resource usage.	Chapter 13, Lesson 2
■ Monitor and analyze security aspects.	Chapter 13, Lesson 2
■ Track bugs that result from customer activity.	Chapter 13, Lesson 2

Evaluate the deployment plan.

Objective	Location in Book
■ Identify component-level deployment dependencies.	Chapter 13, Lesson 3
■ Identify scripting requirements for deployment. Considerations include database scripting.	Chapter 13, Lesson 3

Create an application flow-logic diagram.

Objective	Location in Book
■ Evaluate the complexity of components.	Chapter 13, Lesson 4
■ Evaluate the complexity of interactions with other components.	Chapter 13, Lesson 4

Validate the production configuration environment

Objective	Location in Book
■ Verify networking settings.	Chapter 13, Lesson 5
■ Verify the deployment environment.	Chapter 13, Lesson 5

Exam objectives: The exam objectives listed here are current as of this book's publication date. Exam objectives are subject to change at any time without prior notice and at Microsoft's sole discretion. Please visit the Microsoft Learning Web site for the most current listing of exam objectives: *http://www.microsoft.com/learning/mcp/*.

MCPD Self-Paced Training Kit (Exam 70-549): Designing and Developing Enterprise Applications Using the Microsoft® .NET Framework

Bruce Johnson and
Brian C. Lanham of GrandMasters
with Shawn Wildermuth

PUBLISHED BY
Microsoft Press
A Division of Microsoft Corporation
One Microsoft Way
Redmond, Washington 98052-6399

Library of Congress Control Number: 2006940681

Printed and bound in the United States of America.

1 2 3 4 5 6 7 8 9   QWT   2 1 0 9 8 7

Distributed in Canada by H.B. Fenn and Company Ltd.

A CIP catalogue record for this book is available from the British Library.

Microsoft Press books are available through booksellers and distributors worldwide. For further information about international editions, contact your local Microsoft Corporation office or contact Microsoft Press International directly at fax (425) 936-7329. Visit our Web site at www.microsoft.com/mspress. Send comments to tkinput@microsoft.com.

Acquisitions Editor: Ken Jones
Developmental Editor: Maureen Zimmerman
Project Editor: Laura Sackerman

Body Part No. X13-47926

About the Authors

Bruce Johnson

Bruce Johnson is a partner at ObjectSharp Consulting and is a 25-year veteran of the computer industry. The first half of his career was spent working in the trenches—otherwise known as the UNIX field. The past 14 years have been spent on projects at the leading edge of Microsoft Windows technology—from Microsoft C++ through the myriad versions of Microsoft Visual Basic and ASP up to the present incarnations in Microsoft .NET Framework 3.0. Bruce's experience includes creating commercial Web applications, implementing Web services in a financial institution, and building Windows Forms applications.

As well as having fun with system design and development, Bruce has given more than 200 presentations at conferences and user groups all over North America. He has written columns and articles for numerous magazines and attempts to write regular posts on his blog at *www.objectsharp.com/blogs/bruce*.

Brian C. Lanham

After serving as a nuclear-qualified electrician for six years in the United States Navy, Brian C. Lanham pursued a computer science degree at Pennsylvania State University. During that time, Brian developed C applications for UNIX and DOS. He then moved to Windows and Web applications. Although he has dabbled in Java, .NET is his platform of choice. Brian currently lives in the Roanoke, Virginia, area. He can be reached at *codesailor@gmail.com*.

Shawn Wildermuth

Shawn Wildermuth is a Microsoft C# MVP and is the founder of Wildermuth Consulting Services, LLC, a company that delivers software and training solutions in the Atlanta, Georgia, area. He goes by the moniker "The ADO Guy" and can be contacted through his Web site at *http://adoguy.com*.

A speaker on the International .NET Association (INETA) Speaker Bureau, Shawn has spoken at several national conferences. He is the author of the book *Pragmatic ADO.NET* (Addison-Wesley, 2002) and co-author of *MCTS Self-Paced Training Kit (Exam 70-536): Microsoft .NET Framework 2.0–Application Development Foundation* (Microsoft Press, 2006). He has written articles for a variety of magazines and Web sites, including MSDN, DevSource, InformIT, Windows IT Pro, ServerSide, WindowsDevCenter, and Intel's Rich Client Series. Shawn has enjoyed building data-driven software for more than 20 years.

Mark Blomsma

Mark Blomsma is a Microsoft MVP in Visual C#, a software architect, and owner of Develop-One (*www.develop-one.com*) in Maine. He is a frequent speaker at .NET User Groups and has written articles for a variety of magazines such as *.NET Magazine* and *SDN Magazine*. He specializes in Microsoft .NET technology, enterprise application development, application integration, and software renovation. Visit his blog at *http://blog.develop-one.com*.

Shannon Horn

Shannon Horn delivers training for companies such as Microsoft and AppDev and has been a featured speaker on training videos with Learn-Key. He has also worked with large corporate clients on projects using .NET and Web technologies. Shannon is currently pursuing his third-degree black belt in tae kwon do, plays electric bass guitar, and lives for his kids. You can find out more about him by visiting *http://shannonhorn.spaces.live.com/*.

Mike Snell

Mike Snell has more than 15 years of experience as a software architect and consultant. He has led a number of enterprise-level projects, building client solutions on the Microsoft platform. He has delivered training and mentoring to hundreds of developers. Presently, Mike runs the Microsoft Consulting Practice at CEI (*www.ceiamerica.com*) in Pittsburgh, Pennsylvania. There, with his team of consulting architects, he helps CEI's diverse client base build mission-critical software.

Mike is recognized as a Microsoft Regional Director, a Microsoft Certified Solution Developer (MCSD), and a Project Management Professional (PMP). His co-authoring credits include *MCPD Self-Paced Training Kit (Exam 70-548): Designing and Developing Windows-Based Applications Using the Microsoft .NET Framework* (Microsoft Press, 2007) and *Microsoft Visual Studio 2005 Unleashed* (Sams, 2006).

Val Mazur

Val Mazur, a Microsoft MVP for Visual Developer and Visual Basic, has been developing applications since 1985. Currently working as a .NET developer for a software company in Toronto, Canada, Val specializes in data access technologies. Val is a contributor to Microsoft KnowledgeBase articles related to data access, a moderator for the ".NET Framework Data Access and Storage" and "SQL Server Data Access" MSDN forums, and the author of a number of publicly available .NET components that work with Microsoft Office Excel files (*http://xport.mvps.org*). Contact Val at *vmazur@mvps.org*.

Contents at a Glance

Table of Contents

What do you think of this book? We want to hear from you!

Microsoft is interested in hearing your feedback so we can continually improve our books and learning resources for you. To participate in a brief online survey, please visit:

www.microsoft.com/learning/booksurvey/

What do you think of this book? We want to hear from you!

Microsoft is interested in hearing your feedback so we can continually improve our books and learning resources for you. To participate in a brief online survey, please visit:

www.microsoft.com/learning/booksurvey/

Introduction

This training kit is designed for developers who plan to take Microsoft Certified Professional Developer (MCPD) *Exam 70-549: Designing and Developing Enterprise Applications by Using the Microsoft .NET Framework.* Developers who work on medium- or large-scale development projects will also benefit from the content in this training kit.

We assume that before you begin using this kit, you are familiar with creating enterprise applications by using Microsoft Visual Studio 2005 and ASP.NET 2.0. You should also have a working knowledge of Microsoft Visual Basic or C#. You should have worked on a team throughout the software development life cycle, and you should be familiar with technical envisioning and planning, design and development, and stabilizing and releasing software.

By using this training kit, you'll learn how to do the following:

- Envision and design an application
- Design and develop a component
- Design and develop an application framework
- Test and stabilize an application
- Deploy and support an application

Hardware Requirements

The following hardware is required to complete the lab exercises:

- Computer with a 600-MHz or faster processor (1 GHz recommended)
- 192 MB of RAM or more (512 MB recommended)
- 2 GB of available hard disk space
- DVD-ROM drive
- 1,024 x 768 or higher resolution display with 256 colors
- Keyboard and Microsoft mouse or compatible pointing device

Software Requirements

The following software is required to complete the practice exercises:

- One of the following operating systems:
    - Microsoft Windows 2000 with Service Pack 4
    - Windows XP with Service Pack 2
    - Windows XP Professional, x64 Editions (WOW)

❑ Microsoft Windows Server 2003 with Service Pack 1

❑ Windows Server 2003, x64 Editions (WOW)

❑ Windows Server 2003 R2

❑ Windows Server 2003 R2, x64 Editions (WOW)

❑ Windows Vista

■ Visual Studio 2005 (A 90-day evaluation edition of Visual Studio 2005 Professional Edition is included on DVD with this book.) If you are running Windows Vista, it is recommended that you download and install Visual Studio 2005 Service Pack 1 and Visual Studio 2005 Service Pack 1 Update for Windows Vista. Visual Studio 2005 Service Pack 1 can be downloaded from *http://www.microsoft.com/downloads/details.aspx?familyid=bb4a75ab-e2d4 -4c96-b39d-37baf6b5b1dc&displaylang=en*. (This download is good for the Standard, Professional, and Team Editions of Visual Studio 2005). Visual Studio 2005 Service Pack 1 Update for Windows Vista can be downloaded from *http://www.microsoft.com/downloads /details.aspx?familyid=fb6bb56a-10b7-4c05-b81c-5863284503cf&displaylang=en*.

■ Microsoft SQL Server 2005 Express Edition running on your computer (This can be installed as part of Visual Studio.)

■ The Enterprise Library application (January 2006 version) installed on your computer. ⸱Enterprise Library can be downloaded from *http://msdn.microsoft.com/library/?url= /library/en-us/dnpag2/html/EntLib2.asp*.

■ NMock installed on your computer. NMock is a free mock object library that can be downloaded from *www.nmock.org*.

■ The Northwind Traders database installed and accessible. To install the Northwind database, follow the instructions found at *http://msdn2.microsoft.com/en-us/library /8b6y4c7s(VS.80).aspx*.

■ Web Services Enhancements (WSE) 3.0 for Microsoft .NET installed on your computer. WSE 3.0 can be downloaded from *http://www.microsoft.com/downloads/details.aspx ?familyid=018A09FD-3A74-43C5-8EC1-8D789091255D&displaylang=en*.

IMPORTANT   Visual Studio Team Suite

To complete the lab exercises for Chapter 10, Lesson 1, "Creating a Unit Test Framework," and Chapter 11, Lesson 2, "Testing the Component Thoroughly," you will need to have Microsoft Visual Studio 2005 Team Edition for Software Developers installed on your computer. This is available as part of Visual Studio 2005 Team Suite. You can download a free 180-day trial version of Visual Studio 2005 Team Suite from *http://www.microsoft.com/downloads /details.aspx?FamilyId=5677DDC4- 5035-401F-95C3-CC6F46F6D8F7&displaylang=en*. You will need to uninstall Visual Studio 2005 Professional to install Visual Studio Team Suite on the same computer.

To complete the lab exercises for Chapter 10, Lesson 1, and Chapter 11, Lesson 2, you will need:

■ 256 MB of RAM or more

■ 3.3 GB available disk space to download Visual Studio Team Suite

- 2 GB available disk space to install Visual Studio Team Suite
- One of the following operating systems:
  - ❑ Windows 2000 with Service Pack 4
  - ❑ Windows XP with Service Pack 2
  - ❑ Windows Server 2003 with Service Pack 1
  - ❑ Windows Vista

Using the CD and DVD

A companion CD and an evaluation software DVD are included with this training kit. The companion CD contains the following:

- **Practice tests**   You can reinforce your understanding of the exam content by using electronic practice tests that you customize to meet your needs from the pool of Lesson Review questions in this book, or you can practice for the 70-549 certification exam by using tests created from a pool of 300 realistic exam questions. These questions give you many different practice exams to ensure that you're prepared to take the real thing.
- **Code**   Many chapters in this book include code and sample files associated with the lab exercises at the end of every lesson. Most exercises have a project or solution you can use to start the exercise and a version of the completed exercise for your review. To install the code and sample files on your hard disk, run Setup.exe in the Code folder on the companion CD. The default installation folder is \My Documents\Microsoft Press\MCPD Self-Paced Training Kit Exam 70-549.
- **An eBook**   An electronic (eBook) version of this book is included for times when you don't want to carry the printed book with you. The eBook is in Portable Document Format (PDF), and you can view it by using Adobe Acrobat or Adobe Acrobat Reader.

The evaluation software DVD contains a 90-day evaluation edition of Visual Studio 2005 Professional Edition in case you want to use it with this book.

How to Install the Practice Tests

To install the practice test software from the companion CD to your hard disk, do the following:

1. Insert the companion CD into your CD drive and accept the license agreement. A CD menu appears.

> **NOTE** **If the CD menu doesn't appear**
>
> If the CD menu or the license agreement doesn't appear, AutoRun might be disabled on your computer. Refer to the Readme.txt file on the CD-ROM for alternate installation instructions.

2. Click the Practice Tests item and follow the instructions on the screen.

How to Use the Practice Tests

To start the practice test software, follow these steps:

1. Click Start | All Programs | Microsoft Press Training Kit Exam Prep. A window appears that shows all the Microsoft Press training kit exam prep suites installed on your computer.

2. Double-click the lesson review or practice test you want to use.

NOTE Lesson reviews versus practice tests

Select the (70-549) Designing and Developing Enterprise Applications by Using the Microsoft .NET Framework lesson review to use the questions from the "Lesson Review" sections of this book. Select the (70-549) Designing and Developing Enterprise Applications by Using the Microsoft .NET Framework practice test to use a pool of 300 questions similar to those in the 70-549 certification exam.

Lesson Review Options

When you start a lesson review, the Custom Mode dialog box appears so that you can configure your test. You can click OK to accept the defaults, or you can customize the number of questions you want, how the practice test software works, which exam objectives you want the questions to relate to, and whether you want your lesson review to be timed. If you're retaking a test, you can select whether you want to see all the questions again or only those questions you missed or didn't answer.

After you click OK, your lesson review starts.

■ To take the test, answer the questions and use the Next, Previous, and Go To buttons to move from question to question.

■ After you answer an individual question, if you want to see which answers are correct—along with an explanation of each correct answer—click Explanation.

■ If you'd rather wait until the end of the test to see how you did, answer all the questions and then click Score Test. You'll see a summary of the exam objectives you chose and the percentage of questions you answered correctly overall and per objective. You can print a copy of your test, review your answers, or retake the test.

Practice Test Options

When you start a practice test, you choose whether to take the test in Certification Mode, Study Mode, or Custom Mode.

- **Certification Mode**   Closely resembles the experience of taking a certification exam. The test has a set number of questions, it's timed, and you can't pause and restart the timer.
- **Study Mode**   Creates an untimed test in which you can review the correct answers and the explanations after you answer each question.
- **Custom Mode**   Gives you full control over the test options so that you can customize them as you like.

In all modes, the user interface you see when taking the test is essentially the same but with different options enabled or disabled, depending on the mode. The main options are discussed in the previous section, "Lesson Review Options."

When you review your answer to an individual practice test question, a "References" section lists where in the training kit you can find the information that relates to that question and provides links to other sources of information. After you click Test Results to score your entire practice test, you can click the Learning Plan tab to see a list of references for every objective.

How to Uninstall the Practice Tests

To uninstall the practice test software for a training kit, use the Add Or Remove Programs option in Windows Control Panel.

Microsoft Certified Professional Program

The Microsoft certifications provide the best method to prove your command of current Microsoft products and technologies. The exams and corresponding certifications are developed to validate your mastery of critical competencies as you design and develop, or implement and support, solutions with Microsoft products and technologies. Computer professionals who become Microsoft certified are recognized as experts and are sought after industry-wide. Certification brings a variety of benefits to the individual and to employers and organizations.

MORE INFO   **All the Microsoft certifications**

For a full list of Microsoft certifications, go to *www.microsoft.com/learning/mcp/default.asp.*

Technical Support

Every effort has been made to ensure the accuracy of this book and the contents of the companion CD. If you have comments, questions, or ideas regarding this book or the companion CD, please send them to Microsoft Press by using either of the following methods:

E-mail: tkinput@microsoft.com

Postal Mail:

Microsoft Press
Attn: MCPD Self-Paced Training Kit (Exam 70-549): Designing and Developing Enterprise
Applications Using the Microsoft .NET Framework, *Editor*
One Microsoft Way
Redmond, WA 98052–6399

For additional support information regarding this book and the CD-ROM (including answers
to commonly asked questions about installation and use), visit the Microsoft Press Technical
Support Web site at *www.microsoft.com/learning/support/books/*. To connect directly to the
Microsoft Knowledge Base and enter a query, visit *http://support.microsoft.com/search/*. For
support information regarding Microsoft software, please visit *http://support.microsoft.com*.

Evaluation Edition Software Support

The 90-day evaluation edition provided with this training kit is not the full retail product and
is provided only for the purposes of training and evaluation. Microsoft and Microsoft Technical Support do not support this evaluation edition.

Information about any issues relating to the use of this evaluation edition with this training
kit is posted to the Support section of the Microsoft Press Web site at *www.microsoft.com/
learning/support/books/*. For information about ordering the full version of any Microsoft
software, please call Microsoft Sales at (800) 426-9400 or visit the Microsoft Web site at
www.microsoft.com.

Chapter 1
Evaluating the Technical Feasibility of an Application

Application development projects often have limited budgets and constrained timelines, set by the stakeholders and upper management. These same people typically provide the business vision and funding for the project. They make decisions about which projects to execute based on both the business value of the resulting project and a professional developer's estimate of the effort associated with the project. It is their confidence you need to gain before you will be trusted with the budget to execute the project. This means demonstrating that you understand the business problems you will be trying to solve and that you will be successful in translating their vision into tangible software before budgets and timelines are exhausted. To professional developers, this means reviewing requirements and recommending, evaluating, and refining a design for the application.

This chapter looks at how you move from the vision, goals, and requirements of an application to a proposed solution. This process involves recommending technologies, defining a design, and then vetting your recommendations through the creation of a prototype. You then need to demonstrate the feasibility of the project (and your design) to the visionaries and stakeholders. Ultimately, it will be their confidence in your proposed solution that determines whether a project is funded and moves from idea to implementation.

Exam objectives in this chapter:
- Evaluate the technical feasibility of an application design concept.
    - Evaluate the proof of concept.
    - Recommend the best technologies for the features and goals of the application. Considerations include Message Queuing, Web services, .NET Framework remoting, and so on.
    - Weigh implementation considerations.
    - Investigate existing solutions for similar business problems.

Lessons in this chapter:

Before You Begin

To complete the lessons in this chapter, you should be familiar with developing Microsoft Windows applications with Microsoft Visual Studio 2005, using Visual Basic or C#. In addition, you should be comfortable with all of the following tasks:

- Reviewing goals and requirements for Web and/or Windows applications
- Detailing the functional specifications for an application
- Identifying how .NET architectures and related technologies solve specific business problems
- Understanding distributed n-tier architectures
- Working with object-oriented development concepts
- Reading and working with class diagrams and other technical models

---

Real World

Mike Snell

Not every problem should be solved with code or technology. As technologists, our first instinct to any problem might be to write some code. However, this is often not the best choice. Some problems are too costly in terms of dollars, resources, or time to implement. You need to take a step back and look at a problem not just as a developer but from the perspective of what is best for your organization. You will find that looking at problems with this attitude might change the way you would approach a specific solution. The results of this thinking are beneficial to the organization. However, it also shows your management that you see a bigger picture beyond just the technology and can be relied on to add business value.

Lesson 1: Evaluating Requirements and Proposing a Design

Reaching a common understanding among the developers, the business, and the users is the principal goal of application requirements. Nearly all enterprise applications built by professionals define and document requirements. How those requirements are documented, agreed on, and managed is often unique to each project.

For example, the Microsoft Solutions Framework (MSF) for Agile Software Development defines a work item for what it calls a quality of service (QOS) requirement. This work item represents a requirement that can be classified as a performance, load, availability, stress, accessibility, serviceability, or maintainability requirement. The same methodology includes another work item called a scenario. A scenario is the MSF term for use case. A *use case* defines a path of user activity through the system to reach a specific goal. Together, these work items (QOS and scenario) represent the user view (scenario) and the non-functional view (QOS) of the system.

Consider another example. MSF for Capability Maturity Model Integration (CMMI) defines a work item it calls, simply, "requirement." This requirement work item, however, has a number of subtypes. These subtypes include scenario, quality of service, safety, security, functional, operational, and interface. This methodology groups all requirements together but then allows them to be subgrouped by a category. These subgroups are relatively granular. However, they can be reclassified based on some standard requirement groups such as user requirements (scenario), non-functional requirements (QOS, safety, and security), and functional requirements (functional, operational, and interface).

These two examples are simply the beginning. The definitions of software requirements have been discussed, debated, and written about for many years. Many good books are dedicated solely to the subject of requirements. There are also many standards and methodologies that all take a slightly different perspective on software requirements. The intent here is not to change the way you write requirements. Enough is common among these methods to make them all viable. Rather, this chapter will establish a simple baseline for talking about requirements and then discuss how you evaluate requirements and recommend solutions based on those requirements.

After this lesson, you will be able to:
- Recognize poor requirements and propose improvements.
- Evaluate a set of application requirements for their completeness and feasibility.
- Recommend technologies based on a set of requirements.
- Investigate and evaluate existing alternatives to your recommendations.
- Define a high-level application design based on requirements and recommendations.
- Determine whether an application's design is feasible and practical.

Estimated lesson time: 60 minutes

What Makes a Good Set of Application Requirements?

A good requirement set includes requirements that are defined from multiple perspectives. This makes a lot of sense. All projects have multiple influences. The business (or executive sponsorship) has a set of objectives and goals for the application. Users define specific tasks they need to accomplish. Developers and testers need to know what features will be required to make this application a success. There are also requirements around supporting and maintaining the application, around performance and scalability, and more. The goal is to define enough of these requirements to eliminate unknowns (risk) and to build the right project.

This section will define four types of requirements: business, user, functional, and quality of service. Together, these categories represent the perspectives necessary to define the requirements for the vast majority of (if not all) business applications. They provide a common understanding from the business through to the developer. They also allow the quality assurance team to ensure that the application stays focused and on track. Let's take a look at each requirement category in further detail.

Business Requirement

A *business requirement* defines what the business believes to be important for the success of the project. The business typically represents management or stakeholders who are funding the project. They often define requirements in terms of vision or goals for the application. However, these goals need to be turned into real, tangible requirements.

As an example, consider a business requirement that states, "The new version should allow us to sell the application to new markets." This is a great goal for the system. It helps justify the expense of the development in that it will open up new sales channels and markets and hence increase revenues and profits. However, this goal needs to be translated into real business requirements. Real high-level business requirements derived from this goal might look as follows:

- The system must include metadata support for all named concepts. This will allow companies in different markets to rename these concepts based on their terminology.
- The system must implement an open standard for the exchange of sales data. This will allow all markets to interoperate with the application.
- The application must support the definition of feature packs for specific markets. A feature pack is a set of features that can be turned on or off as a group (think add-in). The application's core should not depend on features inside a given feature pack.

You can see that these are tangible requirements tied to what was a goal for the application to support multiple markets. It is also important to note that these are *high-level requirements*—that is, requirements without detailed specifications. That's okay. The requirements can be kept and tracked at a high level. An application architect or systems analyst will have to translate requirements into specifications and design. However, the specifications and design should not alter, add to, or take away from the requirements. If you see this happening, you need to update your requirements and have them revalidated as appropriate and necessary.

User Requirement

User requirements are the tasks the users must be able to accomplish to meet the objectives of their jobs. Most developers do not have the luxury of a business analyst and are, therefore, accustomed to receiving or documenting user requirements. This typically involves sitting with users and discussing exactly what they do (or need to do) to help them. The following are all high-level user requirements:

- A customer service representative must be able to place an order for a customer.
- A user must be able to query the on-hand inventory to determine the number of units of a given product that are in stock.
- Users must be able to view their order histories in a list. They must be able to select an order from the list and view its details.

  These are not use cases or specifications. The first question a business analyst might ask, for example, is "How?" How does a customer service representative place an order for a customer? The user will then typically detail a number of steps that are involved in this process. These steps represent the use case for "customer rep places order for customer." This use case helps the business analyst understand the requirement. In addition, an architect or systems analyst should define the specifications for the given requirement. This will include the information developers need to know such as what constitutes an order, what fields are required, what rules will be processed, and so on.

Functional Requirement

Functional requirements or *functional specifications* are the features the developers must build to satisfy the other requirements. These requirements are typically defined in great detail to help developers understand exactly what they need to develop. The functional requirements are usually written by a technical lead or architect. They are not the requirements of the users or the business.

A functional requirement, for example, might be to create an administrative user interface for managing the settings of an application. The functional requirement should include the name of the form, the controls used on the form, the input validation rules, the security rules, the classes that should be called to support the form's functionality, and so on.

As you can see, functional requirements can be very detailed. It is often better to do functional design rather than to write functional requirements. This allows you to take advantage of application models, tools such as Visual Studio, and some code (or pseudocode) to define the functionality of the system. Developers often understand these items better. In addition, it saves you the time of documenting these items in two places (in a document and in the physical models).

Quality of Service Requirement

Quality of service (QOS) requirements define the contractual, or non-functional, requirements for the system. QOS requirements typically do not represent specific user problems. Rather, they define the requirements concerning factors such as performance, scalability, and standards. These requirements should not be overlooked. They need to be defined and considered when doing application architecture and development. The following are examples of QOS requirements.

- All middle-tier objects should load from the database within two seconds.
- The application should scale to 50 concurrent users with the current server specifications.
- The application should automatically update itself across the local area network (LAN) connection.
- The system should use Windows-integrated security to identify users and partition data based on a user's group affiliation.

You can see that QOS requirements are very important. They further define what the application must support from a non-functional perspective. You must have this information at the outset to make wise decisions about how you recommend and implement technologies for a given business problem.

Exam Tip   Pay close attention to the exact requirements for any given question on the exam. You need to satisfy all the requirements listed in the question and only those requirements listed in the question. Do not assume anything; pay close attention to only what is written. You have to eliminate the urge to use what your experience tells you and focus solely on what is written in the question.

Use Cases versus Requirements

Use cases and requirements are not the same thing. Use cases are a Unified Modeling Language (UML) model meant to describe a set of user steps to accomplish a task. Requirements define what must be created to satisfy the user's needs. Together, they provide a good view of how the user sees the system. However, you should be wary if you encounter attempts to do away with one in favor of the other.

This happens most often with regard to use cases trying, sometimes successfully, to supplant requirements. These situations are almost always highly agile, involve the client on a day-to-day basis, have small teams, and do not involve a geographically distributed work force. If this is your environment, you might be able to take advantage of use cases in lieu of requirements.

You want to avoid, however, cluttering your use cases with so much specification detail that you can't find the use case anymore. For more traditional environments, consider starting with either requirements or use cases and building the missing item. You typically need both to be successful.

Requirements and uses cases have two different goals. Requirements define what needs to be created for the system to be successful. They are useful for defining scope and determining whether you have met objectives. Requirements are often traced all the way through the implementation process. Project managers and testers create requirements traceability matrices that define how a requirement is realized through the system.

Alternatively, use cases are meant to define a set of steps to reach a common user goal. Use cases are more about the process by which a user reaches a requirement. They help architects, developers, and testers understand how people work and how the system should accommodate their activities. Done correctly, they are not requirements.

Evaluating the Requirements for the Application

When you are presented with a set of requirements, you need to be able to evaluate them and determine whether they are complete, feasible, and sufficient. The categories of requirements that must be present to make a complete set have already been mentioned: business, user, functional, and QOS. You next need to look at these requirements and determine whether they are sufficiently well documented. The following list represents criteria or questions that you can use to determine whether the requirements are sufficient.

- **Requirement perspectives**   Are all requirement perspectives considered? Do you have a definition of the business, user, and QOS requirements? Can you derive the functional requirements and design from this set of requirements?

- **Unambiguous**   Is each requirement written using specifics? Can each requirement be acted upon? You want to make sure that there are no unclear requirements. You want to eliminate phrases such as "the application should be easy to use" from the requirements. This is a goal. A requirement would indicate something such as "the application should implement a task pane of common user actions that are available for a given module."

- **Complete**   Are the requirements complete? You need to identify missing elements in the requirements. You should also indicate where further clarification of one or more requirements is warranted. Perhaps, for example, some requirements need further fleshing out through use cases. If you are having trouble understanding a requirement or designing to it, then it's not complete.

- **Necessary**   Are all the requirements actually necessary to satisfy the goals of the application? This is the opposite of complete. Sometimes business analysts, developers, and architects can add things to the system that are not really required. You need to watch for overzealous requirement definitions that inflate the scope of the project.

- **Feasible**   Are the requirements as documented really feasible? You need to review the requirements against known constraints such as budget, timeline, and technology. It's better to raise red flags during the requirements definition phase than to wait until the project is already over budget.

Thinking of your requirements in these terms will make everyone's job much easier. A good set of requirements will lead to good architecture, good testing, and high user acceptance.

Recommending Best Technologies

There is a big difference between defining application architecture and recommending technologies for an application. These tasks often become intermingled and confused. One should not be a substitute for another. Architects and developers should be asked to look at the requirements for a system and make technology recommendations. These technology recommendations, in conjunction with the requirements, will drive a lot of the application's architecture. Therefore, technology recommendations should precede application architecture.

Ideally, the decision to recommend one technology over another should be driven solely by the requirements. A developer should evaluate the requirements and choose the right technologies to fit. However, in all practicality, these decisions sometimes have more to do with what is available than what is best. If you are faced with this dilemma, factor it directly into your decision process. Make it a requirement to use as much existing hardware and software as you can. If this is validated and justified, you can respect the requirement.

Take a look at how you might recommend certain technologies over others, based solely on the user, business, and QOS requirements (and not on what is available or convenient). Of course, to make recommendations, you must have some familiarity with certain technologies and know how those technologies can be brought to bear on a given solution.

An enterprise application can be broken down into a core set of application layers or components. These items comprise the bulk of your technology recommendation opportunities. It makes sense to review the layers and components that define an enterprise application. The following discussion lists each of these items, defines the options that are available, and provides a decision tree that will help guide you toward recommending one technology over another.

Client

The *client* represents how your enterprise application will be presented to the users. The client is the user's interface with the application. It is what the users see and use every time they work with the application. The following list represents some of the many enterprise client technology options available to you.

- **Windows client**   The standard Windows client. This is a forms-based interface and is built as either a single document interface (SDI) or a multiple document interface (MDI) application. An SDI interface has a single, main form that might load other forms into panels or tabs. Each form is typically a different type. An MDI application has a container that loads forms. These forms often represent multiple versions of the same type. Office Word, Microsoft Office Excel, and Visual Studio are MDI examples.

Recommend this solution when you require a rich, interactive user interface and plan to use the resources of the user's desktop. This model requires the Microsoft .NET Framework on each desktop. The application might connect to shared data on the LAN or even occasionally call out to a Web service or use remoting.

- **Smart Client**   Represents a client that is deployed through a Web browser but that runs as a Windows application on the client's machine. Smart Clients provide a high degree of user interactivity but still work with a Web server to use the pervasiveness of the Internet.

  Recommend this solution when you need to build a Web-based application with a very high degree of user interactivity and you can control the client's operating system. This solution depends on Windows and the .NET Framework being deployed on a user's desktop.

- **Browser-based client**   Represents the standard client enabled through a Web browser. These clients typically target the widest audience with a single solution.

  Multi-browser compliance is often a principal driver when recommending this type of client.

- **AJAX-enabled client**   Represents a browser-based client that takes advantage of Java-Script to enable Windows-like features through a browser (such as Outlook Web Access). This provides users with a highly interactive (and much more usable) experience inside a browser.

  When you recommend this solution, you are typically trying to combine the ubiquity of the Web browser with a high degree of usability. You might sacrifice some browser compatibility, however, or choose to write multiple, down-level versions of the application.

- **Microsoft Office Client**   Represents a client that is built with Office Word, Office Excel, or Microsoft Office Outlook as the principal user interface. You might still call back to a Web server through Web services to exchange data. However, users take advantage of the familiar paradigm of Office to complete their work.

  Recommend an Office client when you are building applications that take advantage of the capabilities of Office (such as spreadsheet or contact management). You also need to ensure that the target version of Office is deployed on each user's desktop.

- **Windows Mobile**   Represents clients that are enabled through handheld devices running the Windows Mobile operating system.

  Recommend this solution when users are highly mobile and need access to information over their handheld devices.

Third-Party Controls

Third-party controls represent developer controls not shipped by Microsoft or embedded in the editions of Visual Studio 2005. Explore the controls that are available to you to weigh build-versus-buy decisions. For example, if your application requires that you integrate with a credit card processor, you should explore the many components available for you to do so. In most scenarios, third-party controls can eliminate risk, reduce costs, and increase delivery time. Some of the many control categories that are available include charting, scheduling, navigation, user interface styling, licensing, reporting, integration, spreadsheets, data grids, and many more.

Application Server

Your enterprise application will most likely involve an application server. An *application server* represents the server that you will recommend to run your code in your middle tier. This is code that is shared by the clients and typically processes business rules and accesses data stores. Most standard Windows clients do not require an application server. However, if you are building a distributed application, you will need an application server.

Typically, architects and developers recommend the software and not many of the hardware specifications. When recommending an application server for your solution, consider the version of Internet Information Server (IIS) required, the version of the .NET Framework you need to target, and the security constraints of the application.

MORE INFO   .NET Enterprise Services

.NET Enterprise Services is a collection of robust operations that perform many complex enterprise-level tasks. Specifically, .NET Enterprise Services supports transactional processing, just-in-time activation, object pooling, and role-based security. You can learn more about .NET Enterprise Services at *http://msdn.microsoft.com/library/default.asp?url=/library/en-us/dnentsrv/html/netenterpriseandcomplus.asp.*

Application Libraries

An *application library* is a set of components (and, many times, source code) that you can download and use in your solution. An application library typically encapsulates a set of features that are common to a lot of applications. For example, the Microsoft Enterprise Library provides features for caching, error management, configuration, and more. Review your application's requirements and determine whether these libraries can be used to help ensure best practices and high quality.

Similar to application libraries are application frameworks. A *framework* is a set of base classes and components that abstract a lot of the architectural plumbing away from the developer.

Frameworks try to offer a cohesive solution to many architecture problems. These typically include managing state between application layers, physically distributing the layers of an application, handling plumbing, and more.

Security

You need to be able to recommend security technologies that you can use to meet the security requirements of the application. For example, you need to determine whether you should implement a custom security model or use Windows security in your application. This typically depends on the user base. If you are writing for the corporate audience and are on a Windows network, it's best to integrate your solution with Active Directory directory services. Alternatively, if your users are not on the same domain and connect across the Internet using a Smart Client or Web browser, consider creating a custom security solution that manages credentials in another data store. Other security recommendations might include how you store and encrypt data and how you connect to that data.

Whether you recommend using Active Directory or creating a custom security, you will want to implement role-based security. *Role-based security* is the binding of system operations to roles rather than to specific users. Users are then associated directly with the roles. This technique is important in enterprise applications because it avoids binding security architecture to the ever-changing user population. Instead, the roles represent an abstraction layer and can be managed more easily.

Asynchronous Messaging

There are situations in which you need to notify another system that an operation occurred, and you do not need to know how the other system responds to that information. In these situations, you can use asynchronous messaging. *Asynchronous messaging* (or, simply, messaging) is a technique whereby one system listens on a message queue. A queue is a data structure that exposes a first-in-first-out (FIFO) protocol much like a line of cars at a drive-up teller window. A message queue is simply a queue of messages. Other systems can then post messages to that queue. The delivering systems send the messages in a fire-and-forget mode. That is, they deliver the messages to the queue and then move on. They do not need to know about how the system responds. Alternatively, the receiving system does not necessarily need to know the delivering system, only that it received a message. The receiving system has the choice of processing the message at its convenience.

You have a few choices available to you for asynchronous messaging. The primary choice is Microsoft Message Queue (MSMQ). This is a proven and robust messaging application with a straightforward yet powerful application programming interface (API). One of the useful features in MSMQ is the ability to use a store-and-forward model. This model allows you to queue messages and process them at a later time. The store-and-forward model allows your application

to continue working even if a server resource is unavailable or if the application is disconnected. You can also create your own custom message queues by using .NET. The .NET Framework also supports integration with MQ Series message queues.

MORE INFO   **Message queues**

The MessageQueue component allows you to build complex messaging into your applications. This
is a large topic. Read more *at http://msdn2.microsoft.com/en-us/library/fzc40kc8.aspx.*

Remote Communication

The very nature of distributed application development calls for remote communication
wherein an application running on one computer must communicate with an application running on another computer. There are many reasons to distribute your application among computers, such as resource management, performance, security, and licensing.

There are several factors to consider when choosing the right remote communication strategy
for your application. One is the remote platform. Is the remote platform known? If so, is it consistent with your existing infrastructure? Another factor is the frequency of communication.
Will communication occur once daily or several times every second? You must also consider
bandwidth. How large are the messages between the local and remote machines?

The .NET Framework 2.0 offers a robust array of technology options for accomplishing inter-
process communication in your distributed application. This can be both positive and negative. It is good to have so many equally viable options; however, it can be challenging to choose
the most appropriate option for a given situation. The two primary offerings include Web services and .NET remoting.

Web Services   Web services allow applications on different platforms and in different technologies to communicate with each other over the Internet. They are units of application logic
providing data and services to other applications. Applications access XML Web services
using standard Web protocols and data formats such as Hypertext Transfer Protocol (HTTP),
Extensible Markup Language (XML), and Simple Object Access Protocol (SOAP), independent of how each XML Web service is implemented.

.NET Remoting   Remoting is the .NET solution for inter-process communication in a distributed environment. Before remoting, Distributed Component Object Model (DCOM) was the
principal means of allowing distributed applications to talk with each other. In some situations, developers would write their own communications mechanisms using raw sockets.
Remoting provides a single API for taking advantage of TCP, IPC, and HTTP (Web services)
communication.

Remoting versus Web Services   Remoting and Web services have many similarities. You
will have the challenge of determining which implementation is best for your application. The

answer, of course, depends on the situation at hand. Some of the factors to consider when choosing between the two are listed in Table 1-1.

Table 1-1   Remoting versus Web Services Considerations

Aspect	TCP Remoting	Web Services
Security	Remoting has more options (and requires more planning) with respect to security. You can establish a trust (along with encryption) between servers using IPSec. You can use IIS to host your remoted types (and take advantage of the security model built into IIS). You can also secure the TCP channel to enable both authentication and encryption of messages.	Web services hosted in IIS can take advantage of Secure Sockets Layer (SSL) for encryption and offer a built-in security model for authentication and authorization.
Interoperability	Choose Remoting if you can restrict your interoperation to just other .NET applications.	Choose Web services if you need to interoperate with other platforms or technologies.
Performance	TCP channels with binary formatters in .NET remoting offer the greatest speed. Choose TCP remoting for speed.	Web services rely on XML for communication. XML inherently marks up the data as much as four times the original size.
Scalability	You can host remote servers with IIS, which offers built-in scalability. Alternatively, you should be able to design and code your remote servers so that they scale.	Web services take advantage of the scalability built into IIS. This can be easier to implement and can often offer more scalability compared to remoting.

Exam Tip   Know the limitations of Web services, .NET remoting, and messaging related to communicating across application domains, servers, and different platforms.

Data Storage

Data storage represents how your application will store and access its data. A lot of options are available; let the requirements of the application lead you toward the best solution. The following list represents some of the options that might be available to you.

- **File-based storage**   This represents storing your data in files in the application's file system. File-based solutions typically involve storing data as XML.

  You would recommend this only for small applications in which a database solution is not available or warranted.

- **SQL Express**   SQL Express is a free database solution available from Microsoft. It provides a starting point for creating small-project databases. It also provides a file-based solution for developers seeking to embed SQL in their application.

  Consider this option when you are constrained by costs, can limit your database requirements to a single CPU, a single gigabyte of RAM, and a 4-GB database size, and you do not require many of the advanced features of a full database solution.

- **SQL Everywhere**   SQL Everywhere (also called SQL Mobile) provides a small, lightweight, highly functional database for handheld devices.

  Recommend this option when you are building mobile solutions that store and retrieve data locally to the handheld device.

- **SQL Server editions and options**   The Microsoft SQL Server family includes standard and enterprise editions. These versions include features such as reporting services, analysis services, data mining, notification, and more. If you encounter these requirements, you need to be aware of how these services can help.

- **Other data storage**   A number of other options are available to you for your solutions. You might, for example, have a requirement to retrieve your data from an Oracle or IBM DB2 database. In either case, you can recommend the right .NET data provider to do so.

MORE INFO   SQL Server editions

There are a lot of editions of SQL Server—one to fit every need. For a good overview of what is available to you, search *http://www.microsoft.com/sql/* for "SQL Server 2005 Features Comparison." This provides an item-by-item comparison of features.

This should give you a good overview of what to expect when recommending technologies for your Windows solutions. Your task should be to focus on the requirements, review them, and make recommendations based solely on these requirements. You should not, for example, be recommending a SQL Express database for an enterprise application with hundreds of concurrent users. Rather, you need to respect these and other requirements and recommend the right solution for the job.

Quick Check

1. Name the common types, or categories, of requirements.
2. What is a quality-of-service (QOS) requirement?
3. What are the characteristics of a good requirement?

> **Quick Check Answers**
> 1. Requirements should be seen from multiple perspectives. These include business, user, functional, and quality of service (QOS).
> 2. A QOS requirement defines a contractual requirement that the system must meet. These requirements are often used to define scalability, performance, and other non-functional requirements.
> 3. A good requirement should be unambiguous, complete, necessary, and feasible.

Investigating Existing Solutions for Similar Business Problems

When you make your technology recommendations, it is wise to consider existing solutions to similar business problems. If you find an existing bit of software, a product, or a third-party component, you can sometimes buy rather than build new. This can save you valuable design, development, and test cycles. For example, you should consider software that might even exist already in your own organization. Often this software can be componentized to support multiple applications. If you resist the urge to reinvent, you keep the development team focused on just the features that make your application unique. Following are some common technologies to consider when looking at making alternate recommendations for your enterprise solutions.

- **Corporate assets**   Always look internally first. Companies spend a lot of money every year solving the same problem many times. You might find that you can turn some existing code into a component and use it for multiple applications.
- **Third-party components and libraries**   This was discussed earlier. There are some great solutions available to you for a low cost in terms of creating reports, charts, and other features.
- **Microsoft BizTalk Server**   BizTalk Server provides a solution for managing business process and integration. The latest version, 2006, provides integration with Visual Studio 2005. It also provides adapters for key applications in the industry. Consider recommending this solution when you have a lot of system integration with key business processes.
- **Host Integration Server**   Host Integration Server provides a server product for integrating with IBM mainframes. This includes connecting with data sources, messaging, and security. Consider recommending this when you have to build an application that has a high degree of interoperability with IBM mainframes.
- **Microsoft Windows SharePoint Services**   This software provides a set of services for creating collaborative portal solutions. You can use .NET Framework 2.0 to build Web Parts and Web Part pages for Windows SharePoint Services Web Storage System (WSS). This can be a great solution for companies seeking to create internal collaborative solutions.

■ **Microsoft Commerce Server**   This software provides a platform for building business applications that center on e-commerce. The latest version, 2007, has been written to work specifically with ASP.NET 2.0, BizTalk Server, SQL Server, SQL Server Reporting Services, and more. You should consider this option when recommending e-commerce applications.

Creating a High-Level Application Design

You have your application requirements. You have evaluated these requirements and confirmed them as good. You then put together a technology recommendation based on the requirements. Your next step is to define a model for the application's high-level design. This design should help document and explain the application you intend to create. Therefore, it must define the technologies that you intend to use and indicate how these technologies will be connected.

How you model your application design is not as important as just modeling it. There are many tools that will allow you to define an application design. You can create boxes and arrows in Microsoft Office Visio, or you can use Visual Studio 2005 Team Architect. The latter provides the application diagram for defining applications, their connectivity, and their configuration. You might not have this tool available to you, but it is a good model of what should be in your high-level application design. Let's take a look.

Visual Studio Team Architect Application Diagram

You add items to your application diagram by using the Toolbox in Visual Studio 2005. Figure 1-1 shows the application diagram Toolbox. Note that you can drag application types from the Toolbox onto the designer. This allows you to indicate which technologies you are recommending for a given solution. You can define Windows applications, ASP.NET Web services, ASP.NET applications, and more. In addition, there are a number of endpoints that you can attach to an application. An architect uses these endpoints to configure which applications communicate and through what means. Let's look at an example.

Figure 1-2 provides a sample application diagram. Note that the application is defined as having two user interfaces. It defines a Web-based application that allows employees to enter timesheets and access paycheck information (EmployeePortal) and a Windows application (Payroll) for the payroll department to process paychecks and report on employee information. The diagram also defines a Web service application (EmployeeServices) and two databases (*HumanResourceDb* and *PayrollDb*).

Figure 1-1   The application diagram Toolbox

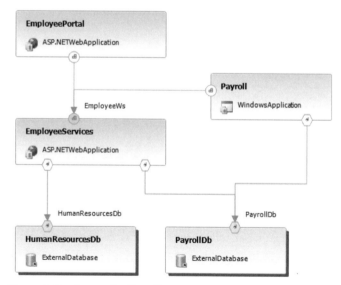

Figure 1-2   An application diagram

Each application on the diagram can be configured in terms of the settings and constraints that are required for the application. Think of this as your application configuration plan. For example, the Payroll client application might define constraints on the client's operating system and version of the .NET Framework. Figure 1-3 shows the Settings And Constraints window in Visual Studio for this application. Note that you define these parameters through this interface. The example indicates that clients must be running Windows XP, Service Pack 2, and the .NET Framework 2.0.

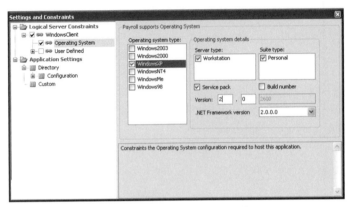

Figure 1-3   The Settings And Constraints window

Defining the application's requirements, making your technology recommendation, and creating a high-level design are the necessary risk-aversion steps to begin your project. You will use this information to define a prototype, refine your design, and begin creating detailed specifications and an application architecture. The next lesson will cover the prototyping process.

MORE INFO   Creating detailed design

Chapter 2, "Creating Specifications for Developers," will cover the process of creating physical models for developers (layers, class, activity, sequence).

Lab: Evaluating Requirements and Recommending Technology

In this lab, you will evaluate a list of application requirements for an enterprise application being built for a health insurance provider. You will use these requirements to make design and technology choices and propose an application design. If you encounter a problem completing an exercise, the answers can be installed from the Code folder on the companion CD.

▶ **Exercise: Review Requirements and Recommend Technologies**

For this exercise, review the following subset of application requirements. You will then follow the steps to arrive at a set of recommendations for the application. The following are key requirements for the application:

❑ R1 Our internal contract specialists will use the application to enter and maintain contract data. A contract is between a health care provider (an external doctor or care group) and the health insurance carrier.

❑ R2 Contract data entry needs to be an intuitive and fast process for users. The contracts are very complex. The interface should be rich enough to aid users in getting contracts done right, quickly.

❑ R3 Health care providers should be able to log on to the application and review their contract details. They should see only their details. They cannot edit or alter the data in any way. However, they can provide feedback with respect to their contract.

❑ R4 Internal users should not have to log on to the application manually. The application should recognize them from their corporate logon information.

❑ R5 The system needs to support up to 75 concurrent users.

❑ R6 The supporting data for the application (claim codes, rates, and so on) is updated quarterly based on a series of four different data feeds. Each feed is a fixed-width file.

❑ R7 The application needs to update the claims processing system with new contract details as they are available. The claims processing system is built on a different platform. You will not have access to the claims processing system or its database. The claims processing system will determine when to process the updates you send.

Follow these steps:

1. Review the application requirements and determine which client technology you should implement, based on the specifics in the requirements.

2. Determine a data storage mechanism for the application.

3. Which technology might you propose to help integrate with the claims processing system (R7)?

4. What additional technologies should you consider for this solution? Consider cost-effective products that satisfy some of these requirements.

Lesson Summary

■ Application requirements should be defined from multiple perspectives, including from the business (or executive sponsorship), the user's, the developer's (functional), and the quality of service (non-functional) viewpoints.

■ A good requirement should be unambiguous, measurable, and actionable. It should not read like a goal nor be left for interpretation.

■ Your functional requirements or functional specifications are better off being defined through application modeling tools rather than as text inside a requirements document.

■ It is important that developers and architects size their recommendations based on real requirements. They should not recommend technologies because they are fashionable or available. Rather, they should do careful analysis and make proper recommendations.

- Always review your recommendations against existing solutions. There might be an off-the-shelf product or an internal company asset that you can use.

- You should start the process of validating your recommendations by creating a high-level application design. This should include your recommendations in terms of technologies, how these technologies integrate to form a solution, and any configuration parameters and constraints of these items.

Lesson Review

You can use the following questions to test your knowledge of the information in Lesson 1, "Evaluating Requirements and Proposing a Design." The questions are also available on the companion CD if you prefer to review them in electronic form.

NOTE   Answers

Answers to these questions and explanations of why each answer choice is right or wrong are located in the "Answers" section at the end of the book.

---

1. You have been given the requirement stipulating that "the data should be stored in the database in a standard, hierarchical format that supports readability and reporting." This is an example of what type of requirement?

   A. Business requirement

   B. Quality of service requirement

   C. User requirement

   D. Functional requirement

2. You intend to write both an e-commerce application and a custom credit card–processing engine that will be used by the e-commerce application. Your application must support 1,000 concurrent users. In addition, the credit card–processing engine should work with multiple credit card companies on different platforms and protocols. Which of the following implementation strategies is best suited to Web services?

   A. The e-commerce client browser communicating with the e-commerce Web server components

   B. The e-commerce middle tier communicating with data services components

   C. The e-commerce middle tier communicating with the custom credit card–processing engine

   D. The custom credit card–processing engine communicating with credit card companies

3. Given the following requirements, which client technology would you recommend?

❑ Users must be able to enter new data as well as view and update existing data. These processes will be controlled through the business rules surrounding each data element.

❑ The application should support up to 50 users.

❑ Users will access the application from their corporate desktops and laptops.

❑ The users expect a highly interactive experience with the application.

❑ The application must be easy to deploy and update.

❑ The application features should be accessible both online and offline.

   A. Microsoft Office application using Office Excel

   B. Standard Windows client

   C. Windows Mobile client

   D. Windows Smart Client

4. Given the following requirements, which data storage technology would you recommend?

❑ Users should be able to work with the application when they are not connected to the LAN.

❑ The application's data is retrieved and aggregated from multiple sources on a monthly basis. After the updated data is posted, users should receive it.

❑ The application should have a small footprint on the user's computer or device.

   A. SQL Enterprise

   B. SQL Express

   C. SQL Everywhere (Mobile)

   D. SQL Standard

5. Which of the following is not supported by MSMQ?

   A. Synchronous messaging

   B. Asynchronous messaging

   C. Data transformation

   D. Priority queuing

Lesson 2: Creating a Proof-of-Concept Prototype to Refine an Application's Design

Enterprise applications often include multiple clients, Web servers, database servers, application servers, frameworks, and networks all working in concert to provide a complete software solution. Suppose you've evaluated the requirements and proposed an appropriate mix of these items. It is then that questions begin to arise regarding the use of things such as multiple threads, component distribution strategies, and inter-application communication techniques. It is best to answer these questions as quickly as possible. A proof of concept is a risk-averse, low-cost means of determining the feasibility of a proposed implementation. It enables you to learn about new technologies, to demonstrate complicated designs, to identify pitfalls, and to improve estimations for your software system.

In this lesson, you will look at how you might create a prototype to answer questions from the requirements and the technology recommendations. You will look at how you can use this prototype to increase the confidence in the project and reduce a lot of the risks associated with it. A prototype is often the step needed to encourage skeptical project stakeholders to approve your project.

After this lesson, you will be able to:

- Choose the type of prototype required for your specific situation.
- Understand the difference between a mockup and a proof of concept.
- Evaluate high-level design decisions through a prototype.
- Evaluate the effectiveness of your prototype.
- Demonstrate the feasibility of the project to stakeholders through the prototype.

Estimated lesson time: 20 minutes

Real World

Mike Snell

Prototyping mitigates (and uncovers) real risks for both the organization and the development team. My team was recently handed a requirements document and asked to put together a set of high-level estimates. We documented a lot of assumptions and made key technology recommendations. Based on this information, we estimated the project to require about six months of effort for our team. The client was pleased with this information and ready to get started. However, this was a new business domain for us and a new client, so we suggested beginning with a three-to-five-week prototyping phase.

> During the prototyping phase, we confirmed the requirements, identified all the user interface (UI) elements, and validated our technology choices. The result was that we uncovered scores of new requirements, an unforeseen set of more than 30 maintenance screens, and implied integration points for which we had not accounted. This was a big surprise to both us and our client. It seems that the project was much bigger than our original estimate of six months. This forced the client to reappraise the need for this software based on its cost. More important, it saved us both from entering into a project in which neither the client nor we would be successful.

What Constitutes a Good Prototype?

A good prototype answers the questions left open from the requirements and technology recommendations. Often, these questions are not so much asked as just exist. This is called a gap. There might be a gap between what a user defines as a requirement or scenario and what the user really wants to see. There might be a gap between what a developer has defined for the application architect and what the project stakeholders understand. There might be a gap between a new architecture that an architect has read about and is proposing and what is truly required. These gaps exist whether they are defined or not. A prototype is meant to reduce the overall project risk by closing some of these gaps.

Mockups and Proof-of-Concept Prototypes

There are many types of prototypes. Some projects create UI prototypes. Others might prototype an architecture consideration. Still others might look at the feasibility of using a specific technology such as BizTalk or Host Integration Server. In fact, every project might have different needs for a prototype. However, for the present purposes, these prototypes can be classified into two principal groups: mockups and proof of concept.

Mockup

A *mockup* is meant to verify the requirements and use cases through the creation of a number of key forms in the system. Mockups are also called *horizontal prototypes* because they reveal a single horizontal picture of the application. They do not go deeply (or vertically) into the other layers of the application such as the business objects and the database. Mockups are a great way to determine whether the requirements are complete and understood. They also help validate the use cases, the navigational structure, and some of the logical interactions of the application.

Mockups do have shortcomings. They do not prove out any of the architecture of the system. They also do not validate the technology decisions. Mockups, however, are a great tool to move from words on paper to something much more tangible. Users often have different opinions when they see something as a picture versus a block of text in a document. Mockups are also useful for defining how the application will look and behave. This removes ambiguity from the implementation and builds early consensus on what will be delivered. The effect is a smoother, faster transition to real working code once development gets started.

Proof of Concept

A *proof-of-concept prototype* is meant to validate the requirements and confirm the technology recommendations and high-level design. A proof-of-concept prototype is also called a *vertical prototype* because it looks at the application through the entire stack or layers of the application (UI, services, business objects, and database). Proof-of-concept prototypes have also been called *reference architectures* because they provide a reference to the development team about just how the system should work from top to bottom. This removes ambiguity, creates a standard, and eliminates a lot of risk.

You create a proof-of-concept prototype by choosing a key use case (or set of use cases) of the application and then building it out through each layer of the design. It makes more sense to prove out a riskier use case than to work with a well-known use case. The latter might be easy, but it lacks the risk reduction you are looking for with a proof of concept.

The Prototyping Process

There are many ways to create mockup-style prototypes. You can use Visual Studio to create screens that connect to dummy data and wire up the navigation. You can also use drawing tools such as Office Visio to simply lay up images that represent the mockup. You might decide to draw the screens on a whiteboard, index cards, or even sticky notes. The process for creating mockups should, however, involve the user. It should be highly interactive because it really is just an extension of the requirements.

A proof-of-concept prototype should, of course, be created with Visual Studio and any other tools (third-party controls, BizTalk, SSIS, and so on) you are trying to review. You can often get developer (or trial) editions of the software for this purpose. If you intend to evaluate, for instance, the feasibility of creating a Smart Client user interface, you should define one by using Visual Studio and an application server. Proof-of-concept prototypes are much more involved than just a mockup. However, their intent is not only to validate key requirements but also to confirm key design decisions.

Creating a Prototype to Evaluate Key Design Decisions

You must make a lot of key design decisions when recommending any technology. These, like all design decisions, come with a certain amount of risk. The risks are usually related to the ability of the technology to satisfy all the requirements and the developer's solid grasp of just how that technology works. The following are all risks that you should consider reducing when proposing technologies. Each of these risks can be mitigated through the creation of a proof-of-concept prototype.

Confirm the Client Technology and Application Container

The application container is the shell that houses the application and provides base services. In a Windows scenario, this is understood to be a main form with the navigation, status indicator, and base functionality such as undo, cut, copy, paste, auto-update, and so on. In a Web application, this might include your master pages, style sheets, themes and skins, the navigation, and any shared controls that you intend to create. There are many other client variations such as Windows mobile, Smart Client, and Office client.

The time to define your application container is in the prototype phase. This allows the technical leaders of the application to set this very key decision about how developers will add user interface elements to the system. It also removes the ambiguity around this key factor. Also, defining the application container through the prototype gives users a better understanding of how the system will operate as a whole even though you will not implement everything the container defines.

Defining User Interface Elements to Confirm Requirements

An application prototype also helps you understand your scope. Work to understand the many forms or screens that will be required for your application and try to list each of these and categorize them by type. A screen type helps you group similar items. The following list offers some screen types you might consider.

- **Data entry form**   Represents a form in which you are requesting the user to enter data for the application.
- **Data list form**   A form that displays a list of data. This list might require paging, sorting, filtering, and so on.
- **Wizard**   You might have a set of forms (or tabs) that work together as a wizard to capture user data.
- **Report**   You might have a number of report-like forms in the system. These reports might allow for data filtering through parameters or viewing the data graphically.
- **Property page**   Represents a form that is used to set and select various properties or settings. These screen types are sometimes implemented in panels or in separate dialog boxes.
- **Navigation and action panes**   These forms are employed by the user to navigate within the system or select key actions. Think of the folder pane in Office Outlook as an example. Depending on your application, you might have one or more of these screen types per module.

When you define the screens and group them, you should also consider their complexity. Complexity of the screen can be defined in terms of its functionality (read versus write), the number of elements on the screen, the user interactivity, and the access to and from the screen. Having this complexity for each screen will help you understand the overall scope for your project better.

Next, create a working prototype of at least one of each screen type. This will ensure that users and developers of the system understand the screen type. You might also have to create reusable base forms or user controls to help during implementation. Having a set of implemented screen types will also add to the overall reference architecture for the development team.

Finally, you might wish to define the actual UI appearance and behavior as part of the prototype phase. This step usually involves creating designs and working with the users to validate those designs. Having these designs at the outset will help set standards for the application and mitigate further risks and possible delays.

Evaluating Web Service and Remoting Recommendations

If you intend to recommend Web services or remoting as part of your application architecture, you need to evaluate them for their effectiveness relative to your constraints. A prototype can help in this regard. When creating the proof of concept, you need to consider all of the following with respect to Web services and remoting.

- How will users be connected to the application server?
- How will the application behave when there is no connection or the connection is slow? Are the results acceptable to the users, or do you have to consider design alternatives?
- How will you manage transaction reliability and ensure no data loss? Will all calls to the application server be synchronous?
- How will you manage concurrency issues? Will the last user to save unknowingly overwrite someone else's changes?

How will you manage security for the services on the application server?

Evaluating Your Proposed Security Model

Your security model should be part of the prototype. This will provide insight into what is required to support the security requirements. When you define a prototype, consider all of the following aspects with respect to security.

- **Feasibility**   You need to be sure that what you are proposing is feasible. If, for instance, you are proposing that each user authenticate through an Active Directory directory service account, you need to make sure that all users have such accounts or that they can be created.

- **Authentication**   You need to confirm your choice for user authentication. Will you need to implement authentication by saving user credentials in a database? Or can you use Windows authentication?

- **Authorization**   You need to confirm your authorization strategy and perhaps filter data based on a user's access rights. You might even need to control this on a field-by-field basis in a business object. You also need to define how you intend to access key resources in the application. Are there files that need to be checked against an access control list? How should the database connection string be stored securely?

- **Connectivity between resources**   You need to validate the feasibility of your proposed high-level design. This might be less of a prototype task and require some discussions with your infrastructure team. For instance, there might be firewall rules that prevent some of your communication decisions between clients and application servers.

- **Data security and encryption**   You need to understand what data in the system is sensitive and requires additional considerations. For example, some data might require that it be encrypted when passed between application layers or stored in the database.

- **Application and data access**   Some features and data in the system will require that you log their use and access. You need to determine which user activities need to be logged, how you intend to do the logging, and how you plan to manage the data in the access log.

Evaluating Third-Party Applications or Controls

Unless you are very familiar with your third-party control or application recommendations, these represent an important piece to consider in the prototype. In fact, any technology that is not familiar should be prototyped. If, for example, you intend to use Windows Workflow Services for the first time, you need to validate your assumptions through a proof of concept. Some third-party control categories you should consider prototyping and evaluating include:

- **General UI**   You might be using these to create unique user interface elements and navigation constructs.

- **Grid control**   You might require a specialized data grid control to manage report-like or spreadsheet-like features.

- **Licensing**   You might need to control licensing for your application or control.

- **Charts and reports**   You might have a requirement to create charts and graphs for the reporting or dashboard features.

- **Data transformation and exchange**   You might use a tool or controls to handle data import and transformation or to generate export files.

Evaluating Proposed Data Access and Storage Methods

The proof of concept phase is also a good time to evaluate your recommendations about data access and storage. If, for example, you are proposing SQL Everywhere be loaded on PDAs and other mobile devices to support offline and synchronization requirements, and you have never done so, you need to prototype. Again, this will help you evaluate your decision in terms of feasibility, practicality, and level of effort.

Evaluating Your State Management Decisions

Your enterprise application must manage state effectively. This includes both ASP.NET and Windows applications. *Application state* defines how data is moved and persisted throughout the layers of an application. There are a number of things to validate in your state management decisions. Some of these include the following considerations.

- **Shared state**   Do users have to be able to share application state as in an auction system? If so, how will this state be shared from one client to another? Through an application server?
- **State persistence**   How will state be maintained on the user's desktop? The application server? Does the user have offline access to this state? Will a stateless load balancer be required? Should state be moved to a state server to increase scalability?
- **Saving state**   How will state move from in-memory to at-rest? Will it be saved locally? How will it get to the database?
- **Caching**   If you have an application server, can some application state be cached on that server and shared? What are the ramifications of the caching strategy in terms of reading old data, updating the cache, and consuming server resources?

Confirming and Refining the Recommended Architecture

Your prototype also offers the chance to refine your architecture recommendations. If, for example, you are proposing to create a framework for the application, then now is the time to validate the feasibility of that framework. You might have the functional requirement to eliminate the need for developers to manage saving and retrieving object data, for example. This type of framework needs to be reviewed and validated through a proof of concept.

You might also want to prove out how you will partition the layers of the application. A good reference architecture will demonstrate to a developer how the code should behave and where it should be located. For example, if you create a user interactivity layer for the application that should be used to house user interface code, then you should prototype just what code goes in this layer and how the controls of the user interface might interact with this code. Prototypes are often as much about validating proposed architectures as they are about evaluating or demonstrating recommended technologies.

Quick Check

1. What is the primary purpose of creating a prototype?
2. What is the difference between a mockup and a proof-of-concept prototype?
3. What is meant by the term *reference architecture*?

Quick Check Answers

1. A good prototype answers the questions left open from the requirements and technology recommendations.
2. A mockup is a horizontal view of the application at the user interface level. A proof of concept takes a vertical slice of the application and implements it through the layers.
3. A reference architecture is an implementation of the architecture through the application layers. For example, it might include a Windows form, a set of business objects, the data access methods, and the data storage solution—all for a single feature or use case.

Demonstrating the Feasibility of the Design

You need to evaluate and prove the effectiveness of the prototype. Remember that your intent is to understand and establish the requirements and design recommendations better. The prototype is meant to build confidence and foster a sense of mutual understanding between users, stakeholders, and the developers—before it's too late.

Go into the prototype phase expecting to find issues with the requirements and design. Do not be afraid to make changes in your assumptions, your design, or your requirements. That is the point. You need to find conflicts between documented requirements and what is practical and feasible. For this reason, spend time evaluating the effectiveness of your prototype. Consider all of the following contingencies.

- **Missing or poor requirements** Did you identify requirements that were incomplete or ambiguous? Were there areas that required additional clarification or use cases?
- **Design challenges** What portions of the application will present additional design challenges? Identify areas that will need more focus. Also, consider whether you need to extend the prototype session to complete this effort.
- **Technology recommendations** Are there different recommendations that you would make, based on the prototype? Did your recommendations satisfy everything you had hoped?
- **Level of effort** The prototype should help you understand how much effort will be required to build the application. Take a look at what was required for the reference

architecture. Now make sure that you have enough time built into the project based on this effort (adjusted for the skills of the team).

- **Usability**   A good gauge of the prototype is, "Does it seem natural to the users, or do they require training to work with the screens?" If your prototype leans toward the latter, you need to keep working.

Finally, you need to take what you've learned from the prototype and put together a presentation for the stakeholders. This will help communicate formally what you've learned and accomplished during the prototype phase. This demonstration will help the stakeholders make the decision to release funds to move the project to the next level.

Lab: Creating a Proof-of-Concept Prototype

The best way to ensure your understanding of this material is to create an actual proof-of-concept prototype. You can use this exercise as your aid for creating a prototype for your next project.

▶ **Exercise: Create a Prototype for Your Project**

Use this exercise as a guide for creating a project prototype. If you don't have a new project, consider each item in the exercise relative to your last (or your current) project. If you were not able to create a prototype for this project, ask yourself, "What risks might I have eliminated if I had created a prototype?" or, "How would things have gone more smoothly if we had started with a prototype?"

1. Read through the application requirements and use cases. Identify the forms that might be required to satisfy the application. List each form and the primary functionality of the form. Look for similarities between the forms. Use these similarities to define form types or groupings.

2. Identify areas of the requirements that seem gray or incomplete. Match these areas to the form types you identified in the previous task. Create a user interface mockup for each of these forms. Review the mockups with the users and get their feedback.

3. Review your proposed architecture with the development team. Find out what questions they have. Do they understand it the same way you understand it? Create a reference implementation of the architecture through the layers. Review this reference architecture with the team and find out whether they now have a better understanding.

4. Confirm the key design decisions you made for the application through the prototype. This might include verifying your security model, understanding how you will use Web services or remoting, or validating your data management technique. You should choose to validate any items that seem risky or not fully understood.

5. Update the requirements, recommendations, and design, based on the prototype. Be sure to track changes. Review how many changes resulted from the prototype.

6. Try to create an accurate estimate of the time it will take to complete the project. Can you get other developers to agree to these estimates? Do you feel the estimates are accurate and complete? If not, what would make them more accurate and complete?

7. Document the lessons the prototype taught you. Put them together in a presentation. This should include your original assumptions, the evaluation, and the revised assumptions resulting from the prototype effort. In addition, add the key screens and other items to the presentation. Take this presentation to the stakeholders and get their feedback.

Lesson Summary

- A prototype is meant to fill in the gaps that remain between the paper definition and the reality of implementation.

- You can define user interface mockups to validate the user interface and navigation of the system. Mockups can be created using index cards, sticky notes, whiteboards, or a drawing tool such as Office Visio.

- A proof-of-concept prototype implements a vertical slice of the application through the layers. This is also called a reference architecture.

- Proof of concepts should use the target technologies for their creation. There are developer evaluation versions of nearly all the technologies you might recommend.

- A prototype should confirm the recommended client type, the application container, the user interface elements, the use of an application server, your security model, the third-party controls you've recommended, the proposed data access and storage methods, your state management decisions, and your overall high-level design.

- Review your prototype to confirm its effectiveness. You need to be comfortable making changes based on your prototype; that is the intention. You also should use the prototype to demonstrate the feasibility of the project to stakeholders.

Lesson Review

You can use the following questions to test your knowledge of the information in Lesson 2, "Creating a Proof-of-Concept Prototype to Refine an Application's Design." The questions are also available on the companion CD if you prefer to review them in electronic form.

NOTE   Answers

Answers to these questions and explanations of why each answer choice is right or wrong are located in the "Answers" section at the end of the book.

---

1. Review the following questions you need to answer with your prototype. Based on these questions, what type of prototype should you create?

❑ How will application state be passed between layers?

❑ How will user data entry be validated?

❑ How will the business rules of the application be enforced?

   A. Vertical prototype

   B. Horizontal prototype

   C. Database prototype

   D. Mockup prototype

2. You need to evaluate quickly the size and magnitude of your user interface. Which of the following prototype steps should you take? (Choose all that apply.)

   A. Define a set of screen types for your application.

   B. List each screen and assign a type and complexity.

   C. Create at least one prototype for each screen type.

   D. Mock up each user interface screen.

3. Which of the following should you consider when evaluating your proposed security model? (Choose all that apply.)

   A. User authentication methods

   B. User authorization methods

   C. Resources control

   D. Connectivity

4. You need to evaluate the effectiveness of your prototype. Which of the following might lead you to believe your prototype was effective? (Choose all that apply.)

   A. A number of gaps were identified in the requirements.

   B. The use cases were validated as correct and sufficient.

   C. Certain areas of the application were exposed as requiring additional focus on the design.

   D. The new technologies that were recommended worked just as expected.

Chapter Review

To further practice and reinforce the skills you learned in this chapter, you can perform the following tasks:

- Review the chapter summary.
- Review the list of key terms introduced in this chapter.
- Complete the case scenarios. These scenarios set up real-world situations involving the topics of this chapter and ask you to create a solution.
- Complete the suggested practices.
- Take a practice test.

Chapter Summary

- You need to look at the requirements of your application from multiple perspectives. These perspectives should include the user, the business, the developers (functional requirements), and the quality of service (or non-functional) requirements. Requirements should not be ambiguous. Instead, they should be clear, measurable, and actionable.

- Developers need to be able to look at a set of requirements and make some technology recommendations. These recommendations should be based solely on the requirements of the system. You should not recommend too much or too little. Do careful analysis and make recommendations that fit these requirements. Don't always assume a build-it stance to satisfy requirements. Consider how an off-the-shelf product or internal asset might decrease time to market and reduce overall risk.

- Application prototypes come in many forms. However, two common forms include mockups and proofs of concept. A mockup helps validate the user interface and navigation of the system. A proof-of-concept prototype takes a vertical slice of the application and implements it across the layers. This helps eliminate risks in the design and gives the developers a reference on which they can model their work. Create an application prototype to confirm the recommended client technology, the application container, the user interface elements (or screen types), the use of an application server, your security model, the third-party controls you've recommended, the proposed data access and storage methods, your state management decisions, and your overall high-level design.

- You need to make sure your prototype is effective. It should not simply demonstrate that you can create simple user interface elements to satisfy basic requirements. Rather, it needs to target the risky, or unknown, elements in the system. You need to evaluate your prototype and make sure it does just that. A prototype means changes to the requirements and recommendations. That is the point.

Key Terms

Do you know what these key terms mean? You can check your answers by looking up the terms in the glossary at the end of the book.

- application library
- application server
- business requirement
- client
- data storage
- framework
- functional requirement
- functional specification
- horizontal prototype
- mockup
- proof-of-concept prototype
- quality of service (QOS) requirement
- reference architecture
- third-party control
- user requirement
- vertical prototype

Case Scenario

In the following case scenario, you will apply what you've learned about evaluating requirements, recommending technologies, and creating a prototype. You can find answers to these questions in the "Answers" section at the end of this book.

Case Scenario: Evaluate Requirements and Propose an Application Design

You are the lead developer at a large healthcare management organization. You have been assigned a project to create an interactive, secure Web site to provide your members and their healthcare providers with information regarding their insurance accounts, claims, and historical records.

Interviews

You attend a meeting to brainstorm on the high-level requirements for the system. This meeting includes key project stakeholders, user representatives, and IT staff. This meeting is being co-facilitated by the lead business analyst and you. The following list presents statements made during the meeting.

- **Member Services Manager** "We have over 50,000 members in 37 states in the United States. Right now, a member's profile is often tracked in multiple systems, depending on his or her location and status. We need to centralize the storage and access to member profile data. The many systems that use member data should be connected to this central view of a member's profile. Each member should be tracked only once.

  "The application should be fast and responsive. When users log on, they should not be frustrated with long wait time (more than five seconds) for any response.

  "We need a clean user interface. The application should be easy to use and approachable. We want users to get to information quickly and efficiently with no confusion."

- **User Representative** "A participating healthcare provider (doctor, pharmacy, and so on) should be able to use the system to look up insurance benefits for a given member. They should be able to find this information based on the member's number. Right now, this is done by phone verification. This application should reduce costs.

  "Our users will require access to the application across the Internet by using any standard, DHTML 4.x–compatible browser."

- **Statistical Reporting and Analysis** "We need to adjust the numbers on the member data every quarter. It's important that we not trace this data back to individual members or member representatives. Rather, we need to do statistical modeling to determine the overall health of our membership. This is done through a third-party application, using complex proprietary algorithms. The data we need is defined by the MemberExtract schema and should be provided as comma-separated values (CSV)."

- **IT Manager** "The application must conform to our security policy. Upon a member's initial request, for example, the application must establish and verify credentials for the member. All subsequent requests will require these credentials. Healthcare providers will be authenticated through previously established credentials. They should continue to have access only to members to whom they provide services.

  "There are four systems that update member profile data. There are another three systems that require read access to this data. Each of these systems will require an update to work with the centralized member profile data. In addition, each of these systems tracks additional information about a member (outside of the profile). It is not within scope to modify this behavior.

  "You should expect up to 1,000 concurrent users working with this data. In addition, users should expect to be able to access the system at all times."

- **Development Manager** "To support the other applications that require access to this member data, we suggest creating a set of services that allow this access. This data can be returned as XML because not all of these other applications are Windows-based. We have created a server to provide this information at *http://contoso/members/memberservice .asmx*. Two service methods are planned: *GetMember(memberId)* and *UpdateMember(memberData)*.

"We are considering using .NET Framework 2.0 for the application. The development team has little experience with this technology. It would be nice if they had some examples to follow."

Questions

While thinking about the statements listed here, answer the following questions.

1. What are the user requirements of the system?
2. What are the business requirements of the system?
3. What are the QOS (or non-functional) requirements of the system?
4. Which requirements represent functional requirements of the system?
5. Which requirements need more detail to make them unambiguous and more actionable?
6. What data storage mechanism might you recommend for the application?
7. What areas of the application seem as though they require additional research through prototyping?

Suggested Practices

To help you successfully master the exam objectives presented in this chapter, complete the following tasks.

Evaluating Requirements and Proposing a Design

For this task, consider completing both practices. If you do not have an application to work with, consider an application that you have used recently. These practices will give you a better feel for your understanding of the material.

- **Practice 1** Spend some time with your business analysts to define application requirements. Work with users to elicit these requirements. Try documenting the requirements and then presenting them back to the users. Refine them based on their feedback. Evaluate these requirements to confirm that they are not ambiguous and can be measured.
- **Practice 2** Take a look at the requirements you created in Practice 1 and consider the technologies you would recommend based on these requirements. Alternatively, find an older set of requirements. Take a look at these again now that you have read this chapter. How would you solve these requirements given today's tools and technologies?

Creating a Proof-of-Concept Prototype to Refine an Application's Design

This task should be common to most senior-level developers. If, however, you have not participated in this process with users, you should strongly consider performing Practice 1. Practice 2 should help you understand how a technology model answers a few questions but presents more. Only a prototype can answer many of these questions.

- **Practice 1** Work with users to define a user interface. Use index cards or a large whiteboard. Have the users describe a scenario of what they need the application to do. You should then draw how the user interface will enable this scenario. This should help you understand expectations, navigation concerns, and interactivity.

- **Practice 2** Define a simple, high-level application design. Document a set of assumptions for the design. Present this design to a small group of developers in a meeting. Listen to how these developers expect to implement the system. List their concerns; try not to elaborate on your design. Now review the list and consider how these questions might be answered through a prototype.

Take a Practice Test

The practice tests on this book's companion CD offer many options. For example, you can test yourself on just the content covered in this chapter, or you can test yourself on all the 70-549 certification exam content. You can set up the test so that it closely simulates the experience of taking a certification exam, or you can set it up in study mode so that you can look at the correct answers and explanations after you answer each question.

MORE INFO   **Practice tests**

For details about all the practice test options available, see the section titled "How to Use the Practice Tests" in this book's Introduction.

Chapter 2
Creating Specifications for Developers

Once you have your requirements, and the stakeholders have given their approval to start, you need to focus on translating those requirements into specifications that can be implemented by developers. This means defining the logical relationships in the system that will provide the team with a common basis as they carry out the software development. It also means imposing the constraints of your technology on the requirements in the form of physical models.

This chapter examines how you review requirements and use cases and defines a logical model from this information. Then you will learn how to apply your technology recommendations and constraints to that logical model. The result will be a set of physical models that take into account both the logical understanding of the application and the physical abilities of the technology. This physical model will serve as a blueprint for developers to help them implement features.

Exam objectives in this chapter:
- Evaluate the technical specifications for an application to ensure that the business requirements are met.
- Translate the functional specification into developer terminology, such as pseudo code and UML diagrams.
- Suggest component type and layer.

Lessons in this chapter:

Before You Begin

To complete the lessons in this chapter, you should be familiar with developing enterprise applications by using Microsoft Windows or ASP.NET. You should also be familiar with Microsoft Visual Studio 2005, using Microsoft Visual Basic or C#. In addition, you should be comfortable with all of the following:

- Reviewing requirements and use cases for an application

- Detailing the functional specifications for an application
- How .NET architectures and related technologies solve specific business problems
- Object-oriented development concepts
- Reading, creating, and working with Unified Modeling Language (UML) (class diagrams and other physical models)
- A drawing or UML tool such as Microsoft Office Visio for creating UML diagrams

---

Real World

The days of a developer designing an enterprise application on a napkin are long over. Contemporary enterprise applications are complex, multifaceted software systems; even relatively straightforward Web applications often have many integration points. We are often asked to build reusable enterprise components for consistent security, logging, and database access across applications. All of these factors increase the overall complexity of our applications. It is this complexity, however, that helps us realize the benefits of distributed, object-oriented systems.

This complexity requires a solid architecture and focused design effort, which means using formal design and formal tools. It also means taking advantage of multiple architects. Working with colleagues through design and implementation decisions will improve your software and reduce project risks. When working together, a formal tool such as UML can be an excellent means for communicating with others in a common design language.

Lesson 1: Create a Logical Model

Software is meant to solve real business problems for real people. These business problems typically have logical concepts, objects, relationships, and attributes. For example, the concept that an automobile has features and options and is sold by a salesperson at a dealership represents a set of tangible, logical objects and relationships. You need to define these logical items so that your software behaves accordingly.

A logical model should not change once it has been defined and agreed upon–that is, unless the real-world concepts on which it is based change. This is unlike software concepts that are affected by technology and other constraints. The logical model gives everyone on the team (users, business analysts, architects, developers, and so on) an understanding of the system from a logical viewpoint. This viewpoint is also more approachable compared to the physical technical models.

This lesson describes how to create logical models by using object role modeling diagrams; it covers the basics of ORM first and then looks at how you can use this tool to document your understanding of the application's requirements in the form of logical relationships.

After this lesson, you will be able to:

- Determine the principal objects (entities) in your system, based on the requirements and use cases.
- Determine the logical relationships between objects.
- Determine the attributes (properties and fields) of an object.

Estimated lesson time: 30 minutes

Object Role Modeling

Object role modeling (ORM) is the process of creating a diagram to represent real-world concepts that define or influence your software. An ORM diagram includes the primary objects (also called entities) in the system, the relationships between those objects, and the attributes–even attribute values–that define those objects. You use the ORM notation to create this logical representation between objects. You could use entity-relationship (ER) diagrams, but they are primarily associated with databases. In addition, class diagrams are associated with physical, object-oriented development. ORM diagrams, on the other hand, offer a purely logical modeling tool for users, business analysts, and developers.

You create ORM diagrams by decomposing the user requirements and use cases for your application and pulling out the objects, relationships, and attributes. You will see this process later in the lesson. First, however, look at how to model this information and how to understand the ORM notation.

The ORM Notation

The ORM notation offers a number of shapes and connectors to define your logical model. However, you can simplify your approach to the notation by understanding a few primary concepts that this discussion begins with. Once you've understood those, you can represent 95 percent or more of your models. These primary concepts include object (or entity), relationship (or fact), and cardinality.

ORM Objects

Objects are represented in ORM diagrams by an oval with the name of the object in the oval. Remember, these are logical models. Therefore, ORM objects are any nouns in the requirements or use case. They do not have to be full-blown physical objects or primary entities. Rather, they represent the logical things that make up the system. For example, consider the following simple use case about an application for purchasing used cars online.

1. Shoppers enter criteria about the type of vehicle they wish to purchase. Purchase criteria include year, make, model, engine size, drive train, and color.

2. The system searches the available inventory for vehicles that most closely match the shoppers' purchase criteria. These vehicles are returned to the shoppers' screens and displayed in a list along with photos and pricing details.

3. Shoppers then select one or more vehicles about which they would like additional information. They are then asked to enter their contact details (name, address, and phone number). This information is forwarded to the next available sales representative, who will contact a shopper to help complete a purchase.

In this small use case, the following would all be considered objects: shopper, vehicle, purchase criteria, inventory, contact details, and sales representative. These might seem clear at first; however, year, make, model, engine size, drive train, color, photo, pricing details, name, address, and phone number are also objects in ORM terms. Figure 2-1 shows these items as objects on an ORM diagram.

NOTE   **Office Visio and ORM diagrams**

Office Visio provides an ORM diagramming tool. If you have the standard Microsoft Office edition, you can create an ORM diagram. This is simply a drag-and-drop diagram. If you have Office Visio for Enterprise Architects (which ships with certain versions of Visual Studio), you can create what is called an ORM Source Model. This is an advanced ORM tool. It provides a fact editor that makes defining objects and relationships much easier. You can also validate your assumptions through examples. Both diagrams are in the database category because they seem to relate to building logical database models. However, ORM diagrams should not be thought of as simply a database tool.

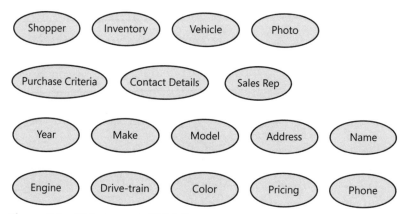

Figure 2-1   Objects on an ORM diagram

ORM Relationship

An ORM relationship defines how two or more objects are related to one another. A relationship between objects in an ORM diagram is represented as a line connecting the objects. Along this line will be a rectangle divided into segments based on the number of objects in the relationship. This is typically two segments because most relationships you model are between two objects (called a binary relationship). However, if you are modeling a relationship that exists among three objects (called a ternary relationship), you need to define all three relationships.

Let's look at some examples. Consider the small use case you saw previously and the objects that were derived from it. The use case defines relationships among each of these objects. These relationships are represented in Figure 2-2.

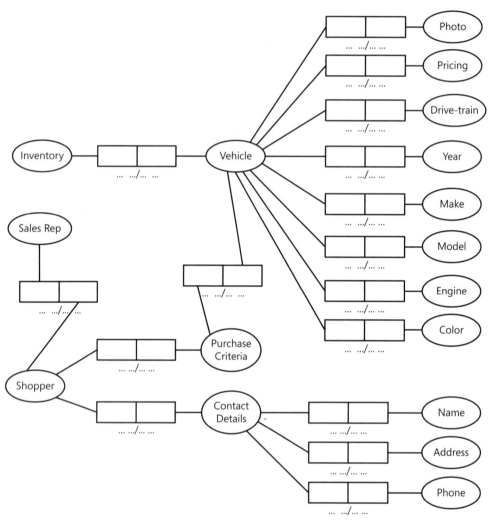

Figure 2-2   ORM relationships

ORM Facts

What is still missing from your diagram are the facts that define the relationship. A fact indicates how two (or more) items are related. This is also called the fact model for your application. Facts don't change. They represent how objects really relate to one another.

You define facts on an ORM diagram by adding text beneath the relationship shape. Note that in Figure 2-2, there is an ellipsis (...) on either side of a slash (/) under each relationship shape. You define the relationship by replacing the ellipsis with text. The slash indicates how you read the relationship. The text on the left side of the slash reads from left to right. The text on the right side of the slash defines the inverse of the relationship. Figure 2-3 shows the model with the facts defined. For example, you read the first fact as "Inventory has Vehicle" and the inverse as "Vehicle is in Inventory."

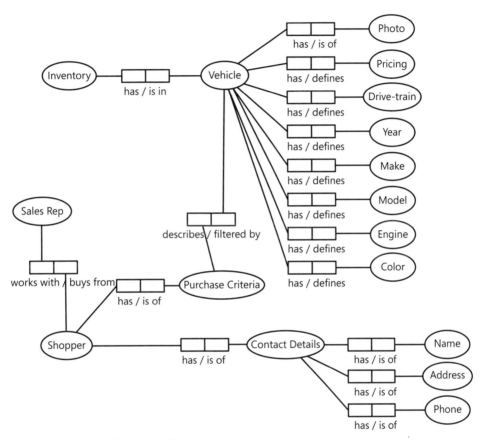

Figure 2-3   ORM relationship facts

ORM Constraints

The constraints are the final thing missing from your model. ORM constraints define how the objects participate in the relationship. This includes defining which items are mandatory and the multiplicity of the relationship. Mandatory items are indicated by a closed (or filled) circle attached to either end of the connection. This closed circle indicates that the given object is mandatory in the relationship. That is, the related item does not exist without the other item.

Multiplicity indicates whether two objects relate to one another as one-to-one, one-to-many, or many-to-many. Multiplicity is indicated with a series of arrows over the relationship shape. Figure 2-4 shows the multiplicity options for ORM relationships.

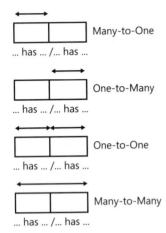

Figure 2-4   ORM relationship multiplicity

Figure 2-5 shows these constraints applied to your sample diagram. For example, you can now read the first relationship (between Inventory and Product) as, "The inventory has one or more vehicles, and each vehicle is in a single inventory." This gives you a very good understanding of your system in terms of objects and the facts that exist between those objects.

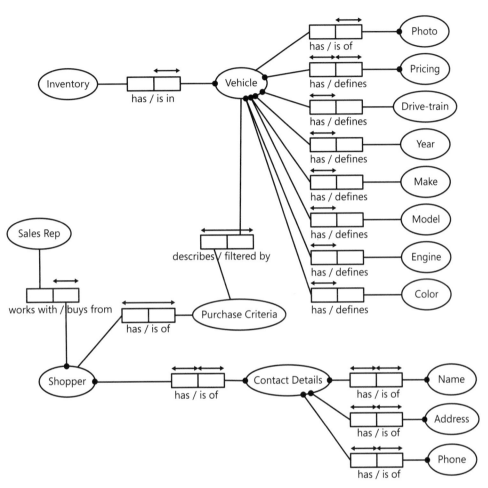

Figure 2-5 The ORM with cardinality

Driving ORM Diagrams from Requirements and Use Cases

You saw in the previous example that you were able to define an ORM diagram from a simple use case. Most use cases and requirements are much more detailed than that simple example. You will want to go over these requirements and use cases line by line and pull out the objects and facts. The objects are easy because they are represented by nouns. The relationships (or facts) are the verb phrases that indicate a connection between objects.

When you first start your ORM diagram, the objects and facts will come quickly and easily. As you progress to a few use cases in, however, you will identify fewer and fewer new objects and fewer new facts. Instead, you might find that you need to rethink or refactor the way you are looking at certain items. You need to look at each statement in the specifications and determine whether your ORM diagram supports the statements found there. If it doesn't, either the statement or the ORM diagram must change. Once these items are aligned, you should have a solid understanding of how the items in your software relate.

Quick Check

1. What is the primary purpose of a logical model of your requirements and use cases?
2. How do you read the relationship between two objects?

Quick Check Answers

1. A logical model defines the facts in the domain for which you are building software. Creating a logical model of your requirements will both validate the requirements and provide a solid understanding of the domain.
2. The relationship is read from left to right, using the text on the left side of the slash under the relationship shape. The inverse relationship is read in the opposite direction, using the text on the opposite side of the slash.

Using ORM Diagrams to Identify Objects, Properties, Methods, Entities, and Fields

Your ORM diagram is a logical view of your objects and relationships. As you continue your design process, you will use the logical model (ORM diagrams and logical architecture) along with your technology recommendations to drive physical models. Your logical models should not change. However, when you apply these logical models to your target technology, you will make decisions that might confuse and even contradict your logical model. This is acceptable because you need to make tradeoffs when moving to the physical model.

Lesson 3, "Create Physical Models for Developers," will examine this process in more detail. The basic concept, however, is that you find the items in the ORM diagram that have the most relationships. These are also items that give an interesting perspective on the system (such as shopper or vehicle). These will become your primary database entities and your classes. The items that relate to these primary entities will themselves sometimes become sub-entities (with their own definition), or they might become database fields and object properties. The relationships will form the basis for your database-stored procedures and your application methods.

Lab: Create a Logical Model

In this lab, you will review a number of high-level application requirements and a simple use case. You will use this information to define the logical objects in the domain and their relationships to one another. You will do so in the context of an ORM diagram.

▶ **Exercise: Review Requirements and Define a Logical Model**

For this exercise, review the following application requirements and simple use case with which you will be working. Then follow the steps listed after that to determine the objects and facts in this domain.

Requirements

- **R1**   The application should be accessible to our automotive research group team, which consists of 80 people in four different locations.
- **R2**   The system needs to support up to 50 researchers entering automotive data concurrently.
- **R3**   Researchers first select an automobile prior to entering or modifying data.
- **R4**   If a researcher cannot find a given instance of a vehicle, he or she will enter the vehicle into the system. A valid vehicle includes a unique combination of make, model, and year.
- **R5**   Researchers classify each vehicle by a category and set of demographic data.
- **R6**   Researchers enter options available for the given vehicle and the price associated with those options.
- **R7**   Vehicles should be reserved for researchers to work on exclusively. Two users should not be able to work on the same vehicle.

Use Case: Researcher Enters Vehicle Data

1. Researcher finds a vehicle in the system with which to work based on the vehicle's make, model, and year. Researcher checks out the vehicle for edit.
2. Researcher enters (or modifies) option data for the selected vehicle. The option data includes the name of the option, the price of the option, and the option exclusions.
3. Researcher categorizes the vehicles based on segment. Segments include car, truck, van, and SUV.
4. Researcher enters demographic information that describes the typical target customer for the vehicle. Demographic information includes age, income, education, and location.
5. Researcher saves the vehicle data and releases his or her reservation on the vehicle.

Lab Steps

The steps for this lab follow. They will lead you to determine the objects in the domain as defined in the requirements and use case listed previously.

1. Determine the objects in the domain. Go through the requirements and use case and pull out all the nouns. Review those nouns and determine whether any represent the same thing. If so, refactor the requirements and use case to use a single representation of any nouns.

2. Create an ORM diagram, using Office Visio. Add the nouns as objects on the diagram.

3. Review the list of objects. Remove any objects that you know are not of interest to your logical model.

4. Define the facts in the system. Go back through each requirement and each line of the use case. Read the phrases that indicate or imply a relationship. Try to model each fact, indicating both the left-to-right relationship and the inverse.

5. Define the constraints on your facts. Go through each fact and verify it with the requirements and the use case. When doing so, consider any constraints that apply to the fact. This should include determining which ends of the relationship are mandatory and the multiplicity of the relationship. When you're finished, lay out your facts on an ORM diagram.

   A diagram showing a solution for this lab, as well as answers to the previous steps in this lab, can be installed from the Code folder on the companion CD.

Lesson Summary

- A logical model is important because your software represents actual concepts. These concepts typically do not change. You need to have a solid grasp of these concepts to make sure your software meets the demands of these real-world concepts.

- An ORM diagram models the logical objects in your software. This includes the relationships between those objects and the constraints that should be put on those relationships.

- An ORM diagram should be thought of as a purely logical view of your objects. It should not represent your classes or your database. You can use your ORM diagrams to drive toward your database and class diagrams. However, this typically means tradeoffs to support the technology. ORM diagrams do not require such tradeoffs. Instead, they should stay faithful to the logical concepts that your software represents.

- The ORM notation uses an oval to represent an object, a line with a relationship box to represent a relationship, and arrows over the box to represent multiplicity. You can write out the relationship as text under the relationship shape on the diagram.

Lesson Review

You can use the following questions to test your knowledge of the information in Lesson 1, "Create a Logical Model." The questions are also available on the companion CD if you prefer to review them in electronic form.

NOTE Answers

Answers to these questions and explanations of why each answer choice is right or wrong are located in the "Answers" section at the end of the book.

---

1. Consider the following statement about your application: "A manager should be sent a shipping exception report by e-mail on a daily basis from the logistics system. If the shipping schedule for an order can't be verified or is in conflict, the manager must manually assign that shipment to a truck, driver, and route." Which of the following represents the logical objects defined in the previous statement?

    A. Order, Shipment, Truck, Driver, Route

    B. Manager, Report, Logistics System, Order, Shipment

    C. Manager, Shipping Exception Report, E-mail, Logistics System, Shipping Schedule, Order, Shipment, Truck, Driver, Route

    D. E-mail, Shipping Report, Verify Shipping Schedule, Assign Shipment

2. Consider the following statement about an application: "A corporate user logs a support request for access to one or more applications." Suppose you have the following objects: corporate user, support request, application access. How would you model the relationships to the Support Request object?

    A. A single unary relationship

    B. Two binary relationships

    C. A single ternary relationship

    D. A quaternary relationship

3. Consider the following statement about an application: "A supervisor approves time sheets." How would you write this fact and the inverse of this fact? (Choose all that apply.)

    A. Supervisor approves Time Sheet

    B. Supervisor has Approval

    C. Time Sheet approved by Supervisor

    D. Approval is of Supervisor

4. Consider the following fact, read left to right: "Shipping Slip has Ship-to Address." What constraints would you attach to this relationship?

    A. Closed circle on Shipping Slip, an arrow over the left side of the relationship shape

    B. Closed circle on Ship-to Address, an arrow over the right side of the relationship shape

    C. No circles, an arrow over the left side and another arrow over the right side of the relationship shape

    D. Closed circle on Shipping Slip, a single, long arrow that covers both the left and right sides of the relationship

Lesson 2: Define Application Layers

A logical architecture helps developers understand how a system is put together, how it works, and how they should add code to it. Logical architectures are not required to make your application work; instead, they are simply a means to explain how it works. It is very difficult for most developers to look at code, or even walk through code, and get a feel for exactly how an application works. Therefore, it can be helpful to define a logical understanding of the layers, components, and communication paths in a system. This also helps architects design the system.

This lesson looks at how you can create and use logical architecture models. First, you will look at defining the layers of your application. Then you will learn how to create a component model. Finally, you will examine how you can describe the communication between the layers and components.

After this lesson, you will be able to:

- Define the logical layers of your application and indicate what code should go into each layer.
- Indicate the communication paths and protocols between the layers in your system.
- Create a logical architecture to define your application.

Estimated lesson time: 20 minutes

Define the Layers of Your Application

The logical layers of your system represent how you plan to divide your code into logical pieces or groups. For example, a three-tier system might define layers to include the user interface, business objects, and database layer. These are considered logical layers because the code is divided logically by what it represents. Physically, the code libraries themselves might run in the same process. In this case, layers are combined for technical tradeoffs or physical reasons. For example, think of a Windows application that defines a set of business objects and stores them inside the same executable as the user interface. These objects run in the same process. However, the code is logically separated; user interface (UI) code goes in the UI layer, and business object code goes in the business object layer.

What Does It Mean to Have Application Layers?

The term *layer* can be thought of as similar to the term *tiers*. "Tiers" was preferred for a time because applications were being built as two-tier and three-tier designs. Tiers in a three-tier application, for example, include the user interface, middle tier, and database tier. A two-tier application has a user interface working with a database directly. The abstraction of code into tiers allows for the innovation (or replacement) of the user interface or database code without rewriting the core of the business logic.

This last concept—the ability to abstract portions of an application so that they can evolve independently—pushed application architectures toward n-tier. More tiers were added to the application. For example, a database tier can be divided into a database abstraction layer for the business objects a database utility (or helper) layer, a stored procedures layer, and the database technology itself. The user interface tier might be split between the strict UI code (events and layout operations) and the code that calls the middle tier. The middle tier can also be divided into sub-tiers. All of these splits represent what are referred to as application layers. Thinking in terms of layers is easier than considering all of these items as tiers in an n-tier design. You can define a name for each layer, and the system will be easier to understand.

Layers provide a clean, logical way to look at an application. Application layers are typically organized from top to bottom. The top is where the user activity happens. The bottom is where the data is stored when at rest. Your application *state*, the data that moves from the database to the user interface, is passed through the layers (from top to bottom and back again). Each layer in the middle represents a view of the state in your application or a service that works on that state. For example, the user interface translates state for display to the user. The business layer works on state and applies business rules to it. The database layer knows how to save state to the database. To gain a logical understanding of a system, you must define the layers and how state is passed among them (the communication paths). Of course, that presents your high-level, logical architecture. You still need to group features into components and define component models.

Layers of a Windows Application

A Windows application can be divided into a number of logical layers. Your decision about which layers to implement and enforce typically depends on your quality of service (QOS) requirements. For example, if your application is a stopgap, possibly throwaway, system with low scalability and maintainability concerns, you might choose to implement only a couple of layers (UI and database). Alternatively, if you are optimizing your architecture for varied physical deployments, high scalability, multiple user interfaces (Smart Client, Mobile, Reports, and so on), and a high degree of reuse, you will opt to abstract your application into many more logical layers—you might even decide to create a framework that supports your layers.

Most enterprise-level applications written today employ some version of the three primary layers: user interface, middle tier, and database. Each of these layers might then be divided into additional layers. The following discussion presents each of these layers and some of their common divisions. Any combination of these layers can comprise a Windows application.

User Interface   A user interface layer provides a window to the application for users. This layer is typically responsible for getting data from the middle tier and displaying it to the user. It is also responsible for controlling how a user interacts with that data. This includes data entry, validation, creating new elements, search, and so on. The UI layer is also in charge of getting the user's modifications back to the middle tier for processing. The user interface layer is often a layer by itself. However, it is also sometimes divided into one or more of the following additional layers:

- **Presentation (or user experience)** This layer defines only the presentation portion of the user interface. This is the portion responsible for laying out the user interface. For a Windows application, think of this code as the code inside of the *FormName.Designer.cs* in Visual Basic or the *InitializeComponent* method in C#. Visual Basic hides this code from the developer. In a Web application, think of this code as the markup code inside the .aspx file. In both cases, Visual Studio is trying to abstract the code for the forms engine and promote the use of the form designer tools.

- **User interface code** This layer is where developers place the code to interact with the user interface. The layer is typically embedded with a Windows form. In ASP.NET, this is the code-behind file. There is a partial class associated to each form or page in both Visual Basic and C#. You put your code in this class, and it is compiled with the form or page. The code that goes in this layer is to respond to events such as loading a form or clicking a button. You might decide to abstract the code to respond to these items into a separate user interface interaction layer. The code that would be compiled with the form or page would then simply delegate calls to this layer. This will increase your reuse if you intend to implement different UIs that perform the same types of activities.

- **Business logic interaction code** You might create this layer if you do not wish to tie the code used to interact with your business layer (middle tier) to the user interface code. This can be helpful if you intend to plan for the replacement of your user interface. For example, you might create a Windows-based client today but have a plan to move to Extensible Application Markup Language (XAML), an Office Client, or something even further.

Middle Tier The middle tier is where you house your business logic. This is often referred to as just the business layer. However, this tier typically includes a lot more than just business logic. It might include components for handling caching, logging, error management, and so on. You might use the Microsoft Enterprise Library (or a similar library) in this tier. The middle tier typically runs on an application server such as Microsoft Windows Server and Internet Information Services (IIS). However, you can create your own middle tiers (using tools such as Windows Services and sockets). The middle tier is sometimes divided into one or more of the following additional layers:

- **Business layer (or business services)** This layer is where you put your domain objects and their business rules. You might be writing stateless components that work with Enterprise Services, real object-oriented business objects that run in process, or simple data transfer objects (DTOs) with processing services that work across remoting channels. In any case, most applications define a business layer. This isolates the business logic so that it can be reused, remain stable (as UIs are rewritten and modified), be easier to change, and so on. For example, a business layer object might be a *Product* class. It might contain properties that define a product and methods that save and load the object. These methods and properties will define the business rules for the given object. These rules should be validated before the object is sent to another layer for processing.

■ **Application layer (or application services)**   This layer represents the plumbing to make your application work and typically solves QOS requirements such as "the application must log errors or cache data for performance." Keep this code isolated from your business logic. Sometimes this code is put into a framework. You can also consider the Microsoft Enterprise Library as part of the application layer. Examples of an application layer might include a *Log* class that contains methods to log certain events such as errors.

■ **Database layer (or database services)**   This layer abstracts the retrieval and storage of data in your database. This code is sometimes combined with the business layer. However, such tight coupling can make the code harder to understand, more brittle to change, and less reusable. For example, the database layer can contain static (or shared) methods that work to save and retrieve data from the database on behalf of the business layer. An example might include a *ProductData* class with a method such as *GetProduct* that returns a *DataSet* with product data. The database abstraction layer is often part of the database layer. However, it typically does not reside on the database server but on the middle-tier application server. That is why it is discussed here.

Database Layer   The database layer represents how you manage the data in your application. For most enterprise applications, this means a relational database such as Microsoft SQL Server. The database layer is responsible for saving, retrieving, and ensuring the integrity of your data and is sometimes divided into one or more of the following additional layers:

■ **Database layer**   See the "Middle Tier" section of this chapter.

■ **Stored procedures**   This layer represents the SQL or managed code used to select, insert, update, and delete data with the database. It also includes any database-defined functions you might create.

■ **Integration services**   This layer represents how the database works with other data sources for integration purposes. In SQL Server, this is SQL Server Integration Services (SSIS) or the earlier Data Transformation Services (DTS).

■ **Database tables, log, and indexes**   This layer represents the actual data in the system, the log of activity, and the indexes used by the database software.

Quick Check

1. What is the purpose of logical application layers?
2. What is the intent of creating multiple (three or more) application layers?

> **Quick Check Answers**
>   1. Logical application layers help developers and architects understand how a system works and where to write their code.
>   2. You abstract code into a layer to mitigate risk. You might be trying to increase reuse, you might be worried about layers changing independently, you might be trying to increase scalability, or you might be trying to isolate developers. The decision to create more than two layers typically revolves around supporting QOS requirements.

Define Communication Between Layers

The application layers define the logical abstractions you intend for the code in the system. You will need to consider how you intend to deploy these logical layers in a physical environment. The environment might constrain your deployment options, or you might have other concerns. For example, you might not be allowed to create a Smart Client designed to work with an application server across an Internet channel. You might have a restriction stipulating that the application server exposed across an Internet channel cannot connect directly into your database server. In this case, you might have to deploy your business logic layer on the application server and your database layer code on another server inside the firewall. The server housing the database layer could then communicate with the database. Clearly, it's important that you be aware of these issues when defining your layers. Imagine if you coupled the layers in the prior example and did not find out about this constraint until it came time to deploy the project. You would be scrambling to decouple this code and would face certain delays and increased costs.

Another deployment issue you need to consider is the communication paths and protocols between the layers. This might not be a concern if you are creating a simple, stand-alone Windows application. However, if you are building anything at the enterprise level, it most likely connects to data in some manner. As you saw in the section of Chapter 1, "Evaluating the Technical Feasibility of an Application," you can use tools such as Visual Studio Team Architect to set these constraints, indicate the communication paths, and define the ports in terms of security and protocol. For your logical architecture, you might decide simply to indicate the layers in the system and their intent and draw arrows between the layers that communicate. On each arrow, you could indicate the intended communication, such as Hypertext Transfer Protocol (HTTP), Transmission Control Protocol/Internet Protocol (TCP/IP), Simple Object Access Protocol (SOAP), and so on. Figure 2-6 shows an example of a logical architecture.

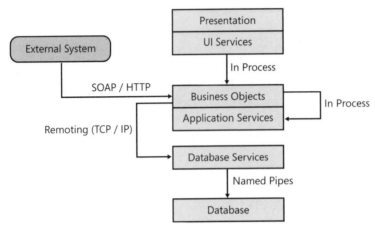

Figure 2-6   An application layer diagram (logical architecture)

This diagram shows the logical layers of the application. Note that, based on deployment constraints, the UI code (presentation and UI services), the business object layer, and the application services layer will all execute in the same process. There is also an external system that will connect to some of the business logic through a Web service. The database services code will be deployed on a different server. Therefore, the communication to this server is through remoting. Finally, the database services code will be the only layer communicating directly to the database; it will do so across named pipes.

Lab: Define Logical Application Layers

In this lab, you will define the logical layers of an application. You will start by reviewing a number of design goals and some functional requirements. You will use this information to propose the logical layers of a solution architecture. You will also add physical constraints to those layers in terms of communication paths and deployment options.

▶ **Exercise: Review Requirements and Define Logical Application Layers**

For this exercise, review the following design goals and some functional requirements. Then perform the steps that follow to determine the application layers and communication paths. The following are the requirements with which you will be working:

Design Goals / Functional Requirements

■ **G1**   The application should be accessible to any employee on the corporate network through a Windows application interface.

■ **G2**   The user interface should be easy to deploy and update.

■ **G3**   The business processing rules should be extracted into their own set of classes and methods. For now, these rules belong to only this application.

- **G4** The database access code will be created by a database developer and not by the developer of each module. All data access should be encapsulated in a common area.
- **G5** All common application functions should be grouped together. We are considering using Microsoft Enterprise Library or something similar to provide these services to the various layers of the application.
- **G6** We are targeting an existing application server for the deployment of the shared business layer. Clients will access this server through remoting.
- **G7** We plan to use the relational database to manage the data and data transactions in the system. This database is accessible from the application server through TCP/IP. Individual clients will not be able to access the database directly.

Lab Steps

1. Determine the user interface layers that you would define.
2. Determine the layers you would define for the middle tier.
3. Determine the layers you would define for the data tier.
4. Draw the recommended layers on a diagram.
5. Determine the communication paths between the layers.
6. Determine the physical processes that will execute each layer in the system.

A diagram showing a solution for this lab, as well as answers to the previous steps in this lab, can be installed from the Code folder on the companion CD.

Lesson Summary

- You define the logical layers of your application to help developers and architects understand how your system works and where their code logically fits.
- A logical architecture indicates the layers in the system and the communication paths between those layers. You abstract code into layers to help mitigate risk and increase reusability. You might also have design goals that you are satisfying with the logical layers in your application.
- An enterprise application is usually split between the user interface layers (presentation and code-behind code), the middle tier (business logic and application services), and the database tier (database abstraction code and the database itself).

Lesson Review

You can use the following questions to test your knowledge of the information in Lesson 2, "Define Application Layers." The questions are also available on the companion CD if you prefer to review them in electronic form.

NOTE   **Answers**

Answers to these questions and explanations of why each answer choice is right or wrong are located in the "Answers" section at the end of the book.

1. Which of the following are benefits of defining application layers? (Choose all that apply.)

   A. Increase code reuse.

   B. Make your code more understandable.

   C. Indicate the library (.dll) that code should go into.

   D. Make your code more maintainable.

2. You have decided to create a separate presentation layer for your user interface. Which of the following code items belong in this layer? (Choose all that apply.)

   A. Windows Forms

   B. Business rules processing

   C. User controls

   D. Database access code

3. You are writing an application that has the following constraints:

   A. The application needs to be written in a very short time.

   B. The application will not be reused. The company is already working on a replacement. However, that will take longer to develop.

   C. The application should support about 10 users.

   D. The application will be accessed by means of a single Windows form.

   E. The application logic is not very complex.

   F. The application will be deployed on each user's desktop (client). Each client will have access to a single, common server running SQL Server.

4. Considering these constraints, which application layers would you recommend?

   A. Presentation→User Activity→Business Objects→Database

   B. User Interface→Business Services→Database

   C. User Interface→Database

   D. User Interface→Application Services→Database

Lesson 3: Create Physical Models for Developers

The physical models for an application indicate how developers should build a system. These are technical models using a technical notation such as UML or the Visual Studio Class Designer. The models take the information from the requirements, use cases, technology recommendations (or high-level architecture), and logical models (ORM diagrams and application layers) and define the components, classes, methods, and messaging between objects.

This lesson looks at how you can define components from the modules, sub-modules, and layers in your application. It then looks at building class models based on the domain you defined in the ORM diagrams. Next, it will cover the purpose of some additional UML models (sequence, collaboration, and activity) that help you understand your system better. Finally, it explores how you can use pseudocode to help developers understand your intent better.

MORE INFO   **The Unified Modeling Language**

This lesson (and this book) is not meant to be a definitive primer on UML. There are many good books that tackle that subject. Rather, this lesson will cover the basic overview of the UML models as they relate to physical models for developers. It will not cover the intricacies of the notation, nor will it cover all of the many models. If you are totally unfamiliar with UML, consider some additional reading on this subject, such as *UML Distilled*, 3e, Martin Fowler (Addison-Wesley, 2003).

> **After this lesson, you will be able to:**
> - Understand the purpose of a component diagram.
> - Understand the purpose of a class diagram.
> - Understand the purpose of an activity diagram.
> - Understand the purpose of sequence and collaboration diagrams.
> - Create entity-relationship diagrams.
> - Create pseudocode to aid developers.
>
> **Estimated lesson time: 35 minutes**

Real World

Mike Snell

I prefer to use UML and other structured modeling notations. Doing so provides a professional framework approach to your designs. A structured notation forces you to think about things you might overlook if you were simply drawing boxes and lines for your design. Issues such as how objects will communicate with one another, which objects create other objects, the lifetimes of objects, and the inner workings of methods are all examples of what should be modeled with a professional notation. The result of using a professional notation will be an increased confidence in and understanding of your architecture—and, often, a better architecture.

Create a Component Diagram

A *component diagram* is used to indicate the components (or code packages) that you will create for your application. A *component* is composed of logically related classes grouped together in a single, deployable unit. You can think of a component as a dynamic-link library (DLL), control, or Web service. Component diagrams are useful for indicating physical dependencies and physical deployment (in conjunction with a deployment diagram). This section examines how you determine the components in your system and how you create a component diagram.

Defining Application Components

When you are working through your requirements, use cases, and logical model, you also work to put things into logical groupings. For example, consider the requirements and use cases for an enterprise human resource application. You will want to group the requirements into modules such as time tracking, payroll, health care, investments, and so on. You then might break these modules into sub-modules and define the set of features within each module and sub-module.

Follow a similar technique for the code elements of your application. You should group the code into physical components that will be used to indicate which library contains a given set of code. These components might follow the same lines as your application layers, or they might follow your modules or even features. For example, if you follow your application layers, you could have a UserInterface component, a BusinessObjects component, and so on. Or you might decide to break some of these layers into multiple components. You might create an Employee component, a Timesheet component, and so on. Each of these might contain business logic for a given module. However, this physical distribution might be based on the choice to encapsulate each module of the application.

Creating a Component Diagram

You create a component diagram by adding components to the diagram and then setting their dependencies. Figure 2-7 shows a sample component diagram. The components are represented with the rectangles that include the two smaller rectangles on their left. Note that each component name is preceded with text indicating its logical layer and then two colons. This text represents the components package. A UML package is a logical grouping of components, classes, and other objects. Here you are using packages to group components by logical layers. For example, the HR Portal UI component is inside the User Interface package.

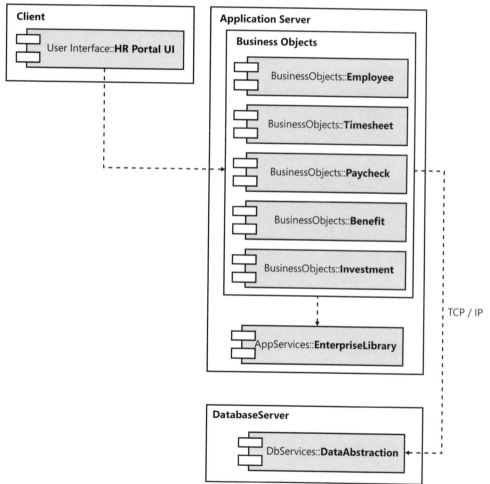

Figure 2-7 A sample component diagram

The outer boxes that surround the components are called nodes. A UML node indicates a deployment container. This is typically a physical piece of hardware. For example, the user interface is running on the *Client* node; the business objects and application services are all on the *Application Server* node. The node concept has also been used to group the business objects. This cuts down on the arrows required to indicate all the dependencies in the diagram.

Create a Class Diagram

A *class diagram* defines the structure of the classes (methods and properties) and the relationship between those classes. A class diagram defines the specification of the system. The classes in the model are static representations of your objects. The model is not meant to show how these classes interact, nor does it show the classes as objects. Rather, it shows the definition of the classes, how they are related, and how they are defined in terms of one another (and in terms of object-oriented design).

The UML defines a model for creating class diagrams. This model represents a notation for entities such as methods, properties, inheritance, associations, data types, and so on. The notation is meant to be technology agnostic. It is focused on object-oriented concepts and not on a particular technology such as .NET or Java. Visual Studio 2005, however, now provides a class diagramming tool. This tool is not meant to follow the UML notation. However, it too defines classes, properties, methods, enumerations, inheritance, dependencies, and so on.

The principal benefit of using Visual Studio is that it is a live model. It represents a two-way synchronization with your code and your diagram. If you build your class models in Visual Studio, the code is stubbed out as well. If you change your code, the model is updated. Therefore, as code is modified, your model is automatically updated. This section will leave the UML and talk about designing classes with the Class Designer.

Defining Classes for Your Application

The classes in your application should derive from your solution architecture (or framework) and your business domain. The solution architecture classes you define are dependent on that architecture. For example, if you intend to create a central class for handling error logging, you create a class called *Logger* or something similar. If you want a base class for managing object security, you create that as part of your framework. The same is true for other framework-like classes such as a database helper class or a cache management class and so on.

The business domain classes also need to respect your solution architecture. If, for example, your architecture dictates that each class must know how to save and create itself from the database, you need to design your business classes accordingly. Perhaps you would create a common interface, for example. As another example, if you are creating your business model by using a pattern such as DTO, you need to create simple domain classes with only fields or properties and then create a set of domain services to work with these classes. The point is that how you define your business domain classes depends on the technical constraints of your overall solution architecture.

The makeup of your business domain itself should be defined based on your logical model. The *business domain* refers to which classes you will define, which classes are composed of other objects (inheritance and encapsulation), and the properties of your classes. If you look back at your ORM diagrams, you will find your primary entities. These are the principal objects that link to a lot of other objects in the model. These objects can be thought of as the perspective objects. That is, they are the objects that you typically start with and from which whose perspective you examine the relationships. They are usually easy to pick out. For example, an *Employee* or *Timesheet* object in an HR application will contain a lot of links and be considered as important to model from their point of view. These objects also participate heavily in the feature set, modules, sub-modules, requirements, and use cases. The other objects in your ORM are sometimes bit players in the domain. At other times, they become simply properties, or even values of properties, of a class.

To create your business domain (class diagram), look through your ORM diagrams and pick out the domain objects and their properties. Then, apply the physical constraints of your technology choices and the constraints of your solution architecture to the class diagram. The result should be a domain model that stays true to your logical model and supports your technology choices.

Creating a Class Diagram

The Class Designer in Visual Studio provides a notation that should be easy to learn for those used to working with UML. The notation represents classes as rectangles. These rectangles, like UML classes, are split into multiple sections (usually two). The top grouping in the class contains the properties of the object; the bottom contains the methods. The notation also allows for the display of items such as fields and nested types. Figure 2-8 shows a sample class diagram for illustration purposes.

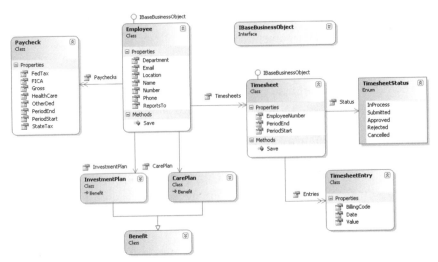

Figure 2-8   A sample class diagram

The Visual Studio 2005 Class Designer has a visual representation of a number of object-oriented elements. These elements include all of the following:

- **Class**   Represented as a rectangle with properties and methods. In Figure 2-8, *Employee*, *Paycheck*, *Timesheet*, *InvestmentPlan*, *CarePlan*, *Benefit*, and *TimesheetEntry* are all classes.

- **Interface**   An interface is represented like a class but has a different color (green). In Figure 2-8, *IBaseBusinessObject* is an interface.

- **Implement interface**   The interfaces that a class implements are represented with the lollypop icon extending from the top of the object. For example, *Employee* in Figure 2-8 implements *IBaseBusinessObject*.

- **Association/Aggregation**   A property that is of a specific type in your domain is indicated by an arrow with the property name on the line of the arrow. *CarePlan* is an example from Figure 2-8.

- **Inheritance**   A class that inherits another class is indicated with the open-ended arrow head (similar to UML). In Figure 2-8, *InvestmentPlan* and *CarePlan* inherit the *Benefit* class.

- **Enumeration**   An enumeration is indicated as a rectangle that is not rounded off (like the classes are). Figure 2-8 has the enumeration *TimesheetStatus*.

- **Other items**   The notation allows you to see a number of additional items. These include *Abstract Class*, *Struct*, *Delegate*, and a *Comment*. You can also show members of the Microsoft .NET Framework. In addition, you can modify the model to show data types and parameters.

Create a Sequence Diagram

A *sequence diagram* shows object interaction during execution (or run time). The model demonstrates the lifetime of these objects and shows the message exchange between them. Object-oriented programming results in many small objects interacting with one another. The objects call one another through a sequence (or chronology) to get work done for the application. The many objects making many calls to one another can make it difficult to understand how they come together to form a complete solution. A sequence diagram is meant to illustrate and clarify just how these objects talk to one another to form a specific solution.

The UML notation dictates how you create sequence diagrams. Objects are listed as rectangles at the top of the diagram with lifelines extending from them. An object lifeline is an indication of how long an object will live before it is disposed of or made ready for garbage collection. The objects themselves are described in the rectangle that sits atop this lifeline. The description that goes in the rectangle is meant to describe an instance of the class. For this reason, you typically write the description as an *Object* or the *Object*, where "object" is the name of the class or variable representing the class.

Figure 2-9 shows a sample sequence diagram. In this example, *EditTimesheetUI*, *Timesheet*, *TimesheetService*, and *TimesheetDataTable* are all objects. This example is meant to show how these objects work together to support the use case, enter timesheet. The design has a user interface form (*EditTimesheetUI*), a domain object (*Timesheet*), an object service for managing the domain object (*TimesheetService*), and a database abstraction class for the object (*TimesheetDataTable*).

Notice the long rectangles that extend along the lifeline of each object. These rectangles indicate when an object is created and when it goes out of scope. For example, the *TimesheetDataTable* object is created twice by the *TimesheetService* during this process.

The messages that pass between objects are indicated by the arrows from one lifeline to another. These messages are meant to be read from top to bottom, left to right (as a sequence). Each message represents a method call, property call, or return value. For example, the Get-Timesheet message represents a call to the *GetTimesheet* method of the *TimesheetService* object. The calls to Entry.Add are depicted as adding data entries to a given timesheet. Return calls are shown as a dashed arrow; return confirmation is an example. All the messages depicted in Figure 2-9 are synchronous. You can also indicate asynchronous messages by using an arrow that has only its lower half.

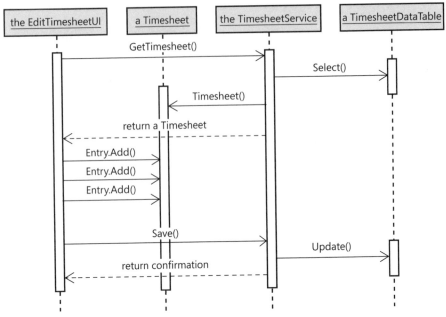

Figure 2-9   A sample sequence diagram

Collaboration Diagram

A *collaboration diagram* shows the same type of interaction between objects as a sequence diagram does. However, the collaboration diagram allows you to lay out the objects in any way you like. The actual sequence is dictated by numbered messages (and not by the model's constraints). Figure 2-10 shows the same sequence diagram shown in Figure 2-10 as a collaboration diagram.

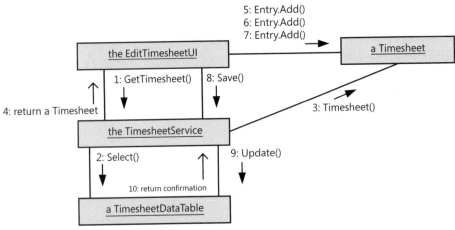

Figure 2-10   A sample collaboration diagram

Quick Check

1. What is the definition of a component? What is the purpose of a component diagram?
2. What is the purpose of a class diagram?
3. When would you use a sequence diagram versus a collaboration diagram?

Quick Check Answers

1. A group of logically related classes and methods comprise a component. A component diagram shows how components work with one another to form a solution and how they are deployed in a physical environment (onto nodes).
2. A class diagram provides a static specification for developers to implement and to help them understand how the classes are structured. It does not provide information about how a class works. It simply alludes to this type of information.
3. You create a sequence diagram to depict the logical sequence between objects across their lifelines. A collaboration diagram does not show an object's lifeline, and the sequence of events is determined only by numbered messages. However, the collaboration diagram allows you to lay out the objects in any spatial order.

Create an Activity Diagram

The UML defines the activity diagram as an answer for flow charting and workflow definition. An *activity diagram* enables you to indicate activities that happen one after another and in parallel. For this reason, the activity diagram is sometimes used to model workflow and the business process associated with use cases. However, the principal intent of an activity diagram is to be a physical model that helps developers understand complex algorithms and application methods. This is the use of the model that this section will discuss.

Figure 2-11 shows the sample activity diagram of a constructor for a fictitious *TimesheetBilling-Codes* class. The closed black circle indicates the start of the method. The arrows indicate the processing flow. Each rounded rectangle indicates an activity in the method. You can see that the example starts with the Get Timesheet Billing Codes activity and moves from one activity to another. You can think of these activities as markers in your method (or even commented sections). These are the things the method must do.

The activity diagram allows you to indicate branches or decisions that must be made in the code. These are represented by the diamonds. The control that comes off of each side of the branch is guarded. That is, it must be labeled as a Boolean condition that must be met for the code to flow in that direction. The first branch in the example is a decision about whether the application is online (as opposed to not being connected to a network). If it is online, the control moves to Check Cache. If not, the control moves to Pull From Cache.

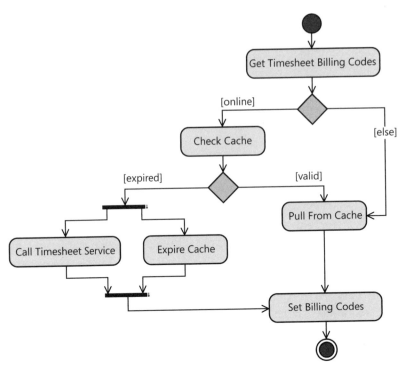

Figure 2-11   A sample activity diagram

The activity diagram also allows you to indicate parallel processing (or multithreading). You do so with a fork. The fork indicates that two processes are happening at once. In the example, both Call Timesheet Service and Expire Cache are forked and in parallel. Once any parallel processing is complete, it is joined. The figure shows a join for the two items executing in parallel. Finally, once the processing is complete, you use a black circle with an outer ring to indicate the completion of the activity.

Create an Entity-Relationship Diagram

The UML does not have a specific diagram for modeling relational databases. This is because the UML is focused on modeling object-oriented systems. The real technique for modeling relational databases is with entity-relationship (ER) diagrams. This section will cover data modeling with ER diagrams.

Normalization

One of the most important considerations when modeling relational databases is to avoid duplicate data. There are several problems with data duplication. First, it leads to excessive, unnecessary storage consumption. Second, it can have an adverse effect on data integrity.

When data is duplicated, each copy of the data needs to be updated; otherwise the data in your database becomes corrupt. Trying to get this data updated simultaneously leads to concurrency issues, record locking, and data-sharing issues that become exponentially more complex for every copy of the same data.

Normalization is the process by which duplicate data is avoided in relational databases. This is accomplished by using separate tables before each entity or copy of the data. This ensures that each table contains data related to a single topic and that related tables are connected. Data modifications in one table, then, are constrained (and linked to) relationships with another. The following describes the four primary normal forms. Note that there is also a fifth normal form not discussed here because it is mostly theoretical.

- **First normal form**   This is the basic level of normalization. Essentially, databases in first normal form are considered two-dimensional in that each entity (table) is appropriately and singularly purposed. Each row in that table represents a unique instance of an entity corresponding to the table definition.
- **Second normal form**   The second normal form requires that the first normal form is achieved. In addition, data that applies to more than one row should be moved into separate tables and linked via foreign keys.
- **Third normal form**   The third normal form requires the second normal form to be achieved. In addition, columns that are not unique to the entity should be removed.
- **Fourth normal form**   This form is also called the Domain/Key Normal Form (DKNF). It is achieved when the third normal form is achieved *and* each record is uniquely identified by a key. Additionally, the domain specifies restrictions on data elements so that data values must fall into specific boundaries. The fourth normal form ensures that the database is free from modification anomalies.

MORE INFO   Normalization

Read more about normalization, from the perspective of a developer, in MSDN at *http://msdn.microsoft.com/library/default.asp?url=/library/en-us/vsent7/html/vxcondatanormalization.asp.*

ER Diagrams

As with other types of modeling, using visual models is generally more effective than text-only models. *Entity relationship* (ER) *diagrams* are the visual means for describing relational systems. ER diagrams consist of a relatively small set of graphical widgets. Typically, entity and relationship widgets are the most commonly used items. Entity widgets represent tables and views. Relationship widgets represent the relationships among entities. Figure 2-12 shows an ER diagram using the Microsoft AdventureWorks sample database. The diagram is created by using Office Visio. It shows tables and columns within those tables and identifies key fields. It also shows relationships among tables.

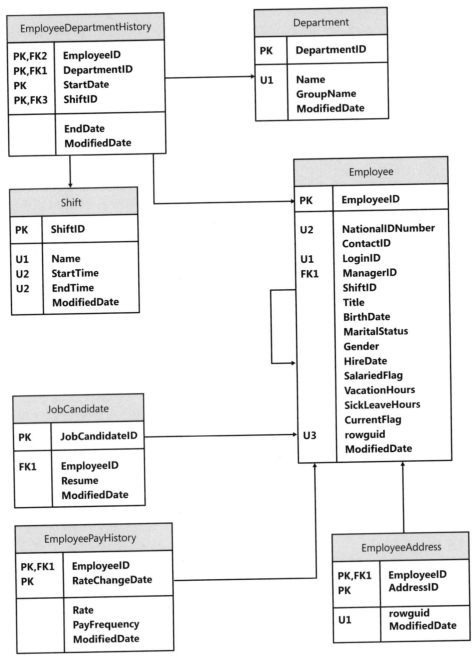

Figure 2-12   Sample entity-relationship diagram

Create Pseudocode

An effective developer model that is often overlooked is pseudocode. *Pseudocode* is not a diagram or a model; it is text that is written like you write code. It does not follow a specific language or notation. It does, however, offer a code-like view of a method for developers who prefer to see code (or are more used to it than models). It can also be an easier (and faster) way to express concepts for architects and designers who are not used to drawing a lot of diagrams (and might also prefer code).

Pseudocode is what you make it. You should strive to mimic some of the structure of your chosen language just to help your developers read it. If, for example, you use C#, you might put curly braces in your pseudocode. If you use Visual Basic, you should consider using *end* statements. However, the code will not compile, will make strange assumptions that code should not make, will take shortcuts, and will generally break the rules. That is the whole point. It is not meant to be real code. The following is an example of some pseudocode for the method defined in Figure 2-11:

```
'VB Public New
  If Application.Online
 If Cache.Expired
       billingCodes = TimesheetService.GetGillingCodes()
       New Thread.execute (call Cache.Expire)
    Else
       billingCodes = Cache.GetGillingCodes()
    End
  Else
    billingCodes = Cache.GetGillingCodes()
  End
  Me.BillingCodes = billingCodes
End    //C# public BillingCodes() {
  If Application.Online {
 If Cache.Expired {
       billingCodes = TimesheetService.GetGillingCodes()
       New Thread.execute (call Cache.Expire)
    } else {
       billingCodes = Cache.GetGillingCodes()
    }
  } else {
    billingCodes = Cache.GetGillingCodes()
  }
  Me.BillingCodes = billingCodes
}
```

Lab: Create Physical Models

In this lab, you will work to define a few physical models for an application. You will first work to create a class diagram. You will then define object interaction diagrams (both collaboration and sequence).

▶ **Exercise 1: Review Object Relationships and Define a Class Diagram**

For this exercise, you will first review a few architectural goals for a Windows application. You will then look at an ORM diagram (Figure 2-13) for a portion of the application that defines the relationships between an employee and a project. You will then work with the design goals and the ORM diagram to define the business services layer. You will specify the business domain by using a class diagram.

Architectural Goals

- All business logic should be encapsulated into a separate business domain layer.
- Each business object should know how to save, update, load, and delete itself.

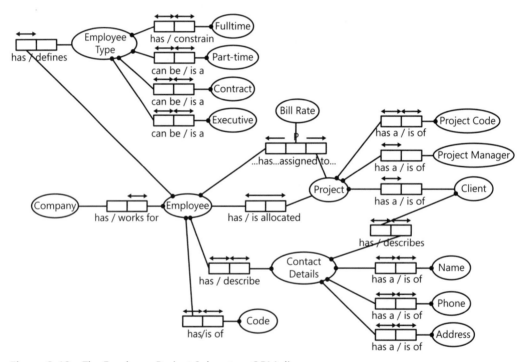

Figure 2-13   The Employee Project Subsystem ORM diagram

Lab Steps

The following steps will lead you through this exercise.

1. Use Visual Studio 2005 to create a new Windows application. Use File | New | Project. You can call this application what you wish; you can create either a Visual Basic or C# Windows application.

2. Add a class diagram to the application. Click Project, choose Add New Item, and select Class Diagram. You can name this diagram whatever you like.

3. Determine the primary objects in the system. Review the ORM (Figure 2-13) and determine which objects have many links from them. Review your choices. Add a class to the diagram for each primary object you chose.

4. From the ORM diagram, determine the objects that represent simple properties of your domain objects. These are objects from the ORM diagram that did not become primary objects, are not relationships, and are not considered values of properties. Right-click a class and choose Class Details to add these properties to each class in the model by using the Class Details window.

5. Determine the association relationships between the classes. These relationships represent properties that link the objects together. You define these relationships by using the Association tool from the Class Designer toolbox. After selecting the Association tool, click and drag from the class that has the association to the class that is the association.

6. Determine the enumerations you wish to define based on the model. These are items that define a property in terms of values. You create an enumeration by using the Enum tool from the toolbox.

7. Determine which objects represent base classes and which should implement inheritance. The ORM model indicates an *EmployeeType* object. This was implemented as an enumeration. However, if some types finish with their own values, you might consider creating an inheritance structure. You would do so by adding the new classes to the model, one for each *EmployeeType*. You would then drag the Inheritance tool from the child class to the base class.

8. Determine any interfaces you wish to define for the system. The architecture goals indicate that each business object needs to save, load, update, and delete itself. Therefore, you might consider implementing a common interface for your business objects. You do so by adding an *Interface* object from the toolbox. You then indicate the methods and any properties that are part of this interface. You can then use the Inheritance tool to indicate which objects implement this interface.

A diagram showing a solution for this exercise, as well as answers to the previous steps in this exercise, can be installed from the Code folder on the companion CD.

▶ Exercise 2: Create an Interaction (Sequence) Diagram

For this exercise, you will review a use case that describes a user submitting an issue to a support system. You will then use this use case along with a description of the classes in your system to create a sequence diagram. The sequence diagram is meant to describe how the physical model realizes the use case.

NOTE   Office Visio for Enterprise Architects

This lab assumes that you are using Office Visio for Enterprise Architects. If you do not have this, you can still use a drawing tool to draw a sequence diagram that mimics the lab.

Submit Trouble Ticket Use Case

Precondition: User has logged on to the system.

1. A user wants to submit an incident report to the trouble ticket system.
2. The system generates a new trouble ticket for the user.
3. The system takes the user to the SubmitIssue form in the application.
4. The user enters the details of the incident.
5. The system saves the incident and generates a trouble ticket tracking number.
6. The tracking number is sent back to the user for tracking purposes.

Submit Issue Architecture Model

- *User*: A class that represents a user in the system.
- *SubmitIssue*: A form in the application that allows a user to submit an incident report.
- *IncidentReport*: A class that represents an issue or incident.
- *TroubleTicketService*: A class that contains methods for submitting a trouble ticket.

Lab Steps

The following steps will lead you through this exercise.

1. Open Office Visio and create a new UML model diagram by using File | New | Software | UML Model Diagram.
2. Add the classes to the model. In the Model Explorer, right-click Top Package and choose New | Class. Name each class and click OK.
3. Define methods for each class. For this exercise, you will simply define those methods you intend to use for the sequence diagram. If you had created your class diagram previously, you would use the full class description as an input into the sequence diagram.

   You add a method to a class in Office Visio by right-clicking the class in the Model Explorer and choosing New | Operation. This opens the UML Operation Properties dialog box. You can use this dialog box to name your operation and indicate its return type, its visibility, and any parameters that are required. You add parameters by clicking the Parameters category on the left side of the dialog box.
4. Add a sequence diagram to the UML model. Right-click Top Package in the Model Explorer and choose New | Sequence Diagram.
5. Drag an Object Lifeline shape onto the diagram for each primary object in the interaction. Double-click each object to define its instance. Select a class from the model as the Classifier. Indicate an instance name in the *Name* field.
6. Align the tops of each object lifeline. Extend each lifeline down about half of the page.

7. Add an activation (long rectangle) to the lifeline of each of your objects. You will use this activation to indicate when the object is created and when it is disposed.

8. Begin connecting your objects by using messages. Each message is defined by a method on the object that is being called. For example, the first message you should create will be from *SubmitIssueUI* to *User*. The message should be the *Load(id)* method. Review the use case and the architecture model and continue to connect objects.

A diagram showing a solution for this exercise, as well as answers to the previous steps in this exercise, can be installed from the Code folder on the companion CD.

Lesson Summary

- A component diagram represents the components in your system (logically related classes and methods) and shows how they work with one another to form a solution. You can show the deployment of components onto nodes. A node typically represents a piece of hardware (such as a server).

- A class diagram illustrates the static specification of classes. This includes methods, properties, fields, and so on. It also shows relationships such as inheritance and encapsulation. The Visual Studio 2005 Class Designer allows you to model classes, structures, enumerations, interfaces, and abstract classes.

- A sequence diagram depicts the messages between objects over a sequence of events. The sequence diagram typically shows multiple objects across a use case.

- A collaboration diagram shows the sequence of events between objects as numbered messages. The collaboration diagram is much like a sequence diagram; however, it allows you to show the objects in any spatial layout.

- An activity diagram indicates the activities in an algorithm or method that happen one after another and in parallel. An activity diagram is like a flow chart.

- Pseudocode is code-like text that is written to show a code-like view of a method. Pseudocode helps developers who prefer to see code to understand a complex algorithm or method.

Lesson Review

You can use the following questions to test your knowledge of the information in Lesson 3, "Create Physical Models for Developers." The questions are also available on the companion CD if you prefer to review them in electronic form.

NOTE   Answers

Answers to these questions and explanations of why each answer choice is right or wrong are located in the "Answers" section at the end of the book.

---

1. Which of the following UML diagrams represents the static structure of the objects in your application?

    A. Component diagram

    B. Collaboration diagram

    C. Pseudocode

    D. Class diagram

2. Which of the following are differences between a sequence diagram and a collaboration diagram? (Choose all that apply.)

    A. A sequence diagram shows message calls over time. A collaboration diagram shows asynchronous messaging.

    B. A sequence diagram uses the model to illustrate sequence and order. A collaboration diagram illustrates this through numbered messages.

    C. A sequence diagram has object lifelines and shows when objects are created and destroyed. A collaboration diagram does not show this information.

    D. A sequence diagram enforces the layout of objects across the top of the page. A collaboration diagram enables you to lay out objects in any spatial manner you choose.

3. Which of the following are good uses for an activity diagram? (Choose all that apply.)

    A. Defining class interactions and groupings

    B. Modeling complex algorithms

    C. Showing a sequence of business events or workflows

    D. Modeling multithreaded methods

4. Which of the following is NOT a part of a UML sequence diagram?

    A. Object

    B. Lifeline

    C. Messages

    D. Branch

Chapter Review

To further practice and reinforce the skills you learned in this chapter, you can perform the following tasks:

- Review the chapter summary.
- Review the list of key terms introduced in this chapter.
- Complete the case scenarios. These scenarios set up real-world situations involving the topics of this chapter and ask you to create a solution.
- Complete the suggested practices.
- Take a practice test.

Chapter Summary

- A logical software model is designed to represent actual concepts from your business domain. The logical model should change only if these concepts change. You can model this domain by using ORM diagrams. These diagrams represent objects as ovals. They show relationships between the objects by using a rectangle that is split in two. You define text under each side of this rectangle to describe the relationship from left to right and the inverse. You place arrows over the relationship rectangle to represent multiplicity. Finally, you can indicate which object or objects are required of the relationship by placing a closed circle on the line pointing to the required object.

- A logical architecture (think layers or tiers) indicates how your system logically works and where (in which layer) developers need to put their code. This model also shows the communication paths between the layers. For example, it can indicate whether the user interface should talk directly to the database layer. Layers also mitigate risk and increase reusability. Most enterprise-level Windows applications define layers for the user interface (presentation and form interaction code), the middle tier (business logic and application services), and the database tier (database abstraction code and the database itself).

- You can use UML and Visual Studio to create physical models for developers. These physical models include component diagrams, class diagrams, activity diagrams, and interaction diagrams (sequence and collaboration). You create a component diagram to show the logical grouping of classes (into components) and the relationships (references) between these components. The component diagram can also show how components are deployed onto nodes (hardware). You create a class diagram to define the static specification of the classes in your domain. A class diagram defines classes, their methods and properties, inheritance and encapsulation, interfaces, enumerations, and so on. You create interaction diagrams to show how objects interact at run time. The UML defines both the sequence and the collaboration diagram to illustrate this information.

A sequence diagram depicts messages between objects over time (left–right, top–bottom). A collaboration diagram shows object call sequences as numbered messages between objects. You can choose how to lay out a collaboration diagram. The sequence diagram notation dictates this for you. You create an activity diagram to illustrate workflow or the activities in a complex algorithm. An activity diagram shows both synchronous parallel activities. Think of an activity diagram as a flow chart.

Key Terms

Do you know what these key terms mean? You can check your answers by looking up the terms in the glossary at the end of the book.

- activity diagram
- business domain
- class diagram
- collaboration diagram
- component
- component diagram
- entity-relationship diagram
- layers
- multiplicity
- node
- object role modeling (ORM)
- pseudocode
- sequence diagram
- state (or application state)

Case Scenario

In the following case scenario, you will apply what you've learned about decomposing specifications for developers. You can find answers to these questions in the "Answers" section at the end of this book.

Case Scenario: Evaluate User Inputs and Create Physical Models

You are a senior developer for a company whose principal business is selling custom-built projects made out of plastics. You have been asked to create a Windows application that will allow the sales team to create a quote for the custom creation of a project and send the quote to engineering for review before sending it to customers. You have been given an application use case and design goals for review.

Use Case: Create Quote and Route for Approval

Precondition: A sales representative has logged on to the system. The sales representative selects the menu option Create New Quote.

1. The sales representative is asked to select the customer for which the quote will be created. If the customer does not exist, the salesperson enters new customer details. Details include customer name, address, phone, and e-mail address.

2. The sales representative is asked to describe the custom product. Description includes type of material (hard or soft plastic), color, dimensions (height, width, length), and a textual description. The user is also asked to provide an attachment that includes a drawing of the request.

3. The sales representative then enters the quantity required, the shipping date requested, possible shipping terms (express, 3-day, or ground), and the payment terms (charge account, net 10, net 30, other).

4. At this point, the sales representative saves the quote in Under Review status. An e-mail notification is first sent to the engineering manager for his or her approval.

5. The engineering manager logs on to the system to review the quote. The user selects the quote requiring approval from a list. The user then reviews the quote details and drawings. If approved, the user enters additional design details and unit-pricing information (costs). The quote status is then set to Engineering Approved and is routed to the production lead. Otherwise, the engineering manager marks the quote as rejected and provides reasoning.

6. The production lead logs on to the system to review the quote. The user selects the quote requiring approval from a list. The user then reviews the quote details surrounding the engineering information and requested production date. If approved, the quote's status is set to Production and Engineering Approved, and the production lead indicates an expiration date for the quote. Otherwise, the quote is marked rejected. In either case, the quote is routed back to the sales representative.

7. The sales representative reviews the approved quote and adds a markup percentage to the unit pricing. The sales representative then generates a copy of the quote to be sent to the customer as an e-mail or fax.

   Post-condition: System marks the selected quote status as Sent to Customer. A version of the quote is then created that cannot be edited. This version is tracked in the system.

Design Goals / Functional Requirements

- The business rules should be encapsulated in objects. Each business object should know how to save and retrieve itself from the database.
- Engineering and production should be able to approve a quote from the Windows application or directly from a corporate e-mail account.
- The application server can access the database server directly because this application sits on the corporate local area network (LAN).

Questions

While thinking about the specifications (use case and design goals) previously listed, answer the following questions.

1. How would you model the domain of the use case by using an ORM diagram?
2. What would a logical architecture model (application layers) look like for this specification?
3. What would a high-level class diagram look like for this specification?
4. How would you create a sequence diagram to describe the object interaction concerning the approval portion of the use case?

Suggested Practices

To help you successfully master the exam objectives presented in this chapter, complete the following tasks.

Define Objects and their Relationships (Create a Logical Model)

Many developers have never created ORM diagrams. However, such diagrams are a great approach to defining a logical model based on requirements and user scenarios. Consider this task to make sure you get experience in creating ORM diagrams. This will help you master this objective.

- **Practice 1** Review requirements and use cases of a new system that has just been designed (preferably) or an older system that you might have worked on. Use this information to define an ORM diagram by using Office Visio. Review this logical representation with a business analyst or user who provided input into the use cases. Determine whether the use case really intended the results of the ORM diagram.
- **Practice 2** Use the ORM diagram you created for Practice 1. Compare it to the domain model (classes or database) that was defined for the system. Determine why tradeoffs were made with respect to the ORM diagrams. Consider whether these were mistakes or

whether the technology dictated an alternative solution. Consider how that might affect the understanding of the system without the ORM diagrams.

Create a Logical Architecture

This task should be familiar to most senior-level developers. They often think of systems in terms of layers. If, however, this is not your experience, you can use this task to master this objective better.

- **Practice 1**   Look back at a few existing projects you worked on. Try to describe the layers of the application. If you can't describe them, try to trace the code. Is the code spread out in many places across the application or was there a disciplined effort to contain the code?
- **Practice 2**   Using the layers you created as part of Practice 1, try to find justification for these layers within the non-functional requirements and design goals.

Create Physical Models for Developers

Class modeling is where application design and coding meet. If you've never created class models (or are unfamiliar with the Visual Studio 2005 Class Designer), this task will provide a good overview of how to use class modeling to help you structure your code better. In addition, if you need more work with UML, follow the practices listed here to create key UML diagrams.

- **Practice 1**   Use Visual Studio 2005 to create a class diagram (or model an existing set of classes). Use the tool to add new methods, properties, and classes to your application.
- **Practice 2**   Create a sequence diagram to describe how a feature of your application works. Pick a feature that you've implemented. Start with its use case and see how well you can describe the messages between your objects without looking at the code. Then compare the sequence diagram to the implemented code.
- **Practice 3**   Convert your sequence diagram from Practice 2 into a collaboration diagram.
- **Practice 4**   Consider the next method you intend to write. Draw an activity diagram to describe the method before you write it. Determine whether this helped you understand the method before you wrote the code.

Take a Practice Test

The practice tests on this book's companion CD offer many options. For example, you can test yourself on just the content covered in this chapter, or you can test yourself on all the 70-549 certification exam content. You can set up the test so that it closely simulates the experience of taking a certification exam, or you can set it up in study mode so that you can look at the correct answers and explanations after you answer each question.

MORE INFO   **Practice tests**

For details about all the practice test options available, see the section titled "How to Use the Practice Tests" in this book's Introduction.

Chapter 3
Design Evaluation

Now that you have designed your application, you will need to evaluate that design. Design evaluation involves examining the properties of your application to determine whether design decisions meet non-functional requirements. In other words, design evaluation requires you to review your design to determine whether it meets common system requirements such as performance, maintainability, scalability, and so on. Evaluating the design at this early phase will enable you to find and correct design mistakes before they become expensive to fix.

Exam objectives in this chapter:
- Evaluate the logical design of an application.
  - ❑ Evaluate the logical design for performance.
  - ❑ Evaluate the logical design for maintainability.
  - ❑ Evaluate the logical design for extensibility.
  - ❑ Evaluate the logical design for scalability.
  - ❑ Evaluate the logical design for availability.
  - ❑ Evaluate the logical design for security.
  - ❑ Evaluate the logical design against use cases.
  - ❑ Evaluate the logical design for recoverability.
  - ❑ Evaluate the logical design for data integrity.
- Evaluate the physical design of an application. Considerations include the design of the project structure, the number of files, the number of assemblies, and the location of these resources on the server.
  - ❑ Evaluate the physical design for performance.
  - ❑ Evaluate the physical design for maintainability.
  - ❑ Evaluate how the physical location of files affects the extensibility of the application.
  - ❑ Evaluate the physical design for scalability.
  - ❑ Evaluate the physical design for availability.
  - ❑ Evaluate the physical design for security.
  - ❑ Evaluate the physical design for recoverability.
  - ❑ Evaluate the physical design for data integrity.

Lessons in this chapter:

Before You Begin

To complete the lessons in this chapter, you should be familiar with Microsoft Visual Basic or C#. You should have successfully completed all the lessons in Chapter 1, "Evaluating the Technical Feasibility of an Application," and Chapter 2, "Creating Specifications for Developers," and you should be comfortable with the following tasks:

- ■ Using SQL Server Management Studio to attach databases
- ■ Using the SQL Server Management Studio Database Designer

Real World

Shawn Wildermuth

I have found the more challenging part of most projects is the consistent use of design principles, including design evaluation. I can sling code in my sleep, but being patient and performing real evaluations of both the physical and logical designs requires a consistent methodology, even when I am pressured by time, price, and resource constraints. I have learned that I cannot assume that the political pressures of a project are not going to get in the way of doing a job; in fact, it is often a symptom of a failed project. Standing strong and making sure I have the time allotted to complete the entire design cycle have helped bring about almost every successful project I have ever worked on.

Lesson 1: Evaluating the Logical Design

Before you can begin the process of actually creating your enterprise application based on the design, you will need to evaluate the design for correctness and completeness. By completing this evaluation, you can ensure that any potential problems with the design are caught as early in the process as possible to reduce the cost of fixing any design flaws.

> **After this lesson, you will be able to:**
> - Evaluate a logical design for standard design criteria.
>
> **Estimated lesson time: 10 minutes**

Evaluation of the Logical Design

In Chapter 2, you worked from use cases to a logical design of your system. Once you have a logical design for a proposed system, you need to evaluate the design based on a set of standard evaluation criteria. In general, this means evaluating the design for performance, maintainability, extensibility, scalability, availability, recovery, data integrity, and use-case correctness. Typically, you can group these evaluations into run-time evaluation (performance, scalability, availability, recoverability, and security), architectural evaluation (maintainability and extensibility), and requirements evaluation (business use case).

Performance Evaluation

Although the logical design of a system is high-level, there are performance considerations that can be evaluated. For instance, you need to evaluate the system tiers and abstraction layers in the design.

As you review the logical design, ensure also that the design is not over-designed into too many tiers. Typically, designing an enterprise application into three logical tiers is sufficient. Creating additional logical tiers is usually an indication of a poor design unless there is very well-thought-out reasoning for the additional tiers.

The levels of abstraction for particular entities should be reviewed to ensure that there are very specific reasons to abstract out particular parts of the design. In particular, you should be looking for extraneous levels of abstraction. Additional levels of abstraction can affect performance by forcing the flow of data across too many objects. By removing unnecessary levels of abstraction, you can ensure that the design has a high level of performance.

The level at which you can do a performance evaluation of the logical design is generally limited to finding redundancies. The level of detail required to determine other performance problems is just not available in the logical design.

Exam Tip   Creating multiple levels of abstraction beyond the three tiers of an application is usually an indication of a performance issue in a logical design.

Scalability Evaluation

The logical design review is also when you should be evaluating the design for scalability. Scalability simply refers to the ability to adapt to an increasing load on the system as the number of users increases. In a logical design, the most important piece of handling scalability is to ensure that you have a separate, logical middle (or data) tier. Remember, the logical design does not specify how you will actually deploy an application on a physical computer but, instead, is a robust design that can accommodate scalability concerns. You can address these concerns by ensuring that the logical design keeps the entire middle (or data) tier as a discrete part of the design.

Availability and Recoverability Evaluations

Your logical design should also take into account the availability and recoverability of your project. High availability is the characteristic of a design that allows for failover and recovery from catastrophic failures. This includes failover ability, reliable transactions, data synchronization, and disaster preparedness. Because the logical design is a fairly high-level view, not all of these availability concerns can be dealt with at the logical level. Instead, try to ensure that your entities can deal with availability solutions.

Your entities should be able to handle high-availability solutions in several ways:

- By using reliable transactions (for example, database transactions, Microsoft Message Queue [MSMQ] transactional messaging, or distributed transactions such as Enterprise Services or distributed transaction coordinator [DTC] transactions)
- By dealing with catastrophic failure by supporting rebuilding corrupted files and configurations in case of a failure to save data outside a transaction
- By allowing for failover to different databases or other data services (for instance, Web services) centers in case of catastrophic hardware failure

Security Evaluation

In evaluating the security of an enterprise application's logical design, you will need to ensure that the application will be able to protect its secrets. Enterprise applications typically will need to access security information to do their work. If you have an enterprise application that uses a database, you will need to ensure that the connection information the application uses is securely placed. This is important because you do not want ill-intentioned people to have access to your application's data. For example, let's say that you have an enterprise application that is used to access sales information for sales people. A copy of this application might be installed on the laptop of a salesperson. If this laptop is subsequently stolen, how do you ensure that the data the application uses is secure?

You can secure data in your enterprise application in several ways: by encrypting sensitive data such as configuration, by limiting local caches of data to only when absolutely necessary, and by using authentication to prevent unauthorized access to the software itself.

For almost every application, sensitive data such as logon information to a Web service or database server that allows access to sensitive data can be dangerous in the wrong hands. By encrypting this data based on Microsoft Windows Data Protection (more often called the data protection application programming interface [DPAPI]), you can encrypt data so that it is decipherable only by a specific user. DPAPI allows you to encrypt data without having shared secrets, as is common with *System.Security.Cryptography*.

MORE INFO   **The data protection API**

To learn more about the data protection API, visit Microsoft.com at *http://msdn.microsoft.com/ library/default.asp?url=/library/en-us/dnsecure/html/windataprotection-dpapi.asp*.

In addition to encrypting data, allow for local caches of data to be minimized on computers. Keeping local copies of data is dangerous because those caches are susceptible to access by people who do not have permission through your application. Caches can also be copied out to easily hidden pieces of hardware, such as to USB memory devices, for use outside of your control. If you do need to keep local caches, such as for an application that is not always connected to a company's servers, then protecting any sensitive data in the cache becomes paramount. Let's say you have a cache of data that contains medical record information. Protecting that data from inappropriate users is your responsibility.

Finally, review the logical design to ensure that unauthorized usage of your application is not possible. Depending on what kind of application you are designing, this can be very important. Suppose you are writing a medical application. Even if you encrypt the sensitive data and never keep a local cache, if you allow people to use your application without verifying their identity, your application will be open to divulging information to which some people should not have access.

Quick Check

1. How should you handle securing sensitive configuration data?
2. What kind of authentication should you use in enterprise applications?
3. What should be your policy about caching sensitive data?

> **Quick Check Answers**
> 1. You should use encryption to make configuration data such as database connection strings protected from unauthorized access. Your applications should allow decryption of the data but should not allow users to view the configuration information directly.
> 2. Using Microsoft Windows authentication (that is, domain authentication) in your applications is preferable to manual authentication methods because the security of identities and passwords can be maintained in a single place.
> 3. Sensitive data should not be cached if at all possible because getting access to those caches—through a variety of means—might compromise your data.

Maintainability Evaluation

Ninety cents out of every development dollar are used to maintain a system, not to build it. That makes the maintainability of a system crucial to its long-term success. Evaluation for maintainability starts here, in the logical design.

The maintainability in the logical design is based on segmenting elements of the logical design into specific tiers. Specifically, each element of the logical design should belong to one—and only one—tier of logical design. The most common problem with a logical design in the realm of maintainability is with entities that cross the data–user interface boundary. For example, if you have an entity in the logical design that is meant to store data about a customer, that same component should not also know how to expose the customer as a Windows Forms control. Separating each of those pieces of functionality will ensure that changes to the user interface and the data layer are discrete. Intermingling user interface and data tiers inevitably creates code that becomes increasingly difficult to maintain.

Extensibility Evaluation

While reviewing the logical design, it is important for you to determine extensibility in your design from two distinct perspectives: Can my design be extended with other components? Are my components extensible?

You should evaluate the logical design and determine which entities in your design can be built on top of other components. Usually, this means determining which classes to extend from the Microsoft .NET Framework itself. Look also at what classes you could use in your own code to build these new objects upon. For example, if you look at a customer entity in the logical design, you might have a common base class that performs data access for your entity objects. On the other hand, you might derive those classes from a class in the .NET Framework (for instance, the *Component* class) to get built-in behaviors.

It is important for you to look for ways to reuse existing code to complete your design instead of rebuilding everything from scratch. Finding components inside the .NET Framework, as well as in your existing code base (if any) to use as the basis of your components, will improve the quality of your project (that is, old code usually means better code) as well as decrease development costs.

In your logical design, look for ways to ensure that the code you write is extensible. One of the reasons you write object-oriented code is to enable code reuse. The more of your application that can be designed to be reused, the better the investment in the technology you are going to make.

Data Integrity Evaluation

Your logical design should also suggest how the data that the enterprise application will work with remains integral during the full life cycle of the application. This means that you will need to ensure that the database not only has a full set of schema, including primary keys, foreign keys, and data constraints, but that the client code determines the correct type of data concurrency to use for your application.

The decision that you make about what type of concurrency to use (optimistic versus pessimistic) will affect the overall safety and performance of your data tier. Typically, optimistic concurrency will perform better but will increase the chance that data will change between updates. Optimistic concurrency implies that data will remain unchanged between retrieving data and saving changes. If data has changed during that time, you will need to determine the best way of handling those changes. Optimistic concurrency generally performs better because there are fewer database and logical locks on the data, so more clients can access data concurrently.

Alternatively, choosing pessimistic concurrency ensures that the data a client is changing cannot be changed by other clients during the time that the client is working with that data. In all but the most severe case, optimistic concurrency is the right decision because it scales out better and performs well.

Business Use-Case Evaluation

At the point of the logical design review, you will need to review the business use cases to ensure that what you have designed continues to meet those needs. You might assume that, because the design was initiated from the use cases, this evaluation is not necessary, but that would be wrong. Much like a conversation that communicates across a room is changed by each listener, it is very common and easy for a designer to make assumptions about what the use cases are. This review of the use cases against the design will almost always find inconsistencies (or ambiguities) that need to be addressed in the logical design.

Lesson Summary

- Evaluating a logical design for run-time attributes such as performance, scalability, availability, recoverability, security, and data integrity will ensure that the logical design will be the best suited to fulfill the requirements.
- Evaluating a logical design for architectural issues such as maintainability and extensibility will ensure that the enterprise application can efficiently mature as a product.
- Evaluating a logical design for completeness against the business use cases will ensure that the logical design meets or exceeds the reason the enterprise application is being written.

Lesson Review

You can use the following questions to test your knowledge of the information in Lesson 1, "Evaluating the Logical Design." The questions are also available on the companion CD if you prefer to review them in electronic form.

NOTE   Answers

Answers to these questions and explanations of why each answer choice is right or wrong are located in the "Answers" section at the end of the book.

---

1. What should you use to protect sensitive data in configuration files?
   A. Use NTFS security to prevent access to configuration files.
   B. Use Windows Data Protection to encrypt the data.
   C. Do not use configuration files; store data inside assemblies.
   D. Use Encryption from the .NET Framework to encrypt the data.
2. To allow for maximum scalability, what is required in the logical design?
   A. Stored procedures
   B. Reliable transaction support
   C. A separate logical data tier
   D. Database failover
3. Each component should exist in how many tiers of your logical design?
   A. One.
   B. Two.
   C. As many as required.
   D. Components should not be tied to a specific tier of the design.

Lesson 2: Evaluating the Physical Design

The logical design of your enterprise application defines how the software will be written. Alternatively, the physical design defines more concrete details of how the software will be segmented and how it will be partitioned on real servers. Evaluating the physical design is just as important as evaluating the logical design.

After this lesson, you will be able to:

- Evaluate the physical design of your enterprise application against standard design criteria.

Estimated lesson time: 10 minutes

Evaluation of the Physical Design

The physical design of an enterprise application includes how the project is going to look when deployed. The big difference in this evaluation and the evaluation of the logical design is the number of concrete details of the design, which include the client deployment (for instance, how the application will be delivered to the client computers) as well as the network topology of what code and data will exist on which type of computer.

Much like the logical design, the evaluation of the physical design is broken up into a series of evaluation categories. These include performance, maintainability, extensibility, scalability, availability, and security evaluations.

Performance Evaluation

The performance evaluation of the physical design starts with a review of the different aspects of the design. These aspects include content, network, and database implementations. Each of these design aspects can adversely affect the final performance of the enterprise application.

You should review the network implementation of the project. The performance of an enterprise application can be greatly improved or destroyed based on how the data tier is implemented in the physical design. Look at how the middle tier is implemented to determine whether access to the tier is helping or hurting performance. There are no firm rules about the right implementation, but separating your data tier into a separate class of computer in the physical design is not always necessary. Typically, you would choose to separate the user interface tier and the middle tier into separate computers if the middle tier will tax the application by using a lot of memory or processor cycles. Because of the added expense of remotely accessing the data across computer boundaries, it is often more economical performance-wise to keep the middle tier on the same computer as the application.

You need to review the database implementation to ensure that it is performing adequately. As part of your performance evaluation, check the database operations to make sure they are performing as expected, both in isolation and under load testing. If this evaluation finds fault, there are many solutions for tuning the database, too numerous to explain in this training kit.

Scalability Evaluation

The scalability evaluation of the physical design is much like the evaluation of the logical design; you need to determine whether the system can adapt to handling higher-sized loads. You do this by reviewing the physical design to ensure that all components—custom components written for the project as well as first and third-party components used in the project—are compatible with moving from an in-process usage to a middle-tier scenario. This usually entails ensuring that all components can handle being moved across process boundaries in an efficient manner.

Availability and Recoverability Evaluation

In reviewing the availability of your enterprise application, you will need to determine what level of availability is required for the application. For example, if you are running a critical customer relationship management system (CRM), it becomes very important for you to handle failover to different computers and even data centers if you have a catastrophic failure such as hardware failure, interruption of Internet access, and so on. Alternatively, if you are building a small internal application, availability is not crucial to your success. The actual availability requirements should be evaluated at this time. This includes more than just ensuring that the deployment strategy takes this into account; you should also consider support for how to have backup databases and Web servers available with the correct version of the code and data. There are different strategies, but usually you will want to use a failover clustered database server for local availability.

The other side of availability is recoverability. Even if you do not need to support failover to new computers, data centers, and so on, you will likely need to support recovering from a failure. This means you need a strategy for backing up any data in the system. This includes database data, event data such as MSMQ and Event Logs, and any other transient data that is crucial to your business.

Security Evaluation

When reviewing the security of your physical design, be aware of the physical design of any communication between your enterprise application and any servers. For example, if your application will access a database server, you will need to ensure that access to that server is secure. Within your organization, this might not be a problem because firewalls and other security measures should keep unapproved people out. But as people are becoming more and more mobile, you will need to deal with an application that can be run outside of your network. In that case, you should use a virtual private network (VPN) to provide safe access to your internal servers. You should never expose your servers to the bare Internet just to allow these remote applications to work. If using a VPN isn't possible, creating proxies to the server, for instance through Web services, is acceptable but often incurs a performance penalty and the expense of securing the Web servers.

Real World

Shawn Wildermuth

Securing enterprise applications in this world of mobile professionals is becoming increasingly difficult. Many organizations I have dealt with have tried to avoid creating a VPN so that mobile professionals could work by using all sorts of other solutions such as Web services, terminal services, and so on. In almost every case, it was easier simply to support a VPN.

If your design uses ClickOnce deployment, you will need to ensure that the Web servers exposing the application are secured like any other Internet-facing server. If you think that a server with a ClickOnce application is not apt to be hacked, you are just inviting trouble.

Maintainability Evaluation

In reviewing the maintainability of the physical design, pay attention to the common-sense approach of the code base. This means that components should use common directory structures and have directory structures of the project mirror namespace usage as much as possible. The key to maintainability is making the code base easy to navigate.

Extensibility Evaluation

The physical makeup of any enterprise application can strongly affect how extensible it is. In general, your review of the extensibility should include a review of what controls and other components are written as part of the project. The location of these controls and components should be as centrally located as possible, so they can be used in applications, if necessary. Writing the same control for different applications is just tedious. Alternatively, copying components from one project to the other breaks the ability for each application that uses a particular component to get the benefits of bug fixes and improvements to the control.

Data Integrity Evaluation

Finally, do an evaluation of the data integrity for your physical design. Unlike the evaluation of the logical design, this evaluation should include an appraisal from the user interface down to the database. Data constraints that are included in the database schema will ensure that the data stays consistent, but you should also include that same constraint higher in the code to reduce the need to go to the database just to find a data inconsistency. For example, if you have a check constraint in the database to ensure that social security numbers are nine digits, your user interface should have validation of that fact so that if an invalid social security number is entered, it is easier to report that to the user to fix than to wait for the data to be sent to the database just to receive a failure message.

Exam Tip   Data validation is not the same as data integrity. Whereas data validation might be required in the user interface of an application, the integrity of relationships between different entities in your data should be maintained both in the data tier of your application and at the database.

Lesson Summary

- Evaluating the physical design should ensure that the deployed project meets the full requirements of a project.
- This physical design evaluation will review the performance, scalability, availability, recoverability, security, maintainability, extensibility, and data integrity of the designed system.

Lesson Review

You can use the following questions to test your knowledge of the information in Lesson 2, "Evaluating the Physical Design." The questions are also available on the companion CD if you prefer to review them in electronic form.

NOTE   Answers

Answers to these questions and explanations of why each answer choice is right or wrong are located in the "Answers" section at the end of the book.

---

1. How should you design domain authentication for remote users without exposing your internal network directly to the Internet?
   A. Open specific ports for your application in the firewall.
   B. Use Web services for all data interactions.
   C. Require all applications to be Web applications.
   D. Use a virtual private network (VPN).

2. Should you validate your data outside the database schema that is already ensured by the database?

   A. Yes

   B. No

3. Should your data tier always exist on a separate computer from the user interface code?

   A. Yes

   B. No

Chapter Review

To further practice and reinforce the skills you learned in this chapter, you can perform the following tasks:

- Review the chapter summary.
- Review the list of key terms introduced in this chapter.
- Complete the case scenarios. These scenarios set up real-world situations involving the topics of this chapter and ask you to create a solution.
- Complete the suggested practices.
- Take a practice test.

Chapter Summary

- Taking the time to evaluate the logical design of your enterprise application will help refine a design as well as ensure that the code that is written from the design is exactly what is required for the project.
- Performing a review of the physical design will ensure that your design is going to meet the requirements as well as perform well once deployed.

Key Terms

Do you know what these key terms mean? You can check your answers by looking up the terms in the glossary at the end of the book.

- logical design
- physical design

Case Scenarios

In the following case scenarios, you will apply what you've learned about how to perform data design. You can find answers to these questions in the "Answers" section at the end of this book.

Case Scenario 1: Review the Logical Design of an Enterprise Application

You work for a small company that needs a meeting-room scheduling application. You will need to create a system that can hold common data such as employees' names, meeting rooms, and the schedule.

Interviews

Following is the comment from the engineering manager, whom you interviewed.

- **Engineering Manager** Our design team has created a logical design that describes the different elements. We need to evaluate that design.

Questions

Answer the following questions for the design team.

1. How will you review the design for business case completeness?
2. How are you going to handle a maintainability review of the design?

Case Scenario 2: Review the Physical Design of an Enterprise Application

You work for a small company that needs a meeting-room scheduling application. You will need to create a system that can hold common data such as employees' names, meeting rooms, and the schedule.

Interviews

Following is the comment from the engineering manager, whom you interviewed.

- **Engineering Manager** Our design team has created a physical design of the different elements as they will exist on specific computer types. We need to review this design.

Questions

Answer the following questions for the design team.

1. How will you evaluate the security of the physical design?
2. How will you evaluate the extensibility of the physical design?

Suggested Practices

To help you successfully master the exam objectives covered in this chapter, complete the following tasks.

Evaluate an Existing Logical Design

For this task, you should complete at least Practices 1 and 2. You can do Practice 3 for a more in-depth understanding of logical design evaluation.

- **Practice 1**   Evaluate a logical design from your organization for flaws based on the criteria outlined in this chapter.
- **Practice 2**   Create a set of recommendations based on the review of the logical design.
- **Practice 3**   Review your recommendations against any changes that have been requested for the project you evaluated to see whether you found the same issues that were discovered after release of the project.

Evaluate an Existing Physical Design

For this task, you should complete at least Practices 1 and 2. You can do Practice 3 for a more in-depth understanding of physical design evaluation.

- **Practice 1**   Evaluate the physical design of an existing project in your organization (perhaps the same project you used in the previous Suggested Practice to evaluate the logical design) against the criteria outlined in this chapter.
- **Practice 2**   Create a set of recommendations based on the review of the physical design.
- **Practice 3**   Review your recommendations against any changes that have been requested for the project you evaluated to see whether you found the same issues that were discovered after release of the project.

Take a Practice Test

The practice tests on this book's companion CD offer many options. For example, you can test yourself on just one exam objective, or you can test yourself on all the 70-549 certification exam content. You can set up the test so that it closely simulates the experience of taking a certification exam, or you can set it up in study mode so that you can look at the correct answers and explanations after you answer each question.

MORE INFO   Practice tests

For details about all the practice test options available, see the "How to Use the Practice Tests" section in this book's Introduction.

Chapter 4

Component Design

A system is composed of many small moving parts, each of which is a small contributor to a larger picture. In enterprise development, these parts are called components. Individual components need to be planned and designed, just as the system architecture does. This chapter will discuss the fundamentals of component design, including database design, component characteristics, high-level design, and feature design.

Exam objectives in this chapter:
- Evaluate the design of a database.
  - Recommend a database schema.
  - Identify the stored procedures that are required for an application.
- Establish the required characteristics of a component.
  - Decide when to create a single component or multiple components.
  - Decide in which tier of the application a component should be located.
  - Decide which type of object to build.
- Create the high-level design of a component.
  - Establish the life cycle of a component.
  - Decide whether to use established design patterns for the component.
  - Decide whether to create a prototype for the component.
  - Document the design of a component by using pseudo code, class diagrams, sequence diagrams, activity diagrams, and state diagrams.
  - Evaluate tradeoff decisions. Considerations include security vs. performance, performance vs. maintainability, and so on.
- Develop the public API of the component.
  - Decide the types of clients that can consume a component.
  - Establish the required component interfaces.
  - Decide whether to require constructor input.

Lessons in this chapter:

Before You Begin

To complete the lessons in this chapter, you should be familiar with Microsoft Visual Basic or C# and comfortable with the following tasks:

- Using Microsoft Office Visio to create UML diagrams
- Using Microsoft Visual Studio 2005 to create class diagrams

---

Real World

Shawn Wildermuth

As enterprise developers, your job of designing solid components is crucial. Component design in large organizations is important because the opportunity to re-use components is greater than in other situations. I have found that as an organization develops, it is important to have good design at all levels of development so that duplicate functionality is not created in different departments. This is a challenge, but if your components are well designed and well documented, it becomes easier to share them within your enterprise.

Lesson 1: Database Design

Before you can deliver data to the user, you will need a good design for storing your data. By building on the Object Role Model (ORM) in Chapter 2, "Creating Specifications for Developers," you will build the required database schema in which to store that data.

After this lesson, you will be able to:
- Define data requirements from the ORM.
- Recommend a data schema.
- Identify the correct use of stored procedures.

Estimated lesson time: 20 minutes

Database Design Basics

Designing databases is easy to do but difficult to do well. The difficulty lies in the apparent simplicity of simply combining tables in a database designer. The problems of bad database design are more obvious in the longer term. Databases are rarely seen as problematic as they are initially created, but they can exhibit problems such as poor performance, lack of data consistency, and difficulty evolving the data model the longer they are in use.

To create a good database design, design the database to be normalized to at least the third normal form (3NF). The 3NF simply states that the data has adhered to a level of consistency and was designed with the principles detailed in Table 4-1.

Table 4-1   Database Design Principles

Name	Description
Atomicity	Each entity in a database should be indivisible and should consist of a single logical entity.
PK Dependence	The primary key for an entity should be required for all entities. For cases in which the primary key is a single column, this is not a problem. For multi-part keys, the entire key should relate to the entire entity.
Attribute Independence	Every attribute for an entity should belong to the entity and only to the entity.

In general, normalizing your database design simply ensures that each of the entities in the database will be independent of each other. These design principles are meant to ensure that your database design can mature and adapt to different requirements over time as well as remain as clean and consistent as possible.

Normalization   Examining normalization in detail is outside the scope of this lesson. For more information on database design and normalization schemes, please refer to *The Art of SQL*, Stephane Faroult and Peter Robson (O'Reilly Media, 2006); and "Database Normalization" in Wikipedia at *http://en.wikipedia.org/wiki/Database_normalization*.

Data Entities

In Chapter 2, you reviewed the requirements to determine what objects are required for your enterprise project. In that review, you created an ORM to determine what sorts of entities the system needed. Now you need to examine the ORM to determine what data entities you need to store in the database.

Data entities define containers for data that you need to store in the database. Typically, a data entity is represented in the database as a single table, but there are exceptions in which a single entity is represented better by multiple tables.

For example, the model shown in Figure 4-1 describes a simple project that will manage customers, sales people, and orders.

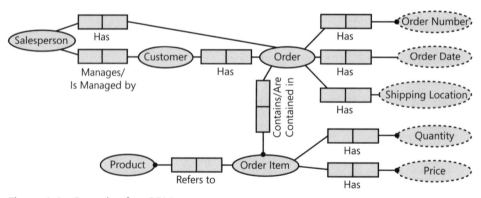

Figure 4-1   Example of an ORM

By reviewing this model, you can confidently create from each of the defined entities a simple database design, as shown in the Entity Relationship Diagram in Figure 4-2.

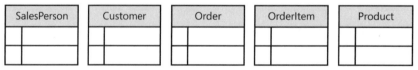

Figure 4-2   An initial database design

In this first pass of the database design, it is important to focus on the entities to be stored. You will have time to delve into the attributes of each entity as you complete the database design.

Figure 4-2 is a good first attempt at a database design, but do not accept the ORM diagrams as the final arbiter of what the database needs ultimately to look like. The final look of the database is called the *database schema*. For example, if you look at Figure 4-1, you will see that it defines a shipping location for an order. It is clear that you need a shipping location for an order, but, taking the long-term view of the design, ask yourself whether there will be other types of locations required as the product matures. In other words, should you normalize locations throughout the database schema into a single table?

For example, will the customer have a location (for instance, the company address for billing)? In addition, the salesperson might have to have a location associated with a particular office on which he or she is working. You could certainly embed this information in the Customer and SalesPerson entities, but wouldn't it be better to abstract the idea of a location and store all locations as a single entity in your system? Alternatively, it might be simpler just to embed this information into each of your entities because the retrieval of the entities will be faster and typically will facilitate writing queries.

So how do you make the decision about how much normalization is the right amount? Normalizing all of your entities to at least the third normal form is almost always the right approach. But be aware that breaking out every type of common data and creating a new entity will invariably cause problems in your database. There is a middle ground between overuse and underuse of reusable entities.

Real World

Shawn Wildermuth

I have seen both sides of the data normalization problem. In some projects I have seen, no formal normalization has occurred, and every table was created with the notion of keys or segmentation of data. Alternatively, I have actually seen over-zealous use of abstracting in database designs. A famous example of this appeared on The Daily WTF Web site at *http://thedailywtf.com/forums/thread/75982.aspx* in which a database was designed to abstract out the notion of a date in the system into a single entity. Because of this, every table in the system had a foreign key constraint to this table. Writing even the most basic query was a nightmare.

In this case, the right answer is to abstract out the location because that is a sizable entity that will likely appear in different places throughout the schema. Making this change in the schema could also necessitate a change in the ORM diagram. Figure 4-3 shows an updated ORM diagram based on the abstraction of the location entity.

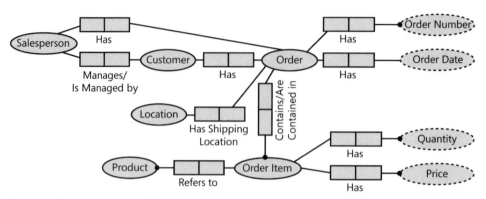

Figure 4-3   An updated ORM

Note that you changed the *ShippingLocation* attribute to a Location entity. The new diagram does not define locations for customers and salespeople because there is no requirement that dictates that. If a new requirement for locations for either of those entities surfaces, your database design will make that change simple, but you should not include relationships in your database design for requirements that do not exist. In Figure 4-4, you can see the addition of this new Location entity.

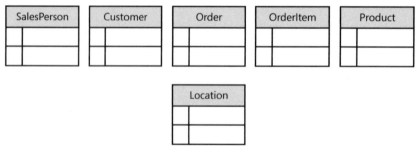

Figure 4-4   An updated database design

Now that you have identified your database entities, you need to determine how to identify each of the entities.

Primary Keys

Once you have defined the entities to be stored in your database, the next step is to define how you want to identify entities uniquely within each database table. Inside the database, this is referred to as a *primary key*. Every table within your database design needs to have a defined primary key. Being able to distinguish a specific row within a table inside the database is crucial to practically all database operations; therefore, it is critically important that you define a primary key for every table.

Although there are several schools of thought about entity identity, it is important to create an identity that is not only unique for each row in a table but to create one that will not change over time. For example, it might be tempting to use a salesperson number for the primary key. This would be fine except that if this salesperson number is visible to users within the resulting system, inevitably there will be a need to change that numbering system. Therefore, it is best always to use a primary key that is not exposed to users directly. In the case of a salesperson number, optimally, you could store that as an attribute in the database table, but make the primary key a different, machine-generated number. For example, if you add primary keys to the earlier table layout for your entities, they would look like the layout in Figure 4-5, which follows.

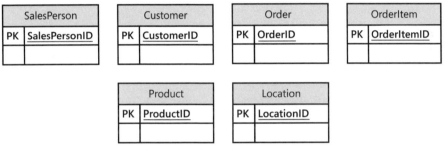

Figure 4-5   A database design with primary keys

In this example, a simple integer specifies a special number associated with each of your entities to specify its primary key. In general, numbers are preferable to other types of primary keys to reduce index fragmentation. Depending on your specific need, you can choose non-numeric primary keys as long as you understand that performance and maintenance issues can result.

Quick Check
1. Should you always use the same types of primary keys for different entities?
2. Why are primary keys important?

Quick Check Answers
1. Although there are exceptions to this rule, in general, you should always use the same kinds of primary keys for different entities. If you use an auto-incrementing number for the primary key of your customer's table, you should also use an auto-incrementing number for the other entities in the data model.
2. Primary keys provide two things: something to uniquely identify each row so that the row can be referred to, without ambiguity, from another row; and an index that makes finding a particular row quick to find.

To create identifiers for each entity in your database design, perform the following steps:

1. Start with any entity in the ORM diagram.
2. Create a new column (or more than one column if you determine you need a multi-part key) in the database design for that entity to hold the identifier for that entity.
3. Ensure that the identifier is both marked required and part of the primary key for that table.
4. Move on to the next entity in the ORM diagram, and return to step 2 for that new entity.

Data Warehousing and Primary Keys

One consideration when defining your primary keys is how your data will be used in large systems. In the case of data warehousing, it might be useful to create truly unique keys. For example, assume you were creating an e-commerce application in which you expect to deploy separate databases for each customer who bought that application. If you had a particularly big customer that bought several instances of your application, that *consumer* might need to merge or warehouse data in each of these instances. If you use a simple numeric primary key, multiple databases will have the same key value pointing at different logical entities.

In those cases, you have two options: You can remap primary keys or use universally unique keys. Remapping primary keys is the process of reassigning keys as you merge databases. This can be laborious and processor intensive but is often the right decision if these instances occur infrequently or if performance of the original system is more important than the processing time during merge. Alternatively, you can use universally unique keys (for instance, with a globally unique identifier [GUID] or other uniqueness). The problem with using universally unique keys is that they generally perform worse than simple unique keys.

The rule of thumb is to remap primary keys by default and use universally unique keys only when you know that merging or warehousing of data across databases will likely occur.

A mapping entity deserves special attention. It is a type used to create a many-to-many relationship in some schema designs. Often, you can define the primary key for these entities to be a multi-part key made of the primary keys of each of the entities. For example, assume that you need a vendor table in your design so that you know from whom to buy your products. Because you might buy products from more than one vendor, you need a way to map vendors to products. Your resulting table will look like Figure 4-6, which follows.

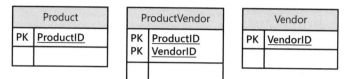

Figure 4-6   A mapping entity example

Once you have settled on your identity fields, you can move on to determining how the different entities are related.

Entity Relationships

When defining your database schema, it is important to define relationships between entities so that the database can ensure that the data stored in the database is consistent and integral. To identify these relationships, you will go back to the ORM diagram for the first indication of which relationships are required. If you look back at Figure 4-3, you will see that specific entities have relationships to other entities. For example, the Salesperson entity shows two relationships: to the Customer entity and to the Order entity.

Using the ORM diagram as your guide in determining these relationships is a good first step. Be cautious not to treat the ORM diagrams as a final arbiter, however. There might be relationships in the diagram that are either implied in the ORM diagram and not obvious or simply missing.

The ORM diagram is also where you will determine the parentage of a relationship. In general, one of the entities needs to be the parent of the relationship. Determine this by looking at the description of the relationship in the ORM diagram. For example, because Salesperson manages Customers in the ORM diagram, you can assume that Salesperson is the parent in the relationship. When one entity is the parent in a relationship, the child will need to store the key of its parent. To extend the parent–child example, you would need to add an attribute to the Customer entity to preserve the Salesperson identifier so that you can determine which Salesperson is the parent of this particular Customer.

Relationships are defined in database schema as foreign-key constraints. The name *foreign-key constraint* indicates that a column in a table uses a key that was defined elsewhere (that is, foreign). Therefore, to create a relationship in the schema, you need a new attribute (or more for multi-part keys) in a table and a foreign-key constraint to ensure the integrity of the relationship. For example, if you create the relationship between the Salesperson and the Customer discussed previously, you will need not only to add a SalespersonID column to the Customer table, but also to create a *foreign key* to ensure that only salespersons currently in the Salesperson table can be used as a Customer Salesperson. Figure 4-7 shows the foreign key and new attribute.

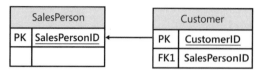

Figure 4-7   A foreign key and new attribute

To identify all the entity relationships, perform the following steps.

1. Start with any entity in the ORM diagram.
2. Look for relationships between that entity and another entity. You can ignore relationships to attributes at this point.
3. Determine the ownership of the relationship from the type and description (for instance, unary, binary, ternary, and so on).
4. Create attributes in the child of the relationship to hold the key of the relationship parent.
5. Create a foreign-key constraint from the child table to the parent table on the new attribute(s) in the child table.
6. If you have more relationships to review in the ORM, choose a relationship, and return to step 3 to determine that new one.

Using these steps, you can add the relationships to your schema to come up with the schema shown in Figure 4-8.

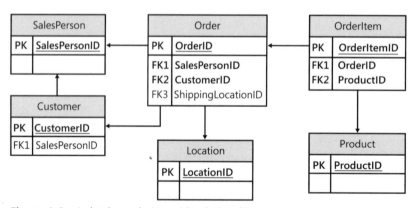

Figure 4-8   A database design with relationships

Typically, when you create relationships, you will also need to determine how you want to propagate changes down a relationship. For example, if an Order entity is deleted, should all OrderItem entities associated with that order also be deleted? In most cases, the answer is yes because you think of Order entities and their OrderItem entities as a logical unit. Alternatively, if an OrderItem is deleted, should the product that was in the OrderItem also be deleted?

When you create a foreign key, you have the opportunity to specify how to propagate that change. Foreign keys allow you to specify a referential action on both the delete and the update of the parent entity. For example, you could specify that when an Order is deleted, the child is also deleted. But you could specify that if the primary key of a product was changed, the change would propagate down to the OrderItem. In most database engines, the referential actions that are detailed in Table 4-2 are supported for both deletions and updates.

Table 4-2   Referential Actions

Name	Description
No action	Nothing is changed in the child.
Cascade	Changes are propagated to the child. For deletions, that means the child is also deleted; for updates, the change is propagated to the child.
Set NULL	When the parent changes or is deleted, the child's foreign key is set to NULL.
Set Default	When the parent changes or is deleted, the child's foreign key is replaced with the column's default value.

Now that you have entities, identifiers, and relationships created, adding the rest of the attributes to your entities is all that is left to do.

Entity Attributes

Ultimately, the goal for defining the database data is usually to store data. Once you have defined your entities and their keys, you can go through the process of determining what data is required for the particular project. The ORM diagrams can indicate data that is required for each entity but will likely not include every piece of information you will need.

In your ORM diagram (see Figure 4-3), several entities actually have attributes associated with them. The Order entity has *OrderNumber* and *OrderDate* attributes. In addition, other entities do not have any defined non-relationship attributes. For example, the Salesperson entity has relationships only to Order and Customer entities. This ORM diagram is indicative of a common problem in ORM diagrams: lack of complete detail about entity attributes. Your role is to determine the real data requirements for each entity.

The task of gathering attribute information about your entities is a fact-finding mission. It is part common sense and part detective work. You must determine which attributes belong, but it is also important not to attempt to add every piece of data you think you might one day need.

To outline the task of gathering this attribute information, look at the Order entity. Currently, the ORM diagram dictates that you have an *OrderNumber* and an *OrderDate*. In addition, you have *ShippingLocation*, *Salesperson*, and *Customer*. Although these are foreign keys, they are also attributes. It is likely that an order in a common e-commerce application will need more attributes. Using common sense, you could assume that there will be a need for some more information about an order. For example, you are going to want to store information about when an order was filled, when it shipped, and, perhaps, even a tracking number. You could also talk with the people responsible for fulfillment, shipment, and payment of orders to see what other information they are going to need. After discussing it with them, you might find that you need to store payment information as part of an order as well. This process might not only determine what attributes are necessary but might also highlight new entities. You might find that, after discussing orders with the accounting people, you will want to store payment information as a separate entity entirely.

When defining attributes, you must also determine whether you should support the notion of *null* for each attribute. Using null in the database indicates that there is no value for a particular attribute. In general, supporting null is a recommended practice because it will reduce your database storage requirements and make indexing more efficient.

In addition to specifying the attributes for each entity, you must also determine what kind of data a particular attribute can store. Depending on the particular database engine you are using, you will want to make informed decisions about how to store each type of data within the database. There are four main types of data that you need to determine how to store in your specific schema: strings, numeric values, date/time values, and Boolean values.

Strings

There are usually three decisions concerning strings: whether to use fixed-length strings, what length to allow, and whether to use Unicode versions. Each of these decisions has implications for the database design.

Fixed-length strings indicate how the database server will be storing the strings. If you use fixed-length strings (for instance, *CHAR* or *NCHAR*), the size of the fixed-length string will be taken up regardless of how big the actual string is. So if you have a *CHAR(10)* but store "Hi" in it, it will still be taking ten characters of memory in the database. Variable-length strings store only the actual string length in them. In that case, a *VARCHAR(10)* with "Hi" stored in it takes the memory of only two characters instead of ten. In general, if your data is fixed length (for example, a two-character status field), use fixed-length strings. If your data will vary (such as with an address), use variable length.

There are different approaches to determining the right length for strings in the database. It is almost always the wrong approach to just make all the strings as long as possible. Limitations to the size of a row (which is different for different database engines) will likely not allow you to make all strings huge. Discussing the requirements with the invested parties will usually yield the right decision about string length. When you think about string sizes, consider strings in a database to be no longer than about 250 characters in length. Anything longer should go into a special type of string that can store huge-sized strings. These are referred to as Large Object Blocks. In Microsoft SQL Server 2005, you would refer to this large string data type as VARCHAR(MAX) or NVARCHAR(MAX). Other databases might refer to these large strings as CLOB (Character Large OBject) or Memo fields. These special types of strings are not stored at the row level, so they can store very large strings (some up to several GB in size). They are a good solution for large, unbounded fields.

You also must determine whether to use Unicode strings in your database. Because Unicode strings can store extended character sets to deal with globalized data, it is almost always the right decision to use Unicode strings by default. Unicode strings take two bytes per character, so choosing all Unicode strings will make all your strings take twice as much memory as non-Unicode strings. The only reason not to use Unicode strings is when row size issues must be managed. For example, a row in SQL Server 2005 can be only 8,000 bytes in size. If you start to contend with row size issues, moving back to non-Unicode strings is an option. Unicode strings are critical to localizing strings inside the database. The decision of whether to use Unicode or not to use Unicode should be weighed against localization. If you have to localize strings, you should use Unicode; regardless of size implications.

Numbers

Storing numeric values in the database is more basic. The decision you have to make concerns what kind of numbers you need to store. For whole numbers only, using an integer-based number is a clear choice. But when storing numbers such as money values, percentages, or large scientific numeric values, you will need to consider carefully the types of data you want to store.

In your schema, you need to store several types of numbers. In the OrderItem entity, you will need quantity and price attributes. Because you do not know what kind of sales items your product needs, using a floating point value for the quantity makes more sense. This allows for non-whole numbers. For example, you could sell items per pound. Also in OrderItem, you need to store a price. Some databases have a data type called *Money* to specify that you are dealing with a monetary number. If you do not have a *Money* data type, you can specify either a floating point number or, more likely, a fixed point number (for instance, NUMERIC[10,2] to mean a ten-digit number with two decimal places).

Date and Time Values

In general, if you need dates and/or time values, most database engines have specific data types associated with dates and times. Usually, there is a data type called *DATETIME* that will store both a date and a time. Be aware that if you store just dates or just times in a *DATETIME* value, you will need to ignore the other part of that value manually.

Boolean Values

Storing Boolean (that is, *True* or *False*) values directly in your schema is a common approach. Because standard SQL does not support Boolean values, some databases do not have specific Boolean data types. For example, SQL Server does not have a Boolean data type but instead has a *BIT* data type that is essentially the same. A *BIT*, however, is not a true False indicator, but instead is a numeric value that can store only zero or one. Generally, zero indicates False, and one indicates True. If your database engine does not support Boolean values as a data type, use a small numeric data type (*BIT, BYTE,* and so on) to indicate the True or False data you require.

Often, you will find that you do not actually need to store Boolean values in the database if other data implies it. For example, in the Order entity, you could have a Boolean value for *HasShipped* as well as for a *ShippedDate.* But the existence of the *ShippedDate* indicates just as easily that an order shipped as having a second field that could get out of sync with the *ShippedDate* field. In those cases, do not create the Boolean attribute if it can be discerned by other data in the entity.

Putting It Together

With this newly gathered information, you can fill in the attributes and new entities in your database design. Your new schema might resemble the image in Figure 4-9.

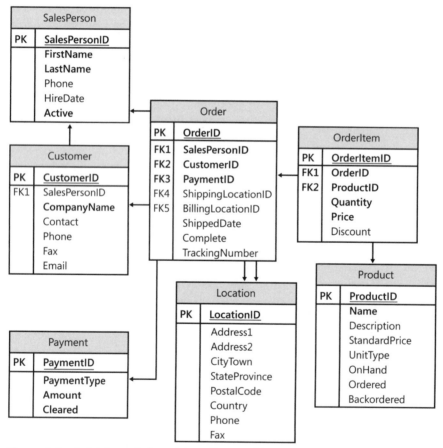

Figure 4-9 A database design with attributes added

Recommend a Data Schema

Now that you have defined all your attributes, there are still some tasks to manage before you can recommend your schema for use in a project. These tasks include defining secondary indexes, adding data constraints, and determining an effective concurrency management strategy.

Secondary Indexing

Secondary indexing is simply the task of determining other indexes to add to a database to make queries more efficient. It is called secondary indexing because when you defined the identifiers earlier in this chapter, every table in your schema got a primary key index to make searching by primary key very efficient. There is a cost for indexing because, as new values are added to your tables, the indexes must be updated with any new values on which they are indexed. With this in mind, you will want to create as few indexes per table as possible, but where necessary, add indexes judiciously.

You are probably responsible for ensuring that it is correct when you recommend a data schema. That does not mean that you cannot elicit advice. If your company employs database administrators, use them to help you make smart indexing decisions.

When you want to determine which secondary indexes you need, look at what types of data are in the schema that will likely cause searches that do not use the primary key. For example, you might choose to add an index on the Order table's *OrderNumber* field so that searching for an order by its order number is a fast search.

Data Consistency

You need your database to help you make your data better. Other parts of the schema recommendation should be any constraints that are necessary to keep your data clean and consistent. For example, you might choose to make the e-mail address in your Customer table uniquely constrained to ensure that the same customer is not entered twice. You might also find that adding check constraints to ensure that data cannot be added to the database violates perceived consistency. For example, the OrderItem table's Discount column should probably have a check clause to ensure that you cannot add a discount greater than 100 percent.

Concurrency Management

When you design a database schema for an application, you will be forced to think a bit about the actual day-to-day use of the data in the database. In general, .NET database access uses disconnected concurrency to deal with sharing data in the database. This means there must be a way to ensure that data in a particular row has not changed since the data was retrieved.

There are several approaches to dealing with concurrency, but most of them do not require changes to the schema recommendation. If you are using a non-SQL Server platform, you will need to perform data comparison to deal with the disconnected concurrency. These types of data comparison techniques do not require that you change your database schema.

Alternatively, if you are using SQL Server, timestamps are a common methodology that is highly efficient. In SQL Server, you can use a timestamp field to support concurrency. A SQL Server timestamp field is not a time field at all, but an eight-byte number that is automatically updated every time the row is updated. You cannot change this number directly, but every update to a row will increase the value of a timestamp field. This means you can use the timestamp to ensure that the row is in the same state as it was when you first retrieved the data. If you are using SQL Server as your database platform, you should use timestamp fields to allow this concurrency management. This means adding a timestamp field to each of the schema tables, as shown in Figure 4-10.

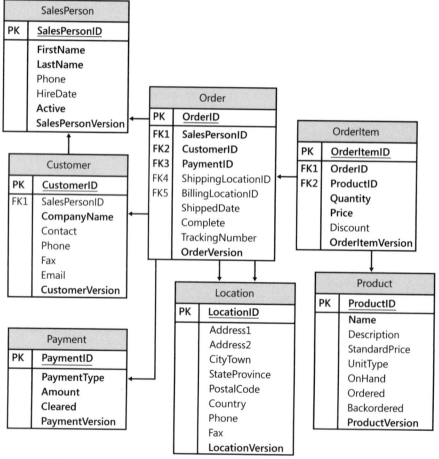

Figure 4-10   A database design with currency fields

Identify Data Procedures

The last step in finalizing your schema design is to identify procedural code that will be required by the schema. Procedural codes are simply stored procedures to perform most tasks that the database requires. Because stored procedures are typically created to perform many common database tasks, you should be concerned only with the Create, Read, Update, and Delete (CRUD) operations for the purposes of the schema design. Typically, this means creating a stored procedure for each one of the CRUD operations. Following are some examples:

- **spCreateCustomer**   Stored procedure to create a new customer
- **spGetCustomer**   Stored procedure to read a customer from the database
- **spUpdateCustomer**   Stored procedure to update a customer
- **spDeleteCustomer**   Stored procedure to delete a customer from the database

Create stored procedures for each of these operations as part of your database design.

Exam Tip   On the exam, be sure to note that stored procedures are expected for most, if not all, database operations. Although in the real world it is often a mix of parameterized queries and stored procedures, in the exam's simplified examples, stored procedures are the right answer.

Lab: Defining Entity Relationships

In this lab, you will review an ORM diagram and identify which relationships are required between the entities.

▶ **Exercise: Reviewing an ORM Diagram**

Review an ORM diagram for relationships and identify them. If you encounter a problem completing an exercise, the completed projects can be installed from the Code folder on the companion CD.

1. Open the Lesson1_ORM.pdf file (or look at Figure 4-3) to view the ORM diagram.
2. Open an instance of SQL Server Management Studio.
3. Attach the DBDesign.mdf database file. This database file (and its log) is located in the Chapter 04/Lesson 1/Before folder, which can be installed from the Code folder on the CD.
4. Open the newly attached instance of the database, and look at the Lesson 4-1 database diagram.
5. Review the ORM diagram to determine which relationships are required, and add them to the database diagram.
6. Save the new diagram to ensure that it is correct. Your resulting diagram should resemble Figure 4-11.

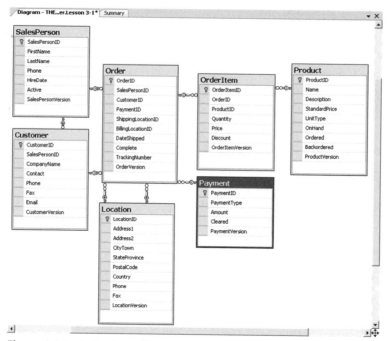

Figure 4-11   A database diagram after adding relationships

Lesson Summary

- Using the ORM diagram, you can determine the entity requirements for a database schema.

- The ORM diagram is a good starting place to determine the data requirements, but reviewing it with stake holders and discerning the requirements by using common sense are both useful to complete real requirements.

- Every data entity in a database schema must have a primary key that is uniquely associated with it.

- Relationships between entities can be identified by referring to the data requirements.

- Finalizing a database schema includes adding clear indexing, ensuring data consistency with constraints, adding concurrency columns if necessary, and identifying stored procedures for use with the schema.

Lesson Review

You can use the following questions to test your knowledge of the information in Lesson 1, "Database Design." The questions are also available on the companion CD if you prefer to review them in electronic form.

NOTE **Answers**

Answers to these questions and explanations of why each answer choice is right or wrong are located in the "Answers" section at the end of the book.

---

1. In an ORM diagram, what could entity relationships be modeled as in the database?

    A. Primary keys

    B. Foreign keys

    C. Mapping tables

    D. Tables

2. What is the purpose of concurrency management?

    A. To ensure that data is consistent across multiple tables in a database

    B. To ensure that data is atomically saved to the database

    C. To ensure that data cannot be overwritten by competing users

    D. To provide a mechanism for propagating changes across tables

3. What is a primary index used for?

    A. To provide uniqueness for each row in a table

    B. To provide for fast searching by primary key

    C. To provide consistency of data across tables

    D. To sort tables

Lesson 2: Designing a Component

In every enterprise, a lot of code is created. Each component in every project is a potential target for reuse. With that in mind, you must design your components with extra care to ensure that your code can be used in other projects within your enterprise. Ensuring that any code created can be used throughout your organization is a key to successful enterprise development.

After this lesson, you will be able to:
- Determine the correct characteristics for a component.
- Create a high-level design of a component.

Estimated lesson time: 20 minutes

Component Characteristics

For each component that you are going to need to design for your enterprise application, you will have to review the client's requirements to plan for the component's requirements. This process involves decisions about how to package the component, where to host the component, and what type of component to build.

Packaging

When reviewing the component you need to build, it is important to determine how the component will be packaged. In many cases, creating a single component is the right decision, but as part of your design criteria, you need to evaluate whether the new component is a single discrete component or a series of related components. For example, an Invoice component might involve creating components for an Invoice or an *Invoice* collection as well as other components for parts of invoices (for instance, Line Items or Payment information).

When determining how many components are necessary, make sure each component is not trying to be too many things to too many people. Typically, this means a component should contain a single logical facility.

In addition, determine how the actual containers for your components will need to be handled. In .NET, components are contained within assemblies. Determining the exact packaging of your components into assemblies has a lot to do with how you want to reuse and deploy your code. You might choose to use a single assembly with most of your components because deploying a single assembly is simpler, and you do not have many applications on a single computer that use the code. Alternatively, you might choose a more granular methodology because you have a larger number of applications, each of which uses only a subset of the total number of components.

For example, if you know that you need to build a component to store your customer information in the database, you could start by assuming that you need a single Customer component. This component would be responsible for reading and writing data to the database for a customer. To start, you can assume a single component, as shown in Figure 4-12.

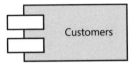

Figure 4-12   Customer component

Your customer might have related components to deal with different objects that they own (such as invoices, payments, and so on.). In this case, a single Customer component is useful. But if the requirement is to store customers and their invoices, you would have to assume that you really need two separate components, as shown in Figure 4-13.

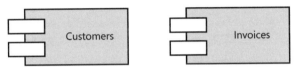

Figure 4-13   Customers and Invoices components

Both of these components could have their own assembly (or package), but because they are so interrelated, it is probably more useful to combine them in a single package. Instead of thinking about what assemblies to create as you design your components, it is more useful to think of packaging throughout an application. This means developing logical assemblies for different types of code. For example, in a typical enterprise application, your packaging might be as simple as a main executable for the user interface, a security package, a data package, and the database. Figure 4-14 shows an example of this structure.

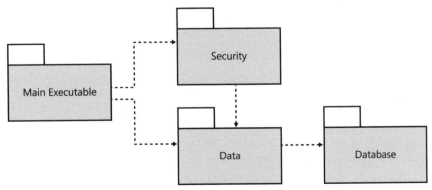

Figure 4-14   Packaging throughout the application

You might find more packages more effective, but in general, separating your user interface from the data is expected in all but the most primitive applications. Now that you have an idea of general packaging throughout your application, you can see clearly that your Customers and Invoices components belong in the data package, as Figure 4-15 shows.

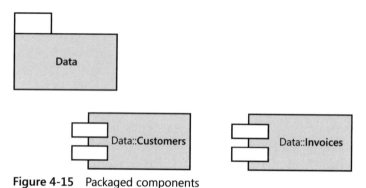

Figure 4-15   Packaged components

Location

When determining the characteristics of your component, you will also need to determine where a component belongs in the architecture. Whether you have designed your architecture to have a physical middle (or data) tier, it should have a logical middle tier to contain data components. So when developing a component, it is important to determine where in the logical tier the component belongs. For example, your Customers and Invoices components belong in the middle tier.

But you might have a component that performs other tasks, such as graphing. That component will more than likely belong in the user interface tier. Deciding that location will help you determine the correct high-level design and what the component interface should look like. This is because if components are to be used across an architecture tier, their locations will probably affect the design and interface of a component.

Type

As the designer of a component, your challenge will be resolving how to capture the functionality of the component while making it accessible to other parts of the application. Your component could be a library of code, a custom control, or a design-time component. Deciding how to share the functionality with the clients of the component requires you to know how it is going to be used. For example, if your component is going to be used to show graphs of data, then creating a custom control makes the most sense. Alternatively, if your component's job is to store information about a specific customer in the database, a custom library makes a lot more sense.

There are no firm rules about how to determine the right type of component to create, but there are some rough guidelines:

- If the component is going to show a user interface, it should be a custom or user control.
- If your component should be usable through the user interface but does not show a user interface (for instance, the Timer component), a design-time component is appropriate.
- If your code does not implement any user interface or design-time experience, most likely it should be a library for consumers of the component to use.

High-Level Design

Once you have the characteristics of your component, you will be ready to design the component. The process of creating the high-level design is not about writing code but about providing the parameters around which code will be created. High-level design requires you to look at your component's role in the bigger picture of the architecture. Creating the high-level design requires consideration of the consistency, life cycle, and design patterns of your component.

Life Cycle

The life cycle of a component is simply taking into account the construction, lifespan, and destruction of the functionality you need. Some components are created and live for long durations, and others perform functional tasks that require very little lifespan at all. Determining the component's life cycle is critical to the design of a component.

For example, in a simple enterprise application, you might create an instance of a component and have it do some work, as Figure 4-16 shows.

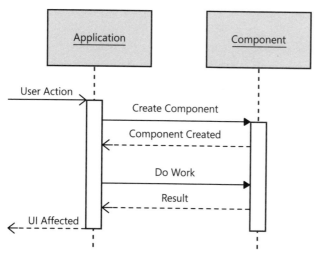

Figure 4-16   A simple component life cycle

In this case, the life cycle is very clear-cut: you create it, you have it do some work, and then you release it for garbage collection. Your class skeleton might look something like this code sample:

```vb
'VB
Public Class SomeComponent
  Public Sub New()
  End Sub

  Public Function DoWork() As Integer
    Return -1
  End Function
End Class
```

```csharp
//C#
public class SomeComponent
{
  public SomeComponent()
  {
  }

  public int DoWork()
  {
    return -1;
  }
}
```

Depending on the construction and any state that the component has, this might be excessive. If you need a component that is stateless and contains functionality that simply processes inputs and returns some sort of data, then a static (or shared in Visual Basic .NET) method might be a better solution. The sequence diagram of that life cycle is more basic, as Figure 4-17 shows.

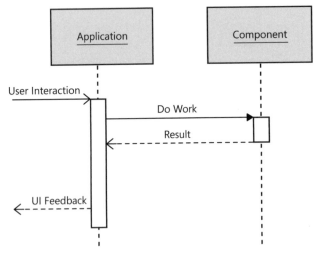

Figure 4-17   A static component life cycle

When you create a skeleton of the code, it might look something like the following:

```vb
'VB
Public Class SomeComponent
  ' Prevent Creation
  Private Sub New()
  End Sub

  Public Shared Function DoWork() As Integer
    Return -1
  End Function
End Class
```

```csharp
//C#
public class SomeComponent
{
  // Prevent Creation
  private SomeComponent() {}

  static public int DoWork()
  {
    return -1;
  }
}
```

Because you are developing for an enterprise application, you might think that you don't need to worry as much about life cycle as you would about other types of applications (for example, Web applications), but that is not true. If your application is long-lived (such as Windows Messenger), keeping instances of classes will cause your application to take increasing memory over time. Typically, try to minimize the use of long-lived objects unless necessary. It is the rare application that can consume all the resources of a computer, so an application should be designed to be well behaved from the start.

To be well behaved, your component should be designed to have a simple life cycle. A simple life cycle implies that the data associated with it should exist for a single instance of the component. In general, this means it is not good practice to hide static data to cache data or attempt to improve performance. By storing instance data at the instance level, you allow the application to control the life cycle of the component. This is important because the nature of the application that uses your component might require it to handle the life cycle differently than you envision its use. If the data needs to be cached, let the application manage that possibility because it can understand the use case for system resources better.

Design Patterns

Rarely do we, as developers, run into problems that are completely unique to programming. This is where design patterns come in. In short, *design patterns* are frequently used frameworks for solving common problems in software development. Design patterns are typically structural solutions for common object-oriented concepts.

While designing your component, it is important to take advantage of design patterns as common solutions to your component structure. For example, one of the most routine design patterns is the singleton. In some instances, you will need to design a class in which only a single instance of the class is appropriate. This is a classic place to use the singleton pattern. There is a design pattern that provides a framework for creating a singleton. For example, a skeleton class using the singleton design pattern would look like this:

```vb
'VB
Public Class Singleton
  ' Prevent Construction outside the class
  Private Sub New()
  End Sub

  ' The single Instance
  Private Shared theSingleton As Singleton = Nothing

  ' The static property to get the instance
  Public Shared Function Instance() As Singleton

    If theSingleton Is Nothing Then
      theSingleton = New Singleton()
    End If

    Return theSingleton
  End Function
End Class
```

```csharp
//C#
public class Singleton
{
  // Prevent Construction outside the class
  private Singleton() {}

  // The single Instance
  private static Singleton theSingleton = null;

  // The static property to get the instance
  public static Singleton Instance()
  {
    if (theSingleton == null)
    {
      theSingleton = new Singleton();
    }

    return theSingleton;
  }
}
```

This pattern for creating a class that exposes a single instance is a reliable method that has been around for years and can help you solve common problems with your design.

There are many design patterns that you can use to design your component. You could spend hours combing through books, Web sites, and blogs to find the right pattern every time you design a component. In general, it is a best practice to start with the Gang of Four design patterns that are outlined in the book *Design Patterns*. The Gang of Four refers to the four writers of that book. See the following More Info box for information about this book and other useful links concerning design patterns.

MORE INFO **Design pattern resources**

■ *Design Patterns*, by Erich Gamma, Richard Helm, Ralph Johnson, and John M. Vlissides (Addison Wesley, 1995). You can find this book at *http://www.awprofessional.com/bookstore/product .asp?isbn=0201633612&rl=1*.

■ "Design Patterns: Solidify Your C# Application Architecture with Design Patterns," by Samir Bajaj, MSDN Magazine at *http://msdn.microsoft.com/msdnmag/issues/01/07/patterns/*.

To Prototype or Not to Prototype

At this point, you should have a good idea of what the design of your component might look like, even if it's only in your head. You now have an important decision to make: "Do I need to prototype the design?"

The decision about whether to prototype comes down to an assessment of the risks of not prototyping. You will need to look at the technological risks to help you make this decision. If the component you are developing is particularly unusual or is using unproved or unfamiliar technology, you are better to create a prototype to test your design.

Prototype a component also when you need to see the component design before the system design is complete. This can include a requirement that the project's proof of concept needs a prototype of your component to ensure that the project is feasible. In some situations, it might be more expedient to have a prototype of the component to satisfy eventual clients.

Expressing the Design

Once you have an idea of the design of your component, you need to capture that design in a way that can be communicated to others. This includes creating activity, sequence, and class diagrams of your component as well as possibly producing pseudocode to represent examples of how the component will be used.

For example, document the design of a fictional component called ProductFactory whose job is to get the information about a specific product from the database and cache products for faster retrieval. You can document your new component in a number of *Unified Modeling Language* (UML) diagrams. First, you could create a simple activity diagram like the one in Figure 4-18 to show the primary flow of the component.

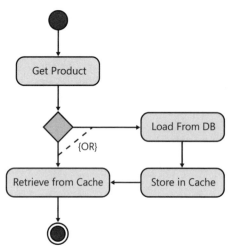

Figure 4-18 ProductFactory component activity diagram

Next, create a sequence diagram to show how you expect the component to be used by clients. The sequence shows not only the timeline flow of work but the interaction between different components. In Figure 4-19, you can see that your ProductFactory component is using the database to get product information.

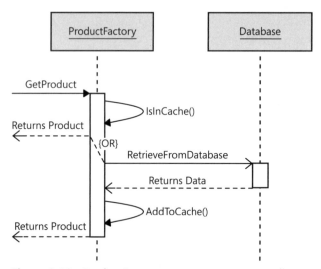

Figure 4-19 ProductFactory component sequence diagram

Finally, you need a class diagram to show the data and operations of your component. In the case of the UML diagrams, using Office Visio to do your diagrams is required because Visual Studio 2005 cannot produce your activity and sequence diagrams, but for your class diagrams, the Visual Studio 2005 class diagram is a richer tool for creating real class diagrams.

For example, you can use Visual Studio 2005 to create a *ProductFactory* class diagram to show the basics of your new class as shown in Figure 4-20.

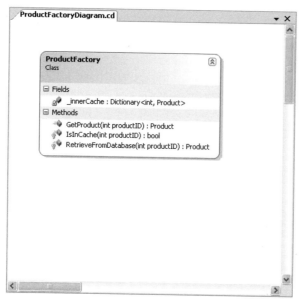

Figure 4-20   ProductFactory component class diagram

MORE INFO   **Creating class diagrams**

For more information about how to create class diagrams in Visual Studio 2005, see the MSDN Documentation at *http://msdn2.microsoft.com/en-us/library/ms304194.aspx*.

BEST PRACTICES   **Iteration**

Design is a very iterative process. As soon as you document your design, it is a good time to review the design to ensure that you have made the best decisions possible for your component. This design–document–review iteration cycle is important to get the right design. Reviewing a design can take the form of a self-analysis or a more formal peer review of the design. No matter how long you have designed software or how accomplished you feel, the more critique the design undergoes, the better it is apt to become.

Design Tradeoffs

There is no such thing as a perfect design. If there were always a single best way to do something, you would not need to design your components, so as you design any component, you will have to make design tradeoffs. This means prioritizing performance, security, and maintainability. Depending on the scenario of your project, each of these priorities might be most important to you. For example, if your application has logon facility but is expected to handle very large loads (such as a news Web site), performance is likely to be the most important factor in your design decision. This does not mean that security and maintainability are not important; it simply means that they take a back seat to performance.

To use the example of an analytical application, you might choose to have more of your back-end data in an unencrypted form to enhance the data-processing performance. In contrast, if you were designing a payroll system, you would want to keep much of the data encrypted and use strong authentication to ensure that the personal data of the employees was well protected. In this case, you would be likely to make security the highest priority, even at the expense of performance or maintainability.

There are no firm rules about which is the most important for a particular component. Only your experience and domain-specific knowledge about the project you are designing will allow you to make design tradeoff decisions.

Lab: Design a Database Logging Component

In this lab, you will design a component for logging information to a file.

► Exercise: Designing a Database Logging Component

In this exercise, you will get requirements for a logging component and design the component.

The following are requirements for the logging component:

- The component allows clients to write out information to a log database.
- The component should also include information about when the information was logged.
- The component should work regardless of what type of project it is used in.

1. In reviewing these requirements, you will need to determine the right packaging for the component. The packaging most likely is a simple .NET in-process component (that is, an assembly).

2. In addition, you might determine that the component can be a simple .NET class that exposes the functionality of logging through a method call that allows log entries to be added to a file.

3. You might decide that the singleton design pattern would be useful for the component, so you would add that to your design.

4. Finally, you decide that the component is a fairly minor one, so prototyping will not be necessary. Your resulting component's class diagram might resemble Figure 4-21.

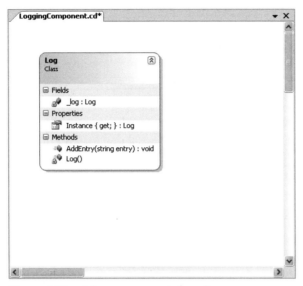

Figure 4-21   A log component class diagram

Lesson Summary

- When designing a component, it is crucial to determine the component's initial characteristics, including packaging, location in the application, and component type.
- While designing a component, understanding its life cycle and following styles of other components in the system are crucial to producing a solid design.
- Most designs can be furthered by reviewing common design patterns to see whether the component to be designed can use an established software solution instead of inventing something completely new.
- Determining whether to prototype a component depends on the complexity of the component, client requirements, and any technological risk factors.
- Using UML to express your design will enable you to communicate the design to a larger audience.
- Reviewing your design tradeoffs will help you ensure that decisions made in the design agree with the overall goals of the project.

Lesson Review

You can use the following questions to test your knowledge of the information in Lesson 2, "Designing a Component." The questions are also available on the companion CD if you prefer to review them in electronic form.

1. How would you package a component that primarily shows a user interface for a Web site?

   A. An executable

   B. A Windows Forms control

   C. An ASP.NET control

   D. A design-time component

2. If you are creating a component that displays data to a user, to which tier should the component belong?

   A. User interface tier

   B. Data tier

   C. Database tier

Lesson 3: Component Features

Now that you have a complete high-level design for your component, you must make decisions about how the component will be implemented. This includes developing the component interface, choosing which features to include in the component, and deciding whether to use existing functionality or create new.

After this lesson, you will be able to:
- Develop component interfaces.
- Determine the correct features for a component.
- Decide whether to implement or inherit functionality.
- Understand the decisions made with respect to working with unmanaged resources.

Estimated lesson time: 20 minutes

Component Interfaces

Working with components is simply a conversation between two objects inside the .NET run time. For components to have that conversation, a common language—the component interface—must be decided on. In other words, the interface for a component includes the constructor, methods, properties, and events of a component. These are also the ways in which a client and a component can have a conversation.

The interface for a component is not necessarily an interface in the .NET sense. The interface of a component can be as simple as a .NET class or as complicated as using interfaces, abstract (or *MustInherit* in Visual Basic .NET) classes, or even a Web service.

Consumers of the Component

Before you design the interface to your component, you must understand the consumer of your component. The code that will consume your component should provide you with key information about what kind of interface you will need. Consumers of the component might expect to use the component as a simple class, in which case, a simple class interface makes the most sense.

In contrast, you might have clients that use the component through remoting. If your component will be accessed as a remote object, you will need to take that into account when defining the interface for your component. Why does remoting a component affect its interface? Remoting assumes that the actual object is across some expensive transport (that is, not in the current AppDomain). Because of this, you will want to allow the consumer to do as many of the operations as possible of the component without a lot of traffic across the transport. In other words, if you expect your object to be remoted, define the interface to avoid being chatty.

In addition, you might be developing a component that will be called through a Web service. If your component will be exposed as a Web service, it must be as atomic and stateless as possible. Web services are more than just another transport layer; they are a disconnected transport. In general, the best practice for using Web services in your components is to make the interface to the component message-based. In other words, a single operation should be able to take a payload that allows as much of the job as possible to be done in a single call. Trying to expose an object across Web services can be challenging if you design a stateful, chatty component.

You must also consider that, because you are writing components for an enterprise application, your component might take the form of a control or design-time component. When you consider who will consume your component, you should try to create components that are easily consumed. This means you may need to create wrappers for special needs or, in the case of creating controls and Web parts, you will likely need to create design-time features such as preview of the control's ultimate user interface (UI) output.

Component Lifetime Interface

Before you start with the rest of the interface for your component, one of the first decisions you will need to make is whether the interface will handle the lifetime of the component. This includes both the construction and garbage collection of your component.

When deciding on how to handle construction of your object, there are several choices. If your component does not have any state but instead will perform some specific task, you might consider using a static class or a singleton design pattern. This pattern means that, generally, no one will create an instance of your class but will instead just call methods on your type. Although this is a powerful pattern, it is useful only in a very narrow use case.

For most components, you will need to decide how to create your objects. In general, asking for initialization data in the constructor is perfectly acceptable. Two-phase construction (for instance, empty constructors plus an "initialization" method) are not considered a best practice. There are always exceptions to this best practice, but in general, accepting initialization data in the constructor is the right thing to do. For example, here is an example of the one-phase versus two-phase interface design:

```vb
'VB
' Prefer single phase construction
' over two phase construction
Public Class OnePhase
  Public Sub New(ByVal someInit As String, ByVal moreInit As Integer)
    ' ...
  End Sub

  ' ...
End Class
```

```
' Don't use two phase construction unless you have a
' compelling reason to use it
Public Class TwoPhase
  Public Sub New()
  End Sub
  Public Sub Initialize(ByVal someInit As String, _
                        ByVal moreInit As Integer)
    ' ...
  End Sub

  ' ...
End Class

//C#
// Prefer single phase construction
// over two phase construction
public class OnePhase
{   public OnePhase(string someInit, int moreInit)
  {
    // ...
  }

  // ...
}
// Don't use two phase construction unless you have a
// compelling reason to use it
public class TwoPhase
{
  public TwoPhase()
  {
  }
  public void Initialize(string someInit, int moreInit)
  {
    // ...
  }

  // ...
}
```

Passing initialization data in the constructor provides clarity of interface and prevents confusion to the users of the component. Passing the initialization data in the constructor also prevents the unexpected side effects of users calling the initialization code twice.

Once you determine what you are going to do with a constructor, look at how you are going to handle the end of a component's life. There are three different ways of dealing with the end of the life of your component, as the following table shows.

Life Cycle Type	Description
Stack-based object	Value types are stored on the stack and are not garbage collected because they are destroyed when the stack is destroyed. This life cycle is very fast and should be used for lightweight objects that are not kept for longer than a method call.
Heap-based object	Objects are garbage collected. Garbage collection occurs when the system is not under load. Most components will fall into this category.
Objects with unmanaged resources	When you need to determine when an object is released, you can implement the *IDisposable* pattern. This is for resources that are not garbage collected (for instance, database connections, IO completion ports, and so on).

In general, you should not use finalizers in your component designs at all. Finalizers allow you to perform clean-up code just before garbage collection occurs. Objects with finalizers are slower to garbage collect and, in almost every case, instead of creating a finalizer, you should be using the *IDisposable* pattern if you need control over your cleanup code.

Design the Interface

Once you understand the life cycle of your component, all that is left is to actually design the methods, properties, and events. Not only must you look at how your component will fulfill its duties, you must also consider how homogeneous the component is as it relates to the rest of the project. Homogeny is important because consistency in how components work will make the development of client components or applications easier for developers.

In this case, homogeny means similarity of interface, naming, and workflow. For example, if the style of the interface of other components in your system is to have overloads for different types of operations, then yours should as well. For example, you might have this *Log* class in your system already:

```vb
'VB
Public Class Log
  Public Sub Write(ByVal message As String)
    ' ...
  End Sub
  Public Sub Write(ByVal message As String, _
              ByVal ex As Exception)
    ' ...
  End Sub
  Public Sub Write(ByVal message As String, _
              ByVal ParamArray args As Object())     ' ...
  End Sub
End Class


//C#
public class Log
```

```
{
  public void Write(string message)
  {
    // ...
  }
   public void Write(string message, Exception ex)
  {
    // ...
  }
   public void Write(string message, params object[] args)
  {
    // ...
  }
}
```

Because this other class creates overloads for different types of messages, you might consider creating multiple methods that take different overloads to follow this stylistic pattern.

Lab: Determine Component Features

In this lab, you will decide how to implement the features of a new component.

▶ **Exercise: Determining the Right Interface for a New Component**

In this exercise, you will review the requirements of a component that will take a name and allow access to different parts of a full name.

1. You are given the following requirements for a component that will be responsible for handling a person's full name:
    ❑ The component should accept a full name or a name in its separate parts when the component is created.
    ❑ The component should allow access to any part of the name separately (for example, FirstName, LastName, MiddleName, and so on).
    ❑ The component should allow retrieval of the full name as a single string.
2. In reviewing these requirements, you determine that a simple class that derives from only the *Object* class is the best approach because this could be used anywhere in the system.
3. You would define two constructors based on the requirements: one to take the full name and one that takes each of the component parts of the name separately.
4. You would define properties for each of the separate parts of the name (for example, FirstName, LastName, and so on).
5. You might determine that the best way to expose the formatted full name is to override the *ToString* method of the base *Object* class.

6. With these decisions made, the class diagram for your resulting class might resemble Figure 4-22.

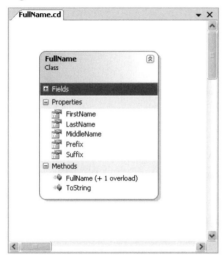

Figure 4-22   FullName component class diagram

Lesson Summary

- Determining a component's interface is a matter of understanding the consumers of a component, what kind of lifetime the component has, and the style of interface on other components in the system.

- Determining how to implement features of a component depends on what functionality is needed. Choosing among extending an existing component, composing a new component by mixing other components, or writing a new component are the three options.

Lesson Review

You can use the following questions to test your knowledge of the information in Lesson 3, "Component Features." The questions are also available on the companion CD if you prefer to review them in electronic form.

NOTE   Answers

Answers to these questions and explanations of why each answer choice is right or wrong are located in the "Answers" section at the end of the book.

---

1. Should the constructor accept initialization data?

    A. Yes

    B. No

Chapter Review

To further practice and reinforce the skills you learned in this chapter, you can perform the following tasks:

- Review the chapter summary.
- Review the list of key terms introduced in this chapter.
- Complete the case scenarios. These scenarios set up real-world situations involving the topics of this chapter and ask you to create a solution.
- Complete the suggested practices.
- Take a practice test.

Chapter Summary

- You can map entities in your design to tables in the database design.
- Creating a complete database schema is crucial to a successful enterprise application design.
- Designing a component requires that you understand both the environment in which a component will be used and where the component fits into the architecture.
- Creating a high-level design of your component is the first step toward completing your component design.
- Reviewing the design for possible uses of design patterns will help your design be that much better in the end.
- Expressing your design in UML diagrams will help you communicate the design to stakeholders and peers for review to ensure that your design meets their needs.
- Designing a well-thought-out interface requires that you understand who will use the component, what kind of lifetime the component will have, and what the stylistic preference for interfaces are within the entire architecture.

Key Terms

Do you know what these key terms mean? You can check your answers by looking up the terms in the glossary at the end of the book.

- consumers
- database schema
- design patterns
- foreign key

- primary key
- Unified Modeling Language (UML)

Case Scenarios

In the following case scenarios, you will apply what you've learned about designing components. You can find answers to these questions in the "Answers" section at the end of this book.

Case Scenario 1: Design an Employee Component

You work for a company that needs to access employee data within many of its applications, some Web-based and some Microsoft Windows–based. You need to be able to expose the data associated with an employee to these different applications.

Interviews

Following is an interview with the engineering manager.

- **Engineering Manager** Both of our development teams will use this component to access the same employee information. There will be no security implications in the data access because it is basic public information (for instance, name, group, and e-mail address).

Questions

Answer the following questions for the component developer.

1. How will you package this component so that I can use it with the Windows-based application I am writing?
2. How will you package this component so I can use it in a Web application?

Case Scenario 2: Design a Database for the Company Library

You are working for a large technology company. They have decided to allow their employees to check out technical books from their internal library, but they want to require the employees to use a small enterprise application to do so.

Interviews

Following is an interview with the engineering manager.

- **Engineering Manager**   We need a database design for a simple library. Each employee can check out up to two books at a time.

Questions

1. How many tables do you expect to have?
2. How are the tables related?

Suggested Practices

To successfully master the exam objectives presented in this chapter, complete the following tasks.

Create a Database Schema

For this task, you should complete at least Practices 1 and 2. You can do Practice 3 for a more in-depth understanding of data design.

- **Practice 1**   Create a database design for a CD collection. Include information about the title, artist, and year of release of each CD. Also, store each song in a separate table.
- **Practice 2**   Create constraints to ensure that each song belongs to a CD.
- **Practice 3**   Add indexes on a commonly used column (for instance, Title) to see how adding indexes can improve the performance of queries.

Design Components

For this task, you should complete at least Practices 1 and 2. You can do Practice 3 for a more in-depth understanding of component design.

- **Practice 1**   Design a component that will show the date and time in separate user interface controls. Make up minimum requirements for the simple component.
- **Practice 2**   Review the design with peers to see whether the design meets minimum requirements.
- **Practice 3**   Implement the design to ensure that it still meets all the requirements.

Take a Practice Test

The practice tests on this book's companion CD offer many options. For example, you can test yourself on just one exam objective, or you can test yourself on all the 70-549 certification exam content. You can set up the test so that it closely simulates the experience of taking a certification exam, or you can set it up in study mode so that you can look at the correct answers and explanations after you answer each question.

MORE INFO   Practice tests

For details about all the practice test options available, see the "How to Use the Practice Tests" section in this book's Introduction.

Chapter 5

Component Development

In Chapter 4, "Component Design," you learned to design a component. Now you will develop that component. Development of a component requires many different decisions. You need to determine exactly how you are going to implement the features, how to handle data in your components, and finally, how to add any common component infrastructure. This chapter will walk you through those three parts of component development.

Exam objectives in this chapter:

- Develop the features of a component.
  - ❑ Decide whether existing functionality can be implemented or inherited.
  - ❑ Decide how to handle unmanaged and managed resources.
  - ❑ Decide which extensibility features are required.
  - ❑ Decide whether a component must be stateful or stateless.
  - ❑ Decide whether a component must be multithreaded.
  - ❑ Decide which functions to implement in the base class, abstract class, or sealed class.
- Develop the data access and data handling features of a component.
  - ❑ Analyze data relationships.
  - ❑ Analyze the data handling requirements of a component.
- Develop a component feedback mechanism.
  - ❑ Develop a component status feedback technique.
  - ❑ Develop an exception handling mechanism.
- Develop a component to include profiling requirements.
  - ❑ Identify potential issues, such as resource leaks and performance gaps, by profiling a component.
  - ❑ Decide when to stop profiling on a component.
  - ❑ Decide whether to redesign a component after analyzing the profiling results.

Lessons in this chapter:

Before You Begin

- To complete the lessons in this chapter, you should be familiar with Microsoft Visual Basic or C#.

Lesson 1: Implementing Component Features

After the design for a specific component is complete, you will need to determine how to implement the features of the component.

After this lesson, you will be able to:

- Determine whether you need to extend, compose, or implement your component's specific features.
- Understand the reasons to make a component stateful or stateless.
- Make decisions about supporting multithreaded environments.
- Know how to deal with unmanaged resources in components.

Estimated lesson time: 30 minutes

Extend, Compose, or Implement?

Before you can implement your component, review the requirements for the component and determine how you are going to fulfill its feature requirements. You need to determine what you must write and what you can build on. Whether you use the expansive Microsoft .NET Framework 2.0, third-party controls, or even other in-house development, you must decide which features you need to build and which features you can reuse from other components. There are three real choices here for any component: extend, compose, or implement.

You might find that a particular class or control is close to what you need but needs customization to meet your needs. In this case, extend the class or control by inheriting from it and adding your customization. For example, you might find that the best way to create a logging component is to extend a *FileStream* class instead of writing the files yourself. If so, you can use the same interface as the *FileStream* class but extend it to do the specific logging that you need. It is important to think of the new component as a type of the class or control from which you are deriving it. In this example, you really want a *LogStream*, not just a log class. Because you want a stream that will write only to a text log, extending the *FileStream* is the right approach. Your *LogStream* class would have a class diagram that resembles Figure 5-1.

You might find that your component needs functionality from a number of different classes or controls. In this case, compose a new component that includes the functionality of all the different classes or controls. The world of controls offers a visual way of thinking about this. You might decide that you need a control that allows users to enter a date and a time as separate pieces of data. You might find that creating a component that is composed of a calendar control and a textbox is the best solution. The new component is not necessarily a calendar control or a textbox but a new type of component that includes both. That is the essence of composition.

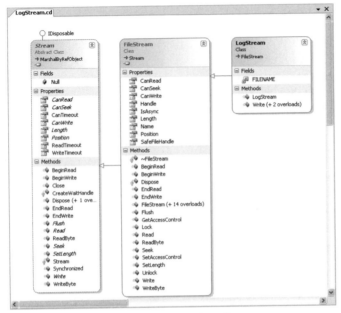

Figure 5-1   LogStream component class diagram

Finally, you might find that neither extending nor composing from existing components will work for your component's features. For example, you might have a component that needs to perform some calculations that are specific to your project, so the only real option is implementing this logic in your own code.

Component implementations will always lean on (or inherit from) other code, even if that code is just the *Object* class. Choosing the right approach to extending, composing, or implementing functionality, however, is crucial to a well-designed and well-implemented component.

Building Class Hierarchies

Sometimes, you decide that you need a hierarchy of classes that make up a component. You might use a class hierarchy so that common functionality can be shared by a variety of component types. This common functionality class is referred to as a base class. The *Stream* class in the .NET Framework is a classic example of this design. The *Stream* class itself is a base class that not only exemplifies the interface that the derived classes will follow but also supports basic functionality that all *Stream*-derived classes will share. Derived classes will specialize the stream for specific purposes. For example, the *FileStream* class is a *Stream* class that writes to a file. There are a number of different streams that are specialized versions of the *Stream* class, including *FileStream, MemoryStream,* and *DeflateStream.*

The *Stream* classes exemplify another decision you must make. Do you need the base class to be abstract? Abstract classes (also referred to as a *MustInherit* class in Visual Basic) are classes that cannot be created. Specifically, only classes that inherit from the abstract class can be instantiated. For example, you might have an *Animal* base class from which a *Cat* class and a *Dog* class inherit. Although cats and dogs are both animals, you cannot create an instance of the *Animal* class itself. All instances of the *Animal* class are actually specializations of the *Animal* class. That is the canonical example of the abstract class. In that case, the *Animal* class would be abstract.

The core concepts of abstract classes and interfaces can be seen as very similar, but they are actually different. An abstract class is used to share not only interface and implementation but also identity. An abstract class is an "is-a" relationship. A *Cat* is an *Animal*. A *Dog* is an *Animal*. Interfaces, on the other hand, define a calling convention or behavior. You might have an *IFeed* interface that defines that you can feed an object. That interface would probably exist on an *Animal* class. But that same interface could also exist on a *ParkingMeter* class. Although you feed an animal and a parking meter differently, the interface in this fictitious *IFeed* interface might define that they both need to be fed.

Component State

One of the most important decisions you will make in developing a component is whether it will be stateful or stateless. Making this determination is simply a matter of establishing whether your component needs to maintain data across multiple calls to itself. In this context, "state" usually refers to any data that is not consumed during a single method call in a component. The decision about whether to be stateful or stateless is not about whether your component needs data to accomplish its task but about where that data is going to exist.

The general rule of thumb is that *stateless* components will scale out better but at the cost of working without local state. For example, assume that you need a component to create an e-mail for a customer to remind him or her of a payment that is due. You might have a stateful component that contains all the data for a customer (as is common with data access layers). You could decide to add the functionality to the existing customer component, which is stateful. When you issue a request for one of these e-mails, you need to get the customer's component and then ask that the e-mail be sent.

As your customer base expands, you might find that reading so many customers out of the database just to send them a routine e-mail is slow because of all the user objects that are being created. That is, it does not scale out well. Instead, create a stateless component that uses the customer identifier to issue the e-mail. Internally, this e-mailing component might use data (such as the identifier you passed to it and the data it retrieved from the database) during the completion of the operation, but it might scale out faster because it could be reused for different customers.

The additional scaling out of the component is accomplished in two ways. No extraneous data is being loaded that the component does not need, and you are avoiding any construction–destruction cycles for every e-mail creation. You can usually tell when a component takes state: it either has a constructor that takes data, or it includes a secondary initialization method (for instance, *Create* or *Init*).

Creating stateful components is not a bad idea. Most created components are stateful. Generally, you can develop stateful components more quickly, and they are required for many components that you will need in your development. However, isolating key components to make them stateless for the purposes of scaling out can be a real boon to most development projects.

Multithreading

Multithreading is using threads in your component to improve your throughput. When working with multithreading in your component, you will need to deal with two issues: thread safety and using multithreading in your component. Thread safety is determining whether your component will be called from multiple threads simultaneously.

Thread Safety

Assuming that your component will be stateful, you will need to determine whether the component will need to support thread safety. Thread safety is simply protection of data within a component from simultaneous access by multiple threads. Thread safety, however, comes at a cost, regardless of which locking scheme you choose to protect your data from multithreaded access. This cost is in development time, component performance, and component testing as well as in debugging difficulties.

It is important for any stateful component that you create to know whether it is valid to use in a multithreaded environment. If it is valid to call the component from multiple threads, you must protect that data. There are components that never need to be *thread safe* because they are always called from a single thread. Typically, you should add thread safety only if your component specifically needs it.

Using Threads

As you implement your component's features, you will need to determine whether to use threads. Introducing threading can improve the performance of a component dramatically by allowing multiple threads to do work simultaneously. At the same time, introducing threading will increase the complexity of your component in both implementation and debugging.

So how do you decide whether to use threading? Introduce threading only when you need it. Not every type of operation will benefit from multithreaded code. Usually, multithreading can help a component when it has an operation that spends much of its time waiting. For example, you might have a component that uses a Web service to retrieve stock prices. Because the retrieval of that information over the Internet might take some time, your component might be waiting just for the results to return. Introducing threading to that component enables you to fire off several threads to retrieve different stock results all at the same time so that requests to the Web service are being made while other requests are pending.

The benefit of adding threading must outweigh the additional complexity. This is a black-and-white rule against which you can measure that decision. You will have to rely on your experience to understand the risk-versus-reward decision.

MORE INFO   **Multithreaded access**

For more information about multithreading, please refer to the chapter titled "Threading" in *MCTS Self-Paced Training Kit (Exam 70-536): Microsoft .NET Framework 2.0–Application Development Foundation* by Tony Northrup, Shawn Wildermuth, and Bill Ryan (Microsoft Press, 2006).

Handling Unmanaged Resources

The common language runtime (CLR) is an environment in which the memory is managed; that is, reference objects are garbage collected. The garbage collector manages memory. After reference objects are out of scope, they are eligible to be reclaimed by the system when the garbage collector cleans up the environment. Other resources, however, are unmanaged. For example, database connections are an unmanaged resource. Even though the local memory associated with a database collection is managed by the CLR, the actual connection is not. If you open a database connection and wait until the garbage collection fires on the connection to close it, the database will end up with many unclosed database connections, which will impede basic performance of the database.

In the .NET Framework, the *IDisposable* interface was created to support unmanaged resources. If you write a component that has unmanaged resources, you must allow for those resources to be cleaned up by the users. You do this by supporting the *IDisposable* interface.

In addition, if you use objects that implement the *IDisposable* interface, you must call the object's *IDisposable.Dispose()* method to clean up their unmanaged resources. This means that if you use an object that supports *IDisposable* within a single call, you should wrap it with a using statement to call the *IDisposable* interface. If you hold on to an object that supports *IDisposable* for longer than a single call (which, for instance, is a member of your component), you must support the *IDisposable* interface so that, in your implementation of the *IDisposable.Dispose()* method, you call your member's *IDisposable* implementation.

In addition to working with members that support *IDisposable*, be aware of other unmanaged resources. Typically, this is when you are retaining resources that are outside the .NET Framework. For example, if you are using an external dynamic-link library (DLL) through interoperability, the DLL is not a .NET component and is, therefore, unmanaged. You must release any resources you use from that DLL, and, by supporting the *IDisposable* interface, you will have a well-defined pattern to clean up any resources.

Quick Check

1. How should you handle unmanaged resources in your own classes?
2. How should you handle classes that have unmanaged resources that you use within your own code?

Quick Check Answers

1. If your class has unmanaged resources, you should implement the *IDisposable* interface.
2. If you are using classes that have unmanaged resources (and, therefore, implement *IDisposable*), you will need to call the *IDisposable.Dispose* method to ensure that all resources are released.

Real World

Shawn Wildermuth

Understanding the implications of unmanaged resources is a crucial skill to have for every level of developer. In my experience in doing a lot of code reviews, not handling unmanaged resources is one of the most common errors in projects. As you create components that use different parts of the .NET Framework, you will need to learn which types of objects support the *IDisposable* interface and which do not. For example, almost all of ADO.NET supports this interface. All classes that derive from *Component* also support this interface. This means a large chunk of the .NET Framework should be dealt with as unmanaged resources. I've learned to tell people to look carefully for this interface.

Lab: Add Handling of Unmanaged Resources

In this lab, you will add support to handle unmanaged resources in an existing component. If you encounter a problem completing an exercise, the completed projects can be installed from the Code folder on the companion CD.

▶ **Exercise: Add Support for Unmanaged Resources**

In this exercise, you will take a partially completed class and add support for handling unmanaged resources.

1. Open the \Chapter05\Lesson 1\Exercise 1\Before project in your preferred language. (C# and Visual Basic are included.)

2. In Microsoft Visual Studio, click File | Open | Project/Solution, and then navigate to \Chapter 05\Lesson 1\Exercise 1\Before.

3. Open the *Logging* class code file.

4. Identify the unmanaged resources (the *FileStream* and *StreamWriter* members).

5. Add the *IDisposable* interface to the *Logging* class.

6. Add the *Dispose* method of *IDisposable* to the *Logging* class.

7. Inside the *Dispose* method, call the *Dispose* methods of *FileStream* and *StreamWriter*.

8. The new *Logging* class might look like the following. (Changes from the Before project are in bold. You can view the completed solution in the After folder.)

```
'VB
Imports System
Imports System.Collections.Generic
Imports System.Text
Imports System.IO

''' <summary>
''' A class for writing information to a
''' standard log file.
''' </summary>
Public Class Logger   Implements IDisposable

  Private Const logFileName As String = "logfile.txt"
  Private logFile As FileStream = Nothing
  Private writer As StreamWriter = Nothing

  ''' <summary>
  ''' Initializes a new instance of
  ''' the <see cref="T:Logger"/> class.
  ''' </summary>
  Public Sub New()
    MyBase.New()
    logFile = File.Open(logFileName, _
                   FileMode.OpenOrCreate, _
                   FileAccess.Write, _
                   FileShare.ReadWrite)
    writer = New StreamWriter(logFile)
  End Sub

  ''' <summary>
  ''' Adds the specified message.
  ''' </summary>
  ''' <param name="message">The message.</param>
  Public Overloads Sub Add(ByVal message As String)
    writer.WriteLine(message)
  End Sub

  ''' <summary>
  ''' Adds the specified message.
```

```
''' </summary>
''' <param name="message">The message.</param>
''' <param name="args">The args.</param>
Public Overloads Sub Add(ByVal message As String, _
                         ByVal ParamArray args() As Object)
  writer.WriteLine(message, args)
End Sub
''' <summary>
''' Performs application-defined tasks associated
''' with freeing, releasing, or
''' resetting unmanaged resources.
''' Implements the Dispose() method of the
''' IDisposable interface
''' </summary>
Public Sub Dispose() Implements IDisposable.Dispose
  writer.Dispose()
  logFile.Dispose()
End Sub
End Class


//C#
using System;
using System.Collections.Generic;
using System.Text;
using System.IO;

/// <summary>
/// A class for writing information to a
/// standard log file.
/// </summary>
public class Logger : IDisposable
{
  const string logFileName = "logfile.txt";
  FileStream logFile = null;
  StreamWriter writer = null;

  /// <summary> `ws 65
  /// Initializes a new instance of
  /// the <see cref="T:Logger"/> class.
  /// </summary>
  public Logger()
  {
    logFile = File.Open(logFileName,
                        FileMode.OpenOrCreate,
                        FileAccess.Write,
                        FileShare.ReadWrite);
    writer = new StreamWriter(logFile);
  }

  /// <summary>
  /// Adds the specified message.
  /// </summary>
  /// <param name="message">The message.</param>
```

```
  public void Add(string message)
  {
    writer.WriteLine(message);
  }


  /// <summary>
  /// Adds the specified message.
  /// </summary>
  /// <param name="message">The message.</param>
  /// <param name="args">The args.</param>
  public void Add(string message,
                  params object[] args)
  {
    writer.WriteLine(message, args);
  }
  /// <summary>
  /// Performs application-defined tasks associated
  /// with freeing, releasing, or
  /// resetting unmanaged resources.
  /// Implements the Dispose() method of the
  /// IDisposable interface
  /// </summary>
  public void Dispose()
  {
    writer.Dispose();
    logFile.Dispose();
  }
}
```

9. Open the *Program* class in the project.

10. Modify the code that creates the instance of the *Logging* class and uses it to support automatic calling of the *IDisposable* interface. The *Program* class might look like the following code.

```
'VB
Class Program

  Public Overloads Shared Sub Main()

    Using theLog As New Logger()
      theLog.Add("Hello Mom")
    End Using

  End Sub

End Class

//C#
class Program
{
  static void Main(string[] args)
  {
    using (Logger theLog = new Logger())
```

```
      {
        theLog.Add("Hello Mom");
      }
    }
  }
}
```

11. Compile the program and fix any coding errors you find. Run the program and, once complete, find the logfile.txt file in the same directory as the executable to ensure that the code worked as expected.

Lesson Summary

- By reviewing existing classes both inside and outside the .NET Framework, you can determine whether to extend an existing class, compose an existing class, or create an entirely new class to meet your functional needs.
- You can determine whether to make the component stateful or stateless by reviewing its requirements.
- Weigh whether supporting the thread safety of your component's data is required.
- You must support the *IDisposable* interface if any of the data in your component is not managed.

Lesson Review

You can use the following questions to test your knowledge of the information in Lesson 1, "Implementing Component Features." The questions are also available on the companion CD if you prefer to review them in electronic form.

NOTE Answers

Answers to these questions and explanations of why each answer choice is right or wrong are located in the "Answers" section at the end of the book.

---

1. If your component uses a component that implements *IDisposable*, do you have to implement *IDisposable* as well?

    A. Yes

    B. No

    C. Yes, but only if the lifetime of the *IDisposable* object is the same as my object

2. When should your component be created as an abstract class (*MustInherit* in Visual Basic)?

    A. To stop instantiation of my class

    B. To force users of my component to inherit from my class to get shared implementation

    C. To force users of my component to write their component to conform to a particular API interface

    D. When my class should be used in only the user interface tier of the system

3. Why avoid making a component thread safe? (Choose all that apply.)

    A. High cost of development

    B. Performance overhead of thread safety

    C. Component will not be used in a multithreaded environment

    D. None; all components should be thread-safe

Lesson 2: Data Access in Components

It is difficult to develop a system that never touches a database in most enterprise-level applications. The database is the central point for data in most companies today. Making components that can consume data is one of the most common tasks for enterprise developers.

> **After this lesson, you will be able to:**
> - Review project requirements to determine the correct data access methodology.
> - Add business logic to your components.
>
> **Estimated lesson time: 10 minutes**

Data Access

As you trudge through the development of your enterprise application, you will likely run into situations in which you need components that must consume, create, or change database data. Data access is the code that enables you to communicate with the database. Data access consists of four operations: create, read, update, and delete. These four operations are often referred to as CRUD operations. Adding any (or all) of these operations to a component makes it a data access component.

Implementing data access in your own components involves reviewing several methods to choose the correct one. These include typed datasets, untyped datasets, and *DataReader* objects as well as Web services.

> **Real World**
>
> *Shawn Wildermuth*
>
> This lesson explains data access by using the .NET Framework alone, but data access in the real world is a different animal. Depending on the requirements of your project, the skill sets of your team, and other factors, you will find that there are many tools to help you accomplish data access. These tools range from simple object-relational mapping products to complex frameworks for building your business objects. As you decide on a strategy for your enterprise applications, become familiar with solutions (both Microsoft and others) and how they match your requirements.

When you build components that consume data, the most basic approach is to access the data by using ADO.NET to implement CRUD functionality. Typically, this means using *DataReader* to get data from the database and using *Command* when you insert, update, or delete. This approach can be efficient, assuming your SQL code is efficient. The *DataReader* class is essentially a forward-only fire hose of data to fill in your component data so other components' data is retrieved from the database quickly. Additionally, using *Command* (in conjunction with stored procedures) to make changes works efficiently because you are working with the database at a very basic level.

Exam Tip   If performance is the most important requirement, then using *DataReader* classes in conjunction with *Command* is the methodology of choice.

Using *DataReader* and *Command* is efficient at run time but at a cost of development time. For example, assume that you have a simple business object that can do all the CRUD functions for contacts. Coding your component to use *DataReader* and *Command* might result in a class design resembling Figure 5-2.

Figure 5-2   Contact component

Much of this class's interface is composed of constructors and methods to get, create, save, and delete a contact (or a list of contacts). The component contains fields to manage if a contact is new (*_isNew*) and if the contact has changes that need to be saved (*_isDirty*). Implementing this class means writing ADO.NET code in each of the data methods (for instance, *GetContact, Save,* and *Delete*). Although this is not difficult, it is labor intensive. For example, here is the *GetContact* method:

```
'VB
Public Shared Function GetContact(ByVal contactID As Integer) _
  As Contact

  ' Get the connection from configuration
  Dim connInfo As ConnectionStringSettings = _
```

```
      ConfigurationManager.ConnectionStrings("AdventureWorks")
   Dim factory As DbProviderFactory = _
      DbProviderFactories.GetFactory(connInfo.ProviderName)


   ' Create the ADO.NET Objects
   Using conn As DbConnection = factory.CreateConnection
     Using cmd As DbCommand = conn.CreateCommand

        ' Setup command to use a stored procedure to
        ' get all the customers data
        cmd.CommandText = "Person.uspGetContact"
        cmd.CommandType = CommandType.StoredProcedure

        ' Add the input parameter
        Dim idParam As DbParameter = factory.CreateParameter
        idParam.ParameterName = "contactID"
        idParam.DbType = DbType.Int32
        idParam.Direction = ParameterDirection.Input
        idParam.Value = contactID
        cmd.Parameters.Add(idParam)
        Try

          ' Open the connection
          conn.ConnectionString = connInfo.ConnectionString
          conn.Open()

          ' Get the data
          Using reader As DbDataReader = _
            cmd.ExecuteReader(CommandBehavior.CloseConnection)

            ' Assuming only one record.
            ' If multiple are returned they are ignored
            If reader.Read Then
              Return New Contact(reader)
            End If

          End Using

        Finally

          If (conn.State <> ConnectionState.Closed) Then
            conn.Close()
          End If

        End Try

     End Using
   End Using

   ' Contact was not found, we return null
   Return Nothing

End Function
```

```csharp
//C#
public static Contact GetContact(int contactID)
{
  // Get the connection from configuration
  ConnectionStringSettings connInfo =
    ConfigurationManager.ConnectionStrings["AdventureWorks"];
  DbProviderFactory factory =
    DbProviderFactories.GetFactory(connInfo.ProviderName);

  // Create the ADO.NET Objects
  using (DbConnection conn = factory.CreateConnection())
  using (DbCommand cmd = conn.CreateCommand())
  {
    // Setup command to use a stored procedure to
    // get all the customers data
    cmd.CommandText = "Person.uspGetContact";
    cmd.CommandType = CommandType.StoredProcedure;

    // Add the input parameter
    DbParameter idParam = factory.CreateParameter();
    idParam.ParameterName = "contactID";
    idParam.DbType = DbType.Int32;
    idParam.Direction = ParameterDirection.Input;
    idParam.Value = contactID;
    cmd.Parameters.Add(idParam);

    try
    {
      // Open the connection
      conn.ConnectionString = connInfo.ConnectionString;
      conn.Open();

      // Get the data
      using (DbDataReader reader =
              cmd.ExecuteReader(CommandBehavior.CloseConnection))
      {
        // Assuming only one record.
        // If multiple are returned they are ignored
        if (reader.Read())
        {
          return new Contact(reader);
        }
      }

    }
    finally
    {
      if (conn.State != ConnectionState.Closed)
      {
        conn.Close();
      }
    }
```

```
    }

    // Contact was not found, we return null
    return null;
}
```

In addition to the simple component that just needs to load itself up with data, you will need related entities. For example, if you had an Order component that had related Order Items, you would want an efficient way to just load up an order, and all related data in the database would be loaded at the same time. It is not intuitive to expect users of the Order component to then load all the Order Items when they need them. Understanding these relationships and modeling them in your components and the database is crucial to creating smart data access components. You can do this by writing related classes that compose the relationships, but this requires even more hand-coded ADO.NET to load related data efficiently.

As you scale out your solution, you can safely remote these objects (or re-factor the factory methods into remotable objects) so that there is a clear upgrade path as your enterprise application needs additional scalability. This method of handcrafting your data access components is preferable when run-time performance and maintainability are high on the list of requirements for your components.

Another solution for performing your data access is to use *DataSet* classes. The *DataSet* class is a container for related data and offers an advantage over raw ADO.NET code in that some of the common data access functionality that you require is built into the *DataSet*. This functionality includes support for related entities, data-binding support in ASP.NET, standard mechanisms for change handling, and support for database-type schema to ensure validation of data before going to the database. In developing your data access components, you can compose your components, using a *DataSet* internally to use built-in functionality instead of having to invent it all yourself. In addition, using *DataAdapter* can both simplify retrieval of multiple entity types and offer efficient ways to update *DataSet* data. However, the disadvantage of using *DataSet* data is that they are not as efficient as handcrafted ADO.NET solutions and are not as agile in evolving into solutions involving remoting.

In addition to using *DataSet* in your code, Visual Studio includes support for using typed *DataSet* classes. Essentially, typed *DataSet* classes are tool-based solutions for generating compile-time, type-safe wrappers around *DataSet* classes. Typed *DataSet* classes in themselves can help you create data access layers quickly. Instead of using *DataAdapter* to actually perform the data access, *DataSet* uses a set of created classes called *TableAdapter*. In some cases, you can use *DataSet* as your components themselves. The Dataset Designer supports a partial class solution for adding your own functionality to the generated classes.

Although the *DataSet* solution takes the least time to develop, there are major problems with an upgrade path for *DataSet*. If you need to move from *DataSet* into real data access components, that will require throwing away the *DataSet* code and creating new code.

Each of these solutions has its advantages and disadvantages. How do you choose which one meets your requirements? Table 5-1 lists general guidelines for which solution to choose and when to choose it.

Table 5-1   Data Access Methodologies

Data Access Method	Requirements
DataReader and *Command*	When performance and scalability are most important and development cost is least important.
DataSet	For a good mix of scalability and development cost with some loss of run-time performance.
Typed *DataSet*	For rapid application design (RAD) or prototyping. There is no good, clear upgrade path from *TableAdapter* to other data access methodologies.

Business Logic

Inside your components, you will need to handle working with the validation and rules that are associated with almost any application. This data-related logic is called *business logic*. It can include anything from ensuring that strings are not too big to fit into the database to more complex interactions such as not allowing new order creation if no credit is available for a particular customer.

Adding this logic to your components requires understanding both the explicit requirements and the implicit requirements. Explicit requirements include logic that is required to implement specific business processes. For example, your requirements might state that when an invoice is finalized, you must calculate the sales tax only for customers who live in certain states. Implicit requirements are more technical in nature, such as validating that data can be stored within the constraints of the database schema and that relationships are maintained. When implementing your data components, you must include functionality for both types of requirements.

Depending on the data access methodology, you will need to determine the correct way to add your business logic. For example, if you are using *DataSet* inside your component, you could use *DataSet* to validate the data against the schema (for example, field-length validation and foreign-key validation) and custom code in your component to perform the more complex business rules.

Lab: Choosing a Data Access Methodology

In this lab, you will review the requirements of a particular enterprise project and suggest a data access methodology that fulfills the requirements.

▶ **Exercise: Choose a Data Access Methodology**

In this exercise, you will review the requirements for an enterprise project and suggest a data access methodology that fulfills those requirements.

■ This project must be delivered by the end of December to be complete in this fiscal year.

■ This project must handle a large number of users. The application it is replacing has more than 1,000 concurrent users.

■ The data the project must deal with is a complex relational database, and the component should be created with the expectation that the data structures will change over time.

1. Based on these requirements, compare using ADO.NET with using *DataReader* and *Command*; using the *DataSet* class; and using typed DataSet datasets.

2. Based on the need to deliver the project quickly, but keeping in mind the ability to scale up, you choose to use *DataSet* inside your components.

Lesson Summary

■ Depending on the performance, development cost, and maintainability requirements of your particular project, you should be able to pick a suitable data access methodology from among *DataReader*, *DataSet*, and typed datasets.

■ By using the data access methodology, you can add business logic to your components in the appropriate way.

Lesson Review

You can use the following questions to test your knowledge of the information in Lesson 2, "Data Access in Components." The questions are also available on the companion CD if you prefer to review them in electronic form.

NOTE Answers

Answers to these questions and explanations of why each answer choice is right or wrong are located in the "Answers" section at the end of the book.

1. Which of the following data access methodologies have built-in support for client-side-schema rules? (Choose all that apply.)

    A. *DataReader* and *Command*

    B. Datasets

    C. Typed datasets

2. How should you add business logic if you are using untyped datasets?

    A. Write custom code, using events on the *DataSet*.

    B. Write *DataSet* containers that perform the business logic.

    C. Use *DataSet* schema.

    D. Both A and C apply.

3. For a project in which you need to complete an application in the shortest amount of time, which data access methodology is acceptable?

    A. *DataReader* and *Command*

    B. Datasets

    C. Typed datasets

Lesson 3: Component Infrastructure

Unfortunately, developing your component's base features is often not enough for real-world systems. Most components should include common infrastructure requirements. These requirements include exception handling and profiling support. In this lesson, you will learn how to plan for this infrastructure.

After this lesson, you will be able to:
- Develop an exception handling mechanism.
- Support profiling in your component.

Estimated lesson time: 10 minutes

Exceptions

As you develop your component, you will need to plan for the unexpected. When your component enters an error condition, it must be able to deal with those conditions. That is where exceptions come in. You must determine when it is appropriate to throw an exception and the right course of action to take if an exception is thrown during your component's execution. These two decisions are discussed separately in this lesson.

Throwing Exceptions

Exceptions are about exceptional events. Ask yourself, "Is this an exceptional case?" It might be perfectly valid for your component to return a value that is indicative of failure without that being an exceptional case. For example, assume you have a Customer component that enables you to retrieve a customer based on the company name. If, when you attempt to find the customer, there is no customer with the specified name, should you throw an exception to indicate that the customer was not found? No, you should return a null (or nothing, in Visual Basic) to indicate that the customer was not found.

Avoid using exceptions for process flow. Exceptions are too heavy for process flow. For example, avoid this sort of code:

```
'VB
Try
  yourComponent.SubmitInvoice()
Catch re As InvoiceRejectedException
  ' ...
Catch ae As InvoiceApprovedException
  ' ...
Catch pe As InvoicePendingException
  ' ...
End Try
```

```csharp
//C#
try
{
  yourComponent.SubmitInvoice();
}
catch (InvoiceRejectedException re)
{
  // ...}
catch (InvoiceApprovedException ae)
{
  // ...}
catch (InvoicePendingException pe)
{
  // ...
}
```

Instead, create a return value that you can use to indicate the results, as follows:

```vb
'VB
Enum SubmissionResult
  Approved
  Rejected
  Pending
End Enum
```

```csharp
//C#
enum SubmissionResult
{
  Approved,
  Rejected,
  Pending
}
```

Then you can use the return value to perform the same process flow without using exceptions:

```vb
'VB
Dim result As SubmissionResult = yourComponent.SubmitInvoice()

Select Case result
  Case SubmissionResult.Approved
    ' ...
    break
  Case SubmissionResult.Rejected
    ' ...
    break
  Case SubmissionResult.Pending
    ' ...
    break
End Select
```

```csharp
//C#
SubmissionResult result = yourComponent.SubmitInvoice();
```

```
switch (result)
{
  case SubmissionResult.Approved:
  {
    // ...
    break;
  }
  case SubmissionResult.Rejected:
  {
    // ...
    break;
  }
  case SubmissionResult.Pending:
  {
    // ...
    break;
  }
}
```

MORE INFO   Scaling your application

For more information about scalability, refer to *Improving .NET Application Performance and Scalability*, J.D. Meier, Srinath Vasireddy, Ashish Babbar, and Alex Mackman (Microsoft Press, 2004).

When should you throw an exception? You should throw an exception only when something exceptional occurs, and you should throw your own exceptions whenever something happens in your code that is unexpected. For example, if you attempt to submit an invoice and find that the invoice is invalid in an unexpected way, throw an exception. If a .NET Framework exception is indicative of the problem (for example, *ArgumentException*), throw that exception. If one does not exist, you should create your own exception class that derives from *System.Exception*.

BEST PRACTICES   Deriving custom exceptions

Prior to the .NET Framework 2.0, it was commonly recommended that all application exceptions derive from *System.ApplicationException*, but that provided a level of isolation with no real purpose. Deriving your own exceptions from *System.Exception* is now the accepted best practice.

Handling Exceptions

When the code inside your component causes an exception to be thrown (that is, not an exception you have explicitly thrown), you must determine whether to allow the exception to propagate or attempt to recover from the exceptional case. Consider the previous example of the Customer component. What happens if the database is not available? The ADO.NET managed provider will throw a *DbException* informing you that it could not locate the database server. At this point, you have two choices: Propagate the exception up the call stack or attempt to recover from the error.

When propagating an exception to the caller, you might find it useful to include contextual information about when the error happened. This is most often done by throwing a new exception and including the current exception as the inner exception. For example:

```
'VB
Try
  Dim result As InvoiceResult = yourComponent.SubmitInvoice()
  ' ...
Catch ex As Exception
  Throw New _
    InvoiceException("Exception thrown while submitting invoice.", ex)
End Try
```

```
//C#
try
{
  InvoiceResult result = yourComponent.SubmitInvoice();
  // ...
}
catch (Exception ex)
{
  throw new
    InvoiceException("Exception thrown while submitting invoice.", ex);
}
```

If you cannot provide any additional information to help determine the source of the exception, you can choose not to catch the exception at all and simply let it flow up to the caller. Often, this is the right approach for exceptions over which you have no control (for instance, *OutOfMemoryException*).

Instead of propagating the exception, you have the choice of attempting to recover from the exception or exiting gracefully. In the case of the unavailable database, you might attempt recovery by retrying the database after a small delay. If the recovery fails, you can either propagate the exception to the caller or attempt to exit gracefully. Both are valid options in different circumstances.

Exam Tip   Avoid deriving your own exceptions from *ApplicationException*; instead, derive them from the *Exception* class. This recommendation has changed from .NET Framework 1.x to .NET Framework 2.0.

Profiling Components

As part of the requirements for any component you develop, expect to profile that component to identify performance issues and resource leaks. *Profiling* a component entails using one of a number of profiling tools to test the effectiveness of the component. These tools are detailed in Table 5-2.

Table 5-2   **Profiling Tools**

Tool	Description
Visual Studio Performance Wizard	Monitors the run-time behavior of your component to report on the effective performance of code. Allows for either sampling or instrumentation. Sampling is useful for testing the effectiveness of a whole system. Instrumentation enables you to test the performance of individual components.
CLR Profiler	Enables you to create memory allocation scenarios under which to test your component or application. Enables you to see how well your application works in a variety of scenarios.
SQL Profiler	Enables you to profile operations inside Microsoft SQL Server. Can help identify inefficient queries, stored procedure compilation issues, and deadlocks.

Before you can use the data in a profile, you must understand the requirements for your component:

- Do you have performance metrics for your component?
- What resource usage is acceptable for your component?
- Under what load scenarios do you need to test the component?

Quick Check
- What is profiling used for?

Quick Check Answer
- To test performance of a component against requirements and to isolate resource leaks.

Simply profiling your component to see how well it behaves will tell you only how it is working, not whether it's working well enough to meet the requirements. Understanding these requirements—or creating them—is crucial to profiling your component.

Lab: Propagating an Exception with Context

In this lab, you will create a new exception class and then use it to wrap an exception that occurs with context. If you encounter a problem completing an exercise, you can install the completed projects from the Code folder on the companion CD.

▶ **Exercise: Propagating the Exception**

In this exercise, you will create a new exception class and use it to propagate context with your exception.

1. In Visual Studio, click File | Open | Project/Solution, and then navigate to \Chapter 05\Lesson 3\Exercise 1\Before.

2. Run the project as it appears in its original form. You will notice that an exception is thrown when the invoice is submitted.

3. Add a new class called *InvoiceException* to the project. You will use this class to propagate the context information.

4. Derive this new class from the *System.Exception* class and create a constructor that takes a string for the message and an exception.

5. In the new constructor, call the base class constructor with the string and exception arguments. The new *InvoiceException* class might look something like the following:

```vb
'VB
Public Class InvoiceException
  Inherits Exception

  Public Sub New(ByVal message As String, _
              ByVal innerException As Exception)
    MyBase.New(message, innerException)
  End Sub

End Class
```

```csharp
//C#
public class InvoiceException : Exception
{
  public InvoiceException(string message, Exception innerException)
    : base(message, innerException)
  {
  }
}
```

6. Go to the *Submit* method of the *Invoice* class and create a *Try/Catch* block around the method body.

7. In the catch portion of the *Try/Catch* block, catch an Exception type of exception and throw your new *InvoiceException,* passing in an informative message and the caught exception. Changes from the Before project are in bold. The completed solution can be viewed in the After folder. The method might look something like the following:

```vb
'VB
Public Function Submit() As SubmissionResult

  Try
    Dim s As String = Nothing

    ' Exception will be thrown here
    Dim length As Integer = s.Length

    Return SubmissionResult.Success
```

```
    Catch ex As Exception
      Throw New InvoiceException("Failure during Invoice Submission.", ex)
    End Try

End Function

//C#
public SubmissionResult Submit()
{
  try
  {
    string s = null;

    // Exception will be thrown here
    int length = s.Length;

    return SubmissionResult.Success;
  }
  catch (Exception ex)
  {
      throw new InvoiceException("Failure during Invoice Submission.", ex);
  }
}
```

8. Compile the program, and fix any coding errors that you find. Run the program under the debugger and, when the exception happens, notice the new exception with the informative message. Also, look at the inner exception to find the original one that was thrown.

Lesson Summary

- You should throw exceptions only in exceptional cases; do not use exceptions for program flow.
- When you propagate exceptions, include contextual information by wrapping them with a more descriptive exception.
- All components should be profiled to isolate performance problems and resource leaks.

Lesson Review

You can use the following questions to test your knowledge of the information in Lesson 3, "Component Infrastructure." The questions are also available on the companion CD if you prefer to review them in electronic form.

NOTE Answers

Answers to these questions and explanations of why each answer choice is right or wrong are located in the "Answers" section at the end of the book.

---

1. When it is appropriate to throw an exception? (Choose all that apply.)

    A. An invalid argument is sent to a method.

    B. While searching for a particular piece of data, it returns with no results.

    C. The system runs out of memory.

    D. The database is not available.

2. You should always include a wrapper exception when throwing an exception.

    A. True

    B. False

3. Why should you profile a component? (Choose all that apply.)

    A. To ensure the component meets all functional requirements

    B. To measure the performance of the component against any performance requirements

    C. To isolate resource leaks

    D. To ensure that the component will compile

Chapter Review

To further practice and reinforce the skills you learned in this chapter, you can perform the following tasks:

- Review the chapter summary.
- Review the list of key terms introduced in this chapter.
- Complete the case scenarios. These scenarios set up real-world situations involving the topics of this chapter and ask you to create solutions.
- Complete the suggested practices.
- Take a practice test.

Chapter Summary

- Implementing component features includes decisions about how to create the desired functionality, including whether to extend, compose, or implement the functionality; whether to build it as a stateless or stateful component; where and how to use threads in the component; and how to deal with unmanaged resources.
- Creating data access components requires an understanding of which data access methodology to choose for your component.
- Adding business logic to a data access component can be accomplished in a number of ways, based on the data access methodology chosen for the component.
- Dealing with component infrastructure includes deciding when and how to deal with exceptions.
- All components should be profiled to ensure that they meet performance metrics and to isolate any resource leaks.

Key Terms

Do you know what these key terms mean? You can check your answers by looking up the terms in the glossary at the end of the book.

- business logic
- profiling
- stateless
- thread safe

Case Scenarios

In the following case scenarios, you will apply what you've learned about how to design components. You can find answers to these questions in the "Answers" section at the end of this book.

Case Scenario 1: Choose a Data Access Methodology

Your company needs data access components to be created for a new application.

Interviews

Following is the engineering manager's interview statement:

- **Engineering Manager**   We have a new application that needs to be brought up to allow employees of the company to request vacation time. The accounting department expected this to be completed already, so we have a severe time constraint on completing this to make them happy.

Questions

Answer the following questions for the engineering manager.

1. Which data access methodology do we need?
2. How can I add the business logic needed to ensure that each employee has only one request pending at a time?

Case Scenario 2: Search for Resource Leaks

The insurance company that you work for released an application about five days ago. There is a problem with the application because it is consuming quite a bit of memory. Your manager needs your help in locating the problem.

Interviews

Following is the manager's interview statement.

- **Manager**   We are under heavy time pressure. The system was not profiled before it went live, and now the system is performing badly and just eating memory. We need you to find out why it is consuming so much memory.

Questions

Answer the following questions for your manager.

1. How do you propose to find the memory issues?
2. Can you isolate the problems to expose which components are causing the problems?

Suggested Practices

To help you successfully master the exam objectives presented in this chapter, complete the following tasks.

Consume an Unmanaged Resource

For this task, you should complete at least Practices 1 and 2. You can do Practice 3 for a more in-depth understanding of how to implement component features.

- **Practice 1** Write a component that uses an unmanaged resource (such as a COM component).
- **Practice 2** Watch the memory consumption if you do not manage the resource.
- **Practice 3** Watch the memory consumption if you do manage the resource.

Create a Data Access Component

For this task, you should complete at least Practices 1 and 2. You can do Practices 3 and 4 for a more in-depth understanding of data access components.

- **Practice 1** Create a new class that exposes data from a database table.
- **Practice 2** Implement the features, using a typed dataset.
- **Practice 3** Re-engineer the component to use *DataSet* and *DataAdapter*.
- **Practice 4** Re-engineer the component to use *DataReader* and *Command*.

Take a Practice Test

The practice tests on this book's companion CD offer many options. For example, you can test yourself on just one exam objective, or you can test yourself on all the 70-549 certification exam content. You can set up the test so that it closely simulates the experience of taking a certification exam, or you can set it up in study mode so that you can look at the correct answers and explanations after you answer each question.

MORE INFO Practice tests

For details about all the practice test options available, see the "How to Use the Practice Tests" section in this book's Introduction.

Chapter 6

Multimedia in Distributed Applications

Although a picture is worth many words, developers have long shied away from the challenge associated with generating the graphics needed by Microsoft Windows and Web applications. This reticence, however, is no longer tenable The world of computing is going toward multimedia, and developers need to move in that direction, too. In this chapter, you will learn what you need to know to join the move toward the use of graphics.

Exam objectives in this chapter:

- Choose an appropriate mechanism to deliver multimedia data across distributed applications by using Web services and Message Queuing.
    - ❏ Evaluate available multimedia delivery mechanisms. Considerations include bandwidth problems, file formats, and sending large attachments.
    - ❏ Design a multimedia delivery mechanism.

Lessons in this chapter:

Before You Begin

To complete the lessons in this chapter, you should be familiar with Microsoft Visual Basic or C# and Windows message queuing, and you should have Web Services Enhancements 3.0 installed on your computer.

Real World

Bruce Johnson

As a developer born without the graphics gene, I've always leaned on others to create dazzling content. But creation of multimedia content is only half the battle. It is necessary to deliver this content, regardless of the client on the other end. This is a need that presents its own set of challenges, one that can test your knowledge of both distributed applications and network engineering.

Lesson 1: How to Choose a Delivery Mechanism

Today's technology is all about choice, and this doesn't change in the world of multimedia and Web services. In this lesson, you will look at the mechanisms and standards that are available to deliver multimedia content in distributed applications.

After this lesson, you will be able to:
- Describe the choices available to deliver multimedia in a distributed environment.
- Identify the differences between the delivery choices.

Estimated lesson time: 40 minutes

What Are the Choices?

Before you can choose the multimedia delivery mechanism for a distributed application, you need to understand what the challenges are. In other words, why does the delivery of multimedia content need to be considered separately from plaintext?

Binary Data and the Internet

Moving binary data across the Internet is not a trivial task. The limitation on binary data and the Internet has to do with the protocols being used. Both HTTP and SMTP support only the 7-bit ASCII character set. That's 128 total characters. As you might suspect, 128 characters are not sufficient to support the majority of languages in the world. And it doesn't come close to enabling the transmission of high-resolution graphics or audio files.

But even with this restriction, you still see pretty pictures on your Web pages, and I'm listening to streaming audio over the Internet as I'm writing this chapter. So how does this happen?

The answer lies in a standard known as *Multipurpose Internet Mail Extensions* (MIME). This standard describes how to *encode* non-7-bit formats, such as images, sound, movies, and other binary files, into the 7-bit ASCII format that the Internet requires. Although MIME helps address the issue of sending multimedia content across the wire for browsers and e-mails, the growing use of Web services and Simple Object Access Protocol (SOAP) means that these applications are no longer the sole consumers of Internet traffic. Can MIME be used to send binary data to a Web service? Let's look at the options.

There are two techniques that are used to place binary data into an XML document. Conceptually, they are roughly equivalent to by-value and by-reference variables.

Binary Data by Value   The by-value approach means that the binary data is placed within the XML document. However, for an XML document to be well-formed, all of the characters in the document must be in the same character encoding, which, for SOAP, means that that the binary data must be encoded into a MIME format such as *base64*. Consider the following XML segment:

```
<a:data xmlns:a='http://www.contoso.com/749tk' >
  <image>asxgp2KrxIE=</image>
  <audio>wsIRE87sDd1=</audio>
</a:data>
```

Although it is feasible to embed encoded data into an XML document, there are some performance implications that have limited its usefulness. First, the necessary data encoding results in a size increase over the original data (base64 is 1.33 times larger for UTF-8 data, for example). This additional size is part of the problem. Because the data is sent inside an XML document, the entire structure needs to be parsed and processed before the data can be extracted. Because parsing XML is a string-related operation, speed can be an issue.

Binary Data by Reference   With the by-reference approach, the binary data is placed outside of the normal XML structure, as the following example shows.

```
<a:data xmlns:a='http://www.contoso.com/749tk' >
  <image data='http://www.contoso.com/749tk/logo.jpg' />
  <audio data='http://www.contoso.com/749tk/anthem.wav' />
</a:data>

--MIME_boundary
Content-Type: image/jpeg
Content-Transfer-Encoding: binary
Content-Location: http://www.contoso.com/749tk/logo.jpg

Asxgp2KrxIE=

--MIME_boundary
Content-Type: sound/wav
Content-Transfer-Encoding: binary
Content-Location: 'http://www.contoso.com/749tk/anthem.wav'

wsIRE87sDd1=

--MIME_boundary--
```

Removing the binary data from the inside of the XML document eliminates some of the performance problems. Although the size of the message hasn't decreased, the XML document no longer needs to be parsed to determine where the binary data begins and ends. This technique is also known as *SOAP with Attachments* (SwA).

In terms of functionally, the SwA approach is a success, but the performance issues don't stop with the larger message size caused by the encoding. The real issue is that there is no information in the message about the size or location of each attachment within the message, so to find a particular attachment, the message needs to be scanned, at least up to the end of the desired attachment. For messages with multiple large attachments, this might not be an optimal approach.

Using DIME to Address the Problem

The next evolution in solving the problem of sending binary data by using SOAP was the *Direct Internet Message Encapsulation* (DIME) standard published as an IETF Internet draft jointly by IBM and Microsoft in 2001. It describes a format for including metadata about the binary data within the message.

Figure 6-1 illustrates the format of a single DIME record. Although describing the details of each field is beyond the scope of this chapter, there are two fields to be aware of. First, the data type that the binary data contains can be identified with the *TYPE_T* field. This enables the recipient of the message to find out whether the data is an image or an audio field, without having to analyze the data itself.

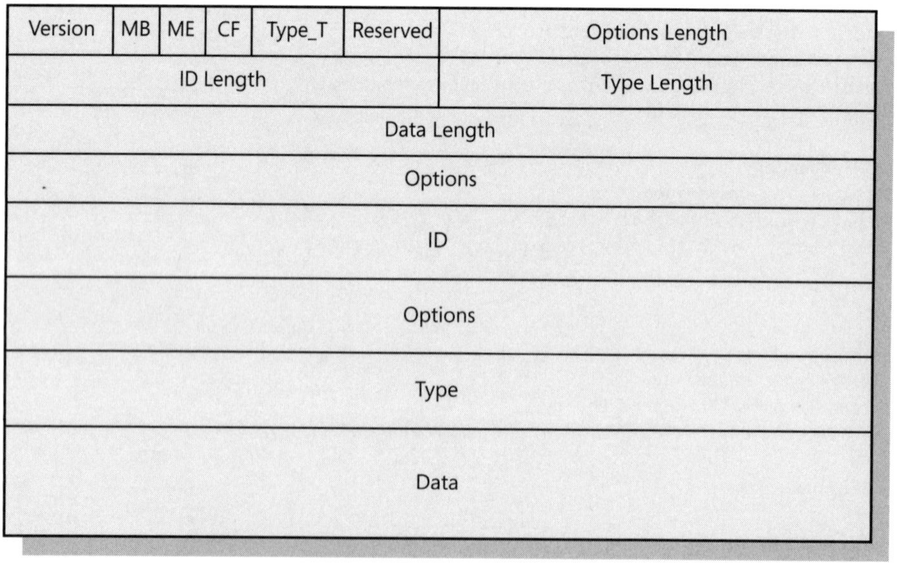

Version	MB	ME	CF	Type_T	Reserved	Options Length
ID Length						Type Length
Data Length						
Options						
ID						
Options						
Type						
Data						

Figure 6-1   The format of a DIME record

It is really the *DATA_LENGTH* field that provides the main benefit of the DIME standard. This field defines how many bytes of data are included in the message. Once the client can determine how long the data is, scanning the message for an end-of-data mark is no long necessary. This has a positive impact on performance.

Although DIME addresses the performance concerns, it is not a perfect solution. At a conceptual level, the flexibility of using XML has been removed. For example, the entire message is no longer a well-formed XML document. Part of it is, but not the entire message, which means that the message can no longer be verified against an XML schema. At least two distinct data models are being used, one for the XML portion of the message and one for the binary data.

These arguments might seem a little esoteric, but they do have some real-world implications. For example, in the SOAP world, WS-Security is the standard for encrypting and signing requests, but with a DIME message, encrypting the SOAP envelope would not result in encryption of the MIME-encoded attachment. Although it is possible to encrypt the attachment manually, the DIME headers need to be handled separately to avoid falling back into scanning the entire message. These problems are not intractable, but they force the developer to know more about the DIME specification than is optimal.

DIME and WS-Attachments

By itself, DIME is simply a definition of how to format an arbitrary number of data records. There is no definition of how the *ID* or *TYPE* fields might be used, nor how DIME and SOAP might be used together. The WS-Attachment standard progresses to this extra step by defining how multiple data records can be combined and referenced and, more important for this chapter, how the packaging can provide attachment capabilities that Web services can use.

More specifically, WS-Attachment allows a SOAP message to be encapsulated within a DIME message. Thus, instead of attaching DIME records to the end of a SOAP request, the SOAP request becomes the payload of the first DIME record in the message.

The WS-Attachment specification also defines the ability to reference other records in the DIME message by using the *ID* field. Within the SOAP request, it becomes possible to reference a specific DIME record. For example, the following XML segment would incorporate the DIME record marked with an *ID* of 0A352496-A98A-4DB0-B2E4-4A5DC8FC17E3

```
<b:responseMesssage>
  <audio
      href="uuid:0A352496-A98A-4DB0-B2E4-4A5DC8FC17E3"/>
  <text>Hello World!</text>
</b:responseMessage>
```

Exam Tip   Keep in mind that even when using the WS-Attachment specification, your ability to compose the SOAP document is eliminated in DIME. For example, WS-Security can't be applied to the attached documents.

MTOM

The most recent standard, and the current best practice, is *Message Transmission Optimization Mechanism* (MTOM). At a high level, MTOM is used to move chunks of binary data to and from Web services without eliminating the XML characteristics of the message. To understand fully how MTOM works, it is necessary to comprehend the *XML-Binary Optimized Package* (XOP) standard.

XML-Binary Optimized Package   If you are trying to improve on DIME, there are really two areas that need to be addressed. One of them is the ability to store binary data efficiently within the XML infoset. This is the area that the XOP targets. The XOP standard describes a mechanism for serializing the XML *infoset* that comprises a SOAP message. This serialization allows binary data to be encoded without stepping outside of the traditional XML. Let's go back to the first XML segment for an example.

```
<a:data xmlns:a='http://www.contoso.com/749tk' >
  <image>asxgp2KrxIE=</image>
  <audio>wsIRE87sDdl=</audio>
</a:data>
```

When the XOP is constructed, the parts of the message that are to be optimized are extracted. The optimizable parts must be in a base64-encoded format. These optimizable parts are then placed back into the package. In the original element (in place of the binary data), a reference to the optimized part is added.

If you think this sounds like the by-reference mechanism described earlier in the chapter, you are right. The improvement that XOP offers is that the base64-encoded data extracted from the message is not necessarily placed back into the package in base64. Instead, the optimized data is stored as a set of binary octets. These octets are a direct representation of the binary data, not an encoded version, so no translation is required. For the preceding example, the XOP package looks like the following.

```
  MIME-Version: 1.0
  Content-Type: Multipart/Related;boundary=MIME_boundary;
      type="application/xop+xml";
      start="<xopsample@contoso.com>";
      start-info="text/xml"
  Content-Description: A sample XOP package

  --MIME_boundary
  Content-Type: application/xop+xml;
      charset=UTF-8;
      type="text/xml
  Content-Transfer-Encoding: 8bit
  Content-ID: <xopsample@contoso.com>
```

```
<a:data xmlns:a='http://www.contoso.com/749tk'>
  <a:image>
    <xop:Include xmlns:xop='http://www.w3.org/2004/08/xop/include'
      href='cid:http://contoso.com/749tk/logo.jpg'/>
  </a:image>
  <a:audio>
    <xop:Include xmlns:xop='http://www.w3.org/2004/08/xop/include'
      href='cid:http://contoso.com/749tk/anthem.wav'/>
  </a:audio>
</a:data>

--MIME_boundary
Content-Type: image/jpeg
Content-Transfer-Encoding: binary
Content-ID: <http://contoso.com/749tk/logo.jpg>

// binary octets for jpg

--MIME_boundary
Content-Type: audio/wav
Content-Transfer-Encoding: binary
Content-ID: <http://contoso.com/749tk/anthem.wav>

// binary octets for wav

--MIME_boundary--
```

There is a subtle element to the XOP standard. Specifically, the standard states that when the optimizable data is removed from the XML document, it is decoded. Once decoded, it is optimized and placed into the separate MIME part. In other words, the binary data is MIME-encoded for insertion into the XML document, MIME-decoded back to its original form, and then optimized. The performance cost of encoding the binary data into base64, only to then decode it, is nil because this process is only conceptual. In any reasonable implementation, the binary data is optimized and injected directly into the package rather than going through all three steps.

MTOM Revisited   So, given that XOP is responsible for the optimization of binary data within an XML document, where does MTOM fit into the picture? The XOP standard can be used to optimize to any XML document. MTOM uses XOP to optimize SOAP messages. If you consider MTOM to be a transformational layer that sits between the client and the Web service, you have a good picture of what happens.

The fact that MTOM is transformational implies that there are two sides to the process. On the server side, the response is converted to an XOP-optimized SOAP message. On the client side, the response is converted from XOP-optimized into the normal SOAP. Therefore, MTOM is only a possibility if both sides of the exchange are capable of processing MTOM messages.

Along with defining how the transformation from SOAP message to XOP and back again takes place, MTOM also places some restrictions on the process to ensure that the transformation is orthogonal. For example, consider the problem of digitally signing a SOAP message containing binary data.

Normally, digitally signing a SOAP message consists of identifying the XML elements that are to be signed and calculating a hash based on the contents. For an XOP package, however, the "contents" are not in the XML element, which makes the digital signature practically useless. However, MTOM says that when signing the element by using WS-Security, the appropriate contents of the XOP package are to be located and then base64-encoded. This encoded value is then used to calculate the hash.

Be aware that the encoding process used for the signature does not change the data as it appears in the XOP package. Instead, the encoding is performed in memory. The correct hash is included in the WS-Security elements and is available for verification by the receiving end).

Quick Check

1. Which standard is used with WS-Attachments?
2. Which standard provides the greatest range of interoperability with applications that are not based on Microsoft .NET Framework?

Quick Check Answers

1. The DIME standard is used with the WS-Attachment standards.
2. The binary-by-reference technique is the most compatible across all non-.NET technologies. DIME is a Microsoft and IBM standard that doesn't have wide vendor support. MTOM is too new a standard to have wide support—yet.

Which Standard to Use?

As with any technology decision, there will always be a number of factors that influence the final choice. The binary data transfer mechanism is no exception. This section will look at the most common factors and the impact they can have on the decision of which standard to implement.

Interoperability

The fact that MTOM is a recognized standard helps greatly when it comes to interoperability. Even DIME, which is less of a standard but still widely available, can be used in both earlier versions of .NET and non-.NET platforms, so, from a pure interoperability perspective, any one of these standards is capable of being used to return binary data from a Web service.

The most recent standard, MTOM, will probably garner the greatest amount of vendor support. Unlike DIME, MTOM is a formal recommendation of the World Wide Web Consortium (W3C). DIME was jointly published by Microsoft and IBM. Although this certainly lends credence to DIME, it was never as accepted as MTOM will be.

Ultimately, the level of interoperability is more a matter of the effort developers have to exert to process the format of the message, so the final consideration will be which tools are available for each environment. Each of the standards is documented in a manner that would allow any other platform to support it; it's just a matter of whether the tools are available or how quickly they can be made available.

Streaming versus Blobs

One of the design choices facing you when considering multimedia and Web services is whether the content should be streamed or sent as a single blob. There are two primary options available to delivering multimedia. When sent as a single blob, the content is basically downloaded to the client as a single file. *Streamed* content is different from the blob-style delivery in that rather than sending the data as a single unit (the file), it is provided as a continuous flow of information. Because of limitations in the standard, it is not currently possible to stream information to a client through a SOAP call. The best that can be done is to pass a URL reference to an externally available stream as part of the result and have the client parse the response and make the streaming request to the URL.

With server-side streaming, the content is fed into the response as a stream of bytes. These bytes are passed on to the client immediately without waiting for the entire response to be completely built. With blobs, the entire response is built on the server. Then, once it is complete, the response is sent to the client as a single blob of content.

The difference between these two is the typical tradeoff between performance and resources. There are two main concerns concerning moving large volumes of data through a Web service boundary. One is the working set that is consumed on the server side. The other is the amount of bandwidth consumed by the base64-encoded content. Using MTOM and its optimized packages already reduces the bandwidth usage significantly. This leaves the working set and memory usage to deal with.

For most Web service requests, the response is built in its entirety before it is sent back to the client. However, if you're dealing with multimedia requests (and, in fact, if you're dealing with any large message), this process can affect the scalability of the application. If every request were returning 10 megabytes (MB) of data, the number of simultaneous requests a system could support would be limited to the RAM on the server, and that limit would probably not be in the thousands.

The solution is to avoid storing the data on the server before sending the request. To help developers implement this pattern, .NET Framework 2.0 includes *IXmlSerializable* support for objects returned from a Web service method.

IXmlSerializable Interface

The purpose of the *IXmlSerializable* interface is to give developers control over the serialization of objects, not just for Web services, but any time an object needs to be converted into an XML format. One of the times the *IXmlSerializable* interface is used is when an object is returned from a Web service method. The current state of the object is serialized into an XML document so that it can be included in the SOAP response message.

The *IXmlSerializable* interface is quite simple to implement. There are three methods in the interface:

- **ReadXml**   Re-create the original state of the object based on its XML representation.
- **WriteXml**   Converts the state of the object into an XML representation.
- **GetSchema**   Returns the schema for the XML representation. Because there is no validation of the XML representation against the schema, a trivial implementation of this method is sufficient.

The trick to implementing a streaming interface for a returned object is to not think of the *IXmlSerializable* interface as creating an XML representation. Instead, think of it as serializing the object into a stream of bytes that can be included inside an XML document (for instance, a SOAP message). That's what the WriteXml method does. On the receiving side, the ReadXml method takes the stream of bytes and rebuilds the object.

NOTE   *IXmlSerializable* and .NET 1.1

The *IXmlSerializable* interface existed prior to .NET Framework 2.0 as an unsupported interface. That is, the interface was used to serialize/deserialize objects passed across Web service boundaries, but it wasn't part of the official product and, as such, could have been changed in a future version. Fortunately, it is now officially part of the .NET Framework.

Along with defining the returned objects as implementing the *IXmlSerializable* interface, the other setting that needs to be changed from stream results into the SOAP response is to turn off the default buffering that ASP.NET provides. This is accomplished by setting the BufferResponse property in the *WebMethod* attribute to False.

```
'VB
<WebMethod(BufferResponse:=False)> _
Public Function GetStreamedData() As StreamingResponse
  ' Implementation
End Function
```

```
//C#
[WebMethod (BufferResponse=false)]
public StreamingResponse GetStreamedData()
{
// Implementation
}
```

There are some limitations to this approach that developers need to keep in mind.

- The performance gain is minimal for small files. More specifically, this approach should be considered only for responses that are larger than 10MB or when keeping server memory usage down is more important than performance.

- Streaming doesn't work if message-level security (for instance, digital signing by using WS-Security) is applied to the SOAP message. Because the entire message needs to be included in the signing process, the response is buffered into memory until complete. This nullifies the memory benefits of streaming.

- Streaming can be used when transport-level security (for instance, Secure Sockets Layer [SSL]) is used.

Binary Data and Message Queuing

Although Web services might appear to be the de facto standard for distributed application communication, there are still many instances when message queuing is the best way to send messages. Many of the problems associated with sending binary data over the Internet don't become a concern when using *Microsoft Message Queue* (MSMQ).

The mechanics of sending an MSMQ message are straightforward.

1. Open a message queue.
2. Create the message content, including setting any properties on the message itself.
3. Use the *Send* method on the message queue to post the message to the queue.

The only real choice faced by a developer is which formatter should be used. The formatter is called when a message is placed into a queue and when a message is retrieved from a queue. The job of the formatter is to serialize and deserialize the message into a particular format, depending on the needs of the sender and receiver.

The .NET Framework is shipped with a number of formatters that handle the most common scenarios. They are the BinaryMessageFormatter, XmlMessageFormatter, and ActiveX-MessageFormatter.

BinaryMessageFormatter   The BinaryMessageFormatter serializes the object into a binary format. All of the fields, both public and private, are converted into a stream of bytes. When the byte stream is deserialized by the receiving application, a clone of the object is created.

From a performance perspective, the BinaryMessageFormatter is the fastest mechanism for placing objects into a message queue. The tradeoff is a lack of flexibility. To receive the message, the receiving application must have access to the assembly in which the class that implements the object is found. After all, only the data associated with the object is transferred, not the behaviors. As a result, the BinaryMessageFormatter is useful only when there is a shared assembly relationship that can be established between the sender and the receiver.

NOTE   Limitations of serialization

Not every data type can be serialized. For example, connections to a database cannot be sent as messages. This makes sense because the connection to the database has a specific process-to-process context associated with it. Moving the connection object—even a clone of the object—to a different computer changes the context.

XmlMessageFormatter   The XmlMessageFormatter serializes the object into its XML representation. The actual format of the representation can be controlled by using attributes, such as *XmlElement* and *XmlAttribute*, on the class definition or by implementing the *IXmlSerializable* interface on the class.

IMPORTANT   Only public properties serialized

Private fields and properties are not serialized by the XmlMessageFormatter. Only the publicly visible properties are serialized. This has the potential to change the state of a deserialized object. If it is critical to maintain the values of the private fields, use the BinaryMessageFormatter.

Although slower than the BinaryMessageFormatter, the XmlMessageFormatter has the advantage of flexibility. The receiver does not need to have the exact class from which the message was created; it just needs one that has the same public properties. As a result, it becomes much easier to maintain compatibility between versions (older versions can ignore nodes in the XML representation that they don't recognize) and to share messages with non-.NET platforms.

ActiveXMessageFormatter   The ActiveXMessageFormatter is used almost exclusively when interoperability with unmanaged applications is required. The formatter converts intrinsic data types (string, integer, dates) into a layout that is understandable by unmanaged applications.

If you run into a situation that these formatters can't handler, there is an extensibility point that allows you to create your own custom formatters. The *IMessageFormatter* interface gives developers the chance to create their own serialization formatter if necessary.

Lab: Using MTOM to Deliver Multimedia

In this lab, you will use the tool set provided in Web Services Enhancements (WSE 3.0) to make the transmission of MTOM messages a very simple process. If you encounter a problem completing an exercise, the completed projects can be installed from the Code folder on the companion CD.

MORE INFO WSE 3.0

For more information about WSE 3.0, visit the Microsoft Web Services and Other Distributed Technologies Developer Center at *http://msdn2.microsoft.com/en-us/library/aa904823.aspx.*

▶ **Exercise 1: Use Options for Sending and Receiving an MTOM Message**

In this exercise, you will mark a couple of options to make sending and receiving an MTOM message transparent to developers.

1. Launch Visual Studio 2005.
2. Open a solution using File | Open | Project/Solution.
3. Navigate to the Chapter06/Lesson1/Lab1/<language>/Before directory. Select the Lab1 solution and click Open.
4. The solution has two projects in it, one for the Service and one for the Client. In the Solution Explorer, expand the MtomService project.
5. Right-click GraphicsService.asmx and select View Code.
6. In the *GraphicsService* class, create a public method called *GetGraphic*. The return value for *GetGraphic* is a byte array, and the method needs to be attributed to indicate that it's a Web method. The resulting method will look like the following.

    ```
    'VB
    <WebMethod()> _
    Public Function GetGraphic() As Byte()
    End Function
    ```

    ```
    //C#
    [WebMethod()]
    public byte[] GetGraphic()
    {
    }
    ```

7. In the *GetGraphic* method, add code to retrieve the file named winter.jpg as an array of bytes and return it. The following line of code is added to the method.

    ```
    'VB
    Return File.ReadAllBytes(Server.MapPath("winter.jpg"))
    ```

    ```
    //C#
    return File.ReadAllBytes(Server.MapPath("winter.jpg"));
    ```

8. In the Solution Explorer, right-click the MtomService project and select WSE Settings 3.0. (If this option isn't available, ensure that WSE 3.0 has been installed on your computer.)

9. On the General tab of the WSE Settings dialog box, check Enable this project for Web Services Enhancements and Enable Microsoft Web Service Enhancement Soap Protocol Factory. On the Messaging tab of the same dialog box, select Optional as the Server Mode in the MTOM Settings section. Click OK.

10. Now move to the client. The MTOM settings in WSE need to be defined as well. Right-click the MtomClient project in Solution Explorer and select WSE Settings 3.0.

11. On the General tab of the WSE Settings dialog box, check Enable this project for Web Services Enhancements. On the Messaging tab of the same dialog box, select On as the Client Mode in the MTOM Settings section. Click OK.

12. In the Solution Explorer, right-click the MtomClient project and select Add Web Reference.

13. Click the Web Services in this Solution link and click the GraphicsService link under the Services column. Then change the Web reference name field to **MtomService**, and click the Add Reference button.

14. To hook up the call to the MtomService, double-click the MtomClientForm in the Solution Explorer. This displays the design surface for the client form.

15. Double-click the Get Image button to create the *Click* event handler procedure.

    At this point, you need to call the Web service to get the byte array for the graphic and then convert it to an *Image* object. This *Image* object is then assigned to the PictureBox that is already on the form. The code to do this, which is placed into the *Click* event handler, is as follows:

```
'VB
Dim ws As New MtomService.GraphicesServiceWse()
Dim ms as New MemoryStream(ws.GetGraphic())
pictureBox1.Image = Image.FromStream(ms)
```

```
//C#
MtomService.GraphicsServiceWse ws = new
    MtomClient.MtomService.GraphicsServiceWse();
MemoryStream ms = new MemoryStream(ws.GetGraphic());
pictureBox1.Image = Image.FromStream(ms);
```

16. The application is now ready to run. Ensure that the MtomClient project is specified as the startup project and click Debug | Start Debugging. The MtomClientForm should appear. Click the GetImage button and, in a few seconds, a pretty winter picture should appear.

▶ **Exercise 2: Sending Binary Data Through MSMQ**

To transmit messages reliably from one process to another, Web Services are not always adequate. This is one of the areas that MSMQ was created to support. In this exercise, you will look at how MSMQ can be used to transmit binary data between two processes.

Before starting on the lab, the BinaryMsmqDemoSetup.bat file must be executed. This script creates the message queue that will be used by the lab. To run the script, you must have local administrator rights because a message queue is being created.

If you encounter a problem completing an exercise, the completed projects can be installed from the Code folder on the Companion CD.

1. Launch Visual Studio 2005.

2. Open a solution using File | Open | Project/Solution.

3. Navigate to the Chapter06/Lesson1/Lab2/<language>/Before directory. Select the Lab2 solution and click Open.

4. In the Solution Explorer, double-click the SendBinaryMsmq form to show the designer surface. Notice that there are two buttons on the form. The Send button will be used to place a message into an MSMQ queue. The Receive button will receive the message and transform the stream of bytes that compose the binary data into a visible image.

5. To start, construct a message that contains binary data and send it to a message queue. Double-click the Send button to create a *Click* event handler procedure.

6. In the *Click* event handler procedure, add the code to instantiate the message queue and message objects.

```
'VB
Dim queue As New MessageQueue(".\private$\BinaryMsmqDemo")
Dim msg As New Message()
```

```
//C#
MessageQueue queue = new MessageQueue(@".\private$\BinaryMsmqDemo");
System.Messaging.Message msg = new System.Messaging.Message();
```

7. Once the *Message* object has been created, the formatter for the message needs to be assigned. For this lab, because you are sending binary data, use the BinaryMessage-Formatter. Add the following code below the just-created queue and message declarations.

```
'VB
msg.Formatter = new BinaryMessageFormatter()
```

```
//C#
msg.Formatter = new BinaryMessageFormatter();
```

8. Next, convert the file to be transferred into a byte stream and assign it to the body of the message. This code is added below the Formatter property assignment.

```
'VB
Msg.BodyStream = new IO.FileStream("winter.jpg", FileMode.New)
```

```
//C#
msg.BodyStream = new FileStream("winter.jpg", FileMode.Open);
```

9. Now send the message. And, to see that you have actually succeeded, display a message about success. This code goes below the BodyStream property assignment.

```
'VB
queue.Send(msg)
MessageBox.Show("Message sent")
```

```
//C#
queue.Send(msg);
MessageBox.Show("Message sent");
```

10. Next is the process of receiving the message and rebuilding the image from the binary data. In the form designer, double-click the Receive button to create the *Click* event handler procedure.

11. The message queue and message objects need to be declared. The following code is added to the procedure.

```
'VB
Dim queue As New MessageQueue(".\private$\BinaryMsmqDemo")
Dim msg As New Message()
```

```
//C#
MessageQueue queue = new MessageQueue(@".\private$\BinaryMsmqDemo");
System.Messaging.Message msg = new System.Messaging.Message();
```

12. Unlike the formatter defined when the message was sent, on the receive side, the formatter for the queue needs to be assigned to the appropriate value. Because you expect binary data to be passed through the messages, this formatter needs to support the binary format. Add the following code below the queue and message declarations.

```
'VB
queue.Formatter = new BinaryMessageFormatter()
```

```
//C#
queue.Formatter = new BinaryMessageFormatter();
```

13. Now retrieve the message from the queue and rebuild the image object from the data in the body. For this lab, the image will be assigned to the picture box on the form. The following code goes below the Formatter property assignment.

```
'VB
msg = queue.Receive()
messageImagePictureBox.Image = New Bitmap(msg.BodyStream)
```

```
//C#
msg = queue.Receive();
messageImagePictureBox.Image = new Bitmap(msg.BodyStream);
```

14. Run the application. On the form that appears, click the Send button to send the message. A message box containing the words "Message sent" should appear. After clearing the message box, click the Receive button. When successful, a pretty image will appear in the *PictureBox* below the buttons.

15. Once you have finished with the application, run the BinaryMsmqDemoTeardown.bat script to remove the queue used by this lab.

Lesson Summary

- Binary data can be transmitted in Web services either by value or by reference. The most recent standards are based on the by-reference approach.

- When using DIME and SOAP with Attachments, one of the problems is the composibility. WS-Security, for example, cannot be applied to the attachments because they fall outside of the SOAP envelope.

- Using MTOM addresses the composibility problem as well as optimizing the binary content for transmission.

- When using MSMQ, the message formatter is the component that transforms the message to and from the appropriate wire-level format.

Lesson Review

The following questions are intended to reinforce key information presented in this lesson. If you are unable to answer a question, review the lesson materials and try the question again.

NOTE Answers

Answers to these questions and explanations of why each answer choice is right or wrong are located in the "Answers" section at the end of the book.

---

1. All of the client computers in your corporate environment are running Windows XP. You need to create a distributed application that maintains the entire state of the object as it is passed between the client and server portions of the application. Which delivery mechanism should you use?

   A. SOAP with Attachments

   B. MTOM

   C. MSMQ with an XmlMessageFormatter

   D. MSMQ with a BinaryMessageFormatter

2. You are creating a Web service that will be consumed by both Java and Windows clients. The graphics returned by the Web service will be encrypted using the WS-Security standard. Which delivery mechanism should you use?

   A. SOAP with Attachments

   B. MTOM

   C. MSMQ with an XmlMessageFormatter

   D. MSMQ with a BinaryMessageFormatter

3. You are creating a Web service that will return large (that is, more than 20MB) audio files. You are concerned about the scalability of the server, so you need to design the delivery mechanism to minimize the impact processing simultaneous requests will have on the server's memory usage. Which delivery mechanism should you use?

   A. SOAP with Attachments

   B. DIME

   C. MTOM, serving the content as streamed data

   D. MTOM, serving the content as one blob

Lesson 2: Challenges in Multimedia Delivery

The technology involved in retrieving the content is only part of the problem in delivering multimedia. Potential issues include network capacity, client capabilities, and licensing. In this lesson, you will learn about the decision points and challenges associated with actually delivering multimedia content.

After this lesson, you will be able to:
- Verify the network capabilities with a network engineer.
- Determine the audio bit rates that should be used for your content.
- Suggest the graphic/video display options that your content requires.
- Prototype a multimedia delivery mechanism.

Estimated lesson time: 15 minutes

Bandwidth Restrictions

Unlike database traffic, multimedia content has a definite impact on network performance. Graphics images tend to be larger than text, and streaming video and audio provide a constant load. Without proper planning, it is possible to bring a network to a halt if too much multimedia content is being used.

Capacity planning for a network is akin to designing the streets of a town. To lay out the streets properly (where *properly* means avoiding traffic jams), you need to know where people start and where they end up. You need to know how many people move over a period of time. All of this must be considered in a plan that must balance the joy of unlimited capacity and the sorrow of paying for unlimited capacity.

Network planning takes the same basic approach as city planning. A network engineer needs to know what the source and destination of packets are, how many are expected to be sent, and when. The details of multimedia content distribution will be of interest to the network engineer engaged in a capacity planning exercise.

The engineer will naturally want to know the types of content that you're planning on delivering. He or she will also be interested in the patterns of usage for the requests. Do they come through steadily over the course of the day? Are there peaks and valleys for the requests? Are there peaks and valleys for the size of the content? All of this information will be needed to ensure that the network capacity is sufficient to support the application.

Quality of Service   With multimedia content, simply having available bandwidth isn't always sufficient. Instead, the latency and point-in-time throughput might be more important. This is especially true when the content is streamed audio or video. Network delays can cause client applications to pause, stutter, and completely fail. For audio and video, this degradation is not only noticeable; it could also cause the application to fail in the eyes of the users.

From a development perspective, there is little you can do to control quality of service. That is usually in the hands of the network experts. What is important, however, is to be aware that there are many different facets to consider when calculating bandwidth. It is rarely as simple as just adding up the capacity of the individual network pipes, and providing the network engineers with the necessary details will go a long way toward ensuring a successful deployment.

Client Requirements

If you spend any time working in multimedia content, you will quickly become familiar with the different components that a client application needs to have installed to access the content. For most formats, whether audio, video, or graphical, that requirement comes in the form of a *codec*. A codec (short for compression/decompression or coder/decoder, depending on whom you talk to) is a piece of software that is responsible for handling the compression and decompression of a stream of content. Figure 6-2 illustrates the position of the codec within the content stream.

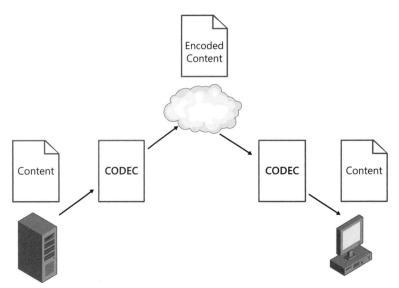

Figure 6-2 Codecs in the stream

When sending multimedia content, it is important to be aware of the codec requirements for the client. This is especially true for video streams because they have a history of being more dependent on the presence of specific codecs.

Audio and Video Options

As has already been mentioned, streaming audio and video can consume a lot of network bandwidth. A number of factors contribute to the actual amount of bandwidth consumed by the content. In addition, the factors also depend on the type of content.

Audio

Audio, whether in a streaming format or when stored as a file, faces some tradeoffs when trying to reduce the size of the content.

Sampling Rate   The sampling rate is the frequency at which analog sound is converted to a digital representation. Consider this to be the number of data points taken per second of sound. Sampling rate is typically measured in hertz (Hz) and is the first determinant in the quality of the sound. CD quality audio is typically 44.1Hz, which is 44,100 samples per second.

As you would expect, there is a tradeoff between sound quality (higher sampling rate) and bandwidth. The higher the sampling rate, the more data is required to reproduce the sound. Less considered is the quality of the original source. If the source is a vinyl album or a microphone, it might not make sense to waste the bandwidth to deliver a CD-quality audio stream.

Compression   There are actually two types of audio compression. The most common standard describes how some information about the sound is eliminated to reduce bandwidth requirements. This is known as audio data compression. The second type of compression (known as audio-level compression) involves eliminating some of the dynamic range of the sound to accomplish the same thing (a reduction in content size, that is).

Most people are familiar with the common types of audio data compression. The MP3 format is one of the more common compression algorithms. From a developer's perspective, the main consideration for audio data compression is whether it is lossless or lossy.

Lossless compression is a descriptive term: all of the information about the original sound is included in the compressed version. The most common format of this type is the Free Lossless Audio Codec (FLAC). Lossy compression uses the inability of humans to hear all frequencies and volumes with the same effectiveness to reduce the size of the audio content. This is the approach taken by MP3 and WMA. The other commonly used Windows audio format, the WAV file, is actually uncompressed.

Video

Video faces many of the same challenges that audio does concerning reducing content size, so although the terminology might be different from the audio options, many of the concepts are the same.

Frame Rate   This is the sampling rate for video. The name comes from the number of still pictures on the reel of tape that was used by mechanical video projectors. Motion pictures typically run at 24 frames per second (fps), whereas digital images are closer to 60 fps. The actual number depends on the specific video format.

Resolution   Resolution is a concept most developers are familiar with due to our ever-present monitors. It is the number of pixels in the horizontal and vertical dimensions of an image. The range can be from 640 x 480 (standard-definition television) to 1920 x 1080 (high-definition television). The desired resolution will depend on the target for the content. If you're streaming video to computer users, using a high-definition resolution will be a waste of bandwidth in most cases.

Compression   Video has the same need for compression that audio does, and perhaps more so, given the amount of information that is required to produce a single frame. Compression techniques usually fall into one of two categories:

- **Intraframe**   Registering the differences between parts of a single frame
- **Interframe**   Registering the differences between contiguous frames

The most common format for video compression is MPEG (Moving Pictures Experts Group), with MPEG-2 and MPEG-4 being the typical implementations.

Digital Rights Management

Digital Rights Management (DRM) is a term that applies to a broad set of technologies associated with managing the intellectual property rights of digital content. In most cases, DRM software handles the monitoring and enforcement of the usage of digital works through a copy protection or a technical protection mechanism.

In Windows, one of the more common mechanisms to implement DRM is with the Microsoft Rights Management Services (RMS).. This application helps administrators control access to protected information on a continual basis. For example, it is possible to require that a person accessing protected content to retrieve a license from the RMS service before it can be played. Access to the license can be granted when the user provides a set of validated credentials. Although RMS isn't the only resource available to provide DRM functionality, it is certainly more than capable of supporting a large number of common scenarios.

Lesson Summary

- The impact that multimedia content has on the network goes beyond the size of the binary data; it also encompasses the number and regularity of the requests for the data.
- If bandwidth considerations are an issue, match the quality and compression to the expected target audience.

Lesson Review

The following question is intended to reinforce key information presented in this lesson. If you are unable to answer a question, review the lesson materials and try the question again.

NOTE Answers

The Answer to this question and explanations of why the answer choice is right or wrong is located in the "Answers" section at the end of the book.

---

1. You are delivering audio content to your client computers, some of which are operating across a 56KB modem connection. You need to minimize the time required to retrieve your content. Which options should you choose? (Choose all that apply.)

    A. Increase the sampling rate for the content.

    B. Decrease the sampling rate for the content.

    C. Use a WAV format for the content.

    D. Use an MP3 format for the content.

Chapter Review

To further practice and reinforce the skills you learned in this chapter, you can perform the following tasks:

- Review the chapter summary.
- Review the list of key terms introduced in this chapter.
- Complete the case scenarios. These scenarios set up real-world situations involving the topics of this chapter and ask you to create a solution.
- Complete the suggested practices.
- Take a practice test.

Chapter Summary

- Delivering multimedia efficiently requires a combination of development and network skills. The choices that have to be made involve areas that fall outside the sphere of comfort for most business application developers.
- The most recently released standards and toolkits make it much easier for developers to deliver multimedia content efficiently.
- Ensure that the content is appropriately rich for the expected target audience. Don't provide more content then the expected bandwidth available to your audience.

Key Terms

Do you know what these key terms mean? You can check your answers by looking up the terms in the glossary at the end of the book.

- base64 encoding
- codec
- Direct Internet Message Encapsulation (DIME)
- encode
- infoset (also XML Information Set)
- *IMessageFormatter* interface
- *IXmlSerializable* interface
- Message Transmission Optimization Mechanism (MTOM)
- Microsoft Message Queue (MSMQ)

- Multipurpose Internet Mail Extensions (MIME)
- SOAP with Attachments (SwA)
- WS-Attachments
- XML-Binary Optimized Package (XOP)

Case Scenario

In the following case scenario, you will apply what you've learned about delivering multimedia in a distributed environment. You can find answer to this question in the "Answers" section at the end of the book.

Case Scenario 1: Delivering Graphics to Multiple Client Applications

You are a corporate developer. An internal application that you are creating provides a near real-time look at the sales volume for the company. The information about sales is rendered as a graphic and used in the corporate portal Web site as well as on the order entry application (a Windows Forms application) used by the sales force.

Your challenge is to design the mechanism used to deliver the graphics to these applications. You already know that the generation of the sales graphic for both of these environments will be performed by a central service. For performance reasons, the service will not generate a new graphic with each request but will cache the graphic, creating a new one every five minutes.

The two client applications (the Web portal and the Windows application) will communicate with this server to request the graphic on a regular basis. In both cases, the client applications will be on different physical computers, although they will always be within the corporation's internal network.

Questions

Answer the following question for your manager.

1. What mechanism should be used to provide the graphics to the client applications? Performance and responsiveness should be the key criteria for the choice.

Suggested Practices

To help you successfully master the exam objectives presented in this chapter, complete the following task.

Create a Web Service That Delivers Dynamic Graphics

For this task, you should complete both practices.

- **Practice 1**   Create a Web service that delivers graphics by using SwA. The Web service exposes a method called *GetGraphicSwa*. The return data type on the method should be a bitmap. Internally, the method uses information in the Northwind Traders database to create a new *Bitmap* object. That object will then be returned from the method.

- **Practice 2**   Create a Web service that delivers graphics by using MTOM. The Web service exposes a method call *GetGraphicMtom*. The return data type on the method will be a bitmap. Internally, the method uses information in the Northwind Traders database to create a new *Bitmap* object. That object will then be returned from the method. In addition, the method needs to be attributed to activate the WSE functionality.

Take a Practice Test

The practice tests on this book's companion CD offer many options. For example, you can test yourself on just one exam objective, or you can test yourself on all the 70-549 certification exam content. You can set up the test so that it closely simulates the experience of taking a certification exam, or you can set it up in study mode so that you can look at the correct answers and explanations after you answer each question.

MORE INFO   Practice tests

For details about all the practice test options available, see the section titled "How to Use the Practice Tests" in this book's Introduction.

Chapter 7
Reusable Software Components

By definition, enterprise applications are within the scope of the entire organization. Because of this, you will experience many opportunities for reuse when developing enterprise applications. Reuse in enterprise applications can take many forms. You might develop a custom class to define some business entity and reuse that definition throughout your development efforts. You might also create an algorithm for executing a specific business process and find that algorithm useful in other applications. Finally, you can purchase a third-party system with common functionality that all enterprise applications can use. Regardless of your situation, reuse is a powerful technique for improving development time, decreasing defects, and ensuring consistency.

The Microsoft .NET Framework offers an excellent balance between building generic software factories and constructing modular, extensible components. This chapter will examine some techniques for identifying reusable components and extending (or restricting) those components. You will also learn about testing and deploying reusable software components. These topics will provide you with the knowledge necessary to identify and extend reusable components in your software development efforts.

Exam objectives in this chapter:
- Consume a reusable software component.
  - ❏ Identify a reusable software component from available components to meet the requirements.
  - ❏ Identify whether the reusable software component needs to be extended.
  - ❏ Identify whether the reusable software component needs to be wrapped.
  - ❏ Identify whether any existing functionality needs to be hidden.
  - ❏ Test the identified component based on the requirements.

Lessons in this chapter:

Before You Begin

To complete the lessons in this chapter, you should be familiar with Microsoft Visual Basic or C# and comfortable with the following tasks:

- Creating an ASP.NET Web page in Microsoft Visual Studio 2005
- Creating class libraries in Visual Studio 2005
- Programming with object-oriented techniques and terms

Real World

Brian C. Lanham

An extremely large number of the applications we create access relational data of some kind. We know this and have probably all written our own data services libraries to wrap common data access routines. When I first started building .NET applications, I wrote a data services library that served me well for years. I still reference it for educational purposes today.

Writing your own reusable components is good in that you have complete control over the functionality. However, it is bad in that you also have complete responsibility for it. It is unlikely that you will think of every possible scenario in which it can be used; therefore, you will likely receive requests for changes. When considering relatively common libraries, you should do some research to see whether someone else has written something similar to your needs.

The Microsoft Enterprise Library 2.0 falls in the category of reusable common functionality. It provides, at no cost, blocks of pre-built, tested, and proven code to perform the more common and, dare I say, mundane routines associated with tasks such as data access, logging, and caching. Another important factor in using existing libraries such as the enterprise library is that it is supported by a community. It is a maintained product. If you find a defect, you can correct it. You can also see whether someone else has corrected it. Using community libraries like that gives you an edge in your development efforts and improves your time to market. Take the time to do some research and see whether something similar to your needs exists. If it supports you only 80 percent of the time, then that's 80 percent less mundane code you have to write, allowing you to focus more on the business.

Lesson 1: Consuming Reusable Software Components

This lesson is segmented into three distinct sections. The first section reviews some techniques for identifying reusable components. You will also learn how to avoid wasting time trying to force reusability. The second section covers the steps appropriate for extending (or restricting) reusable components. This topic will show you how to control and manage reusability. The final portion addresses testing and deploying your extensions and wrappers for reusable components.

After this lesson, you will be able to:
- Identify reusable components.
- Evaluate how a component might be reused.

Estimated lesson time: 90 minutes

Identifying Reusable Components

One of the most important realizations regarding reusability is that not everything is appropriate or available for reuse. Some things are truly singular of purpose and apply in only one situation. This is one of the more important points when dealing with reusable components. If you do not realize this, you might waste time trying to force reuse where there is none.

Whether you are dealing with custom components or third-party software, there are some common attributes when looking for reusability. The next section will explain the common attributes and how to evaluate them.

Evaluating How a Component Might Be Reused

It is generally more important to ask yourself how rather than why a component can be reused. The answer to why a component can be reused is unchanging and consists of adages such as, "Don't reinvent the wheel" and catchphrases such as "Object-oriented programming is all about reuse." What is relevant is how a component can be reused in your organization. That last part is important to remember. If you try hard, you can probably think of how someone can reuse a component in some way. Try to be practical and focus on your current organization in the scope of the strategic technology plan (which is generally three to five years).

Businesses are always changing. In some cases, changes are anticipated and even planned. It is in these situations that you can determine how a component can be reused. For example, suppose some new legislation will become effective within a few months. You might find that some business logic in one system will be applicable to other systems as a result of the legislation. Anticipating this, you can reuse the business logic. As another example, consider mergers and acquisitions. A financial services company might plan to expand and include brokerage services within a year. Anticipating this, you can begin preparing now for system integration opportunities and common financial services business logic. Even in these scenarios, it is unlikely that you will think of everything. However, you have some boundaries within which you can work to focus your reuse efforts.

Unfortunately, when a reusable component surfaces, there are no fireworks, no marching bands, and no announcements. In fact, it is generally quite the opposite. Often reusable components are not recognized until later in the life of the software system. There are some rules of thumb you can follow to identify reusable components. The following listing describes some of the more useful steps you can take to determine whether a component available to you is reusable.

- **Look for a business need**   Talk with your colleagues about their projects. It is possible that they are working on some system that has similar functionality or involves the same business units as yours. You might be able to share recipes for consuming third-party components and define a common set of classes to extend and restrict those components.

- **Consider future efforts and systems integration projects**   When using other systems, whether third-party or custom, it is likely that you will not have that system forever. Even if you have the same product, you will almost certainly change versions. Most scenarios involving other applications are good for wrapping and, potentially, extending those applications with an abstraction layer. Doing this loosely couples any future applications to the existing system. This allows the existing system to change while minimizing the impact on applications that use it. For example, if you are building a system that uses the Human Resources (HR) system for retrieving employee information, you can build a set of classes around the HR system that your application and future applications can use.

- **Review the strategic plan**   Take a look at upcoming projects and the business units they affect. Also look for planned changes in legislation and company policies. These can present appropriate opportunities for reuse in your systems. By anticipating future needs, you can design systems to reuse existing components better and allow more flexibility. For example, suppose you are using a third-party logging component to provide audit trails for a particular application. If you see an upcoming requirement to provide similar audit trails in other systems, you can wrap common logging features and make them readily available for other systems.

- **Inspect access levels**   Not every component can be extended or wrapped. Also, even if a component is visible publicly, some of its members might not be. You need to inspect the component to determine what is available for wrapping. You can investigate the component by using a disassembler or by referencing the component in Visual Studio and using the Object Browser to view its exposed members and their exposed properties and methods.

Reuse Pitfalls

The search for reuse can pull you into a long and drawn-out quest for a perfect design. Here are some common pitfalls to avoid when considering reusability in your design.

- **Do not fabricate a reuse scenario** It can be easy to define a could-happen scenario. This is a two-fold problem. First, there might be many possible scenarios. It is probably cost prohibitive to try to account for all of them. Second, you are going to spend a lot of effort on scenarios that might occur but in reality might never occur.

- **Avoid wrapping an entire system** It might be tempting to create an abstraction layer for the entire functionality of an existing system. For example, if you are building a wrapper to access functionality from the HR system, you might be tempted to wrap the entire HR system. Avoid this; instead, focus on wrapping only the needed functionality. You can always wrap more features later.

Extending and Restricting Reusable Components

Now that you have identified a reusable component, you can use it in its original form but, more likely, you will need to extend it or restrict it in some fashion. This section will discuss forms and techniques of reuse and ways to extend and restrict the functionality of existing components.

Exam Tip When using a component that must be modified to meet requirements, remember that to inherit means to derive a new component from the original component to extend functionality; to wrap means to create an instance of the original component within the new component to restrict functionality.

Choosing Appropriate Reuse Techniques

Almost all reuse comes in one of three rudimentary forms. *Code samples* are blocks of code that are copied and pasted among systems. Perhaps you have a string-parsing routine that your colleague finds useful. You can give her the code (in an e-mail, a text file, and so on), and she can embed that method in her system. *Recipes* are an extension of code samples by which a way to reproduce some behavior is described in terms of consuming an existing component. For example, if your colleague writes a data access component, she can give you a recipe for how to reference that component in your system and how to write code to consume that component. Finally, you can reuse the *binaries* distributed on local or remote systems without distributing them with each project.

Within the three rudimentary forms, there are three basic ways to reuse software. You can use the component in its original form in multiple systems, you can extend component functionality as needed for individual systems, or you can restrict component functionality as needed for individual systems. The following sections will review extending and restricting

components. Using components in their original forms generally falls under the recipes category and should be straightforward.

Extending Components

You might often think of reusing software in terms of either using components without changing them or extending components. This section will discuss ways to extend components.
This discussion assumes that you are extending a binary component. Even if the source code
is available, modifications to the source are not the topic here. Instead, you will learn how to
use inheritance and polymorphism to add your own custom attributes and behaviors to existing software.

Inheriting   The .NET Framework 2.0 supports single inheritance. That means a class can
inherit from only one class. Inheriting from a class is called *implementation inheritance* because
the child or derived class is inheriting the actual implementation or functionality in the parent
or base class. The following code samples show how to inherit in Visual Basic and C#.

```
'VB
Public Class ChildClass
    Inherits ParentClass
```

```
//C#
public class childClass : parentClass
```

You must follow some special rules regarding *constructors* and *destructors* in the context of
inheritance. The following list highlights some of the specifics.

- **Derived class constructors in Visual Basic**   The first line of each constructor in the
  derived class must be a call to the constructor of the base class unless the base class has
  a constructor with no arguments and is accessible to the derived class.
- **Derived class constructors in C#**   If a base-class constructor is not explicitly called by a
  constructor in a derived class, the default constructor is called implicitly. If there is no
  default constructor, the derived class must call a constructor in the base class.

Remember that not every property and method in the parent class is available to the child
class, and this includes constructors and destructors. Access modifiers adorn code elements
to indicate the visibility of individual elements. The following list describes the visibility
adornments available in the .NET Framework and how each affects inheritance.

MORE INFO   **Access levels in Visual Basic**

Access, to an element of a component is determined by how the element is declared and by how
the container of the element is declared. More information about which access levels can be used
on each element type (classes, properties, interfaces, and so on) and the effect of the access level
can be found in the MSDN Library at *http://msdn2.microsoft.com/en-us/library/76453kax.aspx*.

- **Public (VB) / public (C#)**   Members declared as public have unrestricted visibility and are available to any code that can see them, including external and derived classes. Public classes are also unrestricted in visibility, and other classes can inherit from them.

- **Private (VB) / private (C#)**   Private members are available *only to the class in which they are defined*. Private classes must be nested within other classes. All classes declared at the namespace level must be public.

- **Protected (VB) / protected (C#)**   Protected members are visible to other members within the class in which they are defined as well as to classes derived from the class containing their definition. Classes declared as protected must be within another class. All classes declared at the namespace level must be public.

- **Friend (VB) / internal (C#)**   Friend and internal members are visible within the current assembly. Types outside the assembly in which friend and internal members are defined cannot see the friend and internal members. All classes declared at the namespace level must be public.

- **Protected Friend (VB) / protected internal (C#)**   This is the union of the two access modifiers. Using these modifiers in combination allows you to hide members from all but derived classes and other classes in the same assembly.

Exam Tip   Access levels (Public, Protected, and Friend) are important in determining which features (if any) and how those features of a component can be extended, including the entire component. This pertains to the class definition and to member definitions (properties, methods, and events).

In addition to restricting member visibility in classes by using access levels it is also possible to control inheritance. Adorning a class with *NotInheritable* (VB) / *sealed* (C#) prevents derivations of that class. Adorning a class with *MustInherit* (VB) / *abstract* (C#) requires a derived class to be created. The *MustOverride* (VB) / *abstract* (C#) keyword is used in conjunction with *MustInherit* / *abstract* to indicate members of the base class that must be implemented by derived classes. The following code samples demonstrate these techniques.

```
'VB
' The base class cannot be used as is and must be derived.
Public MustInherit Class MyBaseClass

    Public MustOverride Function CalculateInterest(ByVal LoanAmount As _
Decimal, ByVal Term As Integer) As Decimal

End Class

' The derived class cannot, in turn, have another derived class.
Public NotInheritable Class MySubClass
    Inherits MyBaseClass

    Public Overrides Function CalculateInterest(ByVal LoanAmount As _
```

```
Decimal, ByVal Term As Integer) As Decimal
        ' Do some work.
    End Function

End Class
```

```
//C#
// The base class cannot be used as is and must be derived.
public abstract class MyBaseClass
    {
        public abstract decimal calculateInterest(decimal loanAmount, int term);
    }

// The derived class cannot, in turn, have another derived class.
    public sealed class MySubClass : MyBaseClass
    {
        public override decimal calculateInterest (decimal loanAmount, int term)
        {
            // Do some work.
        }
    }
```

Quick Check

- Inheritance is a technique whereby one class can be derived from another—the base class—taking advantage of the functionality of that base class. List the modifiers that can be added to a class declaration with respect to inheritance.

Quick Check Answer

- *NotInheritable* (VB) / *sealed* (C#)   Prevents a class from being used as a base class.
- *MustInherit* (VB) / *abstract* (C#)   Prevents a class from being created. This class can be used only as a base class for a derived class. This is sometimes referred to as an abstract class.

Overriding and Overloading   You do not need to accept the existing implementation of a base class as it is. You can extend the existing implementation by defining new implementations of existing methods. The .NET Framework provides support for overriding and overloading members.

Overriding is replacing a base class member with a derived class member of the same name. The *ToString()* method is an often overridden method. Instead of accepting the default implementation of *ToString*, you can override the implementations in the base class. In Visual Basic and C#, you use the *Overrides* / *override* keywords, respectively, to indicate that a member is overriding another member of the same name in the base class.

Classes can require overriding for some members. Adorning Visual Basic members with the *MustOverride* keyword requires the implementation for that member to be provided by a derived class. In C#, members are declared as abstract to accomplish the same behavior. In Visual Basic, you must also adorn the class with the *MustInherit* keyword if a member is declared as *MustOverride*. In C#, the class containing the abstract member must also be abstract. The following code samples demonstrate this.

```
'VB
Public MustInherit Class MyBaseClass

    Public MustOverride Function CalculateInterest(ByVal LoanAmount As _
Decimal, ByVal Term As Integer) As Decimal

End Class

Public Class MySubClass
    Inherits MyBaseClass

    Public Overrides Function CalculateInterest(ByVal LoanAmount As _
Decimal, ByVal Term As Integer) As Decimal
        Return 15.5
    End Function

End Class
```

```
//C#
    public abstract class MyBaseClass
    {
        public abstract decimal calculateInterest(decimal loanAmount, int term);
    }

    public class MySubClass : MyBaseClass
    {
        public override decimal calculateInterest (decimal loanAmount, int term)
        {
            return 15.5M;
        }
    }
```

In addition to requiring derived classes to implement the necessary functionality, it is also possible to prevent inheritance. You can declare a class as *NotInheritable* (VB) / *sealed* (C#). These keywords allow you to indicate that a class is in its final form and cannot be specialized further. If you want more granularity over inheritance, you can prevent inheritance at the property and method levels. The *NotOverridable* (VB) / *sealed* (C#) keywords are used to indicate that while the class itself may be inherited (and other members overridden), those adorned with these keywords are in their final form in the base class.

The .NET Framework 2.0 adds a new exception type to give you additional flexibility when inheriting from classes requiring overriding. *NotImplementedException* is used when you do not want to provide an implementation. Using this exception allows you to uphold the interface contract associated with inheritance without requiring you to implement features that aren't appropriate. The following samples demonstrate this.

```vb
'VB
Public Class MySubClass
    Inherits MyBaseClass

    Public Overrides Function CalculateInterest(ByVal LoanAmount As _
Decimal, ByVal Term As Integer) As Decimal
        Throw New NotImplementedException
    End Function

End Class
```

```csharp
//C#
    public class MySubClass : MyBaseClass
    {
        public override decimal calculateInterest (decimal loanAmount, int term)
        {
            throw new NotImplementedException();
        }
    }
```

Overloading differs from overriding in that it allows you to provide multiple implementations of the same members. Suppose, for example, that you have an HR system that defines several types of employees in an inheritance chain. In this system, the base class *Employee* is derived by *ExemptEmployee*, and *NonExemptEmployee* classes. Further, suppose a component in the system calculates the amount of vacation time available to an employee. The calculation is, however, different for exempt and non-exempt employees.

Clearly, you can write one method and use conditional logic (the if statement) to determine which calculation to perform. However, if a new type of employee is added to the system, you must modify the conditional logic everywhere that it occurs, and the code becomes unwieldy and difficult to maintain. Instead of using conditional logic, you can use method overloading and polymorphism.

Polymorphism is a word with Greek roots that literally means "many forms." In the context of object-oriented programming, it is a powerful technique for customizing functionality based on particular types. In the preceding scenario, you can use polymorphism to minimize the amount of conditional logic that must be maintained. The following code samples show how to use polymorphism and method overloading in this scenario.

```vb
'VB
Public Class Employee
    Public ReadOnly Property HoursWorked() As Decimal
        Get
            ' Fetch the hours worked from the database.
        End Get
    End Property
```

```vb
End Class

Public Class ExemptEmployee
    Inherits Employee
End Class

Public Class NonExemptEmployee
    Inherits Employee
End Class

Public Class VacationCalculator

    Public Overloads Function GetAvailableVacationHours(ByVal forEmployee _
As ExemptEmployee) As Decimal
        ' Compute
    End Function

    Public Overloads Function GetAvailableVacationHours(ByVal forEmployee _
As NonExemptEmployee) As Decimal
        ' Compute
    End Function

End Class
```

```csharp
//C#
    public class Employee
    {
        public decimal HoursWorked
        {
            get
            {
                // Fetch the hours worked from the database.
            }
        }

    }

    public class ExemptEmployee : Employee {}
    public class NonExemptEmployee : Employee {}

    public class VacationCalculator
    {
        public decimal GetAvailableVacationHours (ExemptEmployee forEmployee)
        {//Compute}
        public decimal GetAvailableVacationHours (NonExemptEmployee forEmployee)
        {//Compute}
    }
```

These code samples show how you can use overloading to replace conditional logic. Overloading is a powerful tool that significantly improves both extensibility and maintainability in your applications. The following code demonstrates how to use the overloaded members polymorphically.

```
'VB
    Public Sub showOverloadingCalls ()
        Dim exEmp As ExemptEmployee = New ExemptEmployee
        Dim nonexEmp As NonExemptEmployee = New NonExemptEmployee

        Dim vc As VacationCalculator = New VacationCalculator

        vc.GetAvailableVacationHours(exEmp)
        vc.GetAvailableVacationHours(nonexEmp)
End Sub
```

```
//C#
        void showOverloadingCalls ()
{
        ExemptEmployee exEmp = new ExemptEmployee ();
            NonExemptEmployee nonexEmp = new NonExemptEmployee();

        VacationCalculator vc = new VacationCalculator();

        // The runtime "knows" which overloaded definition
        // to call based on the method signature.
        vc.GetAvailableVacationHours(exEmp);
        vc.GetAvailableVacationHours(nonexEmp);

}
```

Quick Check

1. Overriding is a technique whereby a derived class can refine the behavior of the base class. List the modifiers that can be added to a function, property, or sub of a class with respect to overriding.
2. Which of these modifiers can be used within the base class?
3. Which of these modifiers can be used within the derived class?

Quick Check Answers

1. There are four modifiers pertaining to overriding. They are:
   - ❑ *Overridable* (VB) / *virtual* (C#) – allows a property or method in a class to be overridden in a derived class
   - ❑ *Overrides* (VB) / *override* (C#) – overrides an Overridable / virtual property or method defined in the base class
   - ❑ *NotOverridable* (VB) / *sealed* (C#) – prevents a property or method from being overridden in an inheriting class
   - ❑ *MustOverride* (VB) / *abstract* (C#) – requires that a derived class override the property or method

> **2.** The base class can use *NotOverridable* (VB) / *sealed* (C#), *MustOverride* (VB) /
>   abstract (C#), and *Overridable* (VB) / *virtual* (C#) to allow or restrict enhancement
>   of the base class functionality by a derived class. The base class can also be a
>   derived class. As a derived class, the base class may use the *Overrides* (VB) / *over-
>   ride* (C#) modifier.
>
> **3.** The derived class must use *Overrides* (VB) / *override* (C#) on properties and meth-
>   ods if the base class has properties or methods marked with *MustOverride* (VB) /
>   *abstract* (C#).

When inheriting, there are times when you want to reference the base class members explicitly. Suppose, for example, that you want to override a method in the base class to add new
functionality, but you do not want to lose the existing functionality. You can reference the
method in the base class directly by using the keyword *MyBase* (VB) / *base* (C#).

Continuing with the employee time management scenario, suppose you have a component to
compute overtime pay. The business logic is the same for all employees. However, in addition
to the base logic, non-exempt employees are to receive an additional hourly payout if the overtime work is between midnight and the beginning of the work day. You can accomplish this by
truly extending the functionality in the base class as the following code samples demonstrate.

```vb
'VB
Public Class Employee
    Public ReadOnly Property HoursWorked() As Decimal
        Get
            ' Fetch the hours worked from the database.
        End Get
    End Property
End Class

Public Class ExemptEmployee
    Inherits Employee
End Class

Public Class NonExemptEmployee
    Inherits Employee
End Class

Public Class OvertimeCalculator

    Public Overridable Overloads Function GetOvertimePay(ByVal _
forEmployee As ExemptEmployee) As Decimal

    End Function

    Public Overridable Overloads Function GetOvertimePay(ByVal _
forEmployee As NonExemptEmployee) As Decimal
```

```
        End Function

End Class

Public Class MyOvertimeCalculator
    Inherits OvertimeCalculator

    Public Overrides Function GetOvertimePay(ByVal forEmployee As _
NonExemptEmployee) As Decimal
        Dim basePay As Decimal
        basePay = MyBase.GetOvertimePay(forEmployee)
        ' Perform custom logic to adjust base pay and return adjusted amount.
    End Function

End Class

Public Class OvertimeTester
    Public Sub Test()
        Dim exEmp As ExemptEmployee = New ExemptEmployee
        Dim nonexEmp As NonExemptEmployee = New NonExemptEmployee
        Dim otc As MyOvertimeCalculator = New MyOvertimeCalculator

        ' This call actually calls the method in the base class.
        otc.GetOvertimePay(exEmp)

        ' This call uses the method in the derived class which,
        ' in turn uses the method in the base class.
        otc.GetOvertimePay(nonexEmp)

    End Sub
End Class

//C#
    public class Employee
    {
        public decimal HoursWorked
        {
            get
            {
                // Fetch the hours worked from the database.
            }
        }

    }

    public class ExemptEmployee : Employee {}
    public class NonExemptEmployee : Employee {}

    public class VacationCalculator
    {
        public decimal GetAvailableVacationHours (ExemptEmployee forEmployee)
        {}
        public decimal GetAvailableVacationHours (NonExemptEmployee forEmployee)
```

```
        {}
    }

    public class OvertimeCalculator
    {
        public decimal getOvertimePay(ExemptEmployee forEmployee)
        { }
        public decimal getOvertimePay(NonExemptEmployee forEmployee)
        { }
    }

    public class MyOvertimeCalculator:OvertimeCalculator
    {
        public override decimal getOvertimePay(NonExemptEmployee forEmployee)
        {
            decimal basePay;
            basePay = base.getOvertimePay(forEmployee);
            // Perform custom logic to adjust base pay and return adjusted amount.
        }
    }

    public class OvertimeTester
    {
        public void Test ()
        {
            ExemptEmployee exEmp = new ExemptEmployee ();
            NonExemptEmployee nonexEmp = new NonExemptEmployee();

            MyOvertimeCalculator otc = new MyOvertimeCalculator ();

            // This call actually calls the method in the base class.
            otc.getOvertimePay (exEmp);

            // This call uses the method in the derived class which,
            // in turn uses the method in the base class.
            otc.GetOvertimePay(nonexEmp)
        }
    }
```

Pitfalls of Extending Components   Extending is a powerful and useful tool. However, there are some potential issues with extending reusable components, especially if doing so with inheritance. The following list highlights some of the more important pitfalls to avoid.

- **Deep inheritance chains**   Like most good things, too much can be bad. Inheritance is no different. The deeper the inheritance chain, the more fragile the super base class becomes. Any change, no matter how small, can have an impact on inherited classes down the line. Avoid creating deep inheritance chains. Consider, instead, refactoring your wrapping classes to include the additional functionality.

- **Excessive overriding**   In some situations, it is appropriate to override functionality in a base class. However, if you override excessively, you are fundamentally changing the class definition. This means that although the derived class is of the same type as the base class, it truly is not like the base class. Instead of trying to force a derived class to be a base class, simply create a new class all to itself.

- **Ignoring security**   If there is security in the base class, it is there for a reason. You should not wrap an existing component for the purpose of bypassing its security mechanism.

Restricting Components

Restricting components is less often considered compared with extending components. Restricting is just as appropriate and valid as extending. Some reasons for restricting functionality include licensing compliance, security, and data protection. This section will review some techniques for restricting the functionality available in reusable components.

Creating Wrappers   When extending components, you can inherit from a base class and add your own functionality as needed. Although some restricting can be accomplished with inheritance, restricting functionality typically requires a slightly different technique. Instead of inheriting from a base class, you can create a wrapper class. The wrapper class is a stand-alone class that contains an instance of the reusable class and exposes limited functionality of that class. It is important to note that because the wrapper class is responsible for instantiating the component, it is also responsible for disposing of the component. Also, the wrapper class is responsible for any threading safety required.

Restricting members is a straightforward technique. You can create the wrapper class so that only those members that you want of the wrapped class are exposed. For example, suppose the existing component has an overloaded method to perform some operation. Now suppose you want to force only one of the several overloaded options. You can simply wrap the component and provide only one way to call the overloaded methods. In this manner, users of your wrapper are forced to follow the constraints you establish. The concept used to house an instance of one class within an instance of another is called aggregation. The following code samples demonstrate wrapping a component.

```
'VB
Public Class ReusableComponent
    Public Overloads Function PerformCalculation(ByVal count As Integer) _
As Decimal
        End Function

    Public Overloads Function PerformCalculation(ByVal count As Integer, _
ByVal weightfactor As Decimal) As Decimal
        End Function

    Public Overloads Function PerformCalculation(ByVal count As Integer, _
ByVal weightfactor As Decimal, ByVal bonus As Decimal) As Decimal
        End Function
End Class

Public Class Wrapper
```

```
    Private _ru As ReusableComponent

    Public Sub New()
        _ru = New ReusableComponent
    End Sub

    Public Function PerformCalculation(ByVal count As Integer, ByVal _
weightfactor As Decimal) As Decimal
        ' This forces the use of only one overloaded member.
        _ru.PerformCalculation(count, weightfactor)
    End Function

End Class
```

```
//C#
    public class ReusableComponent
    {
        public decimal PerformCalculation(int count)
        { }
        public decimal PerformCalculation(int count, decimal weightfactor)
        { }
        public decimal PerformCalculation (int count, decimal weightfactor, decimal bonus)
        { }
    }

    public class Wrapper
    {
        private ReusableComponent _ru;

        public Wrapper()
        {
            _ru = new ReusableComponent();
        }

        public decimal PerformCalculation(int count, decimal weightfactor)
        {
            // This forces the use of only one overloaded member.
            _ru.PerformCalculation(count, weightfactor);
        }
    }
```

If you do want to restrict members with inheritance, there are techniques for that as well. Suppose, for example, that you want to restrict a single item in your base class from being exposed through your derived class. You can suppress the member in question by using a concept called *hiding by name*. This is implemented in Visual Basic with the *Shadows* keyword and in C# by redeclaring the method using the *new* keyword. The following code samples demonstrate hiding by name.

```
'VB
Public Class ReusableComponent
    Public Function PerformCalculation(ByVal count As Integer) As Decimal
```

```
            ' Do some work.
      End Function
End Class

Public Class Wrapper
      Inherits ReusableComponent

      ' This member hides the member of the same name in the base class.
      Private Shadows Function performcalculation(ByVal count As Integer) As Decimal
            MyBase.PerformCalculation(count)
      End Function

End Class

//C#
      public class ReusableComponent
      {
          public decimal PerformCalculation(int count)
          { // Do some work. }
          }

      }

      public class Wrapper : ReusableComponent
          {
              // This member hides the member of the same name in the base class.
              private new decimal PerformCalculation(int count)
              {
                  base.PerformCalculation(count);
              }

          }
```

Invoking Reusable Components Regularly and Asynchronously

When dealing with enterprise applications, you are often required to integrate multiple disparate systems. Furthermore, you might have little or no control over the execution of external applications. You might need to obtain information from one system on a regular cycle. Additionally, you might need information from another system, requiring that system to perform some lengthy processing. Finally, you might need to combine these two scenarios. The .NET Framework offers two reusable components that help you invoke long-running processes asynchronously and regularly.

The BackgroundWorker component is new to .NET Framework 2.0. It allows you to spawn a process on a thread other than the main thread. This can be useful in situations involving long-running and resource-intensive activities. For example, you can perform downloads, run reports, and process batch requests asynchronously.

The BackgroundWorker component uses delegates to keep the owner thread informed of progress and status associated with its execution. To invoke a background process by using the BackgroundWorker component, call the *RunWorkerAsync* method. When finished, the BackgroundWorker component raises the *RunWorkerCompleted* event. Alternatively, you can check the IsBusy property of the BackgroundWorker component to determine whether it is executing a process.

Sometimes, it is desirable to run processes at regular intervals. The Timer component allows you to handle a time event based on a given internal that you specify. For example, suppose you build a workflow system. While users are in the system, you want to check for any updated jobs and tasks periodically and provide some sort of notification to the user that an update is available. You can use the Timer component to accomplish this.

To use the Timer component, you must handle the *Tick* event. This event is fired by the Timer when the specified interval has elapsed (and the timer is enabled). The interval is an *Integer* value indicating the number of milliseconds between tick events. Finally, the Timer component must be enabled to fire events. Controlling the Timer is accomplished by setting the Enabled Boolean property.

You can see how the BackgroundWorker and Timer components can be combined to invoke regularly scheduled yet long-running processes asynchronously. Together or separately, these components provide a powerful toolset for you to integrate applications and to provide a richer user experience. You can integrate applications without frustrating users and without requiring changes to the external applications.

Testing and Deploying Components

Do not assume that existing components have been properly tested or tested at all. Consider performing some black-box testing on reusable components before deploying them. Black-box testing is called that because you cannot see inside the box you are testing. Just as with existing components, you cannot see the code that is performing the work. You have access only to the public (and possibly the protected) interface.

You can perform unit testing to some degree on the component by writing tests to use each available member. This can be useful if you receive regular updates from the component vendor and want to ensure that the component continues to behave as expected between releases. There are several robust testing frameworks, such as NUnit, to help you create and maintain libraries of tests for reusable components. Those topics are beyond the scope of this chapter.

MORE INFO   **NUnit and test-driven development (TDD)**

You can learn more about NUnit and test-driven development as well as download NUnit for free at *http://msdn2.microsoft.com/en-us/library/76453kax.aspx*.

In addition to unit testing, you must perform integration testing on reusable components. You cannot just assume that, once integrated, the component will behave as expected. There are many factors affecting the operations of reusable components. Scalability, performance, and concurrency, among others, can all be affected by integrated components competing for common resources. As with unit testing, integration testing is beyond the scope of this chapter. Be aware, however, of the risks associated with integrating reusable components and of some of the factors affecting successful integration.

When deploying reusable components, you must consider the scope of reuse. For example, if a component is going to be used only within a single application, it can be deployed with that application. However, if it is going to be used by several applications, you might need to deploy it with each application, distribute it to an application server, or register the component with the global assembly cache (GAC) for reuse on a single machine. Also, you must be cognizant of the deployment scenarios so that future deployments do not interrupt service or inadvertently break other applications.

Lab: Consume a Reusable Software Component

In this lab, you will create a reusable component that you can extend and restrict. In Exercise 1, you will create the component. Exercises 2 and 3 will demonstrate extending and restricting, respectively. If you encounter a problem completing an exercise, the complete projects are available on the companion CD in the Code folder.

▶ **Exercise 1: Creating the Reusable Component**

In this exercise, you will create a component for use in the remaining exercises.

1. Start Visual Studio 2005. Create a class library project called **ReusableComponent**.
2. Add a class to the project called **TimeCalculator** with the following definition.

```vb
'VB
Public Class TimeCalculator

    Public Function CalculatePaidTimeOff(ByVal EmployeeType As Short) As Double

        Select Case EmployeeType
            Case 1I ' Exempt
                Return 60D
            Case Else
                Return 20D
        End Select

    End Function

    Public Function CalculateVacation(ByVal EmployeeType As Short) As Double

        Select Case EmployeeType
            Case 1I ' Exempt
```

```
                    Return 60D
            Case Else
                    Return 20D
        End Select

    End Function

    Public Function CalculateHolidays(ByVal EmployeeType As Short) As Double

        Select Case EmployeeType
            Case 1I ' Exempt
                    Return 80D
            Case Else
                    Return 40D
        End Select

    End Function

    Public Function CalculateSickTime(ByVal EmployeeType As Short) As Double

        Select Case EmployeeType
            Case 1I ' Exempt
                    Return 12D
            Case Else
                    Return 6D
        End Select

    End Function

End Class
```

```
//C#
    public class TimeCalculator
    {
        public double CalculatePaidTimeOff(int EmployeeType)
        {
            switch (EmployeeType)
            {
                case 1: // Exempt
                    return 60;
                default:
                    return 20;
            }

        }

        public double CalculateVacation(int EmployeeType)
        {
            switch (EmployeeType)
            {
                case 1: // Exempt
                    return 60;
                default:
```

```
                           return 20;
                }
        }

        public double CalculateHolidays(int EmployeeType)
        {
            switch (EmployeeType)
            {
                case 1: // Exempt
                    return 80;
                default:
                    return 40;
            }
        }

        public virtual double CalculateSickTime(int EmployeeType)
        {
            switch (EmployeeType)
            {
                case 1: // Exempt
                    return 12;
                default:
                    return 6;
            }
        }
    }
}
```

3. Add a class to the project called **BenefitsCalculator** with the following definition.

```
'VB
Public MustInherit Class BenefitsCalculator

    Public Function CalculateSTD(ByVal EmployeeType As Short) As Double

        Select Case EmployeeType
            Case 1I ' Exempt
                Return 240D
            Case Else
                Return 120D
        End Select

    End Function

    Public MustOverride Function CalculateRetirement(ByVal EmployeeType As Short) As
Double

End Class
```

```
//C#
    public abstract class BenefitsCalculator
    {
        public double CalculateSTD(int EmployeeType)
        {
```

```
        switch (EmployeeType)
        {
            case 1: // Exempt
                return 240;
            default:
                return 120;
        }
    }

    public abstract double CalculateRetirement(int EmployeeType);
}
```

▶ **Exercise 2: Extending and Restricting the Component**

This exercise demonstrates extending the functionality of the class created in Exercise 1.

1. Add a class library project called **ExtendingRestrictingComponent**.

2. Add a class called **MyTimeCalculator** to the project that extends and restricts the *Time-Calculator* with the following definition.

```vb
'VB
Public Class MyTimeCalculator
    Inherits TimeCalculator

    ' "My" company does not provide separate sick time.
    ' Instead, it is all vacation time.  Therefore, the
    ' sick time calculation is superfluous.
    Public Shadows Function CalculateSickTime() As Double
        Return 0D
    End Function

End Class
```

```csharp
//C#
    public class MyTimeCalculator : TimeCalculator
    {
        public new double CalculateSickTime(int EmployeeType)
        {
            return 0;
        }
    }
```

3. Add a class called **MyBenefitsCalculator** to the project that extends and restricts the *BenefitsCalculator* with the following definition.

```vb
'VB
Public Class MyBenefitsCalculator
    Inherits BenefitsCalculator

    Public Overrides Function CalculateRetirement(ByVal EmployeeType As Short) As Double

        ' "My" company is a non-profit licensed in the United States.
        ' Therefore, use 403B.
        Select Case EmployeeType
```

```
                    Case 1I ' Exempt
                        Return 403D
                    Case Else
                        Return 0D
                End Select

        End Function

    End Class
```

```
//C#
    public class MyBenefitsCalculator : BenefitsCalculator
    {
        public override double CalculateRetirement(int EmployeeType)
        {
            // "My" company is a non-profit licensed in the United States.
            // Therefore, use 403B.

            switch (EmployeeType)
            {
                case 1: // Exempt
                    return 403;
                default:
                    return 0;
            }

        }
    }
```

▶ **Exercise 3: Testing the Component**

This exercise demonstrates testing the component with a console application.

1. Add a Console Application project called **ReusableComponentTest**.

2. Add the following definition for the console application. This will demonstrate the operation of the outputs of Exercises 1 and 2.

```
'VB
Module Module1

    Sub Main()
        CalculateForAnyCompany()
        CalculateForMyCompany()
        Console.ReadLine()
    End Sub

    Sub CalculateForAnyCompany()

        Dim timecalc As New TimeCalculator
        ' BenefitsCalculator is declared "MustInherit".
        ' Therefore we cannot instantiate it directly.

        Console.WriteLine("Employee Time Calculations - Any Company")
```

```vb
        Console.WriteLine("-----------------------------------------------")

        Console.WriteLine("Exempt Holiday Time: " &
timecalc.CalculateHolidays(1I).ToString)
        Console.WriteLine("Exempt Vacation Time: " &
timecalc.CalculateVacation(1I).ToString)
        Console.WriteLine("Exempt Paid Off Time: " &
timecalc.CalculatePaidTimeOff(1I).ToString)
      Console.WriteLine("Exempt Sick Time: " & timecalc.CalculateSickTime(1I).ToString)
        Console.WriteLine()
        Console.WriteLine("Non Exempt Holiday Time: " &
timecalc.CalculateHolidays(0I).ToString)
        Console.WriteLine("Non Exempt Vacation Time: " &
timecalc.CalculateVacation(0I).ToString)
        Console.WriteLine("Non Exempt Paid Off Time: " &
timecalc.CalculatePaidTimeOff(0I).ToString)
        Console.WriteLine("Non Exempt Sick Time: " &
timecalc.CalculateSickTime(0I).ToString)
        Console.WriteLine()

    End Sub

    Sub CalculateForMyCompany()

        Dim benecalc As New MyBenefitsCalculator
        Dim timecalc As New MyTimeCalculator

        Console.WriteLine("Employee Time Calculations - My Company")
        Console.WriteLine("-----------------------------------------------")

        Console.WriteLine("Exempt Holiday Time: " &
timecalc.CalculateHolidays(1I).ToString)
        Console.WriteLine("Exempt Vacation Time: " &
timecalc.CalculateVacation(1I).ToString)
        Console.WriteLine("Exempt Paid Off Time: " &
timecalc.CalculatePaidTimeOff(1I).ToString)
        ' Notice that we shadowed the sick time calculation and changed the signature.
      Console.WriteLine("Exempt Sick Time: " & timecalc.CalculateSickTime().ToString)
        Console.WriteLine()
        Console.WriteLine("Non Exempt Holiday Time: " &
timecalc.CalculateHolidays(0I).ToString)
        Console.WriteLine("Non Exempt Vacation Time: " &
timecalc.CalculateVacation(0I).ToString)
        Console.WriteLine("Non Exempt Paid Off Time: " &
timecalc.CalculatePaidTimeOff(0I).ToString)
        ' Notice that we shadowed the sick time calculation and changed the signature.
        Console.WriteLine("Non Exempt Sick Time: " &
timecalc.CalculateSickTime().ToString)
        Console.WriteLine()
        Console.WriteLine()
        Console.WriteLine("Employee Benefits Calculations - My Company")
        Console.WriteLine("-----------------------------------------------")
        Console.WriteLine("Exempt STD Time: " &
```

```
          benecalc.CalculateRetirement(1I).ToString)
                  Console.WriteLine("Exempt Retirement Time: " &
          benecalc.CalculateSTD(1I).ToString)
                  Console.WriteLine()
                  Console.WriteLine("Non Exempt STD Time: " &
          benecalc.CalculateRetirement(0I).ToString)
                  Console.WriteLine("Non Exempt Retirement Time: " &
          benecalc.CalculateSTD(0I).ToString)
              End Sub

      End Module

      //C#
          class Program
          {
              static void Main(string[] args)
              {
                  CalculateForAnyCompany();
                  CalculateForMyCompany();
                  Console.ReadLine();
              }

              private static void CalculateForAnyCompany()
              {
                  TimeCalculator timecalc = new TimeCalculator ();
                  // BenefitsCalculator is declared "MustInherit".
                  // Therefore we cannot instantiate it directly.

                  Console.WriteLine("Employee Time Calculations - Any Company");
                  Console.WriteLine("-----------------------------------------------");

                  Console.WriteLine("Exempt Holiday Time: " +
          timecalc.CalculateHolidays(1).ToString ());
                  Console.WriteLine("Exempt Vacation Time: " +
          timecalc.CalculateVacation(1).ToString ());
                  Console.WriteLine("Exempt Paid Off Time: " +
          timecalc.CalculatePaidTimeOff(1).ToString ());
                  Console.WriteLine("Exempt Sick Time: " +
          timecalc.CalculateSickTime(1).ToString ());
                  Console.WriteLine();
                  Console.WriteLine("Non Exempt Holiday Time: " +
          timecalc.CalculateHolidays(0).ToString ());
                  Console.WriteLine("Non Exempt Vacation Time: " +
          timecalc.CalculateVacation(0).ToString ());
                  Console.WriteLine("Non Exempt Paid Off Time: " +
          timecalc.CalculatePaidTimeOff(0).ToString ());
                  Console.WriteLine("Non Exempt Sick Time: " +
          timecalc.CalculateSickTime(0).ToString ());
                  Console.WriteLine();
              }

              private static void CalculateForMyCompany()
              {
```

```
            BenefitsCalculator benecalc = new MyBenefitsCalculator();
            TimeCalculator timecalc = new MyTimeCalculator();

            Console.WriteLine("Employee Time Calculations - My Company");
            Console.WriteLine("-------------------------------------------");

            Console.WriteLine("Exempt Holiday Time: " +
timecalc.CalculateHolidays(1).ToString ());
            Console.WriteLine("Exempt Vacation Time: " +
timecalc.CalculateVacation(1).ToString ());
            Console.WriteLine("Exempt Paid Off Time: " +
timecalc.CalculatePaidTimeOff(1).ToString ());
        // Notice that we shadowed the sick time calculation and changed the signature.
            Console.WriteLine("Exempt Sick Time: " + timecalc.CalculateSickTime(-
1).ToString ());
            Console.WriteLine();
            Console.WriteLine("Non Exempt Holiday Time: " +
timecalc.CalculateHolidays(0).ToString ());
            Console.WriteLine("Non Exempt Vacation Time: " +
timecalc.CalculateVacation(0).ToString ());
            Console.WriteLine("Non Exempt Paid Off Time: " +
timecalc.CalculatePaidTimeOff(0).ToString ());
        // Notice that we shadowed the sick time calculation and changed the signature.
            Console.WriteLine("Non Exempt Sick Time: " + timecalc.CalculateSickTime(-
1).ToString ());
            Console.WriteLine();
            Console.WriteLine();
            Console.WriteLine("Employee Benefits Calculations - My Company");
            Console.WriteLine("-------------------------------------------------");
            Console.WriteLine("Exempt STD Time: " +
benecalc.CalculateRetirement(1).ToString ());
            Console.WriteLine("Exempt Retirement Time: " +
benecalc.CalculateSTD(1).ToString ());
            Console.WriteLine();
            Console.WriteLine("Non Exempt STD Time: " +
benecalc.CalculateRetirement(0).ToString ());
            Console.WriteLine("Non Exempt Retirement Time: " +
benecalc.CalculateSTD(0).ToString ());

        }

    }
```

Lesson Summary

- Inheritance is the ability to extend existing functionality by defining a new class that inherits functionality from an existing class and then adds to it.

- You can control inheritance by forcing or preventing it. You can control access to some members in base classes by using access modifiers such as Public, Private, and Protected.

- Overloading allows you to create multiple definitions of the same member with differing signatures. Overriding allows you to redefine members that are in a base class to provide a custom implementation using the same name.
- Shadowing is a technique that allows you to hide a base class member in a derived class.

Lesson Review

You can use the following questions to test your knowledge of the information in Lesson 1, "Consuming Reusable Software Components." The questions are also available on the companion CD if you prefer to review them in electronic form.

NOTE Answers

Answers to these questions and explanations of why each answer choice is right or wrong are located in the "Answers" section at the end of the book.

---

1. You have found a third-party component that provides much of the functionality you need, but not all. Based on the component's documentation, you learn that the component performs a specific calculation you need. However, your requirements indicate that you need to perform an additional calculation based on the result of that function. You decide to create your own component and inherit the third-party component and override that function. The third-party component declaration is:

```vb
'VB
Public Class AcmeCalculator
Public Function PerformCalc () As Double
End Function
End Class
```

```csharp
//C#
public class AcmeCalculator
{
    public double PerformCalc ()
    {
    }
}
```

You want your new component to be accessible to other assemblies. Which of the following declarations would meet this requirement for your class?

A.
```vb
'VB
Friend Class MyCalculator
    Inherits AcmeCalculator
    Public Overrides Function PerformCalc () As Double
    End Function
End Class
```

```csharp
//C#
intern class MyCalculator:AcmeCalculator
```

```
        {
            Public override double PerformCalc ()
            {
            }
        }
```

B. **'VB**
```
    Private Class MyCalculator
        Inherits AcmeCalculator
        Public Overrides Function PerformCalc () As Double
        End Function
    End Class
```

    // C#
```
    private class MyCalculator:AcmeCalculator
    {
        Public override double PerformCalc ()
        {
        }
    }
```

C. **'VB**
```
    Public Class MyCalculator
        Inherits AcmeCalculator
        Public Overrides Function PerformCalc () As Double
        End Function
    End Class
```

    //C#
```
    public class MyCalculator:AcmeCalculator
    {
        Public override double PerformCalc ()
        {
        }
    }
```

D. The class defined in the third-party component cannot be inherited.

2. You have been given access to three components. The declarations of the components are as follows:

```
Class ComponentA

MustInherit Class ComponentB

NotInheritable Class ComponentC
```

You decide to derive your own component to extend the functionality and use some of the components as they are. Which of the following are valid code samples?

A. **'VB**
```
    Class MyComponent
        Inherits ComponentA
        Inherits ComponentB
```

```
        Dim c as ComponentC


//C#
Class MyComponent:ComponentA, ComponentB
    ComponentC c;
```

B. **'VB**
```
Class MyComponent
    Inherits ComponentA

    Dim b as ComponentB
    Dim c as ComponentC


//C#
Class MyComponent:ComponentA
    ComponentB b;
    ComponentC c;
```

C. **'VB**
```
Class MyComponent
    Inherits ComponentB

    Dim a as ComponentA
    Dim c as ComponentC


//C#
Class MyComponent:ComponentB
    ComponentA a;
    ComponentC c;
```

D. **'VB**
```
Class MyComponent
    Inherits ComponentC

    Dim a as ComponentA
    Dim b as ComponentB


//C#
Class MyComponent:ComponentC
    ComponentA a;
    ComponentB b;
```

3. Which of the following statements are true regarding overriding? (Choose all that apply.)

A. Private methods are *NotOverridable* by default.

B. Public methods are *Overridable* by default.

C. *MustOverride* methods can be contained only in a class declared as *MustInherit*.

D. *MustOverride* methods can contain no code statements.

Chapter Review

To further practice and reinforce the skills you learned in this chapter, you can perform the following tasks:

- Review the chapter summary.
- Review the list of key terms introduced in this chapter.
- Complete the case scenarios. These scenarios set up real-world situations involving the topics of this chapter and ask you to create a solution.
- Complete the suggested practices.
- Take a practice test.

Chapter Summary

- Enterprise applications are applications within the scope of the entire organization. They are not restricted to one business process or even to one business unit and, therefore, provide excellent opportunities to take advantage of reusing components.
- Inheritance is the ability to extend existing functionality by defining a new class that inherits functionality from an existing class and then adds to it.
- You can control inheritance by forcing or preventing it. You can control access to some members in base classes by using access modifiers such as Public, Private, and Protected.
- Overloading allows you to create multiple definitions of the same member with differing signatures. Overriding allows you to redefine members in a base class to provide a custom implementation using the same name.
- Shadowing is a technique that allows you to hide a base class member in a derived class.

Key Terms

Do you know what these key terms mean? You can check your answers by looking up the terms in the glossary at the end of the book.

- abstract class
- aggregation
- component
- control
- inheritance
- polymorphism
- shadowing

Case Scenarios

In the following case scenarios, you will apply what you've learned about reusable components. You can find answers to these questions in the "Answers" section at the end of this book.

Case Scenario 1: Extending a Reusable Component

You have been asked to introduce a third-party loan management application into the organization and integrate the application into several existing custom systems in your technology portfolio. Along with integrating the third-party system, you are also asked to make it so that the function that calculates interest can accept custom interest parameters for theoretical loan calculations. The third-party system's function accepts no parameters and uses system configuration settings.

1. Which of the three forms of reuse (code samples, recipes, and distributed binaries) is appropriate for this scenario?
2. Describe how you will meet the requirement regarding the interest calculation.

Case Scenario 2: Restricting a Reusable Component

You have been asked to introduce a third-party loan management application into the organization and to integrate the application into several existing custom systems in your technology portfolio. The third-party application implements features that the business does not support.

1. Describe how you can hide the functionality that the business does not support.
2. While wrapping one of the third-party classes, you realize that it cannot be instantiated and must be inherited. How do you inherit from this class while still restricting access to members that must be overridden?

Case Scenario 3: Restricting a Reusable Component

You have been asked to integrate a citizen information system with a building permitting system. You are required to prevent changes to the citizen information system while making citizen data available to the permitting system. Additionally, you must restrict some data (such as social security numbers) from being available to the permitting system. Due to a recent audit of the permitting process, you are also required to ensure that the citizen information system has limited access to the functionality available in the permitting system.

1. How will you make citizen information system components available to the permitting system?
2. Describe your technique for restricting the permitting functionality available to the citizen information system.

Suggested Practices

To help you successfully master the exam objectives presented in this chapter, complete the following tasks.

Consume a Reusable Software Component

Complete these tasks to learn more about consuming a reusable component. You should complete all practices.

Practice 1

- Modify the lab to include a new class in the ReusableComponent project. Make the new class require inheriting to access its functionality. Use the *MustInherit* and *MustOverride* combination in Visual Basic and the *abstract* keyword in C#.
- Inherit from the new class with two separate classes. In one class, implement the overridden members. In the other class, throw the new *NotImplementedException*.

Practice 2

- Practice inheritance chains by creating a new class that inherits from a derived class created in Exercise 2 of the lab.
- Create a new public member in the super base class and see how that new member is available in the new derived class.

Practice 3

- Use shadowing to hide base class functionality. Inherit from a base class and then shadow a member of the base class. Experiment with a range of shadowing from completely hiding functionality and information to changing it.
- Use two classes, a worker class and a data class, to experiment with polymorphism. Create a base data class and then inherit from it with two or more derived classes. Then create an overloaded method in the work class to accept arguments of the different types of derived data classes.

Take a Practice Test

The practice tests on this book's companion CD offer many options. For example, you can test yourself on just one exam objective, or you can test yourself on all the 70-549 certification exam content. You can set up the test so that it closely simulates the experience of taking a certification exam, or you can set it up in study mode so that you can look at the correct answers and explanations after you answer each question.

MORE INFO   **Practice tests**

For details about all the practice test options available, see the "How to Use the Practice Tests" section in this book's Introduction.

Chapter 8
Design Logic Implementation

Application logic, or business logic as it is often referred to, is the part of an application that performs the required data processing. It refers to the routines that perform the data entry, update, query, and report processing and, more specifically, to the processing that takes place behind the scenes rather than to the presentation logic required to display the information on the screen. Applications are composed of a user interface and application logic. The user interface and the application logic do not necessarily need to be running on the same computer. If the user interface and application logic are separated, they are then often spoken of as client and application server. To complicate things further, in the case of a Web application, the Web server takes on the role of the client.

Thinking about application logic and how and where to implement it is probably one of the most complicated parts of developing an application. Instead of trying to write "plumbing," you're now programming the code that makes the application unique. When implementing application logic, you will need to consider a number of factors such as the application architecture, data and state management, the deployment model, and, of course, security implications. This chapter will explain the impact of these factors on your application logic and help you choose an appropriate approach for implementing it. Design patterns will, of course, play an important part in solving the challenges that arise when designing the application logic.

Exam objectives in this chapter:
- Choose an appropriate implementation approach for the application design logic.
  - ❏ Choose an appropriate data storage mechanism.
  - ❏ Choose an appropriate data flow structure.
  - ❏ Choose an appropriate decision flow structure.
  - ❏ Choose an appropriate state management technique.
  - ❏ Choose an appropriate security implementation.

Lessons in this chapter:

Before You Begin

To complete the lessons in this chapter, you must have:

- A computer that meets or exceeds the minimum hardware requirements listed in the Introduction at the beginning of this book.
- Completed the labs from Chapter 2, "Creating Specifications for Developers," regarding the creation of documents such as the design diagram and class diagram.
- Read and completed the labs from Chapter 3, "Design Evaluation," regarding evaluation of the logical and physical design.
- Read and completed the labs from Chapter 4, "Component Design," and 5, "Component Development," regarding component design.
- Experience creating and viewing UML diagrams in Microsoft Office Visio 2003 or Visio 2007.
- A basic understanding of what design patterns are and how to apply one in code.

Real World

Mark Blomsma

Deciding how and where to implement application logic is not a trivial matter. I remember working on an application that was built using a 4GL tool. It involved a complex mortgage calculation for customers in multiple countries. The application ran great. Everyone was happy. Then the Internet happened, and the application needed not only to be used by the people in the company but also by customers who needed to log on and request an online quote. The application had to be adjusted to facilitate this extra interface, and although we managed to get things running, the amount of effort was tremendous compared to the problem at hand.

Enterprise applications have one thing in common: they are subject to change. Applications must be designed to allow the addition of new uses and the reuse of the most complex parts of your business logic. In the past, technology boundaries were a big part of the problem, but many standards are available today to enable reuse of your logic. Make your motto "Design for reuse!"

Lesson 1: Implementation Approach Philosophies

Choosing an implementation approach drives how your team will work to implement the logic. There are numerous approaches to take. This lesson will consider two approaches that most developers regard as opposites of the spectrum—waterfall and agile development—and a third, referred to as incremental development.

After this lesson, you will be able to:

■ Consider and evaluate implementation approach philosophies.

Estimated lesson time: 15 minutes

Waterfall Approach

The waterfall approach to implementing an application requires that a designer confer with one or more representatives of the end user organization and write down all the specifications of the application. Usually, the specifications come in a set of functional documents or use cases, written so that the end user can easily read and understand the documents. The end user signs off on these documents, and the documents are then picked up by the technical design team that designs the application, creating a number of artifacts such as class model diagrams, state diagrams, activity diagrams, and data models. The aim of this phase is to write everything down in such detail that a developer will have no problem creating the necessary code. There is a formal handover of the design to both the development team and the test team. After handover, the development team starts coding, and the test team uses the technical design in combination with the use cases to create test cases and test scenarios. Once the development team is finished coding, the code is delivered to the test team. The test team performs the tests they designed based on requirements and detailed design. Any problems will be fixed by the development team. Once the process of testing and fixing is completed, the application is given to the end user for an acceptance test. The end user performs a final check to see whether the application conforms to the initial requirements. If approved, he or she signs off on the finished product, and the project is done.

A project can have more or fewer phases when using the waterfall approach, but the main characteristic is a very formal start and end of every phase, with very formal deliverables.

The advantage of the waterfall approach is that accountability of the team responsible for each phase is higher. It is clear what they need to deliver, when they need to deliver, and to whom they must deliver. Often, the development team will not need to interact with the user. This can be very useful when outsourcing development to a different country.

The main disadvantage to the waterfall approach is that in an environment in which everything is organized in a quite formal manner, flexibility in responding to change is decreased. Even change needs to be organized. Very few companies seem to do this effectively, often resulting in a significant increase in overhead cost. To manage the costs of a project, some companies even go as far as to delay any change in requirements until after initial delivery of the application, effectively delivering an application that does not match end user needs.

Agile Development

Many long-running software development projects have run over their budgets and do not deliver the product on time. The premise of the agile software development philosophy is to minimize risk by developing software in short time boxes, called iterations, which typically last one to four weeks. Each iteration is like a miniature software project of its own and includes all of the tasks necessary to release the increment of new functionality: planning, requirements analysis, design, coding, testing, and documentation. Although an iteration might not add enough functionality to warrant releasing the product, an agile software project intends to be capable of releasing new software at the end of every iteration. At the end of each iteration, the team re-evaluates project priorities.

MORE INFO **Recommended reading**

A number of industry leaders have come together and created the Agile Manifesto. (See *http://www.agilemanifesto.org.*)

The goal of agile software development is to achieve customer satisfaction by rapid, continuous delivery of useful software; always aiming to build what the customer needs; welcome, rather than oppose, late changes in requirements; regularly adapt to changing circumstances; have close, daily cooperation between business people and developers, in which face-to-face conversation is the best form of communication.

The main advantage of agile software development is flexibility in dealing with change, always aiming to deliver according to business needs. The drawback, of course, is an increase in complexity in managing scope, planning, and budget. Another common risk is limited attention to (technical) documentation.

Incremental Development

Incremental software development is a mix of agile and waterfall development. An application is designed, implemented, and tested incrementally so that each increment can be delivered to the end user. The project is not finished until the last increment is finished. It aims to shorten the waterfall by defining intermediate increments and by using some of the advantages of agile development. Based on feedback received on a previous increment, adjustments can be made when delivering the next increment. The next increment can then consist of new code as well as modifications of code delivered earlier.

The advantage is that the formalities remain in place, but change management becomes easier. The cost of testing and deploying an application a number of times will be higher than doing this just once.

Lesson Summary

- There are numerous approaches to developing software. Waterfall, agile, and incremental are the three most common forms.
- The waterfall is more formal and is most useful when user and developer cannot communicate on a daily basis. The agile approach is geared more toward delivering what is needed in a changing environment but requires close interaction between users and developers. The incremental approach helps manage change in a waterfall-style approach.

Lesson Review

You can use the following questions to test your knowledge of the information in Lesson 1, "Implementation Approach Philosophies." The questions are also available on the companion CD if you prefer to review them in electronic form.

NOTE Answers

Answers to these questions and explanations of why each answer choice is right or wrong are located in the "Answers" section at the end of the book.

---

1. Which of the following statements are correct? (Choose all that apply.)
   A. Agile development works best when outsourcing to another country.
   B. Waterfall development creates as much interaction as possible between developer and end user.
   C. Agile development welcomes changes in requirements.
   D. Waterfall development delivers predetermined products.
2. Because agile development welcomes change, it is always better than waterfall.
   A. True
   B. False

Lesson 2: Program Flow Control

Choosing an approach for program flow control is very much an architectural task. The aim is to create a blueprint of your application in which, once you start adding functionality and code, everything just seems to have its own place. If you've ever reviewed or written a high-quality piece of code, you understand this principle. Somehow, without knowing much about the application, by looking at a section of code, you can grasp what the blueprint looks like, and all the pieces of code just seem to come together.

After this lesson, you will be able to:
- Organize your application logic.
- Apply design patterns to organize your code.
- Design your application flow control.

Estimated lesson time: 25 minutes

Organizing Code

The first step in designing your program flow is to organize the code, laying down a set of rules to help create a blueprint, or outline, of the application. Maintenance, debugging, and fixing errors will go more smoothly because code is located in a logical place. After doing the ground-work, you can choose an approach for implementing your application logic.

Design patterns should play an important part in designing your program flow control. Over the years, a lot of code has been written and a lot of solutions have been designed for what turn out to be repeating problems. These solutions are laid down in design patterns. Applying a design pattern to a common software design issue will help you create solutions that are easily recognizable and can be implemented by your peers. Unique problems will still require unique solutions, but you can use design patterns to guide you in solving them.

MORE INFO   Design patterns

To learn more about design patterns, refer to *Patterns of Enterprise Application Architecture*, Martin Fowler (Addison-Wesley, 2002); and *Design Patterns*, Erich Gamma, Richard Helm, Ralph Johnson, and John Vlissides (Addison-Wesley, 1995).

Creating the Blueprint

Layers

The first step is to consider logical layers. Note that layers are not the same as tiers, often confused or even assumed to be the same.

NOTE **Layers versus tiers**

Layers concern creating boundaries in your code. The top layer might have references to code in lower layers, but a layer can never have a reference to code in a higher layer. Tiers concern physically distributing layers across multiple computers. For example, in a three-tier application, the user interface is designed to run on a desktop computer, the application logic is designed to run on an application server, and the database runs on a dedicated database server, and the code on each tier can consist of multiple layers.

Layering assigns responsibilities to specific areas of code. Figure 8-1 shows the three basic layers.

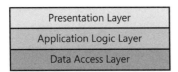

Figure 8-1 Basic three-layer organization

Layering refers to levels of abstraction. The layering shown in Figure 8-1 is true for most applications. These levels are also referred to as the three principal layers and might go by various other names. As a rule, code in the presentation layer might call on services in the application logic layer, but the application logic layer should not be calling method in the presentation layer. The presentation layer should never call on the data access layer directly because doing so would bypass the responsibilities implemented by the application logic layer. The data access layer should never call the application logic layer.

Each layer has its responsibilities, some of which might not be evident by the name, as shown in Table 8-1.

Table 8-1 **Layer Responsibilities**

Presentation	Display of information, collection of user input, command-line input, interfaces with external systems
Application logic	Processing data, managing transactions
Data access	Interaction with data store, messaging systems, remote system access

Layers are just an abstraction, and probably the easiest way to implement the layering is to create folders in your project and add code to the appropriate folder. A more useful approach would be to place each layer in a separate project, thus creating separate assemblies. The advantage of placing the application logic in a library assembly is that this will enable you to create unit tests, using Microsoft Visual Studio or NUnit, to test the logic. It also creates flexibility in choosing where to deploy each layer.

Physical Layers

In an enterprise application, you should expect to have multiple clients for the same logic. In fact, the very thing that makes an application an enterprise application is that it will be deployed to three tiers: client, application server, and database server. The Microsoft Office Access application created by the sales department in your enterprise, although very important to the sales department, does not constitute an enterprise application.

Note that the application logic and data access layers are usually deployed together to the application server. Part of drawing up the blueprint is choosing whether to access the application server by using .NET remoting or Web services. Regardless of choice, you will be adding some code to access easily the remote services in the presentation layer. If you're using Web services to access the services on your application server, Visual Studio .NET will do the work for you and generate proxy code, automatically providing an implementation of the *remote proxy pattern*.

Adding Patterns to Layers

The three basic layers provide a high-level overview. Let's add a couple of structural patterns to create a robust enterprise architecture. The result is shown in Figure 8-2.

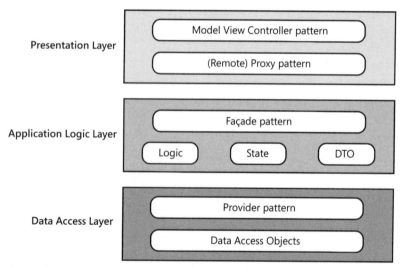

Figure 8-2   Patterns and layers combine to make a robust blueprint

Focus on the application logic layer. Figure 8-2 shows that access to the application logic is using the *façade pattern*. A façade is an object that provides a simplified interface to a larger body of code, such as a class library. A façade can reduce dependencies of outside code on the inner workings of a library because most code uses the façade, thus allowing more flexibility in developing the system. To do so, the façade will provide a coarse-grained interface to a collection of fine-grained objects.

Quick Check

■ Is a three-layer application the same as a three-tier application?

Quick Check Answer

■ No, tiers relate to physical distribution of the application. Layers indicate logical separation of code, assigning responsibility per layer.

Decision Flow

Program flow control, also referred to as decision flow, concerns how you design the services on your application logic layer or, as you've seen in the previous paragraph, how you design the methods on your façade.

There are two approaches to organizing your services:

■ Action-driven
■ State-driven

Action-Driven Approach

When organizing services based on the actions of the user, you will be implementing application logic by offering services, each of which handles a specific request from the presentation layer. This is also known as the transaction script pattern. This approach is popular because it is simple and feels very natural. Examples of methods that follow this approach are *BookStoreService.AddNewOrder(Order order)* and *BookStoreService.CancelOrder(int orderId)*.

The logic needed to perform the action is implemented quite sequentially within the method, making it very readable but also harder to reuse the code. Using additional design patterns such as the table module pattern can help increase reusability.

State-Driven Approach

It is also possible to implement the decision flow of the application in a much more state-driven fashion. The services offered by the application server are more generic in nature, for example, *BookStoreService.SaveOrder(Order order)*. This method will look at the state of the order and decide whether to add a new order or cancel an existing order.

Lab: Designing Application Flow Control

This lab will walk you through the steps of designing the application logic for a specific Web application.

▶ **Exercise: Layering and Application Flow**

Imagine you're working for a company selling books. The company is quite big and has multiple stores. The CEO wants to replace the old mainframe inventory tool with an integrated solution, scanning books as part of inventory management, having an application in the warehouse, a custom cash register application connected to the inventory database, and, of course, a Web application for selling books to Internet users.

1.   Think of the application architecture. Draw a picture of the solution you're creating. Layer the application and think of reuse.

2.   Think of the interfaces you'll want to offer on the application logic layer, which interfaces should be made available to just one application, and which interfaces will be shared across multiple clients. You want to keep it simple by choosing an action-driven interface.

3.   You group your services into four areas: online, register, inventory, and mobile services. You expect each application to make use of the inventory services, but each application will also require a number of unique services due to the nature of the application or device it runs on. The result is shown in Figure 8-3.

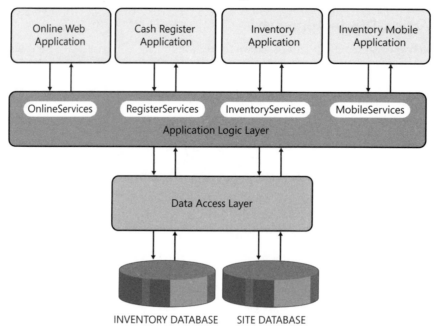

Figure 8-3   Overview of layering, data flow, and data stores

Lesson Summary

- Application flow can be either action driven or state driven.
- Action-driven interfaces lead to more sequential flow implementation of logic. State-driven interfaces are more generic: the application logic determines the flow through the application logic, based on the state of the data.

Lesson Review

You can use the following questions to test your knowledge of the information in Lesson 2, "Program Flow Control." The questions are also available on the companion CD if you prefer to review them in electronic form.

NOTE Answers

Answers to these questions and explanations of why each answer choice is right or wrong are located in the "Answers" section at the end of the book.

1. When implementing application logic using a façade, you can choose to make the interface of your façade action driven or state driven.

    A. True

    B. False

2. You've designed a method that has a signature that looks like *void Save(Order order)* in C# or *sub Save(order as Order)* in Microsoft Visual Basic on the façade of your application logic. In which fashion is this statement designed?

    A. This method is designed in a state-driven fashion.

    B. This method is designed in an action-driven fashion.

Lesson 3: Data Structure Designs

You must make a number of choices while designing your data structures. The first choice is the data storage mechanism, the second is the intended use of the data, and the third is the versioning requirements. There are three ways of looking at data structure designs:

■ Services offer data; data is a reflection of the relational database.

■ Data should be mapped to objects, and services offer access to objects.

■ Data offered by services should be schema based.

Choosing one of the three as the basis for your data flow structure should be done in an early stage of the design process. A lot of companies have a company guideline that forces one of the three choices on all projects, but when possible, you should re-evaluate the options for each project, choosing the optimal approach for the project at hand.

After this lesson, you will be able to:

■ Choose a data storage mechanism.

■ Choose an appropriate data flow structure.

Estimated lesson time: 15 minutes

Choosing a Data Storage Mechanism

When designing your application, you will undoubtedly have to design some sort of data store. The following stores and forms of data storage are available:

■ Registry

■ app.config file

■ XML files

■ Plaintext files

■ Database

■ Message Queuing

Each store has its own unique characteristics and might be suitable to specific requirements.

Registry

Your application should avoid writing data to the registry. In most environments, access to the registry is restricted to administrator accounts and, unless the security settings on your computer have been altered for the worse, you'll get a security exception when trying to do so.

An application can, however, read from the registry. This is useful in that your application might want to store some very sensitive information such as a decryption key. The key can be written to the registry when installing the application. Installing the application would require administrator access to the computer, but running the application requires no special privileges.

The Microsoft .NET Framework 2.0 offers the possibility of encrypting the content of your web.config file, making it extremely rare for you to need to write anything in the registry, but the option is available.

NOTE Reading from the registry

The registry is an invisible place to store a setting. Implementing a fallback when reading from the registry is a good idea. If the setting is not present in the registry, then attempt to read the setting from the web.config file. This is particularly useful when developing in a team in which a configuration file can be easily retrieved from source control, but a registry setting cannot be.

App.config File

The app.config file is a simple text file containing easily understandable XML. It can contain application-wide data such as database connection strings, custom error messages, and culture settings. Being an XML file, the app.config file can consist of any valid XML tags, but the root element should always be *<configuration>*. Nested within this tag, you can include various other tags to describe your settings. To add a configuration file to a Microsoft Windows application in Visual Studio 2005, right-click the project in the Solution Explorer, choose Add New Item, and choose Application Configuration File; the filename needs to be app.config. A file will be added to your Web site containing the following XML.

```
<?xml version="1.0" encoding="utf-8" ?>
<configuration>
</configuration>
```

You can add settings by adding an *appSettings* node or by defining a new configuration section and placing settings in the newly created section. The following sample shows that you've added an entry that can be retrieved by the key *FileLocation*.

```
<?xml version="1.0" encoding="utf-8" ?>
<configuration>
  <appSettings>
    <add key="FileLocation" value="C:\"/>
  </appSettings>
</configuration>
```

The application configuration file is not the right place for writing user-specific settings. If you wish to store some user-specific information, Visual Studio 2005 has a new option called Settings.

▶ **Add a user setting**

1. Open Visual Studio 2005.

2. Start a new Windows application project.

3. Expand the Properties node in the project explorer.

4. Double-click Settings.

5. Add an entry named MyColor.

6. Make it a user setting and assign it the value Red.

   Figure 8-4 shows the screen that you should now see.

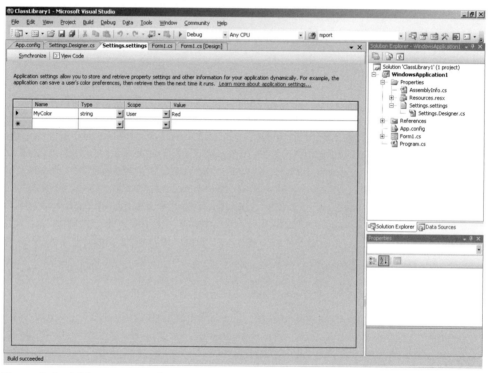

Figure 8-4 Adding a user setting

You have just added a new entry to the settings in the app.config file, but you've used a convenient user interface to do so. If you open the app.config file again, you'll see it now looks like the following.

```xml
<?xml version="1.0" encoding="utf-8" ?>
<configuration>
  <configSections>
    <sectionGroup name="userSettings"
type="System.Configuration.UserSettingsGroup, System, Version=2.0.0.0,
Culture=neutral, PublicKeyToken=b77a5c561934e089" >
```

```
        <section name="WindowsApplication1.Properties.Settings"
type="System.Configuration.ClientSettingsSection, System, Version=2.0.0.0,
Culture=neutral, PublicKeyToken=b77a5c561934e089"
allowExeDefinition="MachineToLocalUser" requirePermission="false" />
      </sectionGroup>
    </configSections>
    <appSettings>
      <add key="FileLocation" value="C:\"/>
    </appSettings>
    <userSettings>
      <WindowsApplication1.Properties.Settings>
        <setting name="MyColor" serializeAs="String">
          <value>Red</value>
        </setting>
      </WindowsApplication1.Properties.Settings>
    </userSettings>
</configuration>
```

You can now add code to your application to write a changed value to the user setting. The settings created using the Settings dialog box are available in code by using the *Properties .Settings.Default* class in C# or the *My* object in Visual Basic.

```
'VB
My.Settings.MyColor = "Blue"
```

```
// C#
Properties.Settings.Default.MyColor = "Blue";
Properties.Settings.Default.Save();
```

When the changed value is saved, the .NET Framework will automatically create a file in the folder *Documents and Settings\<user>\Local Setting\Application Data\<CompanyName>\<app-Name + version>* or equivalent folder, based on the version and language of Windows that you have installed. Note that in Visual Basic, the change is automatically written to the user settings, whereas in C#, an explicit call to *Save* is required.

Retrieving values from the user settings is done by using the same accessors that were used to write the value, as shown in the next code sample.

```
'VB
Dim color as String = My.Settings.MyColor
```

```
//C#
String color = Properties.Settings.Default.MyColor;
```

Note that these same settings can be used to add and modify application settings at design time if the user has sufficient privileges. Application settings cannot be modified at run time.

XML Files

Your application can choose to store data in XML files. You'll have to create a folder structure on your application server to do so. If you are using Web services as the entry point of your application server, be aware that any file in the *Data* folder of your Web application will be protected from browsing. Any data files you place there will be safe. Reading and writing to this directory is possible. The limitations are those of the file systems, in terms of the number of files per directory and, of course, locking issues. If you have one file with all customers, then only one person can lock the file at a time.

XML files are good for storing data that is changed only by a small number of users. If they are very frequently retrieved, you will want to write some code to cache the files.

Plaintext Files

Instead of using XML files for storage, you can, of course, do exactly the same with plaintext files. Instead of using XML to structure your data, you can choose to use a comma-separated file or even fixed ASCII files. XML is a more popular format because the .NET Framework Class Library has rich support for XML files and XML manipulation (located in *System.Xml*).

Database

A database is the data store of choice when you need to either store large amounts of data or service a large number of users.

When choosing a database as the data store for your application, you'll also need to consider availability. If you have multiple applications connecting to the same database, your application might be unavailable whenever database maintenance is done for any of the applications. You can choose to implement a dedicated database, which contains enough data to keep your application running, even when the main database is unavailable. Security considerations might be another reason for not wanting to let every application write data to the same main database. This is especially true if any of the applications is a Web application.

The vast majority of enterprise applications use a relational database as the main store of data.

Message Queuing

Microsoft Message Queue (MSMQ) is a unique data store in that messages are posted to a queue and stored in the queue only until they are processed by a different process. Message queuing can be used to increase the availability of your application. Your application can post messages into the queue, requesting updates to your enterprise database while the database itself might be down for maintenance.

Designing the Data Flow

Considering that the vast majority of enterprise applications use a relational database as the main store of data, you now need to look at how to design the data flow through your application. Remember the three basic considerations when looking at the services that your application will offer to the presentation layer:

- Services offer data; data is a reflection of the relational database.
- Data should be mapped to objects, and services offer access to objects.
- Data offered by services should be schema based.

Data Flow Using ADO.NET

When implementing data-centric services in the application logic layer, you'll design your data flow by using ADO.NET. The .NET Framework Class Library offers an extensive application programming interface (API) for handling data in managed code. Referred to as ADO.NET, the API can be found in the *System.Data* namespace. The complete separation of data carriers and data stores is an important design feature of ADO.NET. Classes such as the *DataSet, DataTable,* and *DataRow* are designed to hold data but retain no knowledge of where the data came from. They are considered data-source agnostic. A separate set of classes such as *SqlConnection, SqlDataAdapter,* and *SqlCommand* take care of connecting to a data source, retrieving data, and populating the *DataSet, DataTable,* and *DataRow.* These classes are located in sub-namespaces such as *System.Data.Sql, System.Data.OleDB, System.Data.Oracle,* and so on. Depending on what data source you wish to connect to, you can use the classes in the correct namespace and, depending on the completeness of the product you're using, you'll find that these classes offer more or less functionality.

Because the *DataSet* is not connected to the data source, it can be quite successfully used for managing the data flow in an application. Figure 8-5 shows the flow of data when doing so.

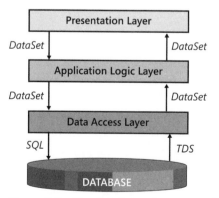

Figure 8-5   The *DataSet* as the center of your data flow

Let's do a walkthrough of this design and imagine that someone has logged on to your bookstore and has ordered three books. The presentation layer has managed the state of the shopping cart. The customer is ready to order and has provided all necessary data. He chooses *submit order*. The Web page transforms all data into a *DataSet* holding two *DataTables*, one for the order and one for orderliness; inserts one *DataRow* for the order; and inserts three *DataRows* for the order lines. The Web page then displays this data back to the user one more time, data binding controls against the *DataSet*, and asks Are you sure? The user confirms the order, and it is submitted to the application logic layer. The application logic layer checks *DataSet* to see that all mandatory fields have a value and performs a check to see whether the user has more than $1,000.00 in outstanding bills. If all is okay, the *DataSet* is passed on to the data access layer, which connects to the database and generates *insert* statements from the information in the *DataSet*.

Using the *DataSet* in this manner is a fast and efficient way of building an application and using the power of the Framework Class Library and the ability of ASP.NET to data bind various controls such as the *GridView* against a *DataSet*. Instead of using plain *DataSet* objects, you can use *Typed DataSet* objects and improve the coding experience when implementing code in both the presentation layer as well as in the application logic layer. The advantage of this approach is also the disadvantage of the approach. Small changes in the data model do not necessarily lead to a lot of methods having to change their signatures. So in terms of maintenance, this works quite well. If you remember the presentation layer is not necessarily a user interface, it can just as well be a Web service. And if you modify the definition of the *DataSet*, perhaps because you're renaming a field in the database, then you're modifying the contract that underwrites the Web service. As you can imagine, this can lead to some significant problems. This scenario works well if the presentation layer is just a user interface, but for interfaces to external systems or components, you will want to hide the inner workings of your application and transform data into something other than a direct clone of your data model, and you will want to create Data Transfer Objects (DTOs). More information about DTOs appears in the next scenario.

NOTE   *DataSets* versus *DataTables* versus *DataRows*

The scenario describes the *DataSet* as the data carrier. If the application you're writing requires inserts or updates to only one table, you can substitute the *DataSet* for the *DataTable*. Similarly, if the presentation layer is interested in only one row of data, you might use a *DataRow* as a data carrier.

NOTE   Table module pattern

The *table module* pattern is a good way to organize code when using *DataSet* objects as the choice for implementing data flow. When using the table module pattern, you implement one class per table to handle all application logic for all rows in a table. These classes can interact with each other to implement complex logic.

Data Flow Using Object Relational Mapping

Data flow using ADO.NET is a very data-centric approach to managing the data flow. Data and logic are discrete. The other side of the spectrum is to take a more object-oriented approach. Here, classes are created to bundle data and behavior. The aim is to define classes that mimic data and behavior found in the business domain that the application is created for. The result is often referred to as a business object. The collection of business objects that make up the application is called the *domain model*. Some developers claim that a rich domain model is better for designing more-complex logic. It's hard to prove or disprove any such claim. Just know that you have a choice, and it is up to you to make it.

Figure 8-6 shows a data flow similar to Figure 8-5 except that now you've added the object relational mapping layer and substituted the *DataSet* objects for different data carriers.

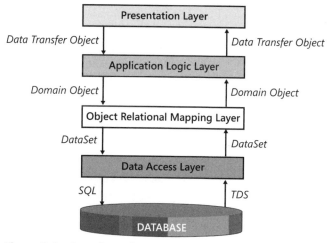

Figure 8-6 Data flow when using object relational mapping

Now do the same walkthrough as you did before; imagine that someone has logged on to your bookstore and has ordered three books. The presentation layer has managed the state of the shopping cart. The customer is ready to order and has provided all necessary data. He chooses *submit order*. The Web page transforms all data into a DTO, holding data for one order and with three order lines, creating the objects as needed. The Web page then displays this data back to the user one more time, data binding controls against the DTO using the ObjectData-Source in ASP.NET 2.0, and asks Are you sure? The user confirms the choice, and the DTO is submitted to the application logic layer. The application logic layer transforms the DTO into a business object of type *Order* having a property for holding three *OrderLine* objects. The method *Order.Validate()* is called to validate the order and check that all mandatory fields have a value, and a check is performed to identify whether the user has more than $1,000.00 in outstanding bills. To do this, the order will call *Order.Customer.GetOutstandingBills()*. If all is well, the *Order.Save()* method is called. The order will submit itself to the object relational mapping layer, where the order and order lines are mapped to a *DataTable* in a *DataSet*, and the *DataSet* is passed to the data access layer, which connects to the database and generates *insert* statements from the information in the *DataSet*. There are, of course, many ways in which object relational mapping can take place, but not all will include transformation to a *DataSet*. Some will create the *insert* statements directly but still use the data access layer to execute that statement.

As you can see, quite a few transformations take place. The use of DTOs is needed because a business object implements behavior, and behavior is subject to change. To minimize the impact of these changes on the presentation layer, you need to transform the data, take it out of the business object and put it in a data transfer object. In Java, the data transfer object is normally referred to as a *value object*.

A big advantage of working with business objects is that it really helps organize your code. If you look back at a piece of complex logic, it is usually very readable because there is very little plumbing code. The disadvantage is that the majority of data stores are still relational, and the mapping of business objects to relational data can become quite complex.

Schema-Based Services

You have just seen two opposites when it comes to managing the data flow. Many variations are possible. A common one is the variant in which a dataset is used as the basic data carrier from user interface to data store, but separate schemas (DTOs) are used for Web services that are called from other systems. The application layer transforms the relational data to a predefined schema. The main advantage of this is that any application that references the service is not depending on any kind of internal implementation of the component. This allows more flexibility in versioning, backward compatibility of interfaces, and the ability to change the implementation of the component while not changing the interface of the service.

Of course, you can use business objects in the Web application and skip the DTO transformation, but this usually works well only if the application logic is deployed together with the Web application. Remember that to call *Order.Save()*, you'll need a database connection. Whether this is desirable is up to you as well as, probably, to your chief security officer.

MORE INFO   **Web service contract first**

WSCF is a popular approach to designing the application layer service interface. The approach focuses on designing the interface first, creating schemas for all methods, before moving on to implementation of these services. You'll find more information on this topic at *http://www.thinktecture.com/WSCF*.

Exam Tip   Data-centric, object relation mapping, and schema-based design should all be familiar approaches when designing the application logic layer.

Lesson Summary

- Deciding on a data store mechanism is the first step in organizing the application logic. One or more multiple stores might be needed, depending on security and availability considerations. Some data can be stored in read-only stores such as the registry or the app.config file.
- Services can be data-centric, object oriented, or schema based.
- The .NET Framework offers a rich API when using *Typed DataSets* to manage data flow.
- Object orientation allows for great flexibility in creating complex code but requires quite some effort to map your business objects to a relational database.
- Schema-based services offer the most flexibility in versioning, backward compatibility of interfaces and the ability to change the implementation of the component while not changing the interface of the service. The cost is a transformation from either a typed dataset or a business object to a service-specific data schema.

Lesson Review

You can use the following questions to test your knowledge of the information in Lesson 3, "Data Structure Designs." The questions are also available on the companion CD if you prefer to review them in electronic form.

NOTE   Answers

Answers to these questions and explanations of why each answer choice is right or wrong are located in the "Answers" section at the end of the book.

---

1. Which of the following data stores are appropriate for maintaining data that is accessed by many users, but updating specific bits of data is done by only a few users? (Choose all that apply.)

    A. Registry

    B. app.config file

    C. XML files

    D. Database

2. You've designed a method that has a signature that looks like *void Save(DataSet order)* in C# or *sub Save(order as DataSet)* in Visual Basic on the façade of your application logic. In which fashion is this method designed?

   A. This method is designed in a data-centric fashion.

   B. This method is designed in an object-oriented fashion.

3. You've designed a method that has a signature that looks like *void Save(RequestSaveOrder order)* in C# or *sub Save(order as RequestSaveOrder)* in Visual Basic on the façade of your application logic. In which fashion is this method designed?

   A. This method is designed in a schema-based fashion.

   B. This method is designed in a data-centric fashion.

Lesson 4: State Management Design

A choice needs to be made about the statefulness of the application logic layer. Options are simple: the layer as a whole is either stateless or stateful. This design choice will be very significant if the application logic layer is deployed to a dedicated application server. The main difference is that a stateful server remembers client data (state) from one request to the next. A stateless server keeps no state information between requests.

> **After this lesson, you will be able to:**
> - Choose an appropriate state management technique.
>
> **Estimated lesson time: 15 minutes**

The application logic layer in a Web application needs to be stateless. Advantages of a stateless application server are that the server is much more robust and much more scalable. When an application server is stateless, it needs to have no prior knowledge of a client when handling a request. Thus it becomes possible to scale out by adding more servers and load balancing requests across multiple servers. When the application server is stateful, then after the initial request, you need to ensure that each request from the same client is directed to the same application server. Another drawback is that the application server is using resources after the client is already gone.

Stateful

A stateful service maintains state across service calls. Let's look at an example. The code shows that a reference to an instance of the service is created, passing the customer ID, 5, as a parameter and, next, it retrieves the name of the customer, not passing any parameter, assuming the service remembers which customer you're referring to. Next, you retrieve the customer address in a similar manner. The service still remembers which customer you're referring to.

```vb
'VB
Private Sub button1_Click(ByVal sender As Object, ByVal e As EventArgs)
    Dim customerId As Integer = 5
    Dim service As MyCustomerService =  New MyCustomerService(customerId)
    Dim name As String =  service.GetName()
    Dim address As String =  service.GetAddress()
End Sub
```

```csharp
//C#
private void button1_Click(object sender, EventArgs e)
{
    int customerId = 5;
    MyCustomerService service = new MyCustomerService(customerId);
    string name = service.GetName();
    string address = service.GetAddress();
}
```

So what happened on the server side? When the service was created, the ID of the customer was used to retrieve the customer from the database. The data was stored as state somewhere in memory, waiting for the next service call. The next call, to get the customer name, comes in, and the service uses that customer in memory to return the name. The same happens when the call for the customer address comes in.

Implementing a service this way results in a lot of network calls and, therefore, the interface of a stateful service is often referred to as a "chatty" interface.

Stateless

A stateless service does not maintain any kind of state across service calls. Again, let's look at an example. The code shows that a reference to an instance of the service is created. No parameter is passed. Next, the name of a customer is retrieved; now the ID of the customer is passed, informing the service of which customer name you actually want. Next, you retrieve the customer address, once again passing the ID of the customer.

```
'VB
Private  Sub button1_Click(ByVal sender As Object, ByVal e As EventArgs)
    Dim customerId As Integer =  5
    Dim service As MyCustomerService =  New MyCustomerService()
    Dim name As String =  service.GetName(customerId)
    Dim address As String =  service.GetAddress(customerId)
End Sub
```

```
//C#
private void button1_Click(object sender, EventArgs e)
{
    int customerId = 5;
    MyCustomerService service = new MyCustomerService();
    string name = service.GetName(customerId);
    string address = service.GetAddress(customerId);
}
```

So what happened on the server side? If implemented using Web services, the only thing that happened was the creation of a local proxy of the service; on the application server, nothing happened yet. Then the first call came in, the service was instantiated, the customer was retrieved from the database, and the name was returned. Next, the client asks for the customer address. On the application server, a new instance of the service is created, the customer is retrieved from the database, and the address of the customer is returned to the client.

Clearly, the scenario is not optimal, and this is important to remember. When implementing a stateless service, the methods on the service should be chunky. That is to say, they should return a chunk of data rather than small snippets.

Web Services

Web services are stateless by default. Using session state on the Web server, it is possible to create a stateful service. This is, however, considered bad design for a number of reasons. Session state increases load on the server even after the server has processed the Web service request, the session and associated memory needs to be maintained Using sessions state complicates scalability when you wish to add a server to handle the requests; a client will need to come back to the same server time and again because this is where the session for that client is managed.

.NET Remoting

.NET remoting allows for three types of objects to be created:

- **Single call**   Single call objects are always stateless.
- **Singleton**   Singleton objects are stateful, and state is shared across all clients.
- **Client-activated**   Client-activated objects are stateful and maintain state until their lease expires or until the client loses its reference to the object. The state is maintained per client.

Quick Check

- What are the choices for implementing state management in the application logic layer?

Quick Check Answer

- The application logic layer is either stateful or stateless.

Lesson Summary

- A server can be stateless or stateful. Web services are stateless by default. The .NET remoting service can be either stateful or stateless.
- Stateless services have chunky parameters and chunky results. Stateful services result in a chattier interface.

Lesson Review

You can use the following questions to test your knowledge of the information in Lesson 4, "State Management Design." The questions are also available on the companion CD if you prefer to review them in electronic form.

NOTE Answers

Answers to these questions and explanations of why each answer choice is right or wrong are located in the "Answers" section at the end of the book.

1. A Web service can never be stateful.

    A. True

    B. False

2. A .NET remoting call configured as performing a SingleCall on a remote object is stateful.

    A. True

    B. False

Lesson 5: Components versus Services

Yet another design choice to make is to choose either components or services. Before going any further, let's define a component and a service.

A software component is a system element offering a predefined service and is able to communicate with other components. A component should encapsulate its inner workings, be reusable, non-context-specific, and a unit of independent deployment and versioning.

Services are the core of the service-oriented architecture (SOA) that defines the use of loosely coupled services to implement the requirements of business processes and software users. A service interoperates based on a formal definition (or contract, most often Web Services Description Language [WSDL]), which is independent of the underlying platform and programming language. The interface definition hides the implementation of the language-specific service.

As you can see, both components and services have a lot of characteristics in common; they both aim to be reusable and offer some sort of interface that hides the inner workings. Services, however, aim to be loosely coupled and try to be platform independent.

After this lesson, you will be able to:
- ■ Choose between components and services as a design solution.

Estimated lesson time: 15 minutes

Loose Coupling

A service aims to offer functionality that is loosely coupled. There are two items that play a role in this. The first is choice of implementation technology, and the second is the design of the service interface.

Technology

A component can be reused by adding a reference to the assembly and accessing classes in the assembly. This introduces tight coupling. Your assembly is compiled against the assembly you've just referenced.

A client that needs to perform a .NET remoting call will need a reference to the interface it tries to call and a reference to all object types used in that interface.

A client that needs to call a Web service has no such dependency. The Web service can be reused by adding a *Webreference* to the Web service. When doing this, Visual Studio will parse the WSDL of the Web service and generate a client proxy that matches the Web service. All object types used in the interface are replicated into local objects. There is no dependency on the implementation of the service as long as the WSDL stays the same. The service can even be replaced by a completely different service as long as the WSDL does not change.

Design

The design of the interface needs to hide the inner workings of the service. In this there is no difference between a component and a service. Suppose you implement an interface with the method *StoreCustomerInSqlDatabase(CustomerRow customer)*. You can implement this as a method on your component or as a Web service. Either way, you're exposing much of the inner workings to the outside world. There are two mistakes. The first is that the name of the method does not just tell you what the method does; it also tries to communicate how it's done. Second, the parameter of the method is a *CustomerRow*, which is a typed dataset version of your customer and matches the data model of your database. If you make any change in your data model, this will change your customer *CustomerRow*, effectively changing your WSDL and requiring change by the applications using your service.

Trying to implement the same method in a schema-oriented manner, the same method would read *SaveCustomer(RequestSaveCustomer request)*. The interface states what will be done, not how it will be done, and the parameter is a specific object holding just the data needed for the request.

Think about loose coupling when designing your application. If reuse is not a requirement, then loose coupling is usually less important also. Consider maintenance, possibilities of versioning, and backward compatibility when designing your service.

Performance

A component can offer functionality as a service without a performance penalty. Using either .NET remoting or Web services to make a service call incurs a performance penalty. This said, implementing the application logic layer as a separate tier, as an application server, allows your application logic to sit closer to the database and to make use of connection pooling when connecting to the database. Processes that are data intensive will profit from being close to the database. Environments with a large number of users will profit from a stateless application service that uses connection pooling.

Platform Independence

Services aim to be platform independent. Services implemented by using .NET remoting are not platform independent. Services implemented by using Web services are. If your application logic is required to offer services across multiple platforms, Web services will be your best choice. At the core of Web services are Simple Object Access Protocol (SOAP) and WSDL, which are industry standards supported by vendors on all platforms.

Exam Tip   The benefits of Web services as opposed to .NET remoting should be clear.

Lesson Summary

- Components offer reuse of application logic but are neither loosely coupled nor platform independent.
- Web services offer reuse of application logic, are loosely coupled, and are platform independent.
- .NET remoting services offer reuse of application logic, are not loosely coupled, and are not platform independent.
- Bad interface design can undo the loose coupling that Web services offers.

Lesson Review

You can use the following questions to test your knowledge of the information in Lesson 5, "Components versus Services." The questions are also available on the companion CD if you prefer to review them in electronic form.

NOTE Answers

Answers to these questions and explanations of why each answer choice is right or wrong are located in the "Answers" section at the end of the book.

1. A component always performs better than a service.
   A. True
   B. False

2. You want to reuse some code that updates the address of a customer. The code will be called by your Customer Service application written in C#, but customers can also log on to your Web site and update their own information. The Web site is written using Java Server Pages. You implement your logic as a:
   A. Component
   B. .NET remoting service
   C. Web service

Lesson 6: Security Implementation

Security concerns authentication and authorization. When implementing your application logic, you'll need to decide whether to implement you authorization just in the presentation layer or also in the application logic layer. This lesson will help you make that choice.

After this lesson, you will be able to:
- ■ Choose an appropriate security implementation.

Estimated lesson time: 15 minutes

Authentication

Authentication is the process of attempting to verify the digital identity of the sender of a request. This section will refer to the sender as the user, but keep in mind that the user, or sender, can be a person using a computer, a computer itself, or a computer program. Your code is running in the application logic layer and will always be accessed by the presentation layer. Thus, you have no direct contact with the original sender of a request. Authentication will have to be implemented in the presentation layer, and the identity of the sender will have to be communicated to the logic layer. The logic layer will have to trust the presentation layer to perform well.

There are several ways of communicating the identity of the original sender:

- ■ When using Web services, use Windows Integrated Security on Internet Information Server to allow only domain users to access the Web services.
- ■ When using .NET remoting, add information about a user to a remoting call by using a custom *ClientChannelSink*.
- ■ Pass the identity of the user as a parameter of the service call.
- ■ Use Web Service Security Enhancements to add identity information to the SOAP request.

Authorization

Authorization refers to allowing methods to be accessed only by those users who have been granted access to them. The default mechanism in .NET is that of role base security. It is based on placing a *principal* on the thread running the current request. The principal contains both the *identity* and a list of roles that have been assigned to the user. A user might, for instance, be assigned the role of both Guest and Author, allowing that user to access functionality designed for both those roles.

For authenticating a user, the application server needs to rely on the presentation layer; authorization, however, is required to make a choice. Does the presentation layer implement authorization to allow the user access to only authorized screens, reports, batches, and services? If so, do you trust the presentation layer enough not to wish to repeat an authorization check in the application layer? Ideally, the application logic layer should minimize its dependencies on the outside world and not rely on the user interface to do the right thing. All authorization checks should be redone at the application server. The façade of the application layer is a great place to check authorization by using attributes. The following code shows an example of using the *PrincipalPermissionAttribute* to specify that only users with the role *RegisteredUsers* are allowed to submit an order.

```vb
'VB
Imports System.Security.Permissions

Namespace MSLearning.TK547.Chapter11.Samples
    '/ <summary>
    '/ BookStoreFacade offers coarse grained access
    '/ to the application domain.
    '/ </summary>
    Public Class BookStoreFacade
        '/ <summary>
        '/ Submit an order for processing.
        '/ </summary>
        '/ <param name="order">The order to be processed.</param>
        <PrincipalPermission(SecurityAction.Demand,
                             Role="RegisteredUser")> _
        Public  Sub SubmitOrder(ByVal order As Order)
        End Sub
    End Class
End Namespace
```

```csharp
//C#
using System;
using System.Security.Permissions;

namespace MSLearning.TK547.Chapter11.Samples
{
    /// <summary>
    /// BookStoreFacade offers coarse grained access
    /// to the application domain.
    /// </summary>
    public class BookStoreFacade
    {
        /// <summary>
        /// Submit an order for processing.
        /// </summary>
        /// <param name="order">The order to be processed.</param>
[PrincipalPermission(SecurityAction.Demand,
                             Role="RegisteredUser")]
        public void SubmitOrder(Order order)
        {
        }
    }
}
```

Implementing security as shown in the preceding code is extremely secure. The common language runtime (CLR) will check the roles of the user before executing *SubmitOrder* and will throw a security exception if the user is not authorized. So you're checking authorization as soon as possible. Throwing an exception is a way to abort the regular flow of a program.

Data-driven authorization is a special scenario. Let's say you have a business rule that only users with role *Employee* are allowed to submit orders of more than $1,000. You'll need to write some application logic to check this. Where could you implement this? You could start adding code to your façade method but, just like layers in the overall architecture, each class in your application logic should have responsibilities. So what are the responsibilities of the façade? Try assigning two responsibilities to the façade, namely, security checks and error logging. Everything else is handled by a secondary class, in this case, the *OrderManager*. The following code shows the result.

```vb
'VB
Imports System.Security.Permissions
Imports System.Threading
Imports System.Security

Namespace MSLearning.TK547.Chapter11.Samples
    '/ <summary>
    '/ BookStoreService is the facade to the
    '/ BookStoreComponent
    '/ </summary>
    Public Class BookStoreService
        '/ <summary>
        '/ Submit an order for processing.
        '/ </summary>
        '/ <param name="order">The order to be processed.</param>
        <PrincipalPermission(SecurityAction.Demand, Role = "Employee")> _
        <PrincipalPermission(SecurityAction.Demand, Role = "RegisteredUser")> _
        Public  Sub SubmitOrder(ByVal order As Order)
            Try
                If order.TotalExcludingTax > 1000 And _
    Thread.CurrentPrincipal.IsInRole("Employee") = False
  Then
                    Throw New SecurityException(
                            "Insufficient privileges to submit
                            an order over $1000.00.")
                End If

                ' delegate processing to order manager
                Dim mgr As OrderManager =  New OrderManager()
                mgr.ProcessOrder(order)
            Catch exception As SecurityException
                ' no need to log security exceptions
                throw
            Catch exception As Exception
                ' log error
            End Try
        End Sub
    End Class
```

```
End Namespace

//C#
using System;
using System.Security.Permissions;
using System.Threading;
using System.Security;

namespace MSLearning.TK547.Chapter11.Samples
{
    /// <summary>
    /// BookStoreService is the facade to the
    /// BookStoreComponent
    /// </summary>
    public class BookStoreService
    {
        /// <summary>
        /// Submit an order for processing.
        /// </summary>
        /// <param name="order">The order to be processed.</param>
        [PrincipalPermission(SecurityAction.Demand, Role = "Employee")]
        [PrincipalPermission(SecurityAction.Demand, Role = "RegisteredUser")]
        public void SubmitOrder(Order order)
        {
            try
            {
                if (order.TotalExcludingTax > 1000 &&
                    Thread.CurrentPrincipal.IsInRole("Employee") == false)
                {
                    throw new SecurityException(
                            "Insufficient privileges to submit
                            an order over $1000.00.");
                }

                // delegate processing to order manager
                OrderManager mgr = new OrderManager();
                mgr.ProcessOrder(order);
            }
            catch (SecurityException exception)
            {
                // no need to log security exceptions
                throw;
            }
            catch (Exception exception)
            {
                // log error
            }
        }
    }
}
```

Note that instead of handling the check for *Insufficient privileges to submit an order over $1000.00* as a security exception, you can also choose to implement this as a domain exception. More about domain exceptions and general exception handling will be discussed in Chapter 5, "Component Development."

NOTE   Web Service Enhancements

Web Services Enhancements (WSE) 3.0 is an add-on to Visual Studio 2005 and to the Microsoft .NET Framework 2.0. It provides advanced Web services capabilities, helping to keep pace with the evolving Web services protocol specifications. These add-ons provide valuable additional functionality when implementing security for Web services. For more information, visit *http://msdn.microsoft.com/webservices*.

Lesson Summary

- The presentation layer needs to implement authentication and communicate the identity of the user to the application logic layer or service.
- The presentation layer will implement authorization, but the application logic layer should also implement authorization.
- The *PrincipalPermissionAttribute* can be used to restrict access to methods to authorized users only.

Lesson Review

You can use the following questions to test your knowledge of the information in Lesson 6, "Security Implementation." The questions are also available on the companion CD if you prefer to review them in electronic form.

NOTE   Answers

Answers to these questions and explanations of why each answer choice is right or wrong are located in the "Answers" section at the end of the book.

---

1. Authentication is best implemented in the application logic layer.
    A. True
    B. False
2. You want to reuse some code that updates the address of a customer. The code will be called by your Customer Service application written in C#, but customers can also log on to your Web site and update their own info. The Web site is written using Java Server Pages. You implement your logic as a Web service. How do you pass the identity of the user?
    A. Implement a custom *ClientChannelSink*.
    B. Pass the identity of the user as a parameter of the service call.
    C. Use Web Service Security Enhancements.

Chapter Review

To further practice and reinforce the skills you learned in this chapter, you can perform the following tasks:

- Review the chapter summary.
- Review the list of key terms introduced in this chapter.
- Complete the case scenarios. These scenarios set up real-world situations involving the topics of this chapter and ask you to create a solution.
- Complete the suggested practices.
- Take a practice test.

Chapter Summary

- Many approaches to implementing applications exist, agile development, the waterfall approach, and incremental development being the most popular.
- Program flow in the application logic layer can be either state driven or action driven.
- Data structure design can be data-centric by using ADO.NET, object oriented by using Object Relational Mapping, or schema driven.
- Application logic is either stateless or stateful. Web services are, by default, stateless.
- Services are the next step up from components, offering what components offer and then some more. Loose coupling and platform independence are the most significant benefits of services.
- Security consists of authentication and authorization. Authentication leads to identification of the user and needs to be implemented in the presentation layer. Authorization needs to be implemented in both the presentation layer and the application logic layer.

Key Terms

Do you know what these key terms mean? You can check your answers by looking up the terms in the glossary at the end of the book.

- ADO.NET
- authentication
- authorization
- design pattern
- exception

Case Scenarios

In the following case scenarios, you will apply what you've learned about design logic implementation. You can find answers to these questions in the "Answers" section at the end of this book.

Case Scenario 1: Scaling Out

Interviews

Following is a list of company personnel interviewed and their statements.

- **IT Manager**   "We're building a Web application because the finance department wants to interview the employees electronically. They claim it is a one-time thing, but I want the basics of the application to be reusable because I've heard rumors that marketing wants something similar for interviewing visitors of our Web site."

- **Head of Finance Department**   "We need this intranet application in two weeks. Our department is financing this application, so it needs to be implemented quick and cheap."

Question

Consider the design of a solution that meets the requirements of both the head of finance and your IT manager.

1. How would you organize the code?
2. How would you ensure reusability of code?

Case Scenario 2: Services

Interviews

Following is a list of company personnel interviewed and their statements.

- **IT Manager**   "The end users need an application to help manage the workflow of contract changes. We need to brainstorm and come up with a solution. The solution needs to be extensible and reusable."

- **End user**   "We need to track work items and attach files to them. It would be nice if, aside from a regular interface, we could have a short list of pending work items in Microsoft Office Outlook."

Question

Consider the design of a solution that meets the requirements of both the end user and your IT manager.

Suggested Practices

To help you successfully master the exam objectives presented in this chapter, complete the following tasks.

Designing Application Logic

- **Practice 1** Create a solution with four projects, a Web site, a Web service, and a class library for application logic and data access. Select a customer in the form, retrieve the customer from the AdventureWorks database, and transform the data into a business object. Implement a *GetOrderTotal()* method on the customer class. Return the data through a Web service and display it in your Web site using a *GridView*.
- **Practice 2** Expand on the solution created in Practice 1 and implement a Web page for adding a customer. Add a Web service to add a customer and store the customer's information in the AdventureWorks database. Use a business object as parameters for the services.
- **Practice 3** Do the same but now use a *Typed DataSet* rather than a business object.

Take a Practice Test

The practice tests on this book's companion CD offer many options. For example, you can test yourself on just one exam objective, or you can test yourself on all the 70-549 certification exam content. You can set up the test so that it closely simulates the experience of taking a certification exam, or you can set it up in study mode so that you can look at the correct answers and explanations after you answer each question.

MORE INFO   Practice tests

For details about all the practice test options available, see the "How to Use the Practice Tests" section in this book's Introduction.

Chapter 9
Logging and Monitoring

Distributed applications have a special place in the hearts of operations personnel. Such applications have two or more individual components, each of which needs to be monitored. Reliability and quality of service (QOS) issues need to be considered, and gathering logging information into a central location (for ease of reporting) is yet one more challenge to deal with. Yes, distributed applications require much more complex care and feeding than the typical Windows Forms application—more even than Web applications because the infrastructure might not necessarily be in place. This lesson discusses the techniques that allow interested parties to keep informed about the status and functions of a distributed application.

Exam objectives in this chapter:

- Choose an appropriate event logging method for the application.
  - ❏ Decide whether to log data. Considerations include policies, security, requirements, and debugging.
  - ❏ Choose a storage mechanism for logged events. For example, database, flat file, event log, or XML file.
  - ❏ Choose a systemwide event logging method. For example, centralized logging, distributed logging, and so on.
  - ❏ Decide logging levels based upon severity and priority.
- Monitor specific characteristics or aspects of an application.
  - ❏ Decide whether to monitor data. Considerations include administration, auditing, and application support.
  - ❏ Decide which characteristics to monitor. For example, application performance, memory consumption, security auditing, usability metrics, and possible bugs.
  - ❏ Choose event monitoring mechanisms, such as System Monitor and logs.
  - ❏ Decide monitoring levels based on requirements.
  - ❏ Choose a systemwide monitoring method from the available monitoring mechanisms.

Lessons in this chapter:

Before You Begin

To complete the lessons in this chapter, you must have:

- A computer that meets or exceeds the minimum hardware requirements listed in the "Introduction" section at the beginning of the book.

- Microsoft Visual Studio 2005 installed on your computer, with either Microsoft Visual Basic .NET or C# installed.

- The Enterprise Library application (January 2006 version) installed on your computer. The Enterprise Library can be downloaded from *http://msdn.microsoft.com/library /?url=/library/en-us/dnpag2/html/EntLib2.asp*.

Real World

Bruce Johnson

When it comes to logging, distributed applications pose an unusual challenge. First, the application has different components running in different systems and directories. The permissions associated with each component can be different. They don't even need to be running at the same time (as in queue-based applications). So gathering all of the information about what is going on within the application and finding a way to synchronize the various inputs is not as trivial as you might hope.

The synchronization aspect is actually one not often thought about. In a truly distributed environment (as opposed to multiple tiers but running on the same physical computer), the question of how to keep track of time is raised. Are all the servers running on the same time—in the same time zone, even? Is a gap expected in processing (back to that queue-based application)? These are questions that need to be addressed to create a good logging mechanism for distributed applications. They are all addressed in this lesson.

Lesson 1: Logging in Distributed Applications

If you read over the exam objectives at the top of this chapter (and you did, didn't you?), you probably noticed that there is a great deal of similarity in the questions that need to be addressed in both logging and monitoring. The main difference between the two is the audience for the information. People who want to see *logging* information usually have different motivations than those who want to *monitor* the application, and that drives the choice of which information to display and the channel through which the data is delivered. In this lesson, the focus is on logging, with the attendant audiences of developers, auditors, and a few select others.

After this lesson, you will be able to:

■ Identify the expected audience for logging data, including the different requirements that they might have.

■ Understand the available options for storing logging data.

■ Decide whether a logging framework is appropriate for your distributed application.

Estimated lesson time: 40 minutes

Who Needs Logging?

This is the key question, isn't it, if only because the people who want the logging information drive the type of information that is required and the way the information is presented. Fortunately, there are only a couple of general categories for interested parties. Unfortunately, each group needs different types of data generated at different levels of granularity. And, just to make it more interesting, they need to get at the data by using different methods. But before you go to that level, let's consider the interested parties.

■ **Developers**   Arguably, this is the most interested party in logging information. The type of data that is needed is also the least structured. Developers normally use logging data to identify the source of sporadic bugs. After all, if the bugs weren't sporadic, or were reproducible outside of the production environment, they would simply create a unit test to duplicate the problem and work from there. In this situation, the developer wants to see the equivalent of checkpoints in the log, each checkpoint indicating the path that was taken while processing the request.

■ **Auditors**   Auditors care about details. More accurately, they care that a set of details can be provided that add up to a specific total. To support this demand, the need to persist detailed information arises. Financial transactions, such as transfers between bank accounts, are a canonical example, but by no means is the need to audit transactions limited to the financial world. Also, it should be pointed out that the type of logging auditors are looking for is not necessarily generated in the same manner as the developer data. Logging doesn't imply that code (C# or Visual Basic .NET code, that is) is required. The logging information could be created using a trigger in the database. That would still qualify as logging data, and it still needs to be accounted for in the design of the distributed application.

■ **Security**   In this age of heightened security, logging requests to access secured resources is a common requirement. The security aspect of logging is a little different than the two groups mentioned so far. Just tracking which requests have succeeded or failed is one thing, but recognizing patterns of failures is also important. In that manner, reaction to attempted security breaches can be quick. For this reason, the security audience is covered in both this lesson and in the one about monitoring.

What Data Is Required?

Once the audience for the data has been identified, the question of which data to log is more easily addressed. Naturally, the specific fields are not something that can be dealt with in a book. Only having intimate details about the application will provide enough information for you to decide exactly what needs to be captured. Based on the audience, however, the data usually falls into the following categories.

■ **General application health**   Is the Web site available? Are the external resources (databases, files, external Web services, and so on) required to satisfy requests available? What exceptions (expected or unexpected) have been thrown?

■ **Performance**   How many requests per second are being processed? How long does each request take?

■ **Security auditing**   What failed attempts to access a secured resource took place? Where did the request come from? How many failed attempts have occurred recently?

Although specifics are beyond the scope of this book, there are a number of guidelines that can be useful in identifying the general types of information that might be required.

Granularity

Granularity is an indicator of the volume of data that is collected during the logging process. It can be broken down into two broad categories.

■ **Course-grained**   Course-grained data is a high-level set of data. The logged data does not include details about individual transactions but, instead, aggregates the details of a group of transactions to reduce the volume of collected data.

■ **Fine-grained**   Fine-grained data collection takes an approach directly opposite to coarse-grained. In fine-grained data collection, detailed, transaction-level information is recorded. As you might imagine, the volume of logged data at this level has the potential to be quite large.

There are times when both coarse-grained and fine-grained data is required, even within the same method. Consider for a moment a distributed application that receives text files containing information about one or more sales orders. This is how electronic data interchange (EDI) works. As part of the processing, information about the number of orders processed and their total value is logged. However, if there is a problem, it might be that operations wants to see detailed information about the individual products in each order. Therefore, the code to log the data needs to change from coarse-grained to fine-grained either at run time (hopefully) or without having to change the source code (a requirement). A solution to this type of situation introduces the concept of logging levels and run-time configuration changes, both of which are covered later in this lesson.

Privacy

As has already been mentioned, successfully accessing a restricted resource might trigger a log entry. However, in certain situations, it is possible that even logging the request, failed or not, might violate someone's privacy. Placing certain types of information into the log file can create a huge security hole. The canonical example is the logging of credit card information for a customer. By now, however, no sane developer would do that. But beyond credit card details, malicious users even use phone numbers and addresses. And whereas the database administrator might make certain that only the appropriate people have access to the customer list, a developer can easily write this "secured" information to a plaintext log file that can be viewed by anyone who knows where to look.

Even if the details of the log don't appear to be privacy violations (as logging credit cards and phone numbers is), users might not want specific information known about them. For example, most people assume that the search keywords they use are privileged information. However, late in 2005, Google was sued by the U.S. government to turn over logs related to some searches that used objectionable words. As it turns out, detailed logs were available because that sort of information is invaluable to Google in terms of both generating revenue and improving search result criteria. But because the detailed logs were available, the government was able to go to a judge and request that they be turned over. This is an instance in which, if less-detailed logs were maintained, the government's ability to request them would have been severely curtailed.

In general, the solution to this problem is to eliminate identifying information from the log. There is nothing intrinsically bad about tracking Web requests, for example, as long as the information necessary to relate the request back to a specific requestor isn't maintained, which is another way of saying that the privacy violation occurs because of the ability to connect logging data to a person, not because of the data being logged—unless, of course, you really need to track the person who makes the request, which puts maintaining security on the logging data at the same level as securing the database.

Synchronization

At the beginning of the lesson, the issue of synchronization was mentioned as being a specific problem in distributed application logging. For a developer trying to find a bug or for an auditor ensuring that a summary log entry is backed up by corresponding detailed entries, knowing which entries belong to which requests is important. If the entire request is handled on a single thread, this isn't a problem. If the request is handled by multiple processes on different physical computers, it is much more of an issue.

Specifically, there are two types of problems that exist in this model. The first is that for log entries to be time-related, the individual servers on which the log entries are generated must be time synchronized. Although there are techniques that can be used to accomplish this, the more servers that get involved, the more challenging it is. The difference between the clocks on different computers is known as *clock skew* and, if precise measurement is not required, knowing the clock skew between pairs of computers is sufficient to adjust the timestamps. The reason for precision as the criterion for assessment is that most algorithms to adjust for clock skew assume that the skew is constant. If it is not, then the timestamps being produced will be accurate only within that range of change.

The second potential problem results from network latency. If, instead of using a synchronized time server or maintaining a set of clock skew pairs, the log entries are submitted to a central logging mechanism, the determining factor of the precision of the timestamp is network latency. There is a small (measurable) delay between the actual event and the generation of the timestamp for the corresponding entry that can be attributed to the time it takes for the request to be sent across the network.

For correlating multiple data entries with a single request transaction in a distributed application, one of the most effective techniques is to use a transaction ID. The idea is, at the start of the request, that a unique identifier for the request is generated. This unique identifier (the transaction ID) flows from call to call, making it always available for use in a log file. By including the transaction ID in the entry, you now have the ability to find all of the log entries associated with a particular request, even if they are physically in different files. Of course, this means that the transaction ID must be passed along from requester to procedures, resulting in a change to the application programming interface (API), which might not be desirable.

Logging Levels

The need to control the granularity of the logged data results in the need to create different logging levels. A *log level* is an indication of how important a particular log entry is to the intended audience, but the names given to the log levels are arbitrary. They could be the name of the audience for the entry or, as is defined in the *Windows Event Log*, they could indicate the severity of the log entry by using the following levels.

- **Error** This is a significant problem with the application. It usually indicates a loss of data or functionality that needs to be addressed immediately.
- **Warning** This is a less significant problem than Error. Although there is no immediate concern, warnings could be an indicator that future problems are possible.
- **Information** This type of entry is used to indicate that an operation of interest has occurred.
- **FailureAudit** This is an audit entry for a failed attempt to access a secured resource.
- **SuccessAudit** This is an audit entry for a successful attempt to access a secured resource.

With logging levels, before an entry is logged, a determination must be made about whether it's appropriate to store it. After all, if you're interested in only Error log entries, then any entry marked as Information should not be saved. Therefore, as part of the mechanism that actually performs the logging, the ability to indicate the logging level must be included along with the ability to indicate the level of interest. Commonly, the level of interest is placed into the appropriate configuration file. Now the logging mechanism can read the .config file and perform the necessary determination about whether the proposed entry should be persisted.

If the log level is placed into the .config file, why would changing a log level even be a question? Wouldn't you just open the .config file in Notepad and change the necessary value? Unfortunately, it is not quite that simple. If the distributed application uses a Web site (such as a Web service), changing web.config causes the virtual directory to restart. This could make aspects of the application in which you were interested disappear. If the distributed application is running as a process, changes to the .config file are not automatically detected and reloaded, so in both cases, some issues still need to be addressed. Fortunately, the Microsoft .NET Framework provides the answer to both.

Changing Log Levels in a Web Application

Start by moving the log level configuration information to a separate file. The name of the file isn't important (you can use logging.config just for narrative purposes), and the contents should look like the section did in the web.config file:

```xml
<?xml version="1.0"?>
<appSettings>
    <add key="LoggingLevel" value="warning" />
</appSettings>
```

After the logging configuration settings have been moved out of web.config, a small change needs to be made to a section in web.config to reference the external file. For the preceding example, the *appSettings* portion of web.config would look like the following.

```xml
<appSettings configSource="logging.config"
    restartOnExternalChange="false">
</appSettings>
```

In the interests of full disclosure, because the section being referenced is *appSettings*, the *restartOnExternalChange* attribute is not normally required. In machine.config, the *appSettings* section already defines the *restartOnExternalChange* attribute to be false, causing any external *appSettings* section to inherit this value by default.

Also, if the portion of the .config file being moved is your own configuration section, the section definition needs to include the *restartOnExternalChanges* attribute, so the custom section definition would resemble the following.

```
<section name="MyAppSettings"
    type="System.Configuration.AppSettingsSection, System.Configuration,
    Version=2.0.0.0, Culture=neutral, PublicKeyToken=b03f5f7f11d50a3a"
restartOnExternalChanges="false" />
```

Changing Log Levels in a Windows Application

The problem with changing log levels in a Microsoft Windows application is exactly the opposite of changing them in a Web application. Whereas a change to web.config is automatically detected and picked up, a change to an application configuration file is not detected at all. App.config information is loaded only when the application starts, so making changes while the application is running cannot affect the level of logging that takes place.

The solution is to use the *FileSystemWatcher* class to monitor the app.config file for any changes. Then, once a change is noticed, the log level setting can be reloaded. At that point, subsequent attempts to create a log entry will be filtered by the new logging level.

Setting up the *FileSystemWatcher* class is straightforward. The Path property indicates the directory that is to be watched. The class actually pays attention to all of the files in a directory, but because the application might not care about all of the files, the Filter property is used to indicate the files for which events will be raised. Finally, the NotifyFilter property specifies the types of file system events (such as file additions, deletions, renames, and so on) that actually raise an event. To monitor a .config file for updates in the application's current directory, the following code would be used.

```vb
'VB
Dim fsw as New FileSystemWatcher()
fsw.Path = Environment.CurrentDirectory
fsw.Filter = "*.config"
fsw.NotifyFilter = NotifyFilters.LastWrite
AddHandler fsw.Changed, AddressOf AppConfigChangeHandler
fsw.EnableRaisingEvents = True
```

```csharp
//C#
FileSystemWatcher fsw = new FileSystemWatcher();
fsw.Path = Environment.CurrentDirectory;
fsw.Filter = "*.config";
fsw.NotifyFilter = NotifyFilters.LastWrite;
```

```
fsw.Changed += new FileSystemEventHandler(AppConfigChangeHandler);
fsw.EnableRaisingEvents = true;
```

The event handler for the *Changed* event (called *AppConfigChangeHandler* in the code) contains all of the work involved with reloading the configuration file. The *RefreshSection* method on the *ConfigurationManager* class is used to indicate that a particular section should be re-read from disk the next time it is accessed.

```
'VB
ConfigurationManager.RefreshSection("appSettings")
```

```
//C#
ConfigurationManager.RefreshSection("appSettings");
```

There are two potential issues that need to be considered before leaving this topic. First, the *RefreshSection* method works correctly only if the configuration file being changed is external to the main app.config file. This means that the section being refreshed needs to be defined using the *configSource* attribute and the actual XML for the section placed in a separate file.

The second potential issue is a little less troublesome. The *FileSystemWatcher* does not respond with absolute accuracy to every single file system event. It is possible that if there were a large number of files changed in a short period of time, the buffer that holds the change information will be overrun, and a change might be missed. However, this is really only a hypothetical issue for the case of changes being made to a configuration file. It is highly unlikely that a large number of changes to a .config file will be made at one time, and the Filter property can be used to reduce the raised events to changes to only a single file.

Data Storage Choices

Both logging and monitoring have the same options available for storing log entries, but from a practical perspective, some types of storage are more optimal for the type of audience that cares about logging. This section, therefore, will focus on the persistence options that are more likely to be found in a logging scenario. For each option, the characteristics will be considered within the context of logging and how the gathered information might be used.

Flat Files

To many developers, "log file" is just another name for a *flat file*. To be sure, the structure of a flat file is simple. Each line in a log file contains the information for one event. The information for an event contains one or more fields related to the event (date, time, description, source, and so on). The structure of each line generally falls into one of the following categories.

- **Comma-delimited** Each field is separated by a comma. This is a common enough file format that Microsoft Office Excel can open it without conversion. The biggest drawback is the restriction placed on the content by the use of the comma as a delimiter: the field value cannot contain a comma. There is a solution to this problem. The value containing the command can be surrounded by single quotes. However, the use of commas, single quotes, and double quotes as special characters places an undue restriction on the content of the log file. Other options are available.

- **Tab-delimited**   Conceptually, a tab-delimited file is the same as a comma-delimited file, but the separator is a tab character, not a comma. The idea is to make the delimiter a character that is seldom used in the field values, and that idea is true enough that problems are rarely seen in the real world.

- **Fixed-length**   Rather than use a delimiter to separate fields, this format specifies the exact size of each field value. The number of characters in each field is fixed, regardless of the field value being stored. This removes the need for field delimiters. As a format, fixed-length has been around for a long time and is now mostly used to maintain compatibility with existing systems. The format can cause some information to be lost (if the field value is too long for the allocated space) or result in large log files (because field values are padded with spaces to fit the defined length).

In a distributed environment, the main drawback to using a flat file to store logging data is that it is normally local to the process that is doing the logging. This is not to say that the log file can't go onto a central shared directory, but if you do so, it's possible that a log entry can't be made because the link to the shared location is unavailable. As well, the security context under which the process is running must have access to the remote share, a right that might be more than the application otherwise requires.

Exam Tip   Keep in mind the negative side of flat files when considering questions related to the data storage options for logging.

Event Log

The event log is the second choice for most developers who are generating logging entries. Unlike the flat file with a schema that is completely flexible, the event log has only a fixed set of fields that can be assigned values. Table 9-1 contains the fields that can be populated in the event log.

Table 9-1   Event Log Fields

Field Name	Description
Source	The name of the application that is the source for the event log. It must be registered on the computer before it can be used.
Message	The string that is the message for the log entry.
Type	The type of log entry. It must be one of the *EventLogEntryType* values.

Table 9-1   Event Log Fields

Field Name	Description
Event Id	An application-specific identifier for the event.
Category	An application-specific subcategory that is associated with the log entry.
Raw Data	A set of binary data that is associated with the log entry.

There is actually more than one log file available for the insertion of event information into the event log. When installed, Windows provides three log files, named Application, Security, and System. The purpose of these logs is to segregate related information, making it easier for the audience to find the desired information. The System log contains entries associated with the operating system and its related processes. The Security log contains successful and failed resource access events. The Application log contains entries associated with non-operating system applications. The Application log is the most likely target for developers.

If you require more log files to further segregate events, you can do that programmatically by using the *CreateEventSource* method on the *System.Diagnostic.EventLog* class.

```
'VB
EventLog.CreateEventSource("Source Name", "Log Name")
```

```
//C#
EventLog.CreateEventSource("Source Name", "Log Name");
```

This statement creates a new event log called Log Name and adds a potential source for events called Source Name. Although this is a simple way to add an event log, there is a permission limitation that restricts when the statement should be used. Administrator rights require the ability to create an event log, so the *CreateEventSource* method shown previously must be run by someone with elevated privileges. Usually, this means that the event logs should be created during the installation of the application, when requiring administrative privileges is much easier to accomplish.

Even writing to the event log requires permissions that are not normally granted to every user. For example, if the distributed application is running as a Web site (such as a Web service), the default ASP.NET user doesn't have the necessary permissions to create an event log entry. As a best practice, the ASP.NET user should run at a low privilege level. With ASP.NET, the suggested level is known as medium trust. By default, medium trust can't add events to the event log. The solution is to create a custom policy based on medium trust that includes access to the event log. Once the custom policy file is configured, it can be referenced by modifying the trust in web.config. The details of how to run ASP.NET using such a custom policy (and the risks involved) can be found in the following reference.

MORE INFO Running ASP.NET in a medium trust environment

For more information about how to run ASP.NET in a medium trust environment, refer to "How to: Use Medium Trust in ASP.NET from Microsoft's Prescriptive Architecture Group." The document can be found at *http://msdn.microsoft.com/library/default.asp?url=/library/en-us/dnpag2/html /PAGHT000020.asp*.

The *WriteEntry* method on the *System.Diagnostics.EventLog* class is used to add a log entry. The simplest overload takes a single string value as a parameter. That value is used as the message portion of a log entry in the Application log with an entry type of Information.

```
'VB
System.Diagnostics.EventLog.WriteEntry("This is the log message")
```

```
//C#
System.Diagnostics.EventLog.WriteEntry("This is the log message");
```

In more complicated overloads, you can specify additional information, including the log to which it will be written (Application, System, Security, or your own log), the event log type, the event identifier, the event category, and an array of bytes (the *RawData* field) to be included with the entry.

Exam Tip The permission requirement for writing to the event log is a commonly forgotten requirement, which makes it more likely to appear on the exam.

Using the event log solves some of the problems associated with a flat file. Although the event log is local to the process creating the log entry, the information can easily be accessed remotely by using the Event Viewer. And the common format in which events are recorded means that third-party applications can be employed to monitor and report on the entries.

However, the cost of this centralization is a lessening of flexibility. With a flat file, developers can define whatever fields they want in whatever order they want. The event log has a set list of fields. The only areas without restriction on the kind of data logged are the *Message* and *RawData* fields. Third-party applications will not be able to process the contents of these fields because the contents don't match a particular schema.

Database

Although the first two data store types are adequate for many situations, neither of them completely addresses the issue of centralized accessibility, and flat files and the event log are not useful for generating reports. Yes, flat files can be used as the input in some reporting engines, but that format is not optimal (to put it mildly), and success depends on the consistency of the format of the log entries. If the need to produce reports about log activity is one of the requirements of the audience, then using a database is an appealing possibility.

Database tables have the same fixed field layout as the event log. However, unlike the event log, the developer is able to define the fields that are stored and can even add more as enhancements to the application dictate. This ability to customize provides a level of comfort that sits well with most developers. As well, the limits of what can be stored are increased from whatever settings are in the event log to whatever the maximum size of a database table is.

From a reporting perspective, there is little question that databases are more than adequate. If Microsoft SQL Server 2000 or SQL Server 2005 is the database being used, then SQL Reporting Services can not only generate professional-looking reports, it can also automate their delivery and retention. In other words, using a database makes it easy to retain, analyze, report on, and manage logging information.

There are two main downsides to using a database. One is the need for a database server. The flat file and event log storage types are provided with Windows. If the data is being stored on the local computer, there is no way that a flat file or the event log will be unavailable. Alternatively, the database needs to be running to act as a data store.

The result of centralizing the data is that an additional point of failure is added to the application, and it is one that might cause critical information to be unavailable. For example, assume the log entries are being used by an auditor. If the database used for logging is unavailable, then the application will be unable to store the information required by the audit. This gap in information is one of the things that annoy auditors.

Placing logging data into a database is a familiar task. For .NET developers, ADO.NET is the most likely mechanism and, given that ADO.NET is well understood by most developers (and that detailed coverage is outside the scope of this book), the following sample code will be simplistic but illustrative.

```vb
'VB
Dim cn As New SqlConnection(connectionString)
Dim cmd As New SqlCommand( _
    String.Format("INSERT INTO LogTable VALUES" & _
    "(GetDate(), '{0}', '{1}')", logType, logMessage))
cmd.CommandType = CommandType.Text
cn.Open()
cmd.ExecuteNonQuery()
cn.Close()
```

```csharp
//C#
SqlConnection cn = new SqlConnection(connectionString)
SqlCommand cmd = new SqlCommand(
    String.Format("INSERT INTO LogTable VALUES" +
    "(GetDate(), '{0}', '{1}')", logType, logMessage));
cmd.CommandType = CommandType.Text;
cn.Open();
cmd.ExecuteNonQuery();
cn.Close();
```

Quick Check

1. Which data storage option is most appropriate if significant reporting on the logged information will be required?
2. Which data storage option is more appropriate if the log needs to be viewable using standard third-party tools?
3. Which data storage option is more appropriate if the information being logged can change format from event to event?

Quick Check Answers

1. From a reporting perspective, using a database as the data store provides the most reporting functionality. Although a flat file can be reported on (even by SQL Reporting Services), that presupposes that the format of every record in the flat file has the same schema. If that's true, then the flat file is also a possibility.
2. The event log is the format that is most likely to be addressed by third-party tools and has the benefit of being a known format that can be processed without additional configuration or mappings.
3. Both the event log and a database suffer from the inflexibility of a set schema. Even though the database table is freely defined by a developer, each record in the table has to have the same structure. Alternatively, a flat file can take on the format and structure as required by the application.

System-Wide Logging

As has already been discussed, the type of logging that needs to take place depends greatly on the audience. The result is that applications usually have logging statements scattered all over the application. It is common to find a single method that has two or three or more logging statements in it, each targeted at a different audience and each going to a different data store. In the majority of cases, the "logging statement" referred to here can be more than one line of source code (perhaps a test to see whether the log entry is required, followed by collecting the logging information and sending it to the log). Trying to keep extra code out of the methods is one of the driving forces behind creating a logging framework.

A logging framework provides a central method through which all logging can be performed. A common interface to such a framework is a single method that takes all of the required details as parameters and generates the necessary log entry. Now only one line of code is needed to perform logging, greatly reducing code clutter.

However, the logging requirements for an application can become even more complicated. What if, for example, event log entries should now be sent to a database? Or the format of the log entries should be changed? Certainly, the centralized method can be modified. But even with such a minimal change to the assembly, thorough testing will be required.

The solution is to use configuration information to control the logging function. By defining the appropriate settings within a configuration file, the destination or format for a log entry could be modified with no change to a running assembly. This ability is made possible with the introduction of a logging framework into an application.

To create a logging framework that is this flexible would be a tremendous undertaking. Fortunately, it is not necessary. There is a number of third-party logging mechanisms available in the .NET world that implement just such elements. One of the more popular frameworks is the Logging Application Block, which is part of the Enterprise Library produced by the Prescriptive Architecture Group at Microsoft. Another is Log4Net, an open-source logging framework based on the Log4j framework. Both of these frameworks are surprisingly fully featured and extensible, providing source code to handle any situations that haven't already been considered.

A common concern as various frameworks are being considered is whether the friction of using the framework outweighs the benefits. The answer comes down to the types of functionality that are needed and how flexible the logging needs to be. In the Enterprise Library, the *Write* method can be configured to route messages to multiple data stores under different conditions, including the severity level and the message source. The configuration for the framework can be modified in the moment, and changes are incorporated into the run-time processing immediately. It is truly (as the name suggests) enterprise-level in terms of functionality. If that is a requirement (or even if it might be), consider using the Logging Application Block. Even if it seems just a little like overkill, it's probably still worth it. After all, the framework includes code that has already been tested by others. And that in itself makes third-party frameworks worthwhile.

Lab: Common Logging Issues

In this lab, you will consider one of the main issues associated with adding logging to a distributed application, specifically, changing log levels in real time. If you encounter a problem completing an exercise, the completed projects can be installed from the Code folder on the companion CD.

▶ Exercise: Changing Log Levels in Real Time

The purpose of this exercise is to demonstrate a technique that allows you to reload configuration files. The assumption here is that the starting point is a simple Windows Forms application with a button that displays the log level as retrieved from the .config file. With the initial implementation, changing the app.config file will not affect the displayed value. In other words, successive button clicks display the same log level, even after it has been changed and saved. Feel free to prove this for yourself after step 7.

1. Launch Visual Studio 2005.

2. Open a solution, using File | Open | Project/Solution .

3. Navigate to the Chapter09/Lesson1/Exercise1/<language>/Before directory. Select the Exercise1 solution and click Open.

4. In the Solution Explorer, double-click the GetConfigValue form to display the design surface. Then double-click the form to create the *Load* event handler procedure.

5. In the *Load* event handler, add code to create the *FileSystemWatcher* object. The Path is set to the current directory. The Filter is set to be any file with a .config extension, and the NotifyFilter is set to raise events when a file is updated.

   ```
   'VB
   Dim fsw As New FileSystemWatcher
   fsw.Path = Environment.CurrentDirectory
   fsw.Filter = "*.config"
   fsw.NotifyFilter = NotifyFilters.LastWrite
   ```

   ```
   //C#
   FileSystemWatcher fsw = new FileSystemWatcher();
   fsw.Path = Environment.CurrentDirectory;
   fsw.Filter = "*.config";
   fsw.NotifyFilter = NotifyFilters.LastWrite;
   ```

6. In the same *Load* event handler procedure, a handler for the *Changed* event needs to be added. This procedure is called when a file system event that matches the NotifyFilter happens to the file (or files) indicated by the Path and Filter properties and the Enable-RaiseEvents property on the *FileSystemWatcher* object is set to true. Add the following code to the end of the *Load* event handler procedure.

   ```
   'VB
   AddHandler fsw.Changed, AddressOf AppConfigChangeHandler
   fsw.EnableRaisingEvents = True
   ```

   ```
   //C#
   fsw.Changed += new FileSystemEventHandler(AppConfigChangeHandler);
   fsw.EnableRaisingEvents = true;
   ```

7. Next, create the *Changed* event handler procedure. From the code added in step 6, the name of this procedure is *AppConfigChangeHandler*. In this procedure, the *AppSettings* section of the configuration file is refreshed. Add the following procedure to the *GetConfig-Value* class.

   ```
   'VB
   Private Sub AppConfigChangeHandler(ByVal sender As Object, _
       ByVal e As FileSystemEventArgs)
       ConfigurationManager.RefreshSection("appSettings")
   End Sub
   ```

```csharp
//C#
private void AppConfigChangeHandler(object sender,
   FileSystemEventArgs e) {
   ConfigurationManager.RefreshSection("appSettings");
}
```

8. Finally, because the official app.config file cannot be refreshed once the application has started, the *appSettings* element must be moved to an external configuration file. In the Solution Explorer, right-click the project and select Add New Item from the context menu. Then, select a template of Application Configuration File and give it a name of **external.config**.

9. Replace the contents of external.config, which were generated automatically, with the following XML document.

```xml
<?xml version="1.0" encoding="utf-8" ?>
<appSettings>
<add key="logLevel" value="Information"/>
</appSettings>
```

10. In the Solution Explorer, right-click the external.config file and select Properties. In the Properties sheet, change the Copy to Output Directory value to **Always Copy**.

11. Open the app.config file. Find the *appSettings* element and replace the entire element (including the opening and closing tags) with the following. The newly added element references the just-created configuration file.

```xml
<appSettings configSource="external.config"></appSettings>
```

12. Launch the application by pressing F5. Click the Get Config Value button and note the log level.

13. Without shutting down the application, go to the external.config file in Visual Studio. Change the value of the *logLevel* attribute to Warning. Save the change.

14. Return to the running application. Click the Get Config Value button again and note that the displayed log level is now Warning.

Lesson Summary

- Logging is useful from both a debugging and an auditing perspective.
- The audience for the logging output needs to be considered when determining the granularity of the messages.
- The ability to change logging levels in the moment is important when the logging is being used for debugging purposes.
- The need for a framework grows as the logging requirements for an application increase.

Lesson Review

You can use the following questions to test your knowledge of the information in Lesson 1, "Logging in Distributed Applications." The questions are also available on the companion CD if you prefer to review them in electronic form.

NOTE Answers

Answers to these questions and explanations of why each answer choice is right or wrong are located in the "Answers" section at the end of the book.

---

1. You company's applications need to be kept running 24 hours a day. To help notify operations of problems, you will be instrumenting your application, but operations doesn't want to be notified of all monitoring messages. Which of the Windows Event Log levels should operations be looking for?

    A. Error

    B. Warning

    C. Information

    D. SuccessAudit

    E. FailureAudit

2. You have created a distributed application that is running on three separate servers within your corporate infrastructure. The servers are running in a secured production environment. The application uses a database that is also deployed in the production environment. The developers don't have access to any of the files on the production servers, although reports can be run against the database. You would like to create a logging mechanism that gives developers access to the information generated by the production application. Which data storage type should you use?

    A. Flat file

    B. Event log

    C. Trace listeners

    D. Database

Lesson 2: Monitoring Distributed Applications

When considering the data that is stored, the differences between logging and monitoring are minimal. In reality, the immediacy of the data is the distinguishing characteristic. Typically, the people monitoring an application want up-to-the-second status. They want to be notified immediately when something unexpected happens. This timeliness requirement has the greatest impact on which data to include and how to deliver it.

The purpose of this lesson is to describe the techniques that can be applied to monitor distributed applications, from both a status and an exceptional-event perspective.

After this lesson, you will be able to:
- Identify the expected audience for the monitoring information.
- Decide which delivery mechanism is most appropriate for the monitoring data.
- Determine whether a system-wide approach to monitoring makes sense.

Estimated lesson time: 35 minutes

Who Needs Monitoring?

This lesson starts with the same question that began the first lesson. Each potential audience for monitoring information has a different set of requirements for the data it wants to see and how it wants that data to be notified.

Operations

The responsibility of operations is to ensure that the applications in the corporate computing environment continue functioning. And the definition of "functioning" has expanded in recent years to include performance and uptime metrics. In this world, keeping track of what an application, especially a distributed one, is doing is a requirement of ensuring a happy user base, so when something goes wrong, the response from operations is more proactive then reactive. Operations people would much rather discover a problem on their own than get panicked calls from the user base.

One of the areas of interest to operations is the health of distributed applications. Because these are normally processes that don't need (or have) a ready user interface, the need to keep track of their status is of paramount importance. For this reason, part of the monitoring that operations likes to see done is checking for service status. This status check should include the availability of any external resources on which the service depends.

Security

The security group (a function often subsumed by operations) also has an interest in monitoring distributed applications. As was noted in Lesson 1, "Logging in Distributed Applications," security logs are of interest to anyone trying to identify systematic failures, but security groups also want to know when the attack is going on. Therefore, not only should security failures be logged (for reporting in the future), but also a notification should be sent immediately to the security group. In this way, the attack can be monitored while in progress, providing the potential for an even closer look at the technique being used.

Security is an issue for monitored applications as well. Even though the events that are raised by monitoring appear to be more ephemeral than logged data, that is an illusion. For an application to be monitored, there must be a listener to accept the notification. The listener will then display the notification to the interested parties in the form of graphs, tables, or other output formats. However, the data is converted to an output format, which means that the data isn't truly ephemeral. It can last much longer than the instant that thinking just about the notification process suggests. This also means that the notifications shouldn't include private details because there is no way to know what happens to the information afterward.

> **Exam Tip**   Keep in mind which groups of users require logging and which require monitoring. Specifically, operations and security will be interested in the immediacy of monitoring whereas auditors, developers, and administrative personnel will be happy with logs.

Data Storage

The process of monitoring demands storage options that are more immediate in their delivery. It is no longer adequate to put the information into a format that will be processed at some later time. The audience for monitoring wants the information now, and anything less than that reduces the value offered by monitoring.

E-mail

The ubiquity of e-mail makes it an obvious choice for delivering monitoring notifications. It has become the bane of anyone who is connected all the time, but in the monitoring world, it is priceless. When an event requires immediate attention, sending notification via e-mail is more likely to be noticed than waiting for someone to check a flat file.

E-mail is also capable of sending notifications beyond the boundary of the corporate infrastructure—the "e-mail everywhere" idea that is embodied in the Blackberrys, cell phones, and personal digital assistants (PDAs) that are so prevalent in the corporate world. For databases, flat files, and the event log, you need to have access to the company network to access the information.

The drawback to e-mail is that it's not truly a data store. Yes, the mail server might save the messages that come and go. And you can search for keywords. But generating a report based on the set of e-mails that you receive will be unsatisfying. E-mail notifications are really a one-time notification. If the information in the event needs to be included in any future reporting or review process, the event should be directed to two separate data stores: the e-mail message for notification and a logging data store (like a database for flat files) for future reporting.

As a warning, it is important not to use e-mail with fine-grained notifications. If you remember the fable, "The Boy Who Cried Wolf," you'll understand the problem. Too many false or unimportant notifications dull the impact of the single critical one that needs to be addressed. The volume of spam that most of us receives is already reducing the imperative to monitor e-mail. To avoid contributing to this situation, the developer needs to ensure that only critical events trigger an e-mail message.

A new class named *System.Net.Mail.SmtpClient* was introduced with .NET Framework 2.0 to assist sending e-mail messages. Two steps are involved in sending the message. The first involves instantiating a *System.Net.Mail.MailMessage* object. The MailMessage contains the subject, the body, and the From and To addresses for the message. The second step uses the *SmtpClient* class to send the message to the mail server. After identifying the mail server by name, the *Send* method submits the MailMessage for processing.

Although this process is simple, it doesn't handle one of the most common requirements for sending e-mails: authentication. Most mail servers require the user to specify a user ID and password before sending an e-mail message. To do this, the *NetworkCredential* class is used in conjunction with the Credentials property on the *SmtpClient* object.s

The *NetworkCredential* class is part of the *System.Net* namespace. A new *NetworkCredential* object is created with the necessary user ID and password. The object is then assigned to the Credentials property. Also, to avoid transmitting the current user's Windows identity, the *SmtpClient* needs to be told that the default credentials should not be sent. The following code sends an e-mail message to an authenticated mail server.

```vb
'VB
Dim message As New MailMessage(fromAddress, toAddress, _
    subject, messageBody)
Dim emailClient As New SmtpClient(mailServerName)
Dim smtpUserInfo = New _
    System.Net.NetworkCredential(txtSMTPUser.Text, txtSMTPPass.Text)
emailClient.UseDefaultCredentials = False
emailClient.Credentials = smtpUserInfo
emailClient.Send(message)
```

```csharp
//C#
MailMessage message = new MailMessage(fromAddress, toAddress,
    subject, messageBody);
SmtpClient emailClient = new SmtpClient(mailServerName);
System.Net.NetworkCredential smtpUserInfo = new
```

```
    System.Net.NetworkCredential(txtSMTPUser.Text, txtSMTPPass.Text);
emailClient.UseDefaultCredentials = false;
emailClient.Credentials = smtpUserInfo;
emailClient.Send(message);
```

Performance Monitor

Although e-mail messages are not truly data stores, the same is not true of the Windows *Performance Monitor*. Also known as the system monitor, this utility straddles the bounds between immediate notification and longer-term data storage. Already, Performance Monitor is capable of tracking many different values updated by managing different parts of the operating systems and running applications. This information, provided in the form of counters, can be retrieved on a recurring basis and displayed in a graphical manner. Figure 9-1 shows the performance monitor with the standard counters included.

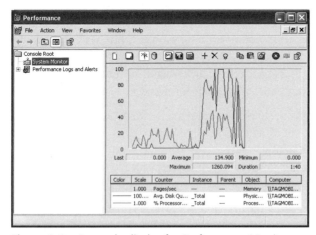

Figure 9-1   A sample display for Performance Monitor

Not only does Windows create a large number of counters for the performance monitor to use, any application has the ability to create its own. So, as you develop your in-house applications, you can seed the code with calls to update performance monitor counters. Then, while your application is running, operations staff is able to view the values on an almost real-time basis, and the viewing (as well as the storage into a more permanent form such as a comma-separated value [CSV] file) takes place by using the same interface as shown in Figure 9-1.

The main benefit of using the performance monitor is the ability to observe the moment-to-moment status of an application. In a monitoring situation, this allows for a dashboard view of the distributed application's status. Add custom counters to your application, and now the operations staff can have an at-a-glance view of the values that are truly important.

Still, there are some drawbacks to using Performance Monitor. A performance counter, unlike all of the techniques described so far, does not allow for an arbitrary message to be sent. It is a numerical value that can only be incremented or decremented, so the performance monitor is good for keeping track of the health and progress of an application, but not good for capturing information that could be used to help solve a problem. For this purpose, more persistent data stores (flat file, database, and so on) are necessary.

Performance counters come in five types.

- **Average**   Measures the counter value over a period of time. The displayed value is the average of the last two measurements. An average is actually a combination of two counters, Performance Monitor: a base counter that tracks the number of samples and a regular counter that tracks the values.
- **Difference**   Displays the difference between two successive measurements. This particular counter cannot be negative, so if the second measurement is less than the first, a value of zero is displayed.
- **Instantaneous**   The counter value displayed at that point in time.
- **Percentage**   The counter value displayed as a percentage. This is different from instantaneous only in the way it is displayed.
- **Rate**   The change in the displayed counter value divided by the change in time. In other words, the rate of change of the counter over time.

The creation of new performance counters can be done either programmatically or directly through the Server Explorer in Visual Studio 2005. Because it is more likely that the counters will be created programmatically, that's the technique this lesson will demonstrate.

The first step is to create the category. The *PerformanceCounterCategory* class has a static method named *Exists*. This method is used to determine whether a particular category has already been defined. If not, the *Create* method can be used to create the category.

The *Create* method can also be used to add counters to the new category. This is an important point because, as it turns out, the only way to add counters programmatically is when the category is created. Counters cannot be added to existing categories. Instead, the category has to be deleted and then re-created with the new and old counters added in.

The creation of a counter uses two separate classes. The first, named *CounterCreationData*, is used to define the information about an individual counter. The second, named *CounterCreationDataCollection*, is a collection of *CounterCreationData* objects. It is an instance of this second object (the collection) that is passed into the *Create* method. At that point, a category will be created that contains all of the defined counters.

```vb
'VB
Dim CounterDatas As New CounterCreationDataCollection()
Dim cntr1 As New CounterCreationData()
Dim cntr2 As New CounterCreationData()

cntr1.CounterName = "DemoCounter1"
cntr1.CounterHelp = "A description of DemoCounter1"
```

```
cntr1.CounterType = PerformanceCounterType.NumberOfItems64
cntr2.CounterName = "DemoCounter2"
cntr2.CounterHelp = "A description of DemoCounter2"
cntr2.CounterType = PerformanceCounterType.NumberOfItems64

CounterDatas.Add(cntr1)
CounterDatas.Add(cntr2)

PerformanceCounterCategory.Create("Demo Category", _
    "A help message for the category", _
    PerformanceCounterCategoryType.SingleInstance, _
    CounterDatas)

//C#
System.Diagnostics.CounterCreationDataCollection CounterDatas =
    new System.Diagnostics.CounterCreationDataCollection();

System.Diagnostics.CounterCreationData cntr1 =
    new System.Diagnostics.CounterCreationData();
System.Diagnostics.CounterCreationData cntr2 =
    new System.Diagnostics.CounterCreationData();

cntr1.CounterName = "DemoCounter1";
cntr1.CounterHelp = "A description of DemoCounter1";
cntr1.CounterType = PerformanceCounterType.NumberOfItems64;
cntr2.CounterName = "DemoCounter2";
cntr2.CounterHelp = "A description of DemoCounter2";
cntr2.CounterType = PerformanceCounterType.NumberOfItems64;

CounterDatas.Add(cntr1);
CounterDatas.Add(cntr2);

PerformanceCounterCategory.Create("Demo Category", _
    "A help message for the category", _
    PerformanceCounterCategoryType.SingleInstance, _
    CounterDatas);
```

MORE INFO *PerformanceCounter* and permissions

Although most accounts can read and update performance counters, the creation of a performance counter category and the counters themselves require a higher level of permissions. The only default groups that have the ability to create categories and counters are Administrators and Power Users. For most distributed applications, this means that the code to add categories and counters to the performance monitor should be included in the installation process, not in the code that is executed while servicing a request.

When updating the numeric value associated with a performance counter, the *Performance-Counter* class contains all of the necessary methods and properties. A *PerformanceCounter* instance is created by specifying the category and counter name in the constructor.

```vb
'VB
Dim pc as New PerformanceCounter("Category", "CounterName")
```

```csharp
//C#
PerformanceCounter pc = new
    PerformanceCounter("Category", "CounterName");
```

Once instantiated, the counter can be updated using one of the methods shown in Table 9-2.

Table 9-2 Performance Counter Update Methods

Method/Property	Description
Decrement	Reduces the value of the counter by one
Increment	Increases the value of the counter by one
IncrementBy	Increases the value of the counter by the specified amount
RawValue	Sets the value directly through a simple assignment

Quick Check

- If you are a member of the operations staff tasked with ensuring that the transactions-per-second performance of an application stays above a certain level, which data storage mechanisms are you most likely to need?

Quick Check Answers

- Either the performance monitor or e-mail could be used in this situation. The correct answer will depend greatly on the type of operations infrastructure that is currently in place in your company. If there is already an operations staff that is keeping an eye on the Web application by using the performance monitor, performance counters are the most likely to be appropriate. However, if there isn't an operations staff, or if the staff doesn't pay attention to performance counter information, delivering notifications through e-mails is a better choice.

System-Wide Monitoring

When choosing a system-wide mechanism, the monitor function has some of the same requirements and options as logging, which is to say that many of the mechanisms mentioned regarding the Logging Application Block can also be used when monitoring. Specifically, the Logging Application Block can be configured so that e-mails are transmitted or performance counters updated in response to logged events from within the application. This provides the same level of configurability, including monitoring levels, multiple destinations, and changing in real time as logging has.

There are two components to using the Logging Application Block. The first involves how to start the process by creating an entry. The second is how to determine where the entry goes.

Creating a Log Entry

The creation of a log entry for the Logging Application Block is done through the *Write* method on the *Logger* class. Although there are a number of overloads that can be used to provide different properties, the one shown in the following code allows for the widest range of choices. The *LogEntry* contains properties such as Categories, ActivityId, Severity, Priority, and EventId that can be associated with each log entry. It also includes a Message property that contains the logged message. An instance of *LogEntry* is created, and the properties assign the desired values, which are then passed into the *Write* method.

```
'VB
Dim log as New LogEntry()
log.Category = "MyCategory1"
log.Message = "My message body"
log.Severity = TraceEventType.Error
log.Priority = 100
Logger.Write(log)
```

```
//C#
LogEntry log = new LogEntry();
log.Category = "MyCategory1";
log.Message = "My message body";
log.Severity = TraceEventType.Error;
log.Priority = 100;
Logger.Write(log);
```

Another property of the *LogEntry* class is ExtendedProperties. This property is a collection of name/value pairs that are included in the log entry. By adding pairs to this collection, the developer can place context information into the logging mechanism. The standard formatters in the Logging Application Block iterate over this collection and place the name and value in the output stream.

Configuring the Block

Place the configuration for the Logging Application Block in the app.config file. Although this allows people to be able to view the definition and modify the configuration details by hand, you shouldn't let people who want to do so near your source code unless those people are very experienced. The flexibility of the logging makes the configuration information quite convoluted. Fortunately, there is another way: the Enterprise Library Configuration utility.

This utility provides a handy user interface to define the settings not just for the Logging Application Block but for any of the application blocks within the Enterprise Library. It is launched from the Start | All Programs | Microsoft patterns and practices Enterprise Library – January

2006 | Enterprise Library Configuration menu option. Figure 9-2 illustrates the configuration utilities interface.

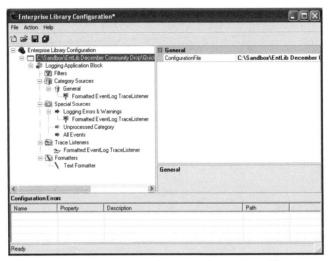

Figure 9-2   The Enterprise Library Configuration utility

In the utility, use the File | Open Application menu option to open the app.config file that needs to be modified. If this .config file hasn't been set up for logging yet, right-click the configuration file on the left side and select New | Logging Application Block from the context menu.

There are three elements that need to be defined to route a logging message: a category source, a trace listener, and a formatter.

- **Category source**   The name of a category to which a message is posted. Along with the name, which is just a string value, there is also a source level that indicates the severity associated with this category.
- **Trace listener**   A reference to a class that monitors trace and debug output. Consider this to be receiving the log messages.
- **Formatter**   A reference to a class that formats the log entry for output. This class determines what the entry will look like when it is delivered to the trace listener.

The logging configuration is built from the bottom up, starting with the formatters. The Logging Application Block includes both binary and text formatters. A custom formatter can also be defined by creating a class that implements the *ILogFormatter* interface. The goal of the formatter is to convert a log entry into a format that can be delivered to the trace listener.

Once the formatter has been defined, it is associated with a trace listener. Again, the Logging Application Block includes a number of trace listeners, including database, e-mail, flat file, and the event log. To create an instance of a trace listener, specify the formatter to be used along with the properties needed by that type of listener. For example, an e-mail trace listener would have Simple Mail Transfer Protocol (SMTP) details, and a database trace listener would include a connection string.

The final step in the configuration process is to define the category. Here, you specify the category name and severity level as well as which trace listener (along with the corresponding formatter). Now when a log message is posted through the *Write* method, the category associated with the message identifies the trace listener to use. Then the formatter associated with the trace listener formats the log message into the appropriate string value. The listener then uses that string value when directing the output to the appropriate destination.

Each category is able to associate with more than one listener. Each log message is directed to all of the listeners for the matching category. This allows more than one destination to be defined for each log entry.

Lab: Monitoring Applications

In this lab, you will explore some of the mechanisms that are available to monitor distributed applications during run time. Specifically, you will be manipulating some performance counters as well as configuring an application to use Enterprise Library to send event notifications as an e-mail. To do the second exercise, you will need to have the IP address (or host name) for an SMTP-compliant mail server. If you encounter a problem completing an exercise, the completed projects can be installed from the Code folder on the companion CD.

▶ **Exercise 1: Adding a Performance Counter**

In this lab, you will demonstrate the technique used to add performance counters to an application. Specifically, you will add a category named Training Kit Counters and, into that category, a counter called Counter1. In subsequent executions of the program, the counter will be incremented by a random number.

The steps are easily mastered, but you must also be aware of the aspect of permissions. To create a performance counter, you need to have Full Control on the following registry key.

`HKEY_LOCAL_MACHINE\SOFTWARE\Microsoft\Windows NT\CurrentVersion\Perflib`

Because providing full control to this registry key is not something that should be done lightly, performance counters and their corresponding categories are usually created at installation time. It becomes a lot more palatable to say that the application needs to be installed by an administrator than it is to say that the application needs to be run by an administrator every time.

1. Launch Visual Studio 2005.
2. Open a solution by using File | Open | Project/Solution.
3. Navigate to the Chapter09/Lesson2/Exercise1/<language>/Before directory. Select the Exercise1 solution and click Open.

4. In the Solution Explorer, double-click the Module1.vb file to display the coding editor. Because this is a Console application, the Main procedure will be shown, and at the moment, it's empty.

5. The first step is to determine whether the counter category already exists. In this manner, you can simply run the same application multiple times and not attempt to create the category each time. Use the *Exists* method on the *PerformanceCounterCategory* class for this purpose. Add the following code to the Main procedure.

```vb
'VB
If Not PerformanceCounterCategory.Exists( _
    "Training Kit Counters") Then
End If
```

```csharp
//C#
if (!PerformanceCounterCategory.Exists("Training Kit Counters"))
{
}
```

6. To add counters to this category, use a *CounterCreationDataCollection* object. Add *CounterCreationData* objects into this collection. Then the collection is passed to the *Create* method. Add the following code to the *If* block created in the previous step.

```vb
'VB
Dim counterCollection As New CounterCreationDataCollection()

Dim newCounter As New CounterCreationData("Counter1", _
    "This is a demonstration counter", _
    PerformanceCounterType.NumberOfItems64)
counterCollection.Add(newCounter)

PerformanceCounterCategory.Create("Training Kit Counters", _
    "This is a demonstration category", _
    PerformanceCounterCategoryType.SingleInstance, _
    counterCollection)
```

```csharp
//C#
CounterCreationDataCollection counterCollection = new
    CounterCreationDataCollection();
CounterCreationData newCounter = new CounterCreationData("Counter1",
    "This is a demonstration counter",
    PerformanceCounterType.NumberOfItems64);
counterCollection.Add(newCounter);

PerformanceCounterCategory.Create("Training Kit Counters",
    "This is a demonstration category",
    PerformanceCounterCategoryType.SingleInstance,
    counterCollection);
```

7. Once you can be certain that the counters have been created, you can use them. Start by declaring a PerformanceCounter variable. Add the following code below the *If* block created in step 5.

```
'VB
Dim counter As New PerformanceCounter("Training Kit Counters", _
    "Counter1", False)
```

```
//C#
PerformanceCounter counter = new
    PerformanceCounter("Training Kit Counters", "Counter1", false);
```

8. For this counter, use the *Increment* method (and the *Random* class) to update the counter's value.

```
'VB
Dim rand As New Random(Convert.ToInt32( _
    DateTime.Now.TimeOfDay.TotalMilliseconds))
Dim incrementValue As Integer = rand.Next(1, 10)
counter.IncrementBy(incrementValue)
```

```
//C#
Random rand = new Random(Convert.ToInt32(
    DateTime.Now.TimeOfDay.TotalMilliseconds));
int incrementValue = rand.Next(1, 10);
counter.IncrementBy(incrementValue);
```

9. The coding for the application is now complete. All that remains is to ensure that it's doing what it's supposed to. Run the application by pressing the F5 key. This needs to be done before using the performance monitor so that the category and counter can be created.

10. Once the application has been run successfully, start the performance monitor by using the Start | Run | Perfmon.exe command.

11. In the performance monitor, click the Add button or use Ctrl+I to reveal the Add Counters dialog box (see Figure 9-3).

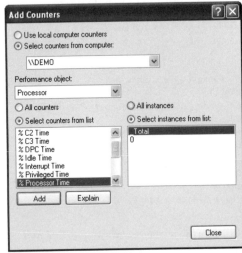

Figure 9-3 Adding counters in the performance monitor

12. Select a *Performance* object of Training Kit Counters. Then select Counter1 and click Add.

13. Click the Close button. The newly added counter is now displayed on the main chart for Performance Monitor. Note the value of the Counter1 counter.

14. Run the lab application once more by pressing F5. Check that the value of Counter1 has been increased.

▶ Exercise 2: E-mail Notifications with the Logging Application Block

In this exercise, you will configure the Logging Application Block to send a notification by using the e-mail trace listener. You will create a Console application that does nothing by calling the *Logger.Write* method. Then you will use the Enterprise Library Configuration utility to direct the output of the log message to the e-mail listener.

1. Launch Visual Studio 2005.

2. Open a solution by using File | Open | Project/Solution.

3. Navigate to the Chapter09/Lesson2/Exercise2/<language>/Before directory. Select the Exercise2 solution and click Open.

4. In the Solution Explorer, double-click Module1 to display the code view.

5. The sole purpose of the Main procedure is to create a log message and submit it to the Logging Application Block through the *Write* method, so you will declare a *LogEntry* class and populate some of the properties. You will add a Training Kit Category as well as two extended properties. Add the following code to the Main procedure.

```vb
'VB
Dim log As New LogEntry()
log.Message = "This is a demonstration log entry"
log.Severity = TraceEventType.Information
log.Categories.Add("Training Kit Category")
log.ExtendedProperties.Add("First Property", _
    "This is the value of the first property")
log.ExtendedProperties.Add("Second Property", _
    "This is the second property's value")

Logger.Write(log)
```

```csharp
//C#
LogEntry log = new LogEntry();
log.Message = "This is a demonstration log entry";
log.Severity = TraceEventType.Information;
log.Categories.Add("Training Kit Category");
log.ExtendedProperties.Add("First Property",
    "This is the value of the first property");
log.ExtendedProperties.Add("Second Property",
    "This is the second property's value");

Logger.Write(log);
```

6. Now that the coding is complete, you can configure the application for logging. Start by launching the Enterprise Library Configuration utility with the Start | All Programs | Microsoft patterns & practices Enterprise Library – January 2006 | Enterprise Library Configuration menu option.

7. Open the app.config file associated with the Console application. Use the File | Open Application menu option and open the Chapter09/Lesson2/Exercise2/<language> /Before/LoggingApplicationBlock app.config file.

8. Add the Logging Application Block portion of the .config file by right-clicking the just-opened application and selecting New | Logging Application Block from the context menu. A Logging Application Block section should be added to the application that has been opened.

9. For convenience, use the existing text formatter. Create a new trace listener by right-clicking the Trace Listeners node underneath the Logging Application Block and selecting New | Email Trace Listener from the context menu.

10. The properties for the trace listener must be set. On the right side of the form, set the Formatter to Text Formatter. Set the FromAddress property to an e-mail address that can be used by the SMTP server that you're about to specify. Normally, this means that both the To and From need to belong to the same domain. The SMTPServer property is given either an IP address or host name that provides e-mail services. Finally, set the ToAddress property to an e-mail address that you can check for the received notification.

11. Next, add a new category. Right-click the Category Sources node and select New | Category from the context menu.

12. Change the name of the category to **Training Kit Category** and change the SourceLevels property to **Information**.

13. Next, add the listener to the category. Right-click the Training Kit Category node and select the New | Trace Listener Reference context menu item.

14. In the created item, set the ReferencedTraceListener to Email TraceListener.

15. Save the configuration changes with File | Save Application.

16. All of the configuration is now in place. Returning to Visual Studio 2005, run the application by pressing F5. The application will run for only a few seconds.

17. At this point, a detailed description of the steps to follow become a little challenging. Open your favorite mail reader and check the e-mail address that you specified in step 10. You should see an e-mail message. (You might have to wait a couple of minutes.) The body of the e-mail message will contain the details of the event as formatted by the TextFormatter.

Lesson Summary

- The focus of monitoring is more on how event information can be delivered to the intended audience and less about how to store the data.

- In many cases, the monitoring event needs to be paired with a logging mechanism. This is because the delivery of an event to a monitoring listener doesn't mean that the data is then available for future review and reporting. E-mail delivery is a good example in that without an additional logging element, there is no easy way to see what events have transpired.

- A logging framework can be useful in a monitoring environment in that the same event can easily be routed to a monitoring store (performance counter or e-mail) and a persistence store (flat file, database, or event log).

Lesson Review

You can use the following questions to test your knowledge of the information in Lesson 2, "Monitoring Distributed Applications." The questions are also available on the companion CD if you prefer to review them in electronic form.

NOTE Answers

Answers to these questions and explanations of why each answer choice is right or wrong are located in the "Answers" section at the end of the book.

---

1. The distributed application that is about to be deployed contains logging statements in a number of areas within the code. You need to determine which of the following areas should be treated as monitoring information (and therefore requiring operations to be notified) as opposed to those that should simply be logged for future review. Which of the following areas should be monitored? (Select all that apply.)

    A. Valid credentials are provided.

    B. Invalid credentials are provided.

    C. A database is successfully accessed.

    D. A request is in an invalid format.

    E. The processing of a request is completed.

Chapter Review

To further practice and reinforce the skills you learned in this chapter, you can perform the following tasks:

- Review the chapter summary.
- Review the list of key terms introduced in this chapter.
- Complete the case scenarios. These scenarios set up real-world situations involving the topcs of this chapter and ask you to create a solution.
- Complete the suggested practices.
- Take a practice test.

Chapter Summary

- The audience for the logging or monitoring information needs to be considered when determining all of the other factors associated with recording the information. It is important to provide the correct level of detail to ensure that valuable information isn't missed or overlooked.
- There are data stores available to support all of the most common logging and monitoring requirements. How the information is pushed into the store means that if a particular requirement isn't supported out of the box, creating the necessary store should be relatively easy.
- There are a number of frameworks that make it easy to implement the vast majority of logging and monitoring scenarios without requiring coding of a centralized logging mechanism. Where appropriate, lean toward using a framework instead of taking a create-your-own approach.

Key Terms

Do you know what these key terms mean? You can check your answers by looking up the terms in the glossary at the end of the book.

- flat file
- granularity
- log level
- logging
- monitoring
- Performance Monitor
- Windows Event Log

Case Scenarios

In the following case scenarios, you will apply what you've learned about logging and monitoring in a distributed environment. You can find answers to these questions in the "Answers" section at the end of the book.

Case Scenario 1: Instrumenting a Distributed Application

You are a corporate developer creating a distributed application that will be available to internal users through a Windows Forms interface and to external users through a Web application. The application will be deployed on multiple servers with a centralized database. The operations group within your company needs to watch the ongoing performance of the distributed application to identify usage patterns as well as address performance issues as soon as such issues are noticed. Also, to help with debugging problems, you would like to place tracing messages at strategic points within the code.

Your challenge is to determine which instrumentation technique should be used to address each of these situations.

Questions

Answer the following questions for your manager.

1. Where should the information used to determine usage patterns be stored?
2. Where should the information about the current health of the Web application be stored?
3. Where should the tracing information be stored?

Suggested Practice

To help successfully master the exam objectives presented in this chapter, complete the following tasks.

Logging Application Events

For this task, you should complete both practices.

- **Practice 1**   Create an unhandled exception handler for an existing distributed application. In the exception handler, make an entry in the event log for every unhandled exception that occurs within the application.
- **Practice 2**   In an existing distributed application, add support for the Logging Application Block. Along with adding the logging code in the appropriate places, add the necessary configuration steps to web.config and create an external logging configuration file so that the logging level can be modified in real time.

Monitoring the Application

For this task, you should complete both practices.

- **Practice 1** For an existing distributed application, add a performance counter category for the application and add a counter representing the number of requests processed. Update the counter every time a successful request is completed.

- **Practice 2** For an existing distributed application, configure the application to send an e-mail every time an unhandled exception is encountered. Do this by creating an unhandled exception handler and using the Logging Application Block to define an e-mail trace listener.

Take a Practice Test

The practice tests on this book's companion CD offer many options. For example, you can test yourself on just one exam objective, or you can test yourself on all the 70-549 certification exam content. You can set up the test so that it closely simulates the experience of taking a certification exam, or you can set it up in study mode so that you can look at the correct answers and explanations after you answer each question.

MORE INFO   **Practice tests**

For details about all the practice test options available, see the "How to Use the Practice Tests" section in this book's Introduction.

Chapter 10
Planning for Testing

Information available as of the publication date of this book indicates that less than five percent of developers use unit testing as part of their day-to-day development activities. One of the reasons that unit testing is not more common is that, in some instances, testing is perceived as being too difficult to do properly. Creating unit tests for the simple cases is, well, simple. However, simple cases are not normally sufficient to create thoroughly tested classes. Complexities can be caused by a number of factors, including the need to handle data retrieval and updates along with external dependencies such as network access, Web services, and database servers. Even with a number of readily available unit testing frameworks for .NET developers, there are a number of common testing scenarios that are either not covered by the current frameworks or are just very challenging to do. This chapter lays out considerations that can make testing a less-challenging prospect.

Exam objectives in this chapter:
- Evaluate the testing strategy.
  - ❑ Create the unit testing strategy.
  - ❑ Evaluate the integration testing strategy.
  - ❑ Evaluate the stress testing strategy.
  - ❑ Evaluate the performance testing strategy.
  - ❑ Evaluate the test environment specification.

Lessons in this chapter:

Before You Begin

To complete the lessons in this chapter, you should be familiar with Microsoft Visual Basic or C# and be comfortable with creating a unit test for one or more of the methods on a class. You should also have one of the following versions of Microsoft Visual Studio installed:.

- Visual Studio Team System for Testers
- Visual Studio Team System for Developers
- Visual Studio Team Suite

Real World

Bruce Johnson

There is nothing like the enthusiastic evangelism of a convert, and that's what I am to unit testing. For more years than I care to admit, I did little or nothing to create structured testing for my applications, much less creating a framework in which tests could be executed on an automated and regular basis to check for newly introduced errors.

I was wrong. Over the past few years, I have seen the benefits of structured testing first-hand, mostly for early bug identification and certainty that implementation changes don't introduce additional errors. So now I try to convince all developers I meet that unit testing is the way to go.

One of the areas of resistance that I get, however, is the difficulty associated with building the tests in the first place. It is true that, in some cases, writing a good test takes more effort than writing the code being tested. But the establishment of a proper testing framework and strategy can go a long way toward eliminating this concern. The goal of this lesson is to describe how to evaluate testing frameworks and solve some of the common problems that arise.

Lesson 1: Creating a Unit Test Framework

For developers, unit testing is the first—and, frequently, the only—type of testing they encounter, and many are resistant to the idea of spending the effort necessary to create good unit tests. Although trying to convince developers of why they should create unit tests is beyond the scope of this chapter, the presence of a good framework for unit testing is the first step in gaining converts. The goal of this lesson is to outline the elements of such a framework and describe how to address some of the more complicated areas.

> **After this lesson, you will be able to:**
> - Design and implement a unit testing framework for your own environment.
> - Evaluate an existing unit testing framework.
>
> **Estimated lesson time: 30 minutes**

What Makes a Good Framework?

Depending on how closely you are following the precepts of *extreme programming* (XP), you might or might not subscribe to the ideas of *test-driven development* (TDD). But regardless of whether you want to write all of your tests before writing the code that will be tested or afterward, the tests must be written. One of the main goals of a unit testing framework is to provide structure for the tests.

As a starting point, let's define some of the components that comprise a unit testing framework.

Test Case

A *test case* is a piece of code that exercises a particular feature of a specific class. The exercising could consist of checking whether a feature works, but it also includes ensuring that the feature fails in the expected way under the right circumstances. For the Visual Studio Team System, a test case normally is implemented as a method in a test class that is decorated with the *TestMethod* attribute.

```vb
'VB
<TestMethod()> _
Public Sub TestCaseExample()
…
End Sub
```

```csharp
//C#
[TestMethod()]
public void TestCaseExample()
{
…
}
```

Test Suite

Although test cases form the lowest level of granularity for unit testing, multiple test cases can be grouped together into a test suite. The main purpose of a test suite is to provide a logical unit of execution for the test. That is to say that you would most likely run all of the test cases in a test suite together to determine the success or failure of a code change.

For .NET, the class that makes up the test suite is indicated by decorating the class declaration with a *TestClass* attribute.

```VB
'VB
<TestClass()> _
Public Class TestClassExample
...
End Class
```

```C#
//C#
[TestClass()]
public class TestClassExample
{
...
}
```

From an implementation perspective, there is a question of whether a test suite should reside in a single class or in many. This is a philosophical question, and the correct answer is going to depend a great deal on your approach. Generally, it is a good idea to define a one-to-one relationship between test suites and the classes that are being tested. That level of granularity works quite well to help developers keep track of where the tests for a particular class can be found. However, the implementation of the test suite might require that more than one class be used.

BEST PRACTICES **One test assembly per code assembly**

In practice, this division of test cases is taken a step further. It is usually a good idea to create one test project for each non-test project. The name of the test project should readily describe the target of the test. For example, the project Contoso.Business would have a test project called Contoso.Business.Test.

Within the test project, there should now be one test class per code class. Again, the name of the test class should make it obvious which class is being tested. (The Contoso.Business.Person class would be tested by the Contoso.Business.Test.Person class).

Test Fixture

Beyond the code that actually performs the test, test suites frequently need additional information. This information could be database scripts that initialize and restore the database, files that are required by the tests, and any other artifact that might be used as part of the testing process. The name given to these artifacts is *test fixtures*. Although they are rarely implemented as code, they are definitely a part of the unit testing framework.

Visual Studio allows files of all types, including all the items that are text fixtures, to be added to projects. The benefit of doing this is that you can track, version, and deploy the test like any code in the project.

Once the fixture has been added to the test project, determine where it will reside when the tests are executed. For non-test projects, this would normally involve copying the fixtures to the bin directory that contains the executables. But the interface that surrounds running unit tests within Team System raises the question of whether it's necessary to move the fixtures on build.

Although it is easy to assume that the project will always be available when the tests are run, that isn't always the case. It is possible to execute the tests through a command-line interface, and this is the normal invocation method when the tests are run as part of a continuous integration regimen. Also, to run the test through the Visual Studio interface requires that all of the project, including the source code, be deployed to the computer that will be running the tests.

Instead, configure the fixtures so that they are moved to the same directory as the test project output file, which is a dynamic-link library (DLL). There are a couple of techniques to accomplish this goal. For instance, you can go into the property sheet for each fixture and set the Copy To Output Directory to Copy Always; or you can select the Test | Edit Test Run Configuration menu item and choose the currently active test run configuration. (By default, this is localtestrun.testrunconfig.) In the dialog box that appears, select the Deployment option on the left, and the screen shown in Figure 10-1 appears.

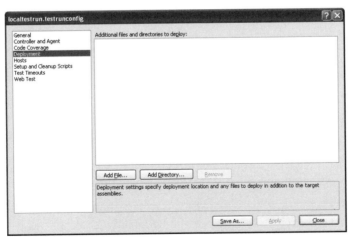

Figure 10-1 Setting the deployment options for a test run configuration

Click the Add Files button, navigate to the fixture to deploy, and click Open. By adding it to this dialog box, you are letting MSTest (the application that actually runs the test) know that this file should be copied to the deployment directory before the test is run. This action takes place as long as the mstest.exe command-line utility is provided with the /runconfig command line switch.

Quick Check

- What are the differences among a test suite, a test case, and a test fixture?

Quick Check Answer

- A test case is a single test against one method in a class. A test suite is composed of one or more test cases. A test fixture is an external resource on which a test case depends. Test fixtures are associated with a test suite.

The Properties of a Good Unit Test

To properly evaluate a unit test, as well as to determine what should be tested and how, it is worthwhile to look at what makes a good unit test. Specifically, a unit test should be CIVIL.

Clear

A good unit test is clear about the intention of the test. Given the propensity for developers not to document the code, a well-designed test suite provides samples of how to invoke the methods in a class as well as of what kinds of errors are expected and when. In other words, unit tests can easily become an important piece of the developer-level documentation for a class.

Of course, unit tests are useful as documentation only if another developer can look at the code and understand the goal and technique. For this reason, treat unit test code with the same level of care you give to production code. Ensure that it's clear, clean, and of clear intention.

Independent

Design unit tests to be as independent of other parts of the application as possible. This includes abstracting out calls to other classes within the application file. This might be done by using a factory pattern to create instances of certain classes. It might seem inefficient and cause more complicated programming, but there is a benefit to this approach in terms of writing testable code.

Unit tests are supposed to exercise a single piece of functionality. Then, if a bug is found, pinpointing the cause is much easier. Maintaining independence of classes enables you to test a class without worrying about whether the subordinate class has been implemented or even whether it is correct.

Very Fast

A unit test should run as quickly as possible. Although there are times when a particular test might need to run longer than a second, this should absolutely be the exception because the longer it takes for a particular test to run, the less often it will be executed. Developers don't like to twiddle their thumbs while waiting for a test suite to complete. They have more important things, such as adding new bugs . . . er . . . functionality to attend to. Although the ideal (zero-length unit tests) isn't possible, by aiming for speed, you can help create tests that will be run more frequently.

Isolated

It should be possible to load and run the unit tests on any system. This means that access to external resources needs to be abstracted out of the system and is performed by isolating the external resource access into a separate class. Then the generation of class instances needs to be implemented through a factory pattern.

By not allowing the unit tests to be dependent on external resources, you help simplify the deployment process. Although it might seem silly to spend time keeping unit tests isolated from external resources, you would not want to spend the first 24 hours installing all the bits and pieces of software required to allow your tests to pass again after you acquire a new computer.

Also, if unit tests are dependent on the presence or absence of external resources, it becomes more challenging to run the tests in other environments. Because a well-designed build integration process includes the execution of unit tests, and the build server is not normally a development server, this is a source of potential trouble.

Finally, if you have any experience writing unit tests, you know that one of the most difficult areas to deal with is simulating the failure of an external resource. If you have no experience with this, try to imagine how you would test a disk-full situation without completely filling up a hard drive. It becomes easier to test extreme scenarios by abstracting external resource functionality into another class.

Limited in Scope

A unit test should concentrate on testing a single entity, partly to conform to the rule about speed stated earlier. More important is the ease in identifying the source of any detected problems. If the test that invokes a single method fails, you have a very good idea where to start your search for a cause.

Exam Tip   The attributes that make up a good unit test can be used to determine which unit tests are considered "good."

What Should Be Tested?

Although the question of which parts of an application should be tested seems like a simple one, there are layers of complexity to the answer. To create an answer that is appropriate to your situation, let's look at all the possibilities.

Public Methods on a Class

Most developers can agree that if your class exposes a public method, there needs to be a test for that method. In fact, it's safe to go a step further. For every public method exposed by a class, there needs to be a test case for every successful path and every failure path through the method. In most cases, there will be more than one test for each method.

Protected Methods on a Class

A protected method is one that is accessible to classes derived from the base class, which makes it a little more difficult to create a test case to exercise it. Still, it is technically a method that is available from outside the class, which means that it should be tested.

The technique to accomplish this is to create a class within the test project that derives from the class being tested. This class can expose the protected methods to the unit testing code through a separate method. By using this technique, all of the protected methods become accessible and, therefore, testable.

Private Methods on a Class

The question of whether private methods on a class should be tested is a contentious one, with smart people propounding both sides of the argument. Following are the arguments for and against testing private methods.

Against Testing Private Methods   By testing private methods, you are tying the test cases too closely to the implementation of the class. If the implementation or the signature of the private methods changes, your tests can show failed results, even though the external behavior of the class hasn't changed.

Also, the code in the private methods should already be covered by tests run against the public methods on the class. Because all that really matters to external users of a class is the public behavior, that level of testing should be sufficient.

For Testing Private Methods   In some instances, the functionality implemented in private methods can be quite complex. If all of the testing on these methods is done indirectly, it becomes much more difficult to develop a set of test cases that provides sufficient coverage for all of the individual methods.

Also, one of the principles of unit testing is to test the smallest possible piece of functionality. By testing private methods, as opposed to the public methods that use them, you are conforming with the principle of limited scope that is one of the properties of a good unit test.

There is no way to identify the best approach to take in this area. Whether you test private methods will depend, at least in part, on your unit testing philosophy. That having been said, one of the reasons for not testing private methods should not be "because I don't know how." It is quite possible to invoke private methods as part of a unit test. By understanding the technique, at least you will be able to make an informed decision about which procedure to follow.

Exam Tip   Creating tests for public methods is fairly clear cut, but because there is no obvious answer for how to deal with private methods, the likelihood is reduced of the issue appearing on the exam.

The key to testing private methods is the *System.Reflection* namespace. It's a little-known fact that the *private* keyword is actually a compiler cue. Attempting to use a method marked as private from outside of the class will cause a compilation error. However, there is nothing in the common language runtime (CLR) that prevents running code from invoking private methods outside of a class, assuming that you have the appropriate permission. That permission is *ReflectionPermission*.

Private methods are invoked by using the *MethodInfo* class. This class contains information about the methods implemented in a specific type. The information for a particular method is retrieved by calling the *GetMethod* method on the *Type* object for a type. Following is an example.

Start by assuming that a class named *Order* has been defined elsewhere. The *Order* class contains a private method called *calculateSalesTax*. The following code gets the *MethodInfo* for *calculateSalesTax*.

```VB
'VB
Dim t As System.Type
t = GetType(Order)
Dim mi As MethodInfo
mi = t.GetMethod("calculateSalesTax", _
    BindingFlags.Instance Or BindingFlags.NonPublic)
```

```C#
//C#
System.Type t;
t = typeof(Order);
MethodInfo mi;
mi = t.GetMethod("calculateSalesTax",
    BindingFlags.Instance | BindingFlags.NonPublic);
```

Once the *MethodInfo* object associated with a particular method is retrieved, the *Invoke* method is used to execute it. The parameters to this method are a specific instance of the object (the *Order* object in this example) and an array of objects that make up the parameter list for the method. If the method being invoked is a static or shared one, the instance parameter is left as null.

```VB
'VB
mi.Invoke(New Order(), New Object(){"orderName"})
```

```C#
//C#
mi.Invoke(new Order(), new Object[]{"orderName"});
```

Web User Interface Testing

This chapter, up to this point, has focused on the testing of various types of methods exposed by a class, but testing a user interface, whether it is a Windows Forms application or a Web page, is a much more challenging endeavor. Because the easier of the two is Web pages, this section will start with that.

If you consider that the procedure for testing a method is, basically, sending a group of input values (parameters) and checking the result, then a Web page should be relatively easy to test. After all, a request, complete with a set of values, is sent to a Web server (the input parameters). The server does what it should and returns a response consisting of an HTML document (the result). It should be a simple process to validate the result to determine the success or failure of the test.

Unfortunately, it's not quite that simple. If you are testing a user interface, the presence or absence of a particular HTML tag might not be the sole determining factor for success. The positioning of the element on the form might be just as important a consideration. The actual positioning depends on how the page within the browser renders, something that is much more difficult to verify solely by looking at the HTML response message.

Still, performing some unit testing on a Web page is a useful addition to a test suite. The easiest way to verify a Web page is to perform XPath queries on the resulting HTML. Thus, queries can be used to determine whether the required elements are present and have the appropriate attributes. Unfortunately, XPath is possible only if the HTML is well formed, which is not the case in many Web pages.

BEST PRACTICES   **Create well-formed HTML**

Although it is not necessary to create well-formed HTML (browsers are capable of handling atrocious HTML), it is a good practice to do so. There is no performance penalty for this, and it allows the Web page to be part of an automated test suite.

If the creation of well-formed HTML is not possible, there are other approaches that can be taken. The general technique involves searching for expected tags. The search can be a simple one, using the *IndexOf* method on the *String* class. Or regular expression matching can be used to determine whether the desired text is present. For example, if you expect a text box with an ID of nameTextBox, you could create a regular expression that would match <INPUT type=text id=nameTextBox.

The biggest problem with this approach is making sure you find the correct tag. In the previous example, a match would not be made if the response contained <INPUT type=text name=nameTextBox id=nameTextBox, even though, from the perspective of a Web browser, the two tags are functionally equivalent.

Windows Forms User Interface Testing

Going from the relatively easy to the almost impossible, consider the options available for unit testing the user interface in a Windows Forms application. When considered from the same perspective as testing methods or Web pages, the model is not similar. Forms don't have a set of input values and a result. The event-driven nature of Windows Forms and the inability to peer at the event handlers conspire to eliminate that as a possibility.

In general, the only way to test a Windows Forms interface is manually; that is, define a set of actions and expected results in a separate document. That document can then be linked as a manual test by using, for example, the manual test found in Visual Studio Team System. With the Team System manual test, running the test causes the document that describes the steps to appear in front of the tester. After following the steps, it falls to the tester to report the success or failure of the test.

Quick Check

1. Is there any reason the public methods on a class should not be tested?
2. Is there any reason the private methods on a class should not be tested?

Quick Check Answers

1. There is no legitimate reason the public methods on a class should not have a test case. In fact, in most cases, each public method should have at least two test cases, one that demonstrates a successful call and one that demonstrates a failed call.
2. Private methods on a class do not need to be tested if testing the public methods provides sufficient coverage. Private methods are more likely to be tested if there is something in the implementation that would give a developer more confidence about the code if it were tested in isolation from the public methods.

Lab: Creating Unit Tests

The arrival of Visual Studio Team System has moved the building of unit tests into the mainstream. Although it was possible to do so with earlier versions of Visual Studio by using third-party tools, the level of integration increases the likelihood that the average developer will start to use unit testing techniques.

Creating a unit test by using Visual Studio Team System is relatively straightforward. The purpose of this lab is to explore a less simple approach that can be used to good effect by developers. If you encounter a problem completing an exercise, the completed projects can be installed from the Code folder on the companion CD.

▶ **Exercise 1: Testing Private Methods**

Although the question of whether private methods should be tested is open for debate, the fact that it is possible is not. This exercise will demonstrate a technique that can be used to invoke and, therefore, test private methods.

1. Launch Visual Studio 2005.

2. Open a solution by using File | Open | Project/Solution.

3. Navigate to the Chapter10/Lesson1/Lab1/<language>/Before directory. Select the Lab1 solution and click Open.

4. In the Solution Explorer, double-click the *MethodInvoker* class. You will place the code to make the call to the private method here.

5. For ease of use, the methods in this class will be static/shared. Start with the method that will be used to invoke both static and instance methods. Create an empty method called *RunMethod*. The method takes a *Type* object, a string as the name of the method to be called, an object that contains an instance of the specified type, an array of parameter objects, and a binding flag. The return value from this method is an object.

   ```
   'VB
   Private Shared Function RunMethod(ByVal t As Type, _
       ByVal methodName As String, ByVal instance As Object, _
       ByVal parameters() As Object, ByVal flags As BindingFlags) As Object
   End Function
   ```

   ```
   //C#
   private static object runMethod(Type t, string methodName,
       object instance, object[] parameters, BindingFlags flags)
   {
   }
   ```

6. Within this method, the first step is to retrieve the *MethodInfo* object for the method that you want to invoke.

   ```
   'VB
   Dim mi As MethodInfo
   mi = t.GetMethod(methodName, flags)
   If mi Is Nothing Then
       Throw New ArgumentException(String.Format("There is no {0} _
           method in type {1}", methodName, t.Name))
   End If
   ```

```
//C#
MethodInfo mi;
mi = t.GetMethod(methodName, flags);
if (mi == null)
  throw new ArgumentException(
    String.Format("There is no {0} method in type {1}",
    methodName, t.Name));
```

7. Once the *MethodInfo* object is available, the *Invoke* method can be used to call it. The following line of code is placed below the code added in step 6.

   ```
   'VB
   Return mi.Invoke(instance, parameters)
   ```

   ```
   //C#
   return mi.Invoke(instance, parameters);
   ```

8. Now that the technique used to invoke private methods has been defined, you can create a couple of publicly exposed methods to use them. Start by creating a method called *RunInstanceMethod*. This method exposes the same parameters as *RunMethod*, with the exception of the *BindingFlags* value. The empty method looks like the following.

   ```
   'VB
   Public Shared Function RunInstanceMethod(ByVal t As Type, _
      ByVal methodName As String, ByVal instance As Object, _
      ByVal parameters() As Object)
   End Function
   ```

   ```
   //C#
   public static object RunInstanceMethod(Type t, string methodName,
      object instance, object[] parameters)
   {
   }
   ```

9. Inside this method, the *RunMethod* private function is called. The *BindingFlags* value is set to indicate that the method is an instance one.

   ```
   'VB
   Return RunMethod(t, methodName, instance, parameters, _
      BindingFlags.Instance Or BindingFlags.Public Or BindingFlags.NonPublic)
   ```

   ```
   //C#
   return runMethod(t, methodName, instance, parameters,
      BindingFlags.Instance | BindingFlags.NonPublic);
   ```

10. The *RunStaticMethod* method is almost identical. The difference is that the parameter list doesn't include an instance of the object being called, and the *RunMethod* call passes a null value instead of a class instance.

    ```
    'VB
    Public Shared Function RunStaticMethod(ByVal t As Type, _
       ByVal methodName As String, ByVal parameters() As Object)
       Return RunMethod(t, methodName, Nothing, parameters, _
          BindingFlags.Static Or BindingFlags.Public Or BindingFlags.NonPublic)
    ```

```
End Function
```

```
//C#
public static object RunStaticMethod(Type t, string methodName,
    object[] parameters)
{
    return runMethod(t, methodName, null, parameters,
        BindingFlags.Static | BindingFlags.Public | BindingFlags.NonPublic);
}
```

11. The last step is to test the code. A *TestClass* has been created that contains a static *Multiply* method that takes two integers as parameters. To call this method, a couple of lines are added to the *Main* method in the *TestMethodInvoker* class. Specifically, these lines call the *RunStaticMethod*, passing the type (*TestClass*), the name of the method, and the parameters.

```
'VB
Console.WriteLine(MethodInvoker.RunStaticMethod(GetType(TestClass), _
    "Multiply", New Object() {2, 3}))
    Console.ReadLine()
End Sub
```

```
//C#
Console.WriteLine(MethodInvoker.RunStaticMethod(typeof(TestClass),
    "multiply", new Object[] { 2, 3 }));
            Console.ReadLine();
```

12. Now launch the project by pressing the F5 key and notice that a 6 is displayed in the console output window.

Lesson Summary

- A unit testing framework consists of test cases aggregated into a test suite. Also part of the framework are test fixtures, which contain non-code artifacts necessary to execute the test cases.

- A good unit test should be CIVIL: Clear, Independent, Very fast, Isolated, and Limited in scope.

- All of the public methods exposed by a class should have unit tests, preferably more than one. The unit tests should exercise not only the successful case but also any expected exception cases.

- Testing protected and private methods is possible. The decision to do so depends on the complexity of the functionality under test.

- User interface testing is a challenging proposition. Although Web pages can be automatically tested, the ability to create unit tests for Windows Forms applications is limited.

Lesson Review

You can use the following questions to test your knowledge of the information in Lesson 1, "Creating a Unit Test Framework." The questions are also available on the companion CD if you prefer to review them in electronic form.

Answers   Answers to these questions and explanations of why each answer choice is right or wrong are located in the "Answers" section at the end of the book.

1. An existing unit test for the *Order* class has failed. The test exercised the *CalculateSalesTax* method. Upon further examination, you discover that the problem wasn't in *CalculateSalesTax* but in the SalesTaxRate property on the *Customer* class, which is used by *CalculateSalesTax*. Which property of a good unit test did the failed test violate?

    A. Clarity

    B. Independence

    C. Very Fast

    D. Limited in Scope

2. A class named *Order* has a method called *AddOrderLine*. The method takes a product number and a quantity as parameters. The product number must be a valid identifier for a product. The quantity must be greater than zero. What is the minimum number of test cases that should be defined on this method to provide adequate functional coverage?

    A. 1

    B. 2

    C. 3

    D. 4

Lesson 2: System-Level Testing

Depending on the size of a development team, the writers of the unit tests might be involved in performing other higher-level testing. For the purposes of this chapter, assume that developers are not directly responsible for performing the system-level tests but might be called on to review the testing plan for completeness and appropriateness. In this lesson, you will look at integration testing, stress testing, and performance testing as they relate to evaluation rather than to execution.

After this lesson, you will be able to:
- Evaluate the integration testing strategy.
- Evaluate the stress testing strategy.
- Evaluate the performance testing strategy.

Estimated lesson time: 30 minutes

Integration Testing

A good starting point for a discussion about integration testing is to identify its place within the universe of testing. Figure 10-2 illustrates the activities associated with both defect injection and defect removal. As you can see, integration testing sits opposite architecture in the hierarchy, which means that integration testing is fundamentally a validation of the architectural design on which the system was built.

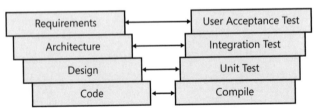

Figure 10-2   The hierarchy of defect injection and removal activities

Figure 10-2 also shows that integration testing comes after the completion of successful unit tests. Integration testing is actually a logical extension of unit testing. A unit test focuses on a small unit of functionality; an integration test spans multiple functional blocks. Integration testing is exercising the interaction between two or more components.

Placing integration testing after unit testing is very important. The goal of unit testing is to ensure that the individual methods are working as expected. If any of the unit tests failed or were incomplete and have not been corrected, it will invariably show up in the integration testing. Otherwise, many hours could be spent poring over the integration boundary of the components involved when the real problem is within a particular class, not at the boundary.

The design of integration tests for an application resembles the design of unit testing. Both a unit test and an integration test operate on the functionality exposed by a component. The difference is in the definition of a component. For a unit test, a component is a class. For an integration test, a component is a collection of classes that function together to provide larger business functionality.

Integration testing is also an iterative process. The test design starts by testing the interface between two components. Then a third component is added, and a different set of tests is defined to test the integration of the three components in unison. The process of aggregating components continues until all the components are in play and functioning together.

A number of different approaches to integration testing are available. Each is valid, and the correct choice depends on the skills and tendencies of the people involved.

Top-Down Integration Testing

The underlying principle of top-down testing is to start with the highest-level modules and work down the hierarchy. By highest-level is meant the modules that involve the greatest number of components. Thus, the high-level logic is tested first. The theory of this approach is that if there is a problem with the high-level logic, why waste time testing the lower-level integrations?

From an implementation perspective, top-down integration testing minimizes the need for *driver* applications to execute lower-level integration testing. It does, however, increase the need for *stub* functionality so that the high-level integrations are isolated from failures with lower-level, untested components.

NOTE Drivers and stubs

In the world of testing, a driver is a piece of code that invokes the item being tested. Drivers form the initialization point for the test and handle any marshaling of data and flow that is required between the tested components. Stubs have the opposite purpose. They emulate lower-level functionality that hasn't yet been tested. For a known set of inputs, the stub returns a set of outputs with no calculation being applied, thus eliminating (hopefully) the possibility of false test results being introduced by the untested components.

Top-down design also suffers from one other failing. In some cases, it is convenient to release some limited functionality for an application. If the top-down approach is taken, it is not possible to do this before all of the integration tests are complete. The reason is that with a top-down approach, the low-level integrations get tested at the end of the testing phase only.

Bottom-Up Integration Testing

As you might have guessed, the bottom-up approach is the opposite of the top-down approach. Integration testing starts with the lowest-level components. You might hear these low-level components referred to as *utility modules*.

By starting with the utility modules, the bottom-up approach minimizes the need for stubs. After all, it's better to use the real, or already-tested, components than stubs that have the possibility of not quite matching reality. But the bottom-up approach increases the need for drivers to coordinate the integration activities of the low-level components.

Also, the bottom-up approach has the same inability to provide the limited functional prerelease that the top-down approach does for essentially the same reason: that no single vertical chain of functionality is completely tested until the entire application is completely tested.

Umbrella or Vertical-Slice Testing

In the umbrella, or vertical-slice, approach, the path of testing occurs along functional and control-flow lines. Integration testing starts with the lowest-level components. Because higher-level components are required to test the lower-level components, they are included in the integration test. In other words, rather than creating drivers and stubs, the test simply includes the real components in the integration processing.

One of the benefits of this kind of testing is precisely that driver and stub creation is minimized. Less code needs to be created, and no false results can be generated through the driver or stub code. However, this approach suffers because identifying the integration points becomes much less systematic. A particular functional chain can be missed when identifying the integration points to test. Umbrella testing does, however, lend itself quite nicely to the early release of partial functionality.

Exam Tip   The arguments for and against the different types of integration tests provide a fertile ground for creating exam questions. Be aware of the types of situations in which each approach is better than the others.

Quick Check

■ If you are developing a product and need to be able to generate previews of new functionality for alpha and beta clients, which integration testing method is most appropriate?

Quick Check Answer

■ The vertical-slice testing approach allows for the release of partially completed applications. Because both alpha and beta releases are partially complete, this is the most likely methodology to use.

Performance Testing

The goal of performance testing is to ensure that an application responds properly to a particular set of conditions. The definition of a proper response relates to elements of speed, typically transactions per second; maximum response time; and average response time. Along with ensuring that the application meets whatever performance criteria have been defined for it, performance testing is also aimed at identifying the bottlenecks in the process with the aim of correction.

There are a number of steps involved in creating a performance test. Figure 10-3 provides an illustration.

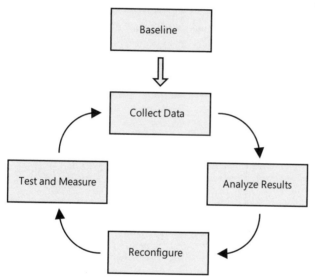

Figure 10-3   Creating a performance test

Baseline

The first and most critical step in performance testing is establishing a baseline. This is done by defining a set of performance objectives, test cases, and metrics that are to be measured. Of these three, the most important are the objectives. A successful performance test needs to have a goal. When tuning an application's performance, it is too tempting to keep fiddling with the configuration settings, trying to squeeze another transaction per second from the application. A performance objective gives you a finish line past which further tuning is not necessary.

Collect Data

This phase of performance testing involves running the test cases and collecting the metrics. Naturally, the specific metrics will vary based on the component being tested. Some of the more common ones include:

- **Processor activity**   % Processor time, context switches per second, processor queue length
- **Memory**   Available memory, pages per second
- **Process**   Page faults per second
- **Network card activity**   Bytes sent/received per second, discarded packets per second

If the available choices are not adequate to measure performance, it is possible to create custom counters. Although there are a number of ways to create a new counter, one of the easiest is to use Visual Studio 2005. In the Server Explorer, expand the server to which the counter should be added until you see Performance Counter. Right-click Performance Counters and choose Create New Category. The dialog box shown in Figure 10-4 will appear.

Figure 10-4   Creating a new performance counter

The name of the category and a description are provided. Then, at the bottom, you can obtain a list of the counters for the category. For each new counter, there is a name, a type, and a description. The type is defined in the *PerformanceCounterType* enumeration, but the ones that you are most likely to use for custom counters include:

- **NumberOfItems32**   Used to count a number of things where the definition of *things* depends on the situation. For example, it would be used if you wanted to count the number of times a method is called or the number of records that were processed.

- **RateOfCountsPerSecond32** Tracks the number of things being counted on a per-second basis.
- **AverageTimer32** Used to measure the average time required to perform a function. It is calculated as the total elapsed time divided by the number of completed items during that time. It is used in conjunction with AverageBase.
- **AverageBase** This is the counter that contains the number of things used in AverageTimer32 counters.

Once the counters have been defined, their use is straightforward. For a standard counter, an instance of the *PerformanceCounter* object is created. Then one of the increment (*Increment*, *IncrementBy*) or decrement (*Decrement, DecrementBy*) methods is used to update the counter. The RawValue method also can be used to set the counter value directly.

If you define average counters, it's a little more complicated. Instances of the counters are created as before. However, the AverageTimer32 type of counter is incremented by the number of ticks to be contained in the average. The AverageBase type of counter is incremented by the number of items that happened during the measured interval. Also, rather than using System.DateTime.Now.Ticks, it is better to use the GetTickCount call because this is the highest-resolution timer available.

Analyze Results

Once the data has been collected, the magic happens. Unfortunately, as in reality, there really isn't any magic. The analysis involves looking at a set of results and identifying the problem. "Identifying the problem" is a deceptively simple statement. There isn't any systemic way to identify areas to improve. The correct answer is terribly dependent on the application, the infrastructure, and the interactions between the components. As a practitioner of performance tuning, I would suggest that, in the absence of obvious causes, you invoke what is called the smell test.

The smell test involves trying to identify those parts of the code where the results are significantly different from the expectations. It could be a query that runs more slowly than expected, a Web page that takes too long to load, or a method that is invoked many more times than expected. These are usually good starting points for the analysis.

Note in the smell test that although the name implies an ad hoc approach to identifying candidates, that is not true. In each of the cases, the trigger should be some measurable data. You can't reliably improve the performance of an application that doesn't have some metric to measure. Otherwise, you have no idea whether the changes made a difference. Although it might be easy to find the easy rewards of performance improvements by making an educated guess, the difference between the metrics will become less and less as the number of iterations increases.

Reconfigure

The reconfiguration phase involves making changes to alleviate the bottlenecks discovered in the Analyze Results phase. Naturally, this can be much harder to accomplish than that simple sentence conveys. And the solution depends on the analysis from the previous step.

Test and Measure

The final step in the circle of performance testing is to test and measure the reconfiguration. The idea behind the iterative nature of performance testing is that it should measurably improve with each cycle. That can be determined empirically only.

There is one other element of the test and measurement process that forms a best practice. While going through this process, make only one change at a time. Frequently, while analyzing the results and checking out the application, multiple areas for improvement become visible. However, changing two variables greatly complicates matters. Although it might not seem likely, it's possible that changing both variables might result in slower performance than changing a single one. The only way to be sure is to keep all variables but one constant for each iteration.

It's very easy to put performance testing and improvements into the same category as performing magic: much hand waving and a few incantations improve performance. But there are a number of dos and don'ts that can help improve the process.

Best Practices for Performance Testing: Dos

- Make sure any logs that are populated by the test are cleared after each run. Log files are frequently text files with new entries added to the end. As these files get too long, they have the potential to skew performance results.

- Ensure that the testing environment mirrors the production environment as closely as possible. Otherwise, you can test and tune areas that don't have any impact once the application goes live.

- If the performance test includes a load element, make sure that some time is included at the beginning of the test to allow for resources to be initialized. As new users enter a system, there are files to be opened, assemblies to be loaded, and other initialization functionality that might skew the earlier iterations of the test. The metrics from the test should not be gathered until the start-up processing is finished.

- If the performance test includes the simulation of a user, ensure that data is randomized to avoid the potential for caching and include wait times (if appropriate) to simulate the typing characteristics of a real person.

- Make sure that all of the computers in the test are being monitored. For some types of tests, elements of the client can become strained when too much memory is being used or connections are insufficient to create the desired load. By watching the client computers, you can ensure that the tests are actually testing what you think is being tested and are not being limited by the client systems.

Best Practices for Performance Testing: Don'ts

- While running a test, ensure that the resources in the tested computers are not crossing thresholds by a significant margin. Performance testing is not the same as load testing, and resource issues can distort results.

- Don't run tests in an environment that has other traffic or activity. The test environment should be isolated from the rest of the corporate network.

- It is not the goal of a performance test to break the system. That's the purpose of a stress test.

Stress Testing

Another name for stress testing might very well be *reliability testing* or *load testing*. The purpose of stress testing is to create a load on all or part of a component and observe how it functions. *Load* means multiple users calling the component simultaneously. Stress testing is actually a specialized form of performance testing. It is closer to destructive testing performed in other fields of engineering. In destructive testing, products are taken up to and then past their breaking point to see what happens. In stress testing, a component is inundated with requests and starved for resources to observe how and when the system breaks down.

Ultimately, creating a proper load is the goal of a stress test design. To do this, identify a process of defining a stress test. Figure 10-5 illustrates the six steps involved in creating a stress test.

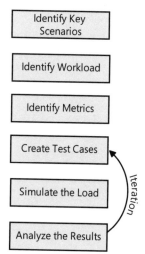

Figure 10-5   The six steps in a stress test

- **Identify key scenarios**   The first step in designing a stress test is to identify the areas that are to be tested. In most cases, it is not worth the cost or resources to stress test every part of the application. After running some basic performance tests and examining the application to find potential areas of concern, you can identify a subset of components as stress candidates.

- **Identify workload**   For each of the scenarios identified in the first step, the target workload must be defined. For a stress test, you would take the normal and peak transaction rates as a starting point. Then you would increase the amount of work performed by the test, based on projected future rates or some factor that you consider reasonable.

- **Identify metrics**   Again, it is not realistic to capture every single metric that you can think of on a stress test. Normally, transactions per second and failure rates are the most likely candidates, but additional information should be captured, depending on the type of component being tested. For example, locking contention and connection pools might be of interest if the test includes a database element.

- **Create test cases**   Once the scenarios, workload, and metrics have been defined, the next step is to create the test case. This includes writing the code that performs the scenario and any additional code of third-party tools to support the metric collection.

- **Simulate the load**   You can choose from a number of options to simulate the load. Third-party tools are available to perform this task, for example. If you are running Visual Studio Team System, however, you have access to the Web Testing tool. Along with providing the ability to make a request to a Web server and determine whether the result is expected, Web Testing allows you to invoke the page (or run the script) as if multiple users are calling the page.

  What if you want to perform unit tests on non-Web components? The Web Testing tool can help out there as well. From its perspective, a Web test looks very much like a piece of code that is executed, which, not surprisingly, is exactly what a regular unit test looks like. If you direct the Web Testing tool to execute a unit test, it will do so in exactly the same manner as it would a Web page test.

- **Analyze the results**   At this point, you have executed a stress test, complete with metrics. The challenge is to analyze these metrics to determine whether there are any problems or, perhaps more important, just where the breakdown point for your application is.

Exam Tip   The key to creating a good performance or stress test is to avoid testing any area that is not directly related to the goal. Either type of test can be invalidated by improper technique, such as repeatedly running the same performance test without considering caching or selecting non-representational data for stress testing.

Quick Check

1. The application you're developing needs to process at least 10 requests per second with 300 active users. Will you be performing a stress test or a performance test?
2. The application that you're developing needs to maintain database integrity even if there is a failure due to too many simultaneous users. Will you be performing a stress test or a performance test?

Quick Check Answers

1. You would be running a performance test because you are required to verify that the application can continue to perform under a certain load. Ideally, the test will not include breaking the application.
2. A stress test involves ensuring that the application fails gracefully, which is what the question is asking. From the perspective of the database, failing gracefully means maintaining database integrity.

Lab: System-Level Testing

Much of what makes system-level testing successful is the application of proper technique, so having a firm understanding of how to structure integration, performance, and stress testing is critical. Still, there are areas in which some technical skills can be applied. If you encounter a problem completing an exercise, the completed projects can be installed from the Code folder on the companion CD.

▶ **Exercise 1: Using Performance Counters**

Sometimes the built-in counters are not adequate when measuring the performance of an application. In this exercise, you will look at the process of adding and incrementing performance counters from within an application.

1. Launch Visual Studio 2005.
2. Open a solution, using File | Open | Project/Solution.
3. Navigate to the Chapter10/Lesson2/Lab1/<language>/Before directory. Select the Lab1 solution and click Open.
4. To start, create a performance category and add some counters. Start by opening the Server Explorer, using the View | Server Explorer menu option.
5. Navigate to your server and expand it to reveal the Performance Counters section. Right-click Performance Counters and select the Create New Category menu option.
6. In the Performance Counter Builder dialog box, name a category **PerformanceDemo** and include any description that you would like.

7. At the bottom left of the dialog box, click the New button. The controls on the bottom right of the dialog box are filled in with some default values. Change name to **Loop-Counter** and type to **NumberOfItems32**.

8. Click the New button again. This adds the counter and again fills the controls with some default values. Change the name to **AverageCounter** and the type to **AverageTimer32**.

9. Click the New button again. Look! More default values are filled in. Change the name to **AverageCounterBase** and the type to **AverageBase**.

IMPORTANT Order matters

The order in which the average counters are created is important. The AverageTimer32 needs to precede the AverageBase with which it is associated. When you add this counter through the Performance Monitor application, only the name of the AverageBase type counter is displayed.

---

10. Click OK to complete the creation of the performance counters.

11. Open the Main routine for the project by double-clicking Program (C#) or Module1 (Visual Basic) in the Solution Explorer.

12. *GetTickCount* is an external function that needs to be invoked through Interop. This means that it needs to be declared. The following code is added to the top of the class that contains Main.

```
'VB
Declare Function GetTickCount Lib "Kernel32" () _
    As Long
```

```
//C#
[DllImport("Kernel32.dll")]
public static extern long GetTickCount();
```

13. In the Main routine, create a loop and increment the LoopCounter counter for every iteration. Start by instantiating the appropriate performance counter and then, inside of a loop, call the *Increment* method.

```
'VB
Dim counter As New PerformanceCounter("PerformanceDemo", _
    "LoopCounter", False)

Dim i As Integer
For i = 0 To 999
    counter.Increment()
Next
```

```
//C#
PerformanceCounter counter = new PerformanceCounter("PerformanceDemo",
    "LoopCounter", false);
```

```
for (int i = 0; i < 1000; i++)
    counter.Increment();
```

14. The next step is to create and use the average performance counters that you created. The instances of the counters are created. Then, within a loop, the *GetTickCount* method is invoked, surrounding a random sleep. Once the sleep is finished, increment both the timer and the base counters.

'VB
```
Dim averageBaseCounter As New PerformanceCounter("PerformanceDemo", _
    "AverageCounterBase", False)
Dim averageCounter As New PerformanceCounter("PerformanceDemo", _
    "AverageCounter", False)

Dim rnd As New Random()
Dim startTime As Long = 0
Dim endTime As Long = 0

For i = 0 To 10
    startTime = GetTickCount()
    System.Threading.Thread.Sleep(rnd.Next(500))
    endTime = GetTickCount()
    averageCounter.IncrementBy(endTime - startTime)
    averageBaseCounter.Increment()
Next
```

//C#
```
PerformanceCounter averageBaseCounter = new
    PerformanceCounter("PerformanceDemo", "AverageCounterBase", false);
PerformanceCounter averageCounter = new
    PerformanceCounter("PerformanceDemo", "AverageCounter", false);

Random rnd = new Random();
long startTime = 0;
long endTime = 0;

for (int i = 0; i < 100; i++)
{
    startTime = GetTickCount();
    System.Threading.Thread.Sleep(rnd.Next(500));
    endTime = GetTickCount();
    averageCounter.IncrementBy(endTime - startTime);
    averageBaseCounter.Increment();
}
```

15. The application is ready to run. To see the results, start the Performance Monitor. Use Start | Run | perfmon to launch the monitor.

16. Within the monitor, add the PerformanceDemo counters. Right-click the graph and select the Add Counters menu item.

17. Select PerformanceDemo from the *Performance* object drop-down list.

18. Click AverageCounter, and then click the Add button. Click LoopCounter, and then click the Add button. Click Close to terminate this dialog box. Your counters have been added to the graph.

19. Now launch the application from Visual Studio 2005 by pressing the F5 key. Pay attention to the behavior of the two PerformanceDemo counters. You might want to remove the default counters to make this easier. If you select one of the counters, you can see the values changing over time.

Lesson Summary

- Integration testing is the mechanism by which the architecture of the application can be verified.

- Integration testing can be done by using a top-down, a bottom-up, or an umbrella approach.

- Performance testing is used to determine how an application responds to a specific set of conditions. It should not be used to try to break the application.

- Stress testing is for verifying the behavior of the application as it is being starved for resources.

Lesson Review

You can use the following questions to test your knowledge of the information in Lesson 2, "System-Level Testing." The questions are also available on the companion CD if you prefer to review them in electronic form.

Answers   Answers to these questions and explanations of why each answer choice is right or wrong are located in the "Answers" section at the end of the book.

1. Your application is using a third-party component to provide some business functionality. At what stage of testing should the interface with this component be tested?

   A. Unit testing

   B. Integration testing

   C. Performance testing

   D. Stress testing

2. You are creating a performance testing strategy for a distributed application. The application is running as a Web service. It has been suggested that a test run consist of a client application that invokes a Web method five times in succession and the average response time be used. Is there anything wrong with this strategy and, if so, what?

    A. No, there is nothing wrong with this strategy.

    B. Yes, there is something wrong with this strategy. The strategy includes using a resource not directly associated with the functionality being tested, namely, the network speed.

    C. Yes, there is something wrong with this strategy. The virtual directory isn't reset after each call to avoid any problems with caching affecting the performance statistics.

    D. Yes, there is something wrong with this strategy. It describes how to perform a stress test, not a performance test.

Lesson 3: The Testing Environment

Creating the appropriate testing environment is an important aspect to consider when testing applications, especially performance testing and stress testing. In general, three aspects of the environment need to be considered: the hardware, the software, and the database. This lesson will discuss the considerations involved in designing a proper test environment, focusing on these three areas.

After this lesson, you will be able to:
- Evaluate the test environment specifications.

Estimated lesson time: 25 minutes

Hardware Environment

When asked what sort of hardware should be used in a test environment, the quick (and usually correct) answer is: exactly the same hardware as the production environment. That simple answer covers most of the basic configuration of a test environment. Of course, there is more to the complete answer than this.

The hardware setup for a unit testing environment is not particularly distinctive. Because all that is being tested is the success or failure of functionality, the hardware really affects only the speed at which a test executes. If database access is required, you can use a central server, or a developer version of the database can be installed on the local computer.

As testing progresses to integration, performance, and stress testing, the configuration of the hardware environment becomes more critical. To be able to state with any kind of certainty that a production application will meet certain quality-of-service guidelines, the performance and stress testing has to be done in an environment that is identical to the production environment, complete with routers, systems and security, and everything else used by the application.

That last sentence deserves some expansion. The ideal performance testing environment replicates the production infrastructure in an isolated environment. This means that all of the hardware, including the networking components, is duplicated. The testing environment should also be isolated from outside influences as much as possible. It shouldn't share databases or database servers with production or even with developers. It shouldn't share Web servers, domain servers, or authentication servers. It shouldn't even share network segments. This isolation, although it might seem extreme, provides the most accurate and dependable results.

As the hardware infrastructure for a testing environment is built, a number of other issues that have the potential to affect performance testing results must also be considered. For most situations, load is generated through a simulation and, in the vast majority of simulations, a single client computer can simulate hundreds of users or more. While running in this mode, it's important to pay attention to the resource metrics on the client computers. Check the network activity, the processor usage, and the page-swapping counters to ensure that the client computers are not being overloaded with the simulation. If they are, the performance test will not generate accurate results.

Software Environment

Like the hardware side, the software configuration for a performance and stress testing environment should mirror the production environment as closely as possible. Any required components, whether part of Windows or from a third party, should be installed and configured in the same manner. Ensure also that only the expected services are running. And, in this case, *expected* means the services that you expect to be running in the production environment.

Real World

Bruce Johnson

One of the greatest hidden dangers in setting up the software in your testing environment is trying to take the easy route. Often, developers about to begin testing have trouble getting the unit tests to run in the test environment, so they start to install the same software that they have on their computers—not the run-time versions, but the developer editions of the software. The number of times Visual Studio is installed on test systems is startling.

This a concern because the installation of a tool such as Visual Studio includes a large volume of software that is usually not needed for the successful execution of the application. Along with extra files, some applications install additional services. If these services are automatically started, they can detract from the native performance of the system. To accurately test an application, it should be running on a system that is as close to the target computer as possible. Unless your application is expected to be running on the same computer as Visual Studio 2005, the testing environment shouldn't have it installed. Please realize that I'm picking on Visual Studio because of developers' familiarity with it. Installing any unnecessary software can result in the same problem.

Data

Quite frequently, if you're creating a business application, there is a database somewhere in the background, and testing with a database presents its own challenges, even in performance and stress testing.

The biggest problem is ensuring that the correct mix of data is available to provide accurate results. In many instances, purely random data is acceptable. For other situations, you might want to skew the randomness so that the data more accurately models reality. Ensuring that the test data models reality as closely as possible is the goal of creating test data.

Real World

Bruce Johnson

The need to make the test data model reality means that it's very tempting to simply use a production database for your testing. It should not be necessary to say just how wrong this is. As much as you might be absolutely positive that there is no way you could ever corrupt the database, that is a risk that most executives would be completely unwilling to take. Data is the lifeblood of most businesses, so the danger of corrupting the information is too great.

It might seem obvious that the next best thing would be to use a copy of the production database. Although this addresses the corruption issue, there are other potential problems. Is any confidential information stored in the database? Is any data subject to the Sarbanes-Oxley Act? Is it possible that privacy laws were violated by copying the data and allowing it to be viewed by people who wouldn't normally need to see it? All of these argue strongly for the next point.

So the starting point for creating test data is to analyze the production data. Check for ranges of values and patterns of entry. For an order entry system, maybe all of the orders are entered during the business week, or the majority are created between 10:00 A.M. and 2:00 P.M. Almost every field will have its own pattern or range. If possible, go to the production database to see what the patterns are. If there are no security or size issues, use a copy of the production data as the test database because the best model for reality is reality. For most developers, however, the creation of realistic test data will be the procedure of choice.

Random Generation Techniques

To help with the process of populating a test database with as realistic a value as possible, here are some techniques for creating random test data.

Random Numbers

When adding random numerical data to a table, SQL provides a function that is invaluable: *RAND()*, but not entirely in the way that you might think. First, consider the need to arrange for a number to fall within a certain range. That can be accomplished with the following SQL statement segment, which returns a random number between 5 and 15.

```
DECLARE @RandomNumber float
DECLARE @RandomInteger int
DECLARE @MaxValue int
DECLARE @MinValue int

SET @MaxValue = 15
SET @MinValue = 5

SELECT @RandomNumber = RAND()

SELECT @RandomInteger = ((@MaxValue + 1) - @MinValue) * @RandomNumber +
    @MinValue

SELECT @RandomNumber as RandomNumber, @RandomInteger as RandomInteger
```

The caveat with *RAND()* is that, when it is used in a SELECT statement, it returns the same value for each record in the result set. Therefore, if you were to execute the following statement

```
SELECT RAND(), EmployeeID from Employees
```

the same random value would be returned for each EmployeeId. The next execution would generate a different random number but, again, the same number for each row. The solution to this problem is convoluted, but it works. Start by creating a view that returns a random number:

```
CREATE VIEW RandomNumber AS SELECT RAND() AS Rnd
```

Next, create a user-defined function that returns the random number from this view.

```
CREATE FUNCTION ReallyRandomNumber() RETURNS FLOAT
AS
RETURN (SELECT Rnd FROM RandomNumber)
```

Once this has been done, you can use the *ReallyRandomNumber* function in a SQL statement to generate a different number for each row:

```
SELECT dbo.ReallyRandomNumber() as Rnd, EmployeeID from Employees
```

Random Dates

Generate random dates by using the *AddDays* method that is intrinsic to the *DateTime* class. To create a random date within a range, you need two values: the bottom of the range and the number of days in the range. Then, generate a random number within the given range and add it to the bottom of the range. The following code generates a random date within the past 1,000 days.

```
'VB
Dim startDate as DateTime = DateTime.Now.AddDays(-1000)
Dim randomInstance As New Random()
startDate.AddDays(randomInstance.Next(1000))
```

```
//C#
DateTime startDate = DateTime.Now.AddDays(-1000);
Random randomInstance = new Random();
startDate.AddDays(randomInstance.Next(1000));
```

Naturally, a similar approach could be employed to work from the top of the range instead.

Random Meaningful Text

Although it's very easy to generate gibberish text by using the *Random* function, selecting meaningful text is a little more complicated. To start with, the universe of possible choices needs to be defined. If you're trying to select a random city or a random name, you have to start with a complete list of all possible cities or names. That list could then be loaded into a collection such as an *ArrayList*. To access a random element, generate a random number between 0 and the number of elements in the collection minus 1 and use that value to retrieve the corresponding text value.

Using DataGenerator

A recently released tool for this purpose can be found in the Visual Studio 2005 Team Edition for Database Professionals. The tool is called DataGenerator. Its purpose is to generate random data for use in various tests. More specifically, it examines the schema of the database and uses that information to determine which type of random data to produce. If the column is numeric, it will generate a random number. If the column contains characters, it will generate random letters.

DataGenerator, however, actually provides more functionality than just creating random data. It has implemented an extensibility point that allows a class to be invoked when data is to be generated. By creating a class that inherits from the *Generator* class and registering it with the DataGenerator tool, you can control the data that is used to populate the database table with a great degree of granularity.

Quick Check

- After deploying an application, you discover that the performance is inadequate. However, you had run performance testing on the application that was successful for the same load prior to deployment. What is the most likely cause for the discrepancy?

Quick Check Answer

- A difference in hardware between the production and test environments is likely. If this is not the case, then the next likely culprit would be that the data in the test environment does not adequately match the production environment.

Lesson Summary

- In a perfect world, hardware will be mirrored between the production and testing environments.

- Extraneous software has the potential to affect performance and stress testing numbers unexpectedly.

- The results of performance and stress testing will be improved (in terms of accuracy) if the underlying data models reality as closely as possible.

Lesson Review

You can use the following questions to test your knowledge of the information in Lesson 3, "The Testing Environment." The questions are also available on the companion CD if you prefer to review them in electronic form.

NOTE   Answers

Answers to these questions and explanations of why each answer choice is right or wrong are located in the "Answers" section at the end of the book.

---

1. You have an application that performs queries against a database. The queries are not ad hoc. During the testing of the application, the performance is adequate. However, once the application is deployed, performance of the queries is slower than expected. Care has been taken to minimize the obvious differences between the two environments. Non-query performance seems to be comparable. What are the most likely causes for the different results in the production environment versus the testing environment?

   A. Differences between hardware in the production environment and in the testing environment

   B. Differences between the background services that are running in the production versus those running in the testing environment

   C. Differences in the data against which the queries are being run

   D. Differences between the versions of software that are running the query

2. You have an application that performs queries against a database. The queries are not ad hoc. Both the test database and production database are installed on a server separate from the production application. The database servers are identical. Care has been taken to minimize the obvious differences in hardware between the two environments. During

the testing of the application, the performance is adequate. However, once the application is deployed, performance is slower than expected. What are the most likely causes for the different results in the production environment versus the testing environment?

- A. Differences between hardware in the production environment and hardware in the testing environment
- B. Differences between the background services that are running in the production environment and those running in the testing environment
- C. Differences in the data against which the queries are being run
- D. Differences between the versions of software that are running the query

Chapter Review

To further practice and reinforce the skills you learned in this chapter, you can perform the following tasks:

- Review the chapter summary.
- Review the list of key terms introduced in this chapter.
- Complete the case scenarios. These scenarios set up real-world situations involving the topics of this chapter and ask you to create a solution.
- Complete the suggested practices.
- Take a practice test.

Chapter Summary

- Creating a framework for performing all types of unit tests is critical to successfully implementing unit testing across an organization.
- Some knowledge of the strengths and weaknesses of an application, from an integration and performance perspective, can help with the design of effective testing at all levels of the application.
- There are a number of options available for most types of testing. Be aware of the choices so that the most appropriate one can be selected for your environment.

Key Terms

Do you know what these key terms mean? You can check your answers by looking up the terms in the glossary at the end of the book.

- driver
- extreme programming
- load testing
- reliability testing
- stub
- test case
- test-driven development
- test fixture
- test suite
- utility modules

Case Scenarios

In the following case scenarios, you will apply what you've learned about how to plan for various testing scenarios. You can find answers to these questions in the "Answers" section at the end of the book.

Case Scenario 1: Choosing the Tests

You are a developer tasked with designing the testing strategy for a Windows Forms application. The application has been developed in three tiers: a graphical front end, a set of classes that implement the business logic for the application, and a database. The application automates a critical line-of-business function that is time-sensitive.

Answer the following question for your manager.

1.   Which tests would you recommend be performed to ensure that a high-quality application is produced?

Case Scenario 2: Choosing the Tests

You are a developer tasked with designing the testing strategy for a Web service that is exposed to partners across a virtual private network (VPN). The ASMX file that identifies the Web methods does nothing other than routing the call to a class that implements the actual business logic.

The partners who call the Web service are using it to retrieve status information for orders that have been placed either through an electronic data interchange (EDI) interface or by phone.

Answer the following question for your manager.

1.   Which tests would you recommend be performed to ensure that an application that meets the requirements is produced?

Suggested Practices

To help you successfully master the exam objectives presented in this chapter, complete the following tasks.

Evaluate the Testing Strategy

■ **Practice 1**   Using a project that you are currently developing, evaluate the tests that are being performed. Are all public methods being tested? Do any private methods require testing? Is there a unit test that should be tested?

■ **Practice 2** Using a project that you are currently developing, add the statements to instrument the application for performance monitoring. Decide on the transactions that should be measured and include the code to track the number of transactions per second that the application processes.

Take a Practice Test

The practice tests on this book's companion CD offer many options. For example, you can test yourself on just one exam objective, or you can test yourself on all the 70-549 certification exam content. You can set up the test so that it closely simulates the experience of taking a certification exam, or you can set it up in study mode so that you can look at the correct answers and explanations after you answer each question.

MORE INFO Practice tests

For details about all the practice test options available, see the "How to Use the Practice Tests" section in this book's Introduction.

Chapter 11
Unit Testing: The First Line of Defense

Unit testing is not a new addition to the developer's arsenal. Developers have been unit testing since the first lines of code were written. Unfortunately, unstructured unit testing produces code that is of only slightly better quality than untested code, and that is not acceptable in today's business environment.

Structured and automated unit testing, however, is something different. Unlike the haphazard technique of the past (in which the developer, looking at the running application, would say, "Hey . . . let's try this"), automated unit testing, when combined with a structured approach to unit test definitions, creates high-quality code with only a marginal increase in the time it takes to produce the code. In some cases, it might take even less overall time to produce the application. The goal in this chapter is to describe how to approach unit testing in a structured manner so that the appropriate increase in code quality can be achieved.

For the examples used in this chapter, the code examples will be based on the Visual Studio Team System. The concepts apply to other testing frameworks, but the syntax and capabilities might be slightly different.

Exam objectives in this chapter:
- Design a unit test.
  - ❑ Describe the testing scenarios.
  - ❑ Decide coverage requirements.
  - ❑ Evaluate when to use boundary condition testing.
  - ❑ Decide the type of assertion tests to conduct.

Lessons in this chapter:

Before You Begin

To complete the lessons in this chapter, you must have:

- A computer that meets or exceeds the minimum hardware requirements listed in the "Introduction" section at the beginning of the book.

- Microsoft Visual Studio 2005 installed on the computer, with either Microsoft Visual Basic .NET or C# installed.
- Visual Studio Team System installed on the computer. Specifically, the Tester or Developer version is required to run the unit tests in the lab for Lesson 2.
- NMock installed on the computer. NMock is a free mock object library that can be downloaded from *www.nmock.org*.

Real World

Bruce Johnson

Unit testing is a new concept to many developers, not because they don't test their code but because of the publicity surrounding test-driven development and tools such as NUnit and Visual Studio Team System. The publicity is actually about how to create unit tests in a structured manner, but that's still a new idea to a surprising number of developers.

The real power of unit testing is the confidence it brings to making changes to the application. A well-designed suite of unit tests means that the implementation of a class can be improved—or bugs fixed—late in the project with minimal risk of introducing new problems. But note that "well-designed" phrase. To take full advantage of the power of automated testing, you need to create a set of unit tests that covers the tested class sufficiently to give you confidence to make the changes. This chapter describes how to design your unit tests to do that. As a developer who has converted to the power of unit tests, I can't stress how useful and freeing this is.

Lesson 1: Identifying Testing Scenarios

The goal is to create a set of unit tests that provides adequate coverage of a class to ensure that the methods work as required. More important, however, the tests need to ensure that changes to the implementation of a method that cause functionality to be different are detected by the tests. That's important enough to repeat. If a change to a method causes the callers of the method to see different behavior, that needs to be flagged by the unit test suite as a problem. This lesson will discuss how to identify the scenarios that need to be addressed by a set of unit tests to achieve this goal.

After this lesson, you will be able to:
- Identify the elements of an interface that need to be tested.
- Create test and use case scenarios to define the unit test boundaries.
- Construct the types of tests that will provide adequate coverage for a class's functionality.

Estimated lesson time: 25 minutes

Anatomy of a Unit Test Suite

Before examining how to construct a successful test suite, consider for a moment what elements comprise a *unit test suite*. First, a single unit test is a piece of code, usually a method, that exercises one specific aspect of the properties or functions of a class. The following code is an example of a simple unit test.

```vb
'VB
<TestMethod()> _
Public Sub AddSuccessTest()
    Dim a As New AdditionClass()
    Dim result as Integer
    result = a.Add(1, 2)
    Assert.AreEqual(3, result)
End Sub
```

```csharp
//C#
[TestMethod()]
public void AddSuccessTest()
{
    AdditionClass a = new AdditionClass();
    int result = a.Add(1, 2);
    Assert.AreEqual(3, result);
}
```

The unit test, in this case, consists of calling the *Add* method and passing in a set of parameters. The result of the method call is then compared to the expected result. If there is a difference (that is, if *Add* doesn't return 3), an exception is thrown. This exception is detected by the unit testing run-time infrastructure and converted to a failed test. Depending on whether you subscribe to the *test-driven development* methodology, the test is created either before the code is written or afterward, but the purpose of the code is the same in both cases: to call a method to see whether the results from the call were what was expected.

Although this example is a unit test, there are a number of other types of tests that can fit into a unit test suite. They are:

- **Web test**   A Web test mimics the use of a Web application through a browser. It sends requests to the Web server and checks whether the response (that is, the Web page) contains the expected elements.
- **Load test**   The purpose of a load test is to test the performance of an application under the stress of multiple users. It is typically associated with a Web application, but it might also be desirable to test the server portion of an n-tier application under the stress of multiple users.
- **Manual tests**   Some tests just cannot be automated. For this reason, Visual Studio Team System includes the concept of a manual test. When this test is run, the user is prompted to follow a set of steps and record the results.

Exam Tip   Because these types of tests are new to Visual Studio 2005, it would not be surprising to see exam items related to which test is appropriate to specific situations.

Characteristics of a Good Unit Test

The creation of a good unit test is important to ensure that it is used regularly. A good unit test has the following characteristics.

- **Runs quickly**   Developers don't like wasting time sitting with nothing to do. And waiting for tests to run qualifies as just that. A test that takes too long to run won't be run often.
- **Tests only one thing**   If a test exercises more than one part of an application, it becomes more difficult to isolate the cause of a failure, and constructing a test suite that provides adequate coverage of functionality is more complex.
- **Clearly reveals its intention**   Unit tests have the side benefit of documenting how a method is used. Other developers should be able to look at the test and understand how methods are to be used.
- **Isolates or simulates environmental dependencies**   This characteristic includes databases, the file system, message queues, networks, and so on. Tests that use these resources are bad for two reasons. First, failures in the external resource will cause a failure in the test, which means that the test is actually testing more than one condition. Also, tests that use external resources will take longer to run.
- **Runs in isolation**   Tests that require special environmental setup are awkward to use at best. At worst, they are the sort of annoying gnat-like problem that developers detest.

Tests that don't run in isolation should be simplified, or the dependent resource should be extracted from the test. A test that runs only on the developer's system is not acceptable under any circumstances.

■ **Uses stubs and mock objects**   This technique allows external dependencies to be eliminated from the application. It is likely that, to use this technique, changes will be made to the code base. In fact, writing code that can easily be tested frequently results in an increase in the use of interfaces.

What to Test

For many developers, looking at a blank unit test is a lot like looking at a blank page while writing. You don't know where to start or what to test, so let's start at the very beginning.

Look to the Interface

The goal of a unit test is to verify the correct functioning of a method. The definition of *correct* might vary based on the values provided as parameters or on some internal state, but the unit tests are still aimed at one of the properties or methods exposed through the interface.

For example, consider a *Product* class that exposes a method called *Load*, which is used to populate the properties of a class by using the values of a specific product as stored in a database. The declaration of the *Product* class looks like the following.

```vb
'VB
Public Class Product
    Public Sub Load(productNumber As String)
        ' code goes here
    End Sub
End Class
```

```csharp
//C#
class Product {
    public void Load(int productNumber) {
        // code goes here
    }
}
```

Given this very simple class definition, what unit tests should be constructed? The following would be a good starting point.

■ **Constructor test**   Determines whether the *Product* class can be constructed with all of the necessary initializations performed correctly.

■ **SuccessfulProductLoad**   Ensures that, for a product number that exists in the database, the values in the database are correctly mapped to the properties in the class.

■ **Dispose test**   If the *Product* class implements the *IDisposable* interface, this test would invoke the *Dispose* method and then ensure that the allocated resources have been properly released.

■ **FailedProductLoad**   Ensures that the method responds appropriately if the specified product number doesn't exist in the database.

What's Out of the Ordinary?

There is rarely a one-to-one relationship between unit tests and the methods being tested. The one-to-one case involves calling a method with a set of parameters that are known to work properly. However, a well-constructed method will validate that the parameters are within an acceptable range, or exceptions will be legitimately raised due to problems within the method. Each of these conditions needs to have a unit test as well.

In fact, to create an effective unit test suite requires developers to think beyond the norm. They need to be aware of how objects are created and destroyed and how the objects react–positively, negatively, and inconclusively–under all circumstances. The developer needs to identify the attributes for each circumstance so that a unit test can be constructed for it.

Consider the following as possible tests that deal with out-of-the-ordinary conditions for the *Load* method.

■ **InvalidProductNumberFormat**   If the product number has a particular format or includes a check digit, a test should be created to ensure that the validation takes place before the database access.

■ **DatabaseInvalidAccess**   This test ensures that the appropriate exception is thrown if the userid and password aren't valid to access the database.

Note that this last test expects that an exception will be thrown, which means that the unit testing framework needs to be able to handle specific exceptions while allowing unexpected exceptions to cause the test to fail. In Visual Studio Team Systems, the *ExpectedException* attribute is used to indicate which exception is expected to be thrown from the test method. For example, the following test indicates that the SqlException exception is expected to be the result of the test.

```VB
'VB
<TestMethod(), ExpectedException(GetType(SqlException))> _
Public Sub LoadInvalidPassword()
    Dim a As New Product()
    a.Load("123abc")
End Sub
```

```C#
//C#
[TestMethod(), ExpectedException(typeof(SqlException))]
public void LoadInvalidPassword()
{
    Product a = new Product();
    a.Load("123abc");
}
```

> ## Quick Check
> - What are the attributes of a good unit test?
>
> ## Quick Check Answer
> - A unit test should test only one thing, use stub and mock objects, be fast, clear, isolated from environmental dependencies, and able to run on different computers without special configuration.

Test Scenarios and Use Cases

Although it might seem a little strange, the starting point for identifying test scenarios is in the requirements of the application. There is a hierarchy of artifacts that exists within the requirements definitions, as illustrated in Figure 11-1.

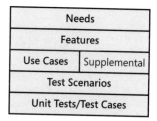

Figure 11-1   The hierarchy of requirement artifacts

Most requirement documents start with a list of the customer's needs. The features the application will implement are derived from those needs with the intention that the customer will use the features to meet them. There is not a one-to-one relationship between needs and features. Features can be combined to meet a particular need. However, if there is a need that is not met by using one or more features, the application is doomed to fail.

The use cases are derived from the list of features for an application.

NOTE   What is a use case?

A use case is a description of how the features will be used to fulfill the customer's needs. It is not programmatic nor does it contain code but, instead, is a step-by-step description of how to use the application. Because the use case normally comes before the coding of the application, the steps provide a framework against which the application can be designed and validated. If done properly, it becomes one of the main building blocks of a user manual.

A flow of events comprises the basic elements of a use case. This is the set of steps that a user goes through to complete the goal. The flow of events is actually composed of more than one element. The first element is termed the "happy" path. This is the sequence that is followed in a use case when everything works as it should. However, use cases typically have more than one flow. These alternate flows occur when something in the happy path goes wrong. For example, a bad password is entered, a product doesn't exist in the database, or a customer isn't approved for credit. The reason isn't as important as the fact that there is a divergence from the main flow of events. Consider the following use case.

Quick $40 Cash Withdrawal from an ATM

The client walks up to the ATM and inserts his or her card. The ATM prompts for the PIN code. The client enters a valid PIN code. The ATM displays a list of options, including a $40 Quick Withdrawal. The client selects the $40 Quick Withdrawal option. The ATM returns the client's card. The client takes the card. The ATM then dispenses $40 in cash. Figure 11-2 displays this set of steps as a flow chart.

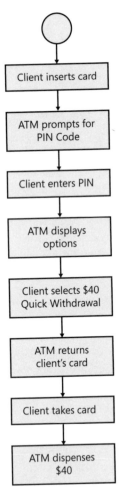

Figure 11-2   The basic ATM cash withdrawal flow

Although this is the simple case, there are a number of decision points that occur within the flow, such as if the client enters an invalid PIN code or the user's bank account doesn't have enough money for a $40 withdrawal. So the more accurate flow chart for the use case would resemble Figure 11-3.

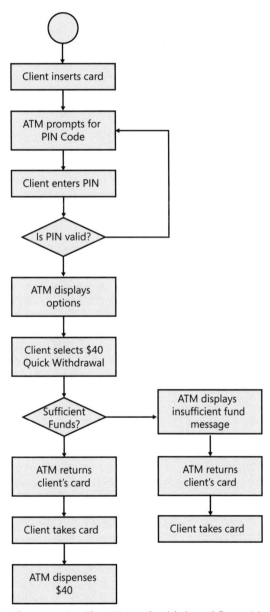

Figure 11-3 The ATM cash withdrawal flow with decisions

Now that you have the event flow associated with a use case scenario, take a look at the test scenarios that can be extracted. First, there is the happy path case that you have already seen. In this situation, everything works as expected. There are two alternative paths that are discernible in the flow chart: when the entered PIN code is invalid and when there are insufficient funds in the user's bank account. Figure 11-4 illustrates the three different paths.

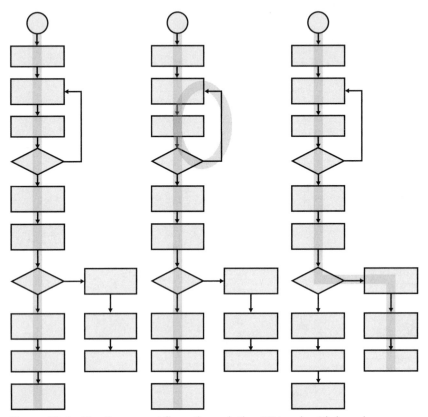

Figure 11-4   The three event flows through the ATM cash withdrawal use case

These paths comprise some of the test scenarios that are associated with the use case, but not all of them. In fact, there is, strictly speaking, an infinite number of test scenarios that can be derived from these paths. The mechanism for trimming the number of scenarios from infinity to something slightly more manageable is covered in the next section. For the moment, consider that there are actually four test scenarios that can be extracted from the paths, not just three.

- The happy path
- The invalid PIN code path
- The insufficient funds path
- The invalid PIN code path followed by the insufficient funds path

In other words, some of the failure paths can be combined to create additional testing scenarios. As you can imagine, if the number of alternate paths in the use case is large, the number of testing scenarios can easily get out of hand. Let's make this a bit more manageable.

Looping

The second test case in Figure 11-4 contains a *looping* situation. Looping occurs when the event flow of a use case loops back on itself. This is why the number of test scenarios is theoretically infinite. You could test the situation in which two PIN codes were entered incorrectly. Or three PIN codes. Or four. You get the idea.

To avoid this situation, trim the number of test scenarios based on an element of moderation. You want to ensure that one loop is included in the testing, perhaps even two. Beyond that, however, continuing to include additional loops into the testing is wasteful, unless, of course, there is a change in logic after a certain number of loops, such as an account lock-out after three failed attempts.

Correlatives

The other technique used to trim down the number of test scenarios is based on the likelihood of collision of flow branches. Going back to your use case example, you could analyze the specifics of each branch to determine whether the combinations need to be included as a separate test scenario.

In your example, you could look at the invalid PIN code entry followed by a valid PIN code entry and conclude that it is unlikely that entering an invalid PIN will affect the insufficient funds case. Therefore, the test scenario combining the invalid PIN and insufficient funds events does not need to be addressed by the unit test suite.

Lab: Identifying Test Scenarios

In this lab, you will walk through the process of identifying the test scenarios for a relatively common use case: creating an online sales order.

The description of the use case is as follows.

1. The user types the Web site address into the browser. The Web site displays the logon page.
2. The user provides a previously registered e-mail address and password. The Web site validates the credentials and presents the main page, which includes the ability to search.
3. The user enters the title of the software to purchase. The Web site returns all of the products whose titles match the entered title.
4. The user adds the software to the shopping cart. The Web site presents the current contents of the shopping cart to the user.

5. The user indicates the desire to proceed to checkout. The Web site requests that the desired shipping address be confirmed.

6. The user confirms the shipping address. The Web site presents the delivery options for shipment.

7. The user selects one of the delivery options. The Web site asks for the credit card information to pay for the order.

8. The user provides the credit card information. The Web site asks for confirmation that the order should be placed.

9. The user confirms that the order should be placed. The Web site displays a confirmation page.

   Now, given this list of steps in the use case, the following exercise will focus on the process of identifying the test scenarios that need to be covered by the unit tests.

▶ Exercise: Identify the Test Scenarios

1. Understand the basic flow of the use case.

   If the steps in the setup are well defined, you should have a good idea of the steps involved in your use case.

2. Define the points in the process at which decisions are made or validations take place.

   Each of these becomes a point at which alternative flows can take place. For this use case, the following table outlines the decision and validation points.

Label	Description
A1	User is not yet registered.
A2	Invalid credentials are provided.
A3	No software was found that matched the provided search string.
A4	The user doesn't want to purchase any of the displayed software.
A5	The user wants to continue shopping after selecting the software.
A6	The user needs to create a new delivery address.
A7	The user cancels the order.

3. Define the list of possible scenarios as the basic flow, plus the alternate flows, plus each combination of alternate flows. Because the invalid-credentials, no-items-found, and continue-shopping scenarios involve a loop, there are alternatives that involve moving backward in the flow.

4. Put the alternatives into the appropriate place in the work flow.

   This makes the determination of correlatives easier to accomplish. Figure 11-5 illustrates where the alternatives fit into the basic flow.

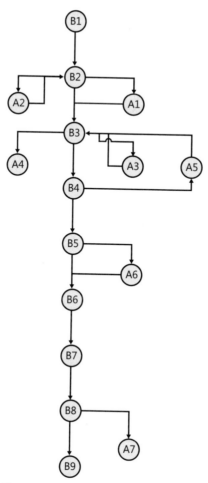

Figure 11-5   The basic flow with alternatives inserted

5. Based on their relative locations, it is strongly suggested that the following combinations of decision points need to be tested.

Combination	Rationale
A1, A2	There might be some relationship between the registration of new credentials and the re-entering of credentials after being invalid. This is not a strong correlation, but they are both associated with gaining access to protected information, which increases its importance.
A3, A5	Both of these decision points involve returning to the B3 step, which increases the likelihood of correlation.

6. Just to provide a rationale for the other alternatives that weren't included, A4 and A7 don't result in users going back into the basic flow and, therefore, don't require any combination testing. Alternative A6 is isolated from the other alternatives by a couple of other steps in the basic flow.

7. The result of this analysis results in the following test scenarios.

Basic Flow	A7
A1	A2 Loop
A2	A3 Loop
A3	A5 Loop
A4	A1, A2
A5	A3, A5
A6	

Lesson Summary

- Unit tests are just one of a number of tests that can help improve the quality of an application.
- A unit test should run quickly, test only one aspect of a class, and be independent of external resources. And did we mention that it should run quickly?
- The interface of a class provides the first set of unit test cases. But understanding how a class is created, destroyed, and used is critical to defining a unit test suite that allows for a high level of confidence of functional coverage.

Lesson Review

You can use the following questions to test your knowledge of the information in Lesson 1, "Identifying Testing Scenarios." The questions are also available on the companion CD if you prefer to review them in electronic form.

NOTE   Answers

Answers to these questions and explanations of why each answer choice is right or wrong are located in the "Answers" section at the end of the book.

1. You have inherited the task of maintaining an existing Microsoft .NET Framework application. The current classes don't have any unit tests defined for them. There is, however, a use case document that describes all of the scenarios for the application. You must define the unit tests that should be included in the suite for each class. What would be your first step?

    A. Look at the public methods that are exposed by the classes.

    B. Create the test scenarios based on an analysis of the use case document.

    C. Perform code coverage analysis on the existing classes to determine which areas need to be tested.

    D. Read the source code to identify the methods that need to be tested.

2. You have a class named *Product* that exposes a method named *Load*. The *Load* method takes a product number as a parameter and fills the class by retrieving the information from a database. Which of the following unit tests are not appropriate for the *Load* method? (Choose all that apply.)

    A. SuccessfulProductLoad test

    B. UnsuccessfulProductLoad test

    C. Constructor test

    D. InvalidDatabaseAccess test

    E. InvalidProductNumber test

Lesson 2: Testing the Component Thoroughly

The key to a successful unit test suite is having all of the functionality exposed by the class under test covered by unit tests, but simply creating more unit tests doesn't necessarily guarantee this. Quality is more important than quantity. The goal of this lesson is to help you improve the quality of the tests as well as identify when more tests are unnecessary.

After this lesson, you will be able to:
- Determine when a component is sufficiently covered by unit tests.
- Identify the relevant properties and the assertions that cover them.
- Isolate unit tests from dependency on external resources.

Estimated lesson time: 45 minutes

Real World

Bruce Johnson

In an ideal world, developers would be able, at will, to change how a class achieves its purpose. After all, changing to find a better way is part of the creative process that motivates many developers. The problem is that developers are also wary of side effects. Many developers have been surprised by making a change to a piece of code only to introduce a new problem in a supposedly complete and separate part of the application.

Here is where confidence in the coverage of a unit test suite is necessary. If the unit tests for a class cover all of the functionality of a class, developers will feel easier about making a change or detecting any side-effect bugs before such bugs wreak havoc on the rest of the application. Further, the test suite can be used on changes made to production code as well, allowing developers to contain the risk associated with bug fixes and minor enhancements. The sighs of relief from developers who are now able to sleep easier is almost deafening.

Code Coverage

Code coverage is actually an interesting conjunction of metrics and reality. As a basic definition, code coverage measures how much of a class is being tested when a particular test suite is executed. Even within that limited scope, however, there are a couple of definitions that are in common use.

Statement Coverage

By general definition, code coverage is a measure of the percentage of statements executed. It is calculated as the number of lines of code that were executed at least once during the unit test, divided by the total number of lines of code. The theory behind this is that if a line of code isn't executed by a test, then any bugs hiding in the code are not likely to be discovered.

Branch Coverage

This type of coverage analysis is also known as *multiple condition coverage*. It assesses the branches that exist within your code and ensures that the unit test suite causes each condition within your code to be evaluated to both true and false. For example, consider a code segment that resembles the following (this sample is pseudocode):

```
If x < 0 Then
    Call MethodOne

If z > 0 or y < z Then
    Call MethodTwo
```

Running this pseudocode through a branch coverage tool will indicate whether x is ever less than 0 (so that Call MethodOne is executed) and whether z is ever greater than 0 and y is ever less than z (so that Call MethodTwo is executed). Notice that, in this second case, both conditions in the OR clause are checked to see whether they are true at least once.

Regardless of which method is used to determine code coverage, the goal is the same: to help identify parts of the code that have not been exercised by unit tests. Implicit in this goal is to reach 100 percent code coverage in your unit tests. Although it might seem as though 100 percent coverage means that all bugs have been removed, that isn't necessarily the case. Consider the following simple but nicely illustrative example.

You have implemented a method called *Divide*, which takes two parameters as follows:

```
'VB
Public Function Divide(a As Integer, b As Integer) As Double
    Return a / b
End Function
```

```
//C#
public double Divide(int a, int b) {
    return a / b;
}
```

Now a unit test is written, calling Divide as follows:

```
'VB
Dim result As Double = Divide(1, 2)
Assert.AreEqual(.5, result)
```

```
//C#
double result = Divide(1, 2);
Assert.AreEqual(.5, result);
```

Would this test pass? Yes, it would. Would the *Divide* method be marked as being covered by a test? Yes, it would. Is there still a bug in the method? Yes, there is. Specifically, if the second parameter is a 0, the DivideByZeroException would be thrown. So is 100 percent testing coverage equal to no bugs? Not at all.

So is code coverage ultimately a useful measure? Yes, because seeing which statements are not being included in the test can help greatly in identifying additional unit tests that need to be added. However, it should not be equated with testing completeness or even adequacy. In general, getting to 80 percent code coverage is quite easy. Anything less than that is probably indicative of a poor suite of tests. Getting from 80 percent to 100 percent is rarely worth the additional effort. The last 10 percent of conditions typically are very difficult to re-create and not worth the time to capture. So a realistic goal for code coverage that maximizes the benefits while minimizing the time is between 80 percent and 90 percent.

MORE INFO   **More details on code coverage**

The principles and philosophy surrounding code coverage is a much deeper topic and requires more space than can adequately be covered in this book. For more information, refer to "Perform Code Coverage Analysis with .NET to Ensure Thorough Application Testing," which is available at *http://msdn.microsoft.com/msdnmag/issues/04/04/CodeCoverageAnalysis/*.

Black-Box Testing

Creating unit tests to increase the code coverage requires, almost by definition, that the tester be familiar with the inner workings of the class. The code has to be seen to know which areas haven't been covered. One form of white-box testing uses details about the implementation of a class to help shape the tests.

Alternatively, black-box testing uses only the inputs, the outputs, and the specifications to create the tests. The correct results are determined by manually applying the specifications to the incoming parameters prior to running the tests. This focus on functionality is why black-box testing is sometimes called functional testing.

The process of defining the unit tests that comprise a black-box test involves varying the values of the input parameters. Completeness of black-box testing is determined by how much of the range of the input parameters is included in the unit test. In an ideal world, all of the values of the input parameters would be included in the unit tests. However, considerations of invalid inputs, sequence of calls, and external resource dependencies, as well as the magic of exponential expansion, make this completely unrealistic. Therefore, instead of trying to cover all of the possible inputs, the unit test writers take representative values and use those to construct the unit tests.

Certainly, simply selecting values and writing unit tests is not sufficient. As most developers are aware, specifications are rarely both clear and complete. Limitation in the language used to write the specifications results in a level of ambiguity that is rarely acceptable in the world of testing. Furthermore, specifications cannot precisely specify every situation that can be encountered, for the same reason that unit tests cannot completely cover the range domain of the input parameters. To make a bad situation worse, users rarely know what they want until they have it. They are much better at identifying what they don't want or want to change after a prototype has been developed, which isn't productive with a test-driven development methodology.

Research into black-box testing techniques has discovered a number of interesting facts. The goal of this research is normally how to maximize the test completeness while minimizing the cost and effort involved; for black-box testing, minimizing cost and effort usually equates to fewer tests. One of the more common techniques to reduce the number of unit tests is through *partitioning*.

The idea behind partitioning is to divide the range of input parameters into groups or partitions. From a functional perspective, all of the values within a partition are the same, so selecting a unit test with just one representative value for the partition should be sufficient to consider the entire partition as tested. As you might imagine, this greatly reduces the number of required test cases. The challenge then becomes determining the partitions for the parameter ranges, something that requires a detailed understanding of the specification but is a more tractable problem.

Boundary Conditions

In the world of black-box testing, boundary conditions are of special interest. Both empirical and anecdotal evidence shows a strong link between boundary test cases and found bugs. This means, at a practical level, that when selecting the values to represent the parameter partitions, it is important to also select values that are exactly on and just outside of the boundary. You might also hear boundary conditions referred to as *edge cases*. The biggest challenge to identifying proper boundary conditions is the same as that which complicates partitioning the input parameters: incomplete or vague specifications.

Quick Check

- Which types of unit test groupings are used to ensure that the coverage of a class by a test suite is adequate?

Quick Check Answer

- Code coverage can be used to identify the areas of the code that are not part of the test suite. Additionally, black-box testing varies the values in the parameter list sufficiently to ensure that many of the edge cases are dealt with.

Assertions

The success or failure of a unit test is determined by whether the test throws an unexpected exception. Although it is certainly possible to throw exceptions by using an *If* statement followed by a throw, that produces a lot of extraneous code. Instead, use the *Assert* class to encapsulate the comparison and throwing the exception.

One of the most commonly used assertions is *AreEqual*, an example of which is shown here.

```
'VB
Assert.AreEqual(3, result)
```

```
//C#
Assert.AreEqual(3, result);
```

This method compares the two objects that are passed into the method and throws an exception if they are not equal. This exception bubbles up to the testing engine as a failure. The complete list of testing methods on the *Assert* class are shown in the following table.

Method	Description
AreEqual	Verifies that the values provided in the first two parameters are equal.
AreNotEqual	Verifies that the values provided in the first two parameters are not equal.
AreNotSame	Verifies that the values provided in the first two parameters refer to different objects. This is different from *AreNotEqual* in that the object reference is being compared, not the logical value.
AreSame	Verifies that the values provided in the first two parameters refer to the same object. This is different from *AreEqual* in that the object reference is being compared, not the logical value.
Fail	This methods throws an exception without comparing any values.
Inconclusive	This method throws an exception that indicates an unfinished test. Although an exception is thrown, the message is different in that it explains that the test hasn't been conclusively performed. It is normally used to create a test method without actually coding it to completion.
IsFalse	Verifies that the value provided in the first parameter is false.
IsInstanceOfType	Verifies that the value provided in the first parameter is the type indicated in the second parameter.
IsNotInstanceOfType	Verifies that the value provided in the first parameter is not the type indicated in the second parameter.
IsNotNull	Verifies that the value provided in the first parameter is not null (or Nothing, in Visual Basic parlance).
IsNull	Verifies that the value provided in the first parameter is null.
IsTrue	Verifies that the value provided in the first parameter evaluates to True.

Data-Driven Testing

When it comes to performing black-box testing by using either of these techniques, a feature is available in the Visual Studio Test System that actually eases the burden of creating partition-driven unit tests. It is called data-driven testing, and it uses the *DataSource* attribute to indicate where the data for the test should come from. Look at an example to gain a better understanding of how it works.

```vb
'VB
<TestMethod(), DataSource("System.Data.SqlClient", _
    "Data Source=LOCALHOST;Initial Catalog=TestDB;" & _
    Integrated Security=True", "UnitTest",  _
    DataAccessMethod.Sequential)> _
Public Sub AddTest()
    Dim obj As New TestClass()
    Dim result as Integer = _
        obj.Add(CType(TestContext.DataRow("TestVal1"), Integer), _
        CType(TestContext.DataRow("TestVal2"), Integer))
    Assert.AreEqual(CType(TestContext.DataRow("Result"), Integer), result)
End Sub
```

```csharp
//C#
[TestMethod(), DataSource("System.Data.SqlClient",
    "Data Source=LOCALHOST;Initial Catalog=TestDB;" +
    Integrated Security=True",
    DataAccessMethod.Sequential, "UnitTest")]
public void AddTest() {
    TestClass obj As new TestClass()
    int result = obj.Add((int)TestContext.DataRow["TestVal1"],
        (int)TestContext.DataRow["TestVal2"]);
    Assert.AreEqual((int)TestContext.DataRow["Result"], result);
}
```

There are two pieces to data-driven testing. The first is the *DataSource* attribute. It is used to define the source of the data used to drive the testing. In the example, you can see that the SqlClient libraries are being used and that a connection string to the data source is being defined. As a result of this combination of parameters, you use as a source any data store that is supported by ADO.NET, which doesn't limit you in any significant way.

The other parameter of particular interest is the latter one. This is the name of the table in the data source that contains the data. The data access method (the third parameter) indicates how the information from the data source is to be processed. The value in the example indicates that the rows in the source are to be processed sequentially. The other option is to process the rows in a random order.

One other declaration overload is important when considering the subject of the *DataSource* attribute. If a single string is passed in, the value can be the name of a connection string within your application configuration file. The following section of an application configuration file provides an illustration of what needs to be done to define the connection.

```xml
<?xml version="1.0" encoding="utf-8" ?>
<configuration>
    <configSections>
        <section name="microsoft.visualstudio.testtools"
type="Microsoft.VisualStudio.TestTools.UnitTesting.TestConfigurationSection,
Microsoft.VisualStudio.QualityTools.UnitTestFramework, Version=8.0.0.0, Culture=neutral,
PublicKeyToken=b03f5f7f11d50a3a"/>
    </configSections>
    <connectionStrings>
        <add name="jetConn"
            connectionString="Provider=Microsoft.Jet.OLEDB.4.0; Data
                Source=C:\testdatasource.mdb; Persist Security Info=False;"
            providerName="System.Data.OleDb" />
        <add name="excelConn"
            connectionString="Dsn=Excel Files;dbq=data.xls;defaultdir=.;
                driverid=790;maxbuffersize=2048;pagetimeout=5"
            providerName="System.Data.Odbc" />
    </connectionStrings>
    <microsoft.visualstudio.testtools>
        <dataSources>
            <add name="jetDataSource" connectionString="jetConn"
                dataTableName="UnitTest" dataAccessMethod="Sequential"/>
            <add name="excelDataSource" connectionString="excelConn"
                dataTableName="Sheet1$" dataAccessMethod="Sequential"/>
        </dataSources>
    </microsoft.visualstudio.testtools>
</configuration>
```

So, given this configuration file, defining *DataSource* with a value of *excelDataSource* would result in the values in the Microsoft Office Excel spreadsheet being used to feed the data-driven test.

Once the data source for the data-driven testing is defined, the second piece of the puzzle is to use the data. This is done through the TestContext.DataRow property. The *TestContext* class is used to pass information about the unit test into the test itself. This includes details such as the deployment directory and the URL (for Web-based tests). In the *TestContext* class, the DataRow property exposes an individual row as retrieved from the data source.

The Visual Studio Test System unit test engine queries the data source and then executes the method marked with *DataSource* once for each row in the source. The information for that row can be retrieved through the DataRow property. This is a *DataRow* object, so the individual column values are accessed through the indexer property. For example, TestContext.DataRow [Result] would retrieve the value of the Result column in the current row. As you can see from the original code, those values can now be passed into the method under test and included in the determination of the success or failure of the unit test.

Isolating Components

Some of the problems with components that have dependencies on external resources have already been discussed from a testing perspective. Mostly, the problems fall into the categories of speed and complexity of test setup. Although it's easy to say that components should be designed with a minimum of dependencies, the reality is that, sometimes, that's not possible. Older classes that were designed before the latest wave of unit testing tools are also likely to fall into this category. In this instance, the need to retrieve data from a particular database might be hard-coded into the implementation. This inflexibility can make it difficult to construct unit tests.

As it turns out, the most common example of dependencies results from needing to access a database. This is the example covered in the next section. Specifically, you will examine the case in which business logic is accessing a data access component, which, in turn, talks to a database server.

As it turns out, the process of isolating components for testing purposes starts with the design. The link between the business logic and the data access component needs to be interface-based. Figure 11-6 illustrates what the interface design is trying to accomplish.

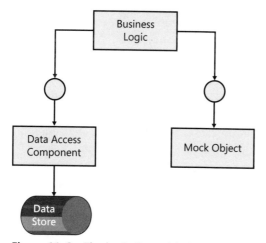

Figure 11-6   The basic flow with the alternatives inserted

The idea behind isolating components lies in the interface. When the application runs in production, the data access component is instantiated and used. When the application is being tested, an object that emulates the data access component is instantiated. The name given to the object that does the emulation is called a *mock object*.

NOTE   Mock objects

A mock object is an object that mimics the interface of another object. Mock objects are generally used in testing or as *stubs* for objects that have yet to be implemented. The most common usage is testing, in which mock objects emulate hard-to-replicate testing conditions such as network failure or out-of-range data.

Design becomes a factor when the business logic component needs to determine which object to instantiate. This is accomplished by implementing the instantiation logic as a factory pattern or by using a dependency injection pattern. The factory pattern involves calling a method that instantiates an object instead of using the new statement directly. The factory uses some information about the environment (a setting in the application configuration file, for example) to determine which object should be returned. The dependency injection pattern involves passing the dependent value (the mock or real object) into the constructor for the class. Either one of these approaches results in a class that is more easily tested without having an external resource available.

When running in production, it would be the real data access component. When running in test, it would be the mock object. The business logic application doesn't know which object was returned, and it doesn't care. Because the returned object implements the interface, the business logic component just calls the object and continues on.

Although it would be possible for a developer to create mock objects for all of the situations that have external dependencies, why would they want to? Not that mock objects aren't useful; they are, but the coding behind them is trivial and monotonous. Writing such code is a task that most developers would go out of their way to avoid. NMock is a solution to this problem.

NMock is a dynamic mock object library for use in .NET applications. It can be downloaded at no charge from *www.nmock.org*. NMock's purpose is to generate mock objects that take on a specific interface, thus allowing them to be used in the testing scenario that was just described. The term *dynamic* comes from the fact that it actually uses reflection to determine which methods the mock object needs to expose. As a result, the creation of a mock object can be accomplished by passing a *Type* object to the method that constructs the object or by using a generic version of the same method. For example, the following code will create an object that implements the *IDataAccess* interface.

```vb
'VB
Dim mocks as New Mockery()
Dim mockObject as IDataAccess
mockObject = mocks.NewMock(Of IDataAccess)()
```

```csharp
//C#
Mockery mocks = new Mockery();
IDataAccess mockObject = mocks.NewMock<IDataAccess>();
```

Having an object that implements *IDataAccess* is nice but, from a testing perspective, relatively limited in its usefulness. To be able to use the mock object in test, it needs to be able to react more naturally with the calling application. For example, the *IDataAccess* interface might contain a *Load* method that returns the number of objects loaded. Although the mock object would have a method called *Load* with the appropriate signature and return value, calling the method would always return 0. In the context of the caller's business logic, a return value of 0 doesn't allow for cases that actually require the retrieval of values to be tested.

The solution to this problem within NMock is the *Stub* class. This class is used to add to the list of requests that the mock object recognizes and responds to. The *Stub* class has a set of cascading methods. First, the *On* method takes the mock object that is being stubbed out. Next, the *With* method indicates the parameter values that are to be paired with the response. Finally, the *Will* method specifies the return value for the method. So, for example, if there is an *Add* method that takes 1 and 2 as parameters and returns a 3, the *Stub* call would look like the following.

```
'VB
Stub.On(obj).With(1, 2).Will(Return.Value(3))
```

```
//C#
Stub.On(obj).With(1, 2).Will(Return.Value(3));
```

Where the *Stub* gets used depends on the pattern. For a dependency injection pattern, the *Stub* is called within the test method after the mock object has been created. The configured mock object is then passed into the constructor.

Alternatively, if the factory pattern is used, the factory becomes responsible for using *Stub* because it's the factory that creates and returns the mock object. From a testing perspective, this is a more awkward approach because the factory is external to the testing assembly and must be kept in sync. However, in some instances, the factory is the best design to work with and, therefore, might be useful in larger or more complex applications.

Quick Check

- What is the benefit gained by using mock objects in a testing scenario?

Quick Check Answer

- A number of areas are very difficult to test on an on-demand basis, such as ensuring that your method functions properly if a network fails.

Lab: Testing with Mock Objects

In this lab, you will use the mock objects implemented in NMock to demonstrate how they can be used to remove a dependency on an external resource. The scenario that you will be implementing is a unit test on a method called *LoadProduct* in a business logic class called *BusinessLogic*. The *LoadProduct* method takes a product number as the parameter and returns a *Product* object. Because the *LoadProduct* method would normally interact with a database, a mock object will be used to take the place of the data access component, and then the mock object will be added to the *BusinessLogic* class through the dependency injection pattern.

If you encounter a problem completing an exercise, the completed projects can be installed from the Code folder on the companion CD.

▶ **Exercise: Unit Testing with Mock Objects**

1. Launch Visual Studio 2005.

2. Open a solution using File | Open | Project/Solution.

3. Navigate to the Chapter11/Lesson2/Lab1/<language>/Before directory. Select the Lab1 solution, and click Open.

4. In Solution Explorer, double-click IProductDataAccess to display the code view. Notice that the only method described in this interface is called *LoadOne*. *LoadOne* takes a single string (the product number) as a parameter and returns a *Product* object. When you're finished, you can close this file.

5. In Solution Explorer, double-click the BusinessLogic file to display the code view. Already implemented in the class is a constructor, which instantiates a private data access component, an instance of the *RealProductDataAccess* class. The class also implements the *IProductDataAccess* interface.

6. Add a second constructor to the class. This constructor will be marked as internal and takes a data access component as a parameter. Add the following code below the currently defined constructor.

   ```
   'VB
   Friend Sub New(dac As IProductDataAccess)
       productDac = dac
   End Sub
   ```

   ```
   //C#
   internal BusinessLogic(IProductDataAccess dac) {
       productDac = dac;
   }
   ```

   Because the constructor is marked as internal or Friend, it is visible only to classes within the assembly. You will create a separate assembly to perform the tests. You need to use the *InternalVisibleTo* attribute to include the test assembly as being available to see and access the internal/Friend constructor.

7. Add the following above the *BusinessLogic* class declaration.

   ```
   'VB
   <assembly:InternalsVisibleTo("MockObjectDemoTest")>
   ```

   ```
   //C#
   [assembly:InternalsVisibleTo("MockObjectDemoTest")]
   ```

8. Next, create the unit test assembly. Select the Test menu, and choose the New Test menu item.

9. Select the Unit Test template. Set the TestName to BusinessLogicTest, and the Add to Test Project drop-down to Create new C#/VisualBasic test project. Click OK.

10. You will be prompted for the name of the project to create. Name it **MockObjectDemoTest**, and click OK.

11. Two references must be added to the newly created test project. First, add a reference for the MockObjectDemo project. In Solution Explorer, right-click the MockObjectDemo-Test project, and select Add Reference from the context menu.

12. Select the Project tab in the Add Reference dialog box. Click the MockObjectDemo project, and then click OK.

13. Add a reference to NMock. Again, right-click the MockObjectDemoTest project in Solution Explorer, and select Add Reference from the context menu.

14. Select the Browse tab in the Add Reference dialog box. Navigate to the directory in which NMock was installed, and select the NMock.dll file. Click OK.

15. When the unit test was created, the BusinessLogicTest file was opened. In that file, there is a method called *TestMethod1*. Change the name of the method to **TestLoadProduct**.

16. Configure the mock object to return the desired value for your test. Start by declaring a *Mockery* object. Then create an instance of the *IProductDataAccess* interface by using the *NewMock* generic method. Add the following code to the *TestLoadProduct* method.

    ```
    'VB
    Dim mocks as New Mockery()
    Dim dac As IProductDataAccess
    dac = mocks.NewMock(Of IProductDataAccess)()
    ```

    ```
    //C#
    Mockery mocks = new Mockery();
    IProductDataAccess dac = mocks.NewMock<IProductDataAccess>();
    ```

17. The newly created mock object needs to be configured to return a *Product* object. The following code goes below the *NewMock* statement.

    ```
    'VB
    Dim productResult As new Product()
    productResult.ProductNumber = "123"
    productResult.Description = "Test Product"

    Stub.On(dac).Method("LoadOne").With("123").Will(Return.Value(productResult));
    ```

    ```
    //C#
    Product productResult = new Product();
    productResult.ProductNumber = "123";
    productResult.Description = "Test Product";

        Stub.On(dac).Method("LoadOne").With("123"). // keep with next line
            Will(Return.Value(productResult));
    ```

18. Finally, call the method, and check to see whether the desired results were returned. Add the following code below the just added statements.

    ```
    'VB
    Dim businessObject As New BusinessLogic(dac)
    Dim result As Product
    Result = businessObject.LoadProduct("123")
    ```

```
Assert.AreEqual("123", result.ProductNumber)
Assert.AreEqual("Test Product", result.Description)

//C#
BusinessLogic businessObject = new BusinessLogic(dac);
Product result = businessObject.LoadProduct("123");

Assert.AreEqual("123", result.ProductNumber);
Assert.AreEqual("Test Product", result.Description);
```

19. Launch the Test Manager with the Test | Windows | Test Manager menu option.

20. Click the *TestLoadProduct* method. Then right-click the method, and select the Run Checked Tests option from the context menu. Notice that, in the Test Results, the method is marked as passing.

Lesson Summary

- Although code coverage is useful in identifying areas that could be covered by unit tests, it should not be used to determine the completeness or correctness of the testing effort.

- Black-box testing involves the creation of unit tests based on specifications only. The challenges involve vague specifications and ensuring adequate coverage of the range of values for the input parameters.

- Mock objects are used to reduce the dependency of unit tests on external resources.

Lesson Review

You can use the following questions to test your knowledge of the information in Lesson 2, "Testing the Component Thoroughly." The questions are also available on the companion CD if you prefer to review them in electronic form.

NOTE Answers

Answers to these questions and explanations of why each answer choice is right or wrong are located in the "Answers" section at the end of the book.

1. You are designing and managing the testing process for a commercial application. You need to specify a code coverage level that balances the quality of the application against the time that it needs to be delivered. What percentage of lines should be covered before signing off on the unit testing as acceptable?

   A. 70 percent

   B. 80 percent

   C. 90 percent

   D. 100 percent

2. In which of the following scenarios would it not be necessary to use a mock object to create an easily repeatable unit test?

    A. Need to retrieve the system's current time

    B. Need to access a file on a remote computer

    C. Need to calculate the total cost of an order, given the cost of each order line

    D. Need to call a Web service method

Chapter Review

To further practice and reinforce the skills you learned in this chapter, you can perform the following tasks:

- Review the chapter summary.
- Review the list of key terms introduced in this chapter.
- Complete the case scenarios. These scenarios set up real-world situations involving the topics of this chapter and ask you to create a solution.
- Complete the suggested practices.
- Take a practice test.

Chapter Summary

- One of the goals of unit testing is to provide a level of confidence for developers to change code with a minimum of concern about introducing side-effect bugs.
- Determining what to test is a multi-pronged process. The interface provides the obvious choices for methods and properties, but code coverage and black-box testing techniques can add exception and range tests, which contribute to the completeness of the testing.
- Designing for testability is important, especially when the class under test depends on external resources. It is very difficult to eliminate external dependency for existing classes that were not designed appropriately.

Key Terms

Do you know what these key terms mean? You can check your answers by looking up the terms in the glossary at the end of the book.

- edge case
- looping
- mock object
- multiple condition coverage
- partitioning
- stub
- test-driven development
- unit test suite

Case Scenarios

In the following case scenarios, you will apply what you've learned about identifying and implementing unit tests. You can find answers to these questions in the "Answers" section at the end of the book.

Case Scenario 1: Unit Testing for a Web Application

You are a corporate developer creating a Web application that will be available to users on the Internet. One of your responsibilities is to create a unit testing plan for the application, but the resources available to you are not infinite, and the delivery date for the Web site is fast approaching. Your challenge is to decide on the appropriate testing approach.

Questions

Answer the following questions for your manager.

1. Which types of unit tests should be used and on which components?
2. What is the best approach to ensure that the unit tests cover the application to the appropriate level?

Case Scenario 2: Identifying External Dependencies

You are a corporate developer creating a Windows-based application that will be available to users on your corporate intranet. The application gathers information from an external Web service as well as from the company database. This information is then displayed in a graphical representation. The specifics about which Web service to invoke and the credentials to use are stored in a configuration file. The information from the two data sources is updated every 30 seconds.

One of your responsibilities is to identify the areas in which a mock object will be required to unit test the components of the application reliably.

Questions

Answer the following questions for your manager.

1. What are the external dependencies for the application?
2. Which of the external dependencies should use mock objects to help with testing?

Suggested Practices

To help you successfully master the exam objectives presented in this chapter, complete the following tasks.

Create Unit Tests for Legacy Classes

For this task, you should complete both practices.

- **Practice 1** Using the black-box testing technique (and assuming that the specifications are available), develop a set of unit tests for an older component. Either the specifications for the class can be used to generate the functionality, or the current client application can be examined to see which methods are called, how they are called, and what is returned.
- **Practice 2** Once the unit tests have been created, use code coverage analysis to suggest areas in which additional unit tests can be added. Aim to get the code coverage to 90 percent.

Take a Practice Test

The practice tests on this book's companion CD offer many options. For example, you can test yourself on just one exam objective, or you can test yourself on all the 70-549 certification exam content. You can set up the test so that it closely simulates the experience of taking a certification exam, or you can set it up in study mode so that you can look at the correct answers and explanations after you answer each question.

MORE INFO Practice tests

For details about all the practice test options available, see the "How to Use the Practice Tests" section in this book's Introduction.

Chapter 12

Stabilizing the Application

Unit testing is but the first step in getting an application ready for release into the cold, cruel world. Yes, it's nice to know your way forward is clear, but that is just the beginning. The next step for the tested components is to become integrated with the other components in the application.

Before coming to that point, however, there is one more step for the component-level code. No one can reasonably claim that getting a successful set of unit tests means that the application is bug free, so instead of depending purely on unit tests, implementing a code review can help greatly in the reduction of defects in the application.

The goal of this chapter is to discuss the concepts that are involved in both of these elements. By the end, you will have gone a lot further toward understanding the process of creating high-quality applications.

Exam objectives in this chapter:
- Perform a code review.
- Perform integration testing.
    - Determine if the component works as intended in the target environment.
    - Identify component interactions and dependencies.
    - Verify results.
- Resolve a bug.
    - Investigate a reported bug.
    - Reproduce a bug.
    - Evaluate the impact of the bug and the associated cost and timeline for fixing the bug.
    - Fix a bug.

Lessons in this chapter:

Before You Begin

To complete the lessons in this chapter, you must have:

- A computer that meets or exceeds the minimum hardware requirements listed in the "Introduction" section at the beginning of the book.

- Microsoft Visual Studio 2005 installed on the computer, with either Microsoft Visual Basic .NET or C# installed.

- The Northwind database installed and accessible. To install the Northwind database, follow the instructions found at *http://msdn2.microsoft.com/en-us/library/8b6y4c7s(VS.80).aspx*.

Real World

Bruce Johnson

Many developers look at the code review process as being a pain in the lower portion of their anatomy. "After all," they think, "I'm the only one who understands the intricacies of what I'm developing. What possible advice could someone else offer about my code that would make it better?"

Unfortunately, they're wrong—not about understanding the details, necessarily, but about the benefits of code review. Having an in-depth understanding of the topic is useful in a code review, but it isn't a requirement. Consider, for example, the impact that software design patterns have had on development. It is widely accepted that there are commonly found scenarios that can be solved over and over again by taking the same approach. The software design pattern concept works at the code level, too.

It is possible to look at a piece of code and see potential problems that have nothing to do with the functionality of the code. Are input parameters in the correct range? Are the right type of exceptions being thrown? Is there a flaw in the programming logic that stands out? Any of these could cause a defect that might or might not be caught by unit tests. Finding these types of problems before the application goes live helps reduce the cost associated with fixing them.

Lesson 1: The Code Review Process

Computers are stupid. Yes, they're incredibly fast at doing what they do, but all they do is follow directions very fast. They are not capable of understanding what users expect of them. Add a zero to an invoice amount. Attempt to divide by zero. Use an object that hasn't yet been instantiated. When encountering such situations, the computer will assume that's what you meant to do, regardless of how illogical it is to you.

This means that, in the vast majority of cases, defects introduced into the application are caused by the developer, although not intentionally, of course. The computer, however, is only doing what is asked of it. The question becomes, "How can you keep computers from doing the stupid things a user tells it to do?"

***

After this lesson, you will be able to:
- Identify the elements of an interface that need to be tested.
- Create test and use case scenarios to define the unit test boundaries.
- Construct the types of tests that will provide adequate coverage for the functionality of a class.

Estimated lesson time: 20 minutes

***

Why Review Code?

Finding bugs is an area that unit testing is supposed to address—and it does, or at least some of it. But unit testing is not sufficient by itself. Gaps in the specifications, errors in assumptions, and even mistakes all contribute to this problem. Ultimately, the more eyes that can look at a block of code, the less likely that a defect will exist.

There are many types of reviews that run the gamut from informal to formal. Some of the more common ones are described in the next sections.

Inspection

This is the most formal of the choices for a code review. The basic groundwork for this procedure, called the *Fagan Inspection*, was developed by Michael Fagan in the mid-1970s. The steps are refined from many iterations to determine the technique that is most effective. The result is a very formal situation that involves between three and six participants.

In general, the participants are assigned roles for the review. Possible roles are the:

- **Reader** Responsible for just reading the code that is being reviewed to the other participants. This is not necessarily the author and, in fact, a good argument can be made to not have the author perform this task. Having another person present the code to the assemblage allows the author to see it from a fresh perspective.

- **Reviewer**   This person is included in the review because of his or her technical expertise. He or she is responsible for a critical analysis of the code from that perspective.
- **Observer**   This person's realm of knowledge is in the domain covered by the code. In other words, he or she knows what the application is supposed to do from a business perspective.
- **Moderator**   This person is in control of the review meeting. His or her job is to ensure that the meeting stays on topic. He or she will record any decisions that are made and act as an arbiter during the process.

Any defects that are discovered are recorded in great detail. This includes not only the location (easily determined because the inspection process is focusing on only a small part of code) but also the severity, the type (algorithmic, documentation, error handling), and the phase at which the error was introduced (developer error, requirements gap, design oversight).

The strength of a formal inspection is also one of the problems. People who spend a lot of time looking at the code will undoubtedly find a lot of defects. But it takes many people time to find those defects. Studies performed over the past 20 years have shown that other techniques find almost as many defects with less investment in time by the staff. For this reason, formal inspections have fallen out of favor with many companies.

Code Walkthroughs

A code walkthrough is a less-formal version of an inspection. You might also hear the term *peer review* used to describe the same process. Regardless of the name, walkthroughs usually involve the author of the code presenting to a group of one or more colleagues. The colleagues, using an attitude of constructive criticism, of course, comment on the code. This includes identifying deficiencies in standards, error handling, parameter validation, and any other apparent technique issue.

The elements presented at a code walkthrough include some or all of the following aspects.

- **Design**   This is a description of the code block at a high level. The purpose is to give the reviewer a better idea of the choices that had to be made and why the code chose what was implemented.
- **Code**   This is the source code that is being reviewed. Typically, the reviewer will be looking for clarity, fulfillment of requirements, adequate consideration given to performance, correctness of algorithms, and proper adherence to standards (such as exceptions and input validation).
- **Test Plan**   Because the code must have passed a unit test suite before reaching the walkthrough stage, there must be a set of unit tests for the block of code. The reviewer needs to see the test so that suggestions can be made about areas that haven't yet been addressed.

Although a code walkthrough does find similar errors to those found in a formal inspection, the lack of formality makes it hard to measure the difference. Formal inspections also generate a number of metrics that can be used to improve the review process. That isn't possible with a code walkthrough because information such as the type of problem and the point at which it was introduced aren't recorded.

Pair Programming

The rise of *extreme programming* techniques has brought the benefits of *pair programming* to the forefront. The premise behind pair programming is quite simple. Instead of having one developer work on a piece of code, two developers are used—two developers working at a single monitor.

MORE INFO Extreme programming

Extreme programming is the most popular of a number of agile software development methodologies. The reason for the term *agile* is that the methods are aimed more at adaptability of development than at predictability. It starts with the premise that requirements are a moving target, so defining all of the requirements at the beginning is very difficult, if not impossible. Therefore, by creating many releases with smaller intervals between each, the development team can "spiral in" on the user's needs.

There are a number of benefits to pair programming, not all of which have to do with code review. Because this is a chapter on code review, the following benefits relate only to aspects of a code block that relate to the code review process.

- **Better code** Not only does the quality of the code produced by a pair of developers improve, but the number of defects decreases. There is a constant check on the code being written so that, overall, the quality level of code rises. There is also less likelihood that a developer will become sidetracked, resulting in time wasted on unproductive areas.
- **Better design** One of the keys to good code in the long term is the ability of a developer to "do the right thing" even if it means the code takes longer to write. It is very easy for a single developer, when faced with a choice between a quick path to the solution and one that takes longer to code but results in a better long-term design, to choose the quick path. Yes, the code is written faster, but it's not in the best interest of the application. When one developer is paired with another developer, the tendency is to choose the better design.
- **Greater responsibility** In environments in which pair programming is practiced and the pairs are rotated on a regular basis, there is a greater feeling of ownership in the code base. Although this might seem trivial, developers who feel ownership of code are much more likely to make decisions that benefit the code over making their development process easier. This results in an application that is in a better position to withstand the inevitable changes and enhancements that will come later in the life cycle.

Of course, pair programming isn't without its problems, but most of them revolve around the logistics of setting up a pair programming environment, not with the quality of code produced. In this area, the biggest drawback to pair programming is that the code is still developed in relative isolation. True, there are two people instead of one looking at the code. But those two still have close ties to the results and, therefore, might not see defects that are readily apparent to an outsider. For this reason, it is a good idea to combine pair programming with some other code review process to ensure that the maximum benefit of the process is achieved.

Over the Shoulder Review

At the bottom of the list (in terms of formality) is the over-the-shoulder review. This usually consists of a developer pulling a colleague into the cubicle and talking him or her through the code that is being written. The author drives the review, describing the design choices, demonstrating the code, and answering any questions the reviewer might have. Suggestions are frequently implemented while the review is still going on.

Although this type of review does have a positive effect on the number of defects found in an application, there are some drawbacks. The very informality that makes it easy to implement can also be a problem. Because there is nothing official, there is no way for a programming manager to ensure that reviews take place on all code checked in an application. There are no metrics or reports that can be used to improve the process.

Also, the informality frequently leads to some of the code in an application not being reviewed. This is especially true after the bulk of an application has been developed, or the application has already entered its maintenance phase. When an informal approach is taken, a large number of small changes get checked into the main branch of a project without review. Rationale such as "It's just not worth the effort" or "It was only a small change" might be heard. This is not the best way to ensure a consistent level of quality across a code base.

Quick Check

1. What is the code review methodology that applies the least structure to the process?
2. What is the code review methodology that would be used in an environment that requires high adherence to software development standards?

Quick Check Answers

1. Of the techniques described in this chapter, the over-the-shoulder review has the least rigid application.
2. The inspection methodology is the most structured, requiring adherence to a set of standards, appropriate roles in the review, and a feedback mechanism for improvement.

Code Review Excuses

As was noted in the preceding section, there are a number of different types of code reviews available. Regardless of the level of formality involved, there should be one that fits within your organization. And even the least formal increases the quality of the code and reduces the number of defects. There can be no good reason for avoiding code reviews in the development process.

Or can there be? This section gives a list of the most common code review avoidance reasons, along with how the issues can be addressed.

Too Much Code

For any significantly sized application, the number of lines of code can easily get into the tens and hundreds of thousands. In chunks of 200–300 lines, that can eat up a lot of valuable developer time.

For applications that are being newly created, there is little that can be done to avoid this. As with most daunting tasks, addressing a little at a time can help, but ultimately, all of the code needs to be reviewed.

For modified applications, however, the review effort is much lighter. The trick is to make sure that only the modified code is reviewed. There are certainly tools that will highlight the differences between the current code and the modifications. By focusing on the changes, the amount of effort involved is greatly decreased.

Logistics

Having teams in multiple locations can make the code review process difficult, from more than just the technical perspective, too. If you've ever been in a room full of developers, you know how difficult it is to get them to focus on the conversation at hand. The life of a developer is a busy one and there are always more important tasks that need to be addressed.

This problem is multiplied across a virtual connection. It is even easier to be distracted by other things on the desktop. This problem isn't easily solved, unfortunately. Discipline and ensuring that all parties contribute regularly is the best way to deal with the issue. Developers expected to provide an opinion on a regular basis will pay attention during the in-between times.

Preparation Time

The efforts required to prepare for a code review are significant. In many cases, it takes longer to prepare properly for a code review than to participate in the review itself. Documentation, design notes, and other materials must be put together and then read by the attendees.

To reduce preparation time, spread it across the entire project. A tool such as nDoc can help by automatically combining code comments into an easily viewable document. Tools such as

Visual Studio Team System that map requirements and design documents to work items and the associated code can help to cut down on the preparation time also.

Consistency or Lack Thereof

For a code review process to be successful, there must be a level of consistency. A block of code cannot be accepted by one reviewer but rejected by another. If this happens, the developers will become frustrated, and they will seek out the easy reviewers for their code.

The solution is to ensure that there is a consensus among the reviewers. This implies that a checklist or published standard must be created. For a summary of the types of questions that should make up this checklist, read the next section in this chapter.

Using a standard of some kind actually has an additional benefit. By documenting how certain situations need to be addressed and publishing them to the developers, you help standardize the coding style across the development team. This means that, when facing a code review, reviewers can focus on the parts of the application that are out of the ordinary rather than rehashing the same old coding patterns.

Reluctant Developers

You have already read about some of the less obvious ways (for instance, not paying attention during the meeting) that developers show their reluctance to be involved in the code review process. However, developers have also used other, more overt techniques that, in some companies, have made code reviews look much closer to public humiliations.

The key to avoiding this situation lies with management. Whether a development manager or a designate is heading the code review, the leader must make clear the boundaries placed on participation. Managers should make an effort to ensure that criticism remains constructive rather than becoming destructive. It is possible, even when egos are involved, to keep the tone of the code review positive and productive.

What Should a Review Look For?

One of the main questions surrounding code reviews is what the outcome should be. What sorts of problems should be subject to review? The following sections describe the main areas of review and the sorts of questions that should be asked in each one. Naturally, there will be some individual variation, so feel free to add and subtract from these as required.

Design

The first place to start a code review is with the design. This means that the work item against which the code is written needs to be discussed and dissected. The choices the developer makes in writing the code are eligible for discussion as well. This is one of the areas in which keeping egos in check is important because, in many cases, the design decisions are more subjective than objective.

The main questions for this section include:

- Is the design understandable?
- Is there a strong relation between the design and the implementation?
- Are all the functions in the design coded?
- Does the design address the issue observed by the work item?

Coding Standards

This area of focus for a code review starts with the assumption that the development team has a published set of coding standards and guidelines. If your team doesn't have such a document, start by creating one. Although it can be fun to debate how to capitalize method names and create strings, the creation of a standard must not devolve into an examination of minutiae. Instead, publish a clear document with some simple standards. These standards will be expanded as situations arise—and they will probably arise out of code reviews. But having a document, any document, is more important than its contents.

Once the coding standards are in place, the main questions associated with this section become:

- Does the code adhere to the coding standards?
- Is the intent of the code understandable?
- Are any constants embedded in the code that should be extracted as a constant or static property?
- Does the documentation of the method include a description of all the parameters and the return value? Are there any range limitations on the parameters? Does the method throw any exceptions?

Maintainability

Beyond coding standards lies the *maintainability* of the code. Although it is common knowledge that a large portion of the code of an application maintains it after its initial deployment, that knowledge is frequently not applied to the actual coding.

Developers, in general, like solutions that are cute and tricky. The pride that is displayed by concise code is dangerous for the next person trying to understand what is being done and modifying it to support the latest enhancement. Therefore, the code review should take steps to ensure that the code is easily envisioned by the next developer to touch it. The questions that arise from this goal are:

- Are the comments found in the code accurate?

- Are the comments found in the code necessary?
- Are any constraints or attributes documented, such as units of measure associated with any variables? This question assumes that the constraints and attributes aren't obvious from the names of the variables.
- Are there unit tests for any changes (assuming that the code review is for a modification)?
- Do the unit tests provide adequate coverage of new code?
- Is the code understandable?

Documentation

Getting developers to document their code is just as easy as getting children to eat their vegetables when their dessert is sitting in front of them. Like the suggestion from the "Coding Standards" section, it is necessary to create documentation guidelines that developers must meet to check their code into production. The standards should include where the documentation is placed, what it should consist of, and how it can be changed.

The questions that arise from this area are:

- Is any functionality that is visible to the user described in the user manual?
- Does the implementation in code match the description in the documentation?
- Are any command-line arguments documented?
- Are any configuration settings documented?
- If this is a change to an existing application, are the changes described in the appropriate document?

Security

This is an area that has gained a great deal of attention lately, and the importance placed on security questions depends on the audience for the application. If a Web application is being developed for commercial deployment, the security issues must be addressed closely. Likewise, if it is a commercial Windows Forms application, the security and privacy questions will be high on the list of concerns. For internal applications, the need to address security issues is much less, although not nonexistent.

As for the questions to ask, they are many and varied, and they depend on the type of application that is being developed. The easiest way to deal with security issues is to have a checklist for each type of application, which the MSDN folks have nicely provided at *http:// msdn.microsoft.com/library/default.asp?url=/library/en-us/dnnetsec/html/CL_Index_Of.asp.*

Performance

Again, the importance of this section depends on the audience for the application. That isn't to say that performance isn't important for any application, but in this particular case, you're thinking about reviewing code for performance issues in the absence of any anecdotal evidence of a performance problem.

Outside of the questions to ask, there are two areas to focus on for performance questions: frequently executed code paths and loops that execute many times. Within these boundaries, there are a number of improvements to look for.

- **Resource cleanup**   If there are resources being allocated and not released, these are definite implications for performance and scalability. It is important to ensure that the code review considers the appropriate use of *Dispose* and the *using* statement.
- **Exceptions**   Although proper exception handling is an important part of any application, developers sometimes go overboard. Throwing exceptions is a relatively slow process and should, therefore, not be used to control flow within the application.
- **String management**   It is fairly common knowledge that StringBuilder is faster than string concatenations after a certain number. This number is traditionally assumed to be three. Even though it is common knowledge, though, it should still be examined as part of the code review. Common knowledge has a tendency to be known not nearly as commonly as might be hoped.
- **Threading**   The use of threads within an application should be a signal that intense examination of the code is required. The complexity associated with ensuring that race conditions, dead locks, or other multithreading issues don't arise is significant.
- **Boxing**   The boxing of a variable involves two operations: heap allocation and a memory copy. Although this is sometimes necessary, excessive boxing is usually indicative of other design issues. For example, it is quite common for developers to create a *struct* (which is a class that is supposed to be allocated on the stack) and then place it in an ArrayList, which requires that they be allocated on the heap. This sort of pattern is exactly what code reviews are intended to catch.

Quick Check

- What are the six areas on which a code review should focus its efforts?

Quick Check Answer

- The six areas are coding standards, design, documentation, maintainability, performance, and security.

Lesson Summary

- Code reviews are an adjunct to unit tests in terms of ensuring that high-quality code is created. Unit tests are necessary, but the more eyes that see the code, the more likely that areas not covered by unit tests will be discovered.

- The level of formality in a code review is usually a function of how much process is found in the company. The more process, the more likely the code review is to follow a strict procedure.

- There are a number of excuses that are used to avoid implementing code reviews in an organization. Most of them are solvable, and the benefits of code reviews outweigh the costs.

Lesson Review

You can use the following questions to test your knowledge of the information in Lesson 1, "The Code Review Process." The questions are also available on the companion CD if you prefer to review them in electronic form.

NOTE   Answers

Answers to these questions and explanations of why each answer choice is right or wrong are located in the "Answers" section at the end of the book.

1. You are part of a team of 10 developers working on a commercial software application. The software is a critical line-of-business system that your clients use. To help ensure that the quality of future releases is high, management has decided to order a code review for changes and enhancements to the applications. Which type of review is most likely to be implemented by your company? (Choose all that apply.)

   A. Inspections

   B. Code walkthroughs

   C. Pair programming

   D. Over-the-shoulder reviews

2. You are the only developer in a small manufacturing company. Your job involves working on the internal applications for the company. Most of the applications you create integrate with a packaged application that runs the company's line-of-business functions. Your manager was a developer until a year ago, when she took this position. Which type of review is most likely to be implemented by your company? (Choose all that apply.)

   A. Inspections

   B. Code walkthroughs

   C. Pair programming

   D. Over-the-shoulder reviews

Real World

Bruce Johnson

Isolating integration testing is a challenge for some developers. It is very easy to combine unit and integration testing within a unit test suite. After all, integration testing technically includes interfacing with external resources such as a database, and many unit tests include that within their purview.

Unit tests, however, are supposed to run independently from external resources, as one of the rules of a good unit test says. Therefore, it really falls to integration testing to deal with this part of the testing phase. This is also where the completeness of design is put to the test because components that have been tested in isolation get worked out in unison. In other words, communication is the key to the process, and that is what makes it so interesting for developers to work on.

Lesson 2: Integration Testing

When put into the context of evaluating component connectivity to external resources, integration testing is a logical extension of unit testing. After all, unit tests are supposed to work on a component, absent of external dependencies, whereas integration tests evaluate two (or more) components to ensure that the dependencies work as they're supposed to.

Although there are many similarities between the two types of tests, there are still some idiosyncrasies that make integration testing worth studying. The purpose of this lesson is to describe the process involved with integration testing.

After this lesson, you will be able to:
- Identify the differences between integration testing and unit testing.
- Create an integration testing plan.
- Determine the assemblies on which an application or method is dependent.

Estimated lesson time: 30 minutes

Integration Testing Defined

An integration test is a piece of code that combines several units of code (or components) and tests the integration between them. The focus of the tests should be the integration boundaries. Indeed, a good strategy should address each of the boundaries. If you think that sounds easy, well, it is and it isn't. It is relatively easy to identify the tests that need to be run, but the number of tests that need to be written can get very large very quickly.

Beyond the question of boundaries, there are other aspects of integration testing that you need to consider. Besides ensuring compatibility among the components, this is also where performance, security, and globalization come into play for the first time. This adds to the burden of designing the tests that make up the integration phase.

Even with well-defined boundaries, it takes a lot of effort to design a good unit test properly because of the exponential number of interdependencies. Consider a test that covers three separate components, each of which interacts with the other. That's a total of eight separate boundaries that need to be tested. Add a fourth component, and the number goes up to 16. This number can easily get out of control.

These numbers, however, are not the only problem. There is also the situation of cascading dependencies. Class *A* calls class *B*, which then calls class *C*. In an ideal world, the integration between class *A* and class *B* would be testable independently of class *C*. This is true not only in an ideal world, but also in a well-defined integration test. More on that shortly.

As with unit tests, there are a number of characteristics that make up a good integration test. In general, the goal of these rules is to reduce the complexity of design as follows.

- Integration tests should operate on only a few classes. As a good rule of thumb, focus on a single class and the classes with which it collaborates. If there are any cascading dependencies, the classes past the first level should be implemented by using mock objects where possible.

- Integration tests must be isolated. They should include any setup and teardown. This includes adding any records to the database, adding files to the file system, and ensuring that previously created files have been deleted. In addition, once the test has completed, the added resources need to be removed. The test should be repeatable.

- Integration tests cannot be order dependent. If tests need to run in a particular order, they are not independent, as is required in the previous rule.

- Integration tests must be fast. This has nothing to do with reduced complexity, but fast integration tests reduce developer frustration, which is just as important.

Steps in Integration Testing

Although it seems that integration testing can be ad hoc in nature, it's much better to have a strategy in mind. The specific steps might be slightly different, depending on the application and the infrastructure, but the following is a list of steps that cover most scenarios. Of course, you're free to add and subtract for your own situation, certainly, after the first two steps.

1. Create a test plan.
2. Execute the use case test cases for the integration.
3. Execute the load testing test cases.
4. Execute the stress testing test cases.
5. Execute the globalization test cases.
6. Execute the security test cases.

Create a Test Plan

The test plan for integration testing consists of a list of the scenarios that need to be addressed by the test. There are a number of documents referenced to arrive at this list. For example:

- Functional specifications for the application
- Requirement document for the application
- Any performance and globalization requirements for the application
- Deployment expectations for the application

The detailed test plan will list all of the possible use cases for the integration of the components. It will also consider the exceptional flows within the use cases and the various input types for the cross-component calls. This includes both valid and invalid inputs.

Execute the Use Test Cases

Of course, the step between creating the test plan and executing the test cases is to implement the test cases in code. For a developer of your caliber, that should be no problem. Now the test cases need to be executed–the normal flow cases and the exception cases.

These two scenarios (normal and exception flow) will be part of any integration testing plan. They are the pieces that show the integration is functioning as expected and should be working before moving on to any of the other integration tests.

In the exception flow tests, there could be some challenges. It is getting close to the point where mock objects are not the desired solution because even though mock objects are designed to emulate the real object, there could be edge case functional differences that cause problems to bubble up to the integration test. So, whenever possible, use the real external resource as part of the test rather than the mock version.

This does mean that, occasionally, you will need to make minor changes to the application code to simulate extreme situations in the external resource, such as tweaking the data access code to simulate the inaccessibility of a database. However, even though these changes are acceptable, they should be minimized because it might violate some corporate policies about not changing the code under test between the time of testing and the time of deployment.

Execute the Load Testing Test Cases

Load testing is used to ensure that the application meets the performance objectives as laid out in the requirements document. Although performance has been considered at the unit test and code review levels, there are times when the work performed by one component has a negative impact on the performance of a separate component. Running the integration test cases under a controlled load environment allows any speed or scalability issues to be addressed. For more information about load testing, refer to Chapter 10, "Planning for Testing."

Execute the Stress Testing Test Cases

Beyond the load testing scenarios is stress testing. Although load testing views the behavior of the application under a reasonable load, stress testing deliberately goes past the boundary of the acceptable number of users. It loads the application under a large number of requests to observe how it behaves or fails. The goal of this type of testing is normally to identify synchronization problems, memory leaks, and other artifacts that don't normally reveal themselves in a system under stress.

Execute the Globalization Test Cases

If your application has any globalization elements, this is where they are tested. Because of this, it is also the area of greatest challenge for setup and teardown. For example, if your application needs to support Japanese, French, and German, you should run the globalization test on each of these versions of Microsoft Windows to verify that Japanese will run on a Japanese version of Windows XP, for example, or that Japanese will run on an American version of Windows XP with the culture set appropriately. As you can imagine, the setup for this type of test is not insignificant.

Execute the Security Test Cases

Although security should be an element of unit tests and code reviews, it is an area of particular interest to integration testing. The boundary between components is where most of the security issues are found, or, more accurately, where they occur because they frequently aren't found until it's too late.

There are two levels at which security testing can be performed.

- **Black-box testing**   The focus of this testing should be on the integration boundary. One of the precepts of service-based architecture is to not trust identity across boundaries. This integration boundary is one of the possible boundaries to consider, so the idea is to ensure that access to the called method is still secured appropriately. Frequently, this is accomplished by simulating the production environment and testing for security in the normal way.
- **White-box testing**   White-box integration testing is not concerned with the individual problems in the collaborating components. Instead, it is ensuring that the addition of a new component doesn't significantly affect the application threat model that has already been developed. If it does, then the additional threats will be added to the model where appropriate.

Quick Check

- When looking at where to focus integration tests, on which areas should the test cases be concentrated?

Quick Check Answer

- In general, integration tests should focus on the boundary cases. That is, the tests should concentrate on the places where one component interacts directly with another component. Other areas of interest include globalization, security, and performance.

Component Dependencies

To be able to create the integration tests that have been discussed, especially when there are *cascading dependencies*, you need to identify the dependencies associated with each method. Although this might seem to be an easy thing to accomplish, that isn't always the case. Let's start with the simple case before moving on to the more complicated one.

File-Level Dependencies

A file-level dependency is a file that is required for your application to run. Any application you create will have a number of such dependencies in the form of the assemblies that make up the Microsoft .NET Framework. It also includes any assemblies that you have created. It is this list that really needs to be retrieved because it is safe to assume that the .NET assemblies have already been tested sufficiently to preclude inclusion in the integration test phase.

There are two parts required for obtaining the necessary information. The first is the list of assemblies that are referenced by the assembly under test. This can easily be retrieved by using the *Assembly.GetReferencedAssemblies* method. This returns an array of assembly objects that are referenced by the assembly making the call.

```
'VB
Dim a As [Assembly] = System.Reflection.Assembly.GetExecutingAssembly()
Dim an As AssemblyName
For Each an In a.GetReferencedAssemblies()
   Console.WriteLine(String.Format("{0},{1},{2}", an.Name, _
      an.Version, an.CultureInfo.Name))
Next

//C#
Assembly a = System.Reflection.Assembly.GetExecutingAssembly();
foreach (AssemblyName an in a.GetReferencedAssemblies()) {
   Console.WriteLine(String.Format("{0},{1},{2}", an.Name,
      an.Version, an.CultureInfo.Name));
}
```

This isn't quite simple enough, however. The assemblies that are returned could, in turn, reference other assemblies, which means that to retrieve a complete dependency tree, there must be a series of calls to *GetReferencedAssemblies*. The details of how to accomplish this can be found in the lab for this section.

Beyond the assembly references, there is another piece of information that is useful to have: the assemblies that are called from each method. In this manner, as the test planner examines the integration tests necessary for each method, the test plan knows which assemblies need to be included in the test. There are a number of ways to accomplish this goal. The two most difficult ones would be to parse the source code or the Intermediate Language (IL) code, looking for the code structure associated with making a call. Although this is possible, it requires a lot of effort. A better approach is to use the incredibly useful .NET Reflector tool written by Lutz Roeder. It is available at *www.aisto.com/roeder/dotnet*. Figure 12-1 shows a sample screen shot.

As Figure 12-1 shows, the right side of the form displays the depends-on and used-by lists for the select method. So, at the very least, it is possible to look at what the dependent assemblies are. If you are so inclined, .NET Reflector also includes an application programming interface (API) that makes it possible to extract the same information programmatically and place it into a format that is amenable to automatic processing.

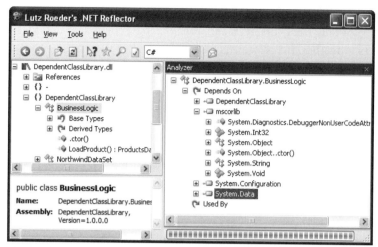

Figure 12-1   A screen shot of .NET Reflector

Distributed Dependencies

Unfortunately, file-level dependencies are not all that is required by an application. Sometimes an application will access external applications through a different mechanism such as Web services, .NET remoting, or COM+. In each of these cases, the complete list of dependencies is much harder to obtain.

It is possible to recognize that the external resource is being accessed. In almost every case, an instance of a proxy class is created and the external resource is accessed through that interface. This proxy class will appear as a *dependent assembly* as outlined in the preceding "File-Level Dependencies" section.

However, the external resource will have dependencies of its own. Perhaps calling the .NET remoting component will result in a database being updated, or the Web service is actually hosted by a third party. In these cases, they might not be easily configurable for testing, which means that true integration testing is very challenging. You can use the same mock object approach that unit testing uses, but then you're not really testing the integration, just your expectations. And that is what integration testing is all about—ensuring that your expectations (as demonstrated in your code) actually match reality.

Lab: Identifying Dependent Assemblies

In this lab, you will create a simple program that retrieves a list of dependent assemblies for an application. The application will not only list the dependent assemblies but will also include all of the dependent assemblies of the dependent assemblies—right up to the point at which a complete list has been gathered.

The biggest challenge to this program is to keep track of the assemblies that have already been added to the list. Not only does this keep the work manageable; it also provides a stopping point for the recursive method that you are going to create. Once there are no assemblies in the *GetReferencedAssemblies* array that have not been processed, the list is complete for that level. The following steps describe how to create the application.

If you encounter a problem completing an exercise, the completed projects can be installed from the Code folder on the companion CD.

▶ **Exercise: Retrieve a List of Dependent Assemblies**

1. Launch Visual Studio 2005.

2. Open a solution, using File | Open | Project/Solution.

3. Navigate to the Chapter12/Lesson2/Lab1/<language>/Before directory. Select the Lab1 solution, and click Open.

4. In the Solution Explorer, notice that there are two applications already present. The first is a Windows Forms application that contains one form. The second is a Class Library project that defines a single class called *Product*. The Windows Forms application displays a form containing a button. The *Click* event for the button instantiates *Product* and calls the *Load* method. The *Load* method retrieves a list of products from the Northwind Traders database and returns them in a *DataSet*. This *DataSet* is then bound to the grid that appears on the form.

5. In the Solution Explorer, expand the DisplayDependentAssemblies project. Double-click the Program file (or Module1 file in Visual Basic). This opens the file in the code view. You will see an empty *Main* method.

6. Start with the recursive method to traverse the dependent assemblies. Define the method signature to take the name of the assembly and the list of already processed dependent assemblies.

```
'VB
Sub buildDependencyList(assemblyName As String, _
    dependentAssemblies As Dictionary(Of String, String))
End Sub
```

```
//C#
static void buildDependencyList(string assemblyName,
    Dictionary<string, string> dependentAssemblies) {
}
```

7. Load an *Assembly* object based on the assemblyName parameter.

```
'VB
Dim a As Assembly = Assembly.Load(assemblyName)
```

```
//C#
Assembly a = Assembly.Load(assemblyName);
```

8. If the assembly hasn't already been processed, call the *GetReferenceAssemblies* method. The following code is added below the previous code declaration.

```vb
'VB
If Not dependentAssemblies.ContainsKey(a.FullName)
End If
```

```csharp
//C#
if (!dependentAssemblies.ContainsKey(a.FullName)) {
}
```

9. Within this *If* block, the name of the assembly is added to the dependentAssemblies variable. Then the referenced assemblies are retrieved.

```vb
'VB
dependentAssemblies.Add(a.FullName, a.FullName)
Dim an() As AssemblyName
an = a.GetReferencedAssemblies()
```

```csharp
//C#
dependentAssemblies.Add(a.FullName, a.FullName);
AssemblyName [] an = a.GetReferencedAssemblies();
```

10. Once the list of reference assemblies is retrieved, it needs to be compared against the already processed list. If the references are not there, the recursive procedure needs to be called. Add the following code below the *GetReferencedAssemblies* call.

```vb
'VB
Dim name As AssemblyName
For Each name In an
    If Not dependentAssemblies.ContainsKey(name.Name) Then
        dependentAssemblies.Add(name.FullName, name.FullName)
        buildDependencyList(name.FullName, dependentAssemblies)
    End If
Next
```

```csharp
//C#
foreach (AssemblyName name in an)
    if (!dependentAssemblies.ContainsKey(name.Name)) {
        dependentAssemblies.Add(name.FullName, name.FullName);
        buildDependencyList(name.FullName, dependentAssemblies);
    }
```

11. Once the method to build the list of reference assemblies is created, it needs to be called. Back in the *Main* method, add the following code.

```vb
'VB
Dim dependentAssemblies As New Dictionary(Of String, String)
Dim rootAssembly As Assembly = Assembly.LoadFrom("DependentApplicationsDemo.exe")
buildDependencyList(rootAssembly.FullName, dependentAssemblies)
```

```csharp
//C#
Dictionary<string, string> dependentAssemblies =
    new Dictionary<string, string>();
```

```
Assembly rootAssembly = Assembly.LoadFrom("DependentApplicationsDemo.exe");
buildDependencyList(rootAssembly.FullName, dependentAssemblies);
```

12. Once the list is built, it needs to be displayed. Add the code to do this to the top of the *Main* procedure.

```
'VB
Console.WriteLine("The dependent assemblies are: ")
Dim assemblyName As String
For Each assemblyName in dependentAssemblies.Values
    Console.WriteLine(assemblyName)
Next
Console.ReadLine()
```

```
//C#
Console.WriteLine("The dependent assemblies are: ");
foreach (string assemblyName in dependentAssemblies.Values)
    Console.WriteLine(assemblyName);

Console.ReadLine();
```

13. Run the application. Notice that the output includes both the *DependentApplicationsDemo* and *DependentClassLibrary* assemblies.

Lesson Summary

- Integration tests focus on the interactions that take place on the boundaries between components.
- Along with interface areas, integration tests also look at globalization, performance, and security because the interface is where weaknesses are likely to appear.

Lesson Review

You can use the following questions to test your knowledge of the information in Lesson 2, "Integration Testing." The questions are also available on the companion CD if you prefer to review them in electronic form.

NOTE   Answers

Answers to these questions and explanations of why each answer choice is right or wrong are located in the "Answers" section at the end of the book.

1. You have just completed the development and unit testing on a component. You need to create a plan for integration testing of the component with the other assemblies in the application. What would be the first step to create the plan ?

   A. Review the public methods that are exposed by the class.

   B. Review the use case document to determine when the class is to be used.

    C. Look at the unit tests already written for the class.

    D. Look at the dependent assemblies for the class.

2. You have just finished the unit testing on a component that interacts with both an external Web service and a local database. The URL for the Web service and the connection string for the database are defined in the application configuration file. The next step is to define the areas on which the integration testing will focus. Which of the following parts of the component should not be targeted during integration testing?

    A. Calling the Web service

    B. Accessing the local database

    C. Security associated with the Web service and database access

    D. Retrieving the configuration information

Chapter Review

To further practice and reinforce the skills you learned in this chapter, you can perform the following tasks:

- Review the chapter summary.
- Review the list of key terms introduced in this chapter.
- Complete the case scenarios. These scenarios set up real-world situations involving the topics of this chapter and ask you to create a solution.
- Complete the suggested practices.
- Take a practice test.

Chapter Summary

- It is very difficult for one person to create an application that considers every possible scenario. The more people who examine the code, the more likely that different, unconsidered perspectives will arise that can improve the overall quality.
- Don't let the excuses that exist for not performing code review prevent you from implementing it. The gain in quality is worth any small drop in productivity that might occur.
- When testing the integration of two or more components, focus on the assumptions made by each at the point of contact. This area is a frequent source of bugs because of the possibility of miscommunication between the two developers—even if the same developer worked on both sides.

Key Terms

Do you know what these key terms mean? You can check your answers by looking up the terms in the glossary at the end of the book.

- cascading dependency
- dependent assembly
- extreme programming
- Fagan Inspection
- maintainability
- pair programming
- peer review

Case Scenarios

In the following case scenarios, you will apply what you've learned about the code review process. You can find answers to these questions in the "Answers" section at the end of this book.

Case Scenario 1: Determine the Code Review Requirements

You are a corporate developer who is part of a team that is creating a Windows application that will be deployed to the 1,500 users in your corporate network and will also be available to users on the Internet. The application is not mission critical, but it is highly visible because it will be used daily by the user base. To make it even more challenging, some of the details of the requirements have been shifting on a regular basis.

One of your tasks is to ensure that the application is coded to a relatively high standard of quality. To this end, you have implemented a standard of at least 85 percent code coverage by unit tests. To maintain the desired standard of coding, however, management has decided to include a code review process. Some of the developers are starting to rebel against what they claim is a "productivity-draining and worthless" exercise.

Your challenge is to recommend the code review methodology that will achieve the desired level of quality without overburdening the development team with an unneeded process.

Question

Answer the following question for your manager.

1. What type of code review methodology would you recommend and why?

Case Scenario 2: Integration Testing for a Web Application

You are a corporate developer creating a Web application that will be available to users on the Internet. The application retrieves data from a database as well as updating the database with new records. Also, two Web service calls are made, one to a local Web service to retrieve status information and a second to a third-party company to perform address input validation and cleansing. One of your responsibilities is to create an integration testing plan for the application. Your challenge is to decide on which areas the integration testing should focus.

Questions

Answer the following questions for your manager.

1. On which areas of the application should integration testing focus?
2. What is the best approach to ensure that the integration tests are an accurate representation of the integration issues?

Suggested Practices

To help you successfully master the objectives presented in this chapter, complete the following tasks.

Perform a Code Review

- **Practice 1** Find a piece of code that you wrote six months or more ago. It should be using the same technologies that you are currently using, if possible. Examine the code with a critical eye toward techniques and practices that you have since discovered to be sub-optimal.

Perform Integration Testing

- **Practice 1** Find a piece of code that calls or is called by external resources or other assemblies. Evaluate the interactions for areas that should be included in an integration test. Design and implement the implementation test, using the steps outlined in Lesson 2, "Integration Testing."

Take a Practice Test

The practice tests on this book's companion CD offer many options. For example, you can test yourself on just one exam objective, or you can test yourself on all the 70-549 certification exam content. You can set up the test so that it closely simulates the experience of taking a certification exam, or you can set it up in study mode so that you can look at the correct answers and explanations after you answer each question.

MORE INFO   Practice tests

For details about all the practice test options available, see the "How to Use the Practice Tests" section in this book's Introduction.

Chapter 13
Evaluating Application Performance

This chapter discusses how to track the performance of an application and decipher the results. You will learn how to interpret performance data to identify potential problems and create a performance baseline. You will also learn how to monitor how an application is used to identify bugs as well as security and resource recommendations. You will gain an understanding of how components interact with and depend on each other to streamline application deployment. Finally, you will determine how to configure a production environment to accommodate a deployed application.

Exam objectives in this chapter:
- Evaluate the performance of an application based on the performance analysis strategy.
  - ❏ Identify performance spikes.
  - ❏ Analyze performance trends.
- Analyze the data received when monitoring an application.
  - ❏ Monitor and analyze resource usage.
  - ❏ Monitor and analyze security aspects.
  - ❏ Track bugs that result from customer activity.
- Evaluate the deployment plan.
  - ❏ Identify component-level deployment dependencies.
  - ❏ Identify scripting requirements for deployment. Considerations include database scripting.
- Create an application flow-logic diagram.
  - ❏ Evaluate the complexity of components.
  - ❏ Evaluate the complexity of interactions with other components.
- Validate the production configuration environment.
  - ❏ Verify networking settings.
  - ❏ Verify the deployment environment.

Lessons in this chapter:

Before You Begin

To complete the lessons in this chapter, you must have:

- A computer that meets or exceeds the minimum hardware requirements listed in the introduction at the beginning of the book.
- Microsoft Visual Studio 2005 and the Microsoft .NET Framework 2.0.

Real World

Shannon Horn

Just prior to the turn of the millennium, I was contracted to resolve Year 2000 (Y2K) issues in custom software packages for the two largest motion picture libraries in the entertainment industry, located in Santa Monica, California, and Universal City, California. As it turned out in most custom software scenarios, the Y2K issues were easy to resolve. However, as an additional task, I was asked to create a central data repository.

My clients accumulated these large motion picture libraries by continually acquiring smaller motion picture companies and adding the motion pictures in the library of the smaller company to their own. However, generally, the motion pictures in the libraries of acquired companies continued to be managed using the software that was implemented by the acquired company. After many years, my clients had to juggle the task of managing data stored in a plethora of database management systems, including some custom ones. The abundance of database management systems created a bottleneck when users needed to analyze data across the entire library.

The central data repository that I was to create was intended to simplify the analysis of data across the whole library while leaving motion picture data in the database management system in which it was stored. I was also asked to create a wizard to enable users to work easily with data by using the repository. The result was an extract, transform, and load (ETL) solution similar to SQL Server Data Transformation Services (DTS). I needed to create a wizard that performed well, simplifying the lives of hundreds or even thousands of users.

My clients and I accomplished our goal by planning performance well in advance. We created a performance model while designing the repository and continued to update the model throughout development. The performance model included multiple performance baselines reflecting the target deployment environments as well as use cases focusing on the needs of entry-level users and administrators.

Lesson 1: Evaluating Application Performance

This lesson describes why performance plays a vital role in a successful application and when to plan performance. It also describes how to identify performance concerns and bottlenecks, and how performance results are used.

After this lesson, you will be able to:

- Describe why tracking application performance is important.
- Determine when to plan application performance.
- Identify application performance bottlenecks.
- Understand how to develop an application performance baseline and when a baseline should be modified.

Estimated lesson time: 15 minutes

Why Track Application Performance?

Users will complain if your application performs slowly. Yet, in most scenarios, application performance is an afterthought at the beginning of development; therefore, consider application performance testing in the initial stages of the application development life cycle. Those test results can be used to improve application design, determine application health, and document minimum and recommended business requirements that the application needs to fulfill. The three categories of application performance that are generally measured and monitored are application response time, throughput, and resource use (CPU, memory, and so on).

Performance Modeling

The first step to take when considering the performance of an application is to create a model of the anticipated performance metrics of the application and validate that model. Performance modeling is the process of prototyping an application to determine what resources your application will require to perform well and continue performing well. Performance modeling allows you to incorporate performance concerns into the application design to ensure that the end result will comply with performance requirements.

The performance model should be created in the design phase of the application life cycle. Performance modeling is an iterative process, and the model should be continually updated throughout the development cycle. The performance model should document and incorporate any known business requirements as well as any other design models that might affect performance, such as the security model. The performance model should also identify target deployment environments and can be created by using the tool of choice. However, Microsoft Office Word is typically used to create models.

A performance model validates the design of an application, and you can use it to identify flaws early in the development life cycle. You can create a performance model through a standard eight-step process, as listed here.

- Identify key usage scenarios that represent target deployment execution environments for the application.
- Identify the user and transaction workloads that an application must support.
- Identify performance objectives and business requirements for the application. Performance objectives include anticipated application response time, application throughput, and resource use. For instance, a business requirement might be that an application must consume particular Web services.
- Identify application budget constraints. These include both financial budget constraints and physical resource constraints.
- Identify processing steps. The processing steps implemented by an application must be broken down and individually optimized to improve performance. Processing steps are typically represented like a use case or sequence diagram.
- Allocate budget. This step assigns portions of the operating budget to individual processing steps.
- Evaluate your model. Evaluate the assignment of the operating budget to processing steps to ensure that it complies with performance objectives and business requirements.
- Validate your model. Once a performance model is in place, it must be evaluated through testing. Thoroughly test a performance model under varying conditions, using multiple platforms, resources, and loads.

The primary output of a performance model is a *performance baseline*, or benchmark, that is used to predict how an application will perform with given resources and loads. A performance baseline is required to determine whether an application is performing well or poorly in a scenario, while the application is being tested, and when it is deployed to production. A recorded performance baseline can take the form of recorded performance metrics associated with a given application execution environment (operating system, software resources, hardware resources, network resources, and so on) .

MORE INFO Performance modeling

For more information about performance modeling, visit the topic entitled "Performance Modeling" in the MSDN library, located at *http://msdn.microsoft.com/library/default.asp?url=/library/en-us/dnpag/html/scalenetchapt15.asp.*

Quick Check

1. When should a performance model be created?
2. What are the most common performance objectives?
3. What is the primary output of a performance model?

Quick Check Answers

1. Application performance should be considered early in the application development life cycle. A performance model should be created in the design phase of the development cycle and continually updated as the application evolves.
2. The most common performance objectives tested are response time, throughput, and resource use.
3. The primary output of a performance model is an application performance baseline. A performance baseline indicates the normal operating metrics for an application in a given execution environment.

Identifying Application Performance Spikes

A performance spike is a noticeable and dramatic increase in the use of processor time, memory resources, disk activity, or similar resource usage by an application. How do you determine whether an application is using more resources than normal? You identify an increase in resource usage by comparing application resource usage to the performance baseline created for the application.

When comparing application performance data to a performance baseline, there are several things to be aware of. For example, applications typically use more resources while the application is starting up; this is common behavior for all applications. Although the time required to start an application is normally miniscule compared to the time during which the application runs, application resource usage data might more accurately represent run-time resource usage and identify performance spikes if application startup resource usage values are eliminated from overall usage data.

One of the primary things you try to avoid by analyzing application performance data is memory paging. As each application (process) is loaded, the operating system assigns a portion of the available memory to the application. The amount of memory assigned to the application is called the application's working memory set. In 32-bit versions of Microsoft Windows, a working set can be up to 4 gigabytes (GB) in size. However, because most systems don't have 4 GB of memory available, the working sets for most applications are much smaller and, furthermore, an application might not be actively using all of the memory assigned to its memory working set. As more applications are started, the operating system might begin to run out of memory to assign to applications. If this occurs, Windows will borrow memory from the working sets of less-active applications. When the operating system can no longer borrow memory from applications, it will begin to page, or persist, the contents stored in memory to the hard disk. Reading from and writing to a hard disk is significantly slower than reading from and writing to memory. Hence, the performance of all applications will suffer dramatically if paging occurs.

Note that if anything in the execution environment of an application changes permanently, the performance baseline should be updated to reflect the impact of the change. Any change could affect application performance. For instance, if the number of users increases, a greater load will be placed on the application. Conversely, if the amount of memory available on the server hosting an application is increased, the server will have more memory available to assign to application memory working sets, paging is less likely to occur, and, as a rule of thumb, the overall performance of all applications hosted on the server will increase.

To be able to identify a performance spike, you must first define an acceptable variance from the performance baseline. An application will not use a consistent quantity of any single resource or combination of resources but will fluctuate resource usage based on several factors, including available resources and application loads. There is no generic rule that is used to identify performance spikes. You must determine for your application and execution environment what performance metrics fall outside of an acceptable variance from the performance baseline. For example, you could determine that if your application uses more than 256 MB of memory, it is operating beyond expected limits.

Once acceptable application performance variances have been defined, you can use Performance Monitor to define and configure alarms to perform actions if application performance ventures beyond your variances.

MORE INFO   Memory paging

For more information on excessive memory paging, review the help topic entitled "Make sure you have enough memory" in the Performance Monitor help file.

Analyzing Application Performance Trends

Once a performance baseline has been created, conduct further research and planning to predict how an application will use resources as loads are placed on it and, conversely, how much hardware will be required to support an application under given loads. Predictive application resource use planning based on a performance baseline and thorough testing is called *capacity planning*. Capacity planning is used to predict future performance through thorough testing by identifying application performance trends.

Capacity planning can be slightly complex and include some light algebraic calculations. The goal of capacity planning is to estimate the cost of each user or transaction supported by an application. If a known cost can be placed on each user or transaction supported by an application with a given execution environment, application behavior can be more precisely predicted using anticipated loads.

MORE INFO   Capacity planning

For more information on capacity planning, visit the topic "How To: Perform Capacity Planning for .NET Applications" in the MSDN library, located at *http://msdn.microsoft.com/library/default.asp?url=/library/en-us/dnpag/html/scalenethowto06.asp*.

Lab 1: Documenting Application Performance Metrics

In this lab you will walk through the process of creating a performance model by using simulated application information. If you encounter a problem completing an exercise, the completed projects can be installed from the Code folder on the companion CD.

▶ **Exercise: Create a Performance Model**

In this exercise you will create a performance model. You are a developer for Adventure Works, which sells sporting goods through retail outlets nationwide. You have been assigned the task of creating an enterprise application to manage, as a service for customers, fantasy football teams and leagues. Significant prizes are awarded to winners. The application will be installed on kiosks located in stores; it will store data in a central database located at the corporate office and will be networked throughout all retail outlets to provide as close to real-time results as possible. Adventure Works requires that the application perform well.

1. Create a performance model design document by using Office Word or your editor of choice. The design document should describe the application being developed. Performance metrics are commonly displayed in a narrative format or in a table format.

2. Identify and list key scenarios. There will be only a single user profile for the application, so the development team created a quick use case to identify football enthusiasts who are store customers as the primary users of the application.

3. Identify and list workload. Based on sales and marketing data, the anticipated workload will be 1,500 concurrent users at any given time; however, the user workload could potentially increase to 3,000 users during the lunch hour between noon and 1 P.M.

4. Identify and list performance objectives. The use case anticipates that each user will log on to the application and navigate to the team stats screen or weekly results screen. This navigation sequence will require four screens to be displayed within a minute.

5. Identify and list budget. Each retail location kiosk will have a 20-GB high-speed hard disk, 512 megabytes (MB) of RAM, and an in-store broadband connection to link to the central database.

6. Identify and list processing steps. The primary sequence followed by a user will be to log on to the application, review the home screen for the application, and navigate to the team stats screen or the weekly results screen. Additional screens manage user profiles and draft information.

Additional steps would normally be required to create a performance baseline. These steps include assignment of the budget to processing steps, testing, and evaluation.

Lesson Summary

■ Application performance is a key factor in a successful application. The three most common performance objectives are response time, throughput, and resource use.

■ A performance model should be created in the design phase of the application development life cycle to ensure that the resulting application meets business performance requirements. The output of a performance model is a performance baseline from which you can determine whether an application is performing well or poorly in a given execution environment.

■ Performance trends should be identified to plan future capacity needs and growth. As the workload of an application grows, you might observe performance spikes, and you can use the baseline to identify these.

Lesson Review

You can use the following questions to test your knowledge of the information in Lesson 1, "Evaluating Application Performance." The questions are also available on the companion CD if you prefer to review them in electronic form.

NOTE Answers

Answers to these questions and explanations of why each answer choice is right or wrong are located in the "Answers" section at the end of the book.

1. What does resource use include?

A. CPU use

B. Budget use

C. Memory use

D. Developer time use

2. Which of the following are key steps used to create a performance model?

   A. Identifying key scenarios

   B. Identifying localized resources

   C. Identifying payloads

   D. Identifying workloads

3. What is a primary concern to be aware of when analyzing performance data?

   A. Memory idle time

   B. Hard disk size

   C. CPU idle time

   D. Memory paging

Lesson 2: Analyzing Monitoring Data

This lesson discusses how to monitor application performance metrics by using existing tools that are external to an application. It also discusses how to instrument applications internally to capture detailed and application-specific metrics. Furthermore, this lesson illustrates how to extend the knowledge of monitoring application metrics to deal with bugs identified in production.

> **After this lesson, you will be able to:**
> - Use external tools to monitor application performance metrics.
> - Instrument .NET applications by using code to record specific metrics.
> - Understand how to track bugs identified through user interaction.
>
> **Estimated lesson time: 20 minutes**

Monitoring Resource Use

Lesson 1, "Evaluating Application Performance," discussed why application performance metrics are important. Lesson 2 discusses how to monitor application performance metrics. Application performance metrics can be monitored through two methods: tools external to an application or code internal to an application.

Monitoring Tools

The most straightforward method of monitoring application performance metrics is to use a tool external to the application that is designed for this purpose. Microsoft offers several performance monitoring tools, and many third-party monitoring tools are available on the market.

Windows Performance Monitor   Windows Performance Monitor is included with Microsoft Windows NT, Windows 2000, Windows XP, Microsoft Windows Server 2003, and Windows Vista. Because Windows Performance Monitor is easily accessible and free to use, it is the most commonly used performance monitoring tool. It can be used to monitor multiple performance metrics for multiple applications simultaneously, and it can be used to monitor performance metrics of the operating system and services.

Each performance metric that is monitored using Performance Monitor is referred to as a counter, and Performance Monitor maintains a collection of counters that are registered and available for monitoring. Performance metric counters are inactive until they are added to the list of counters actively being monitored. Several counters are automatically registered in Performance Monitor by the operating system, and most services and server-level applications that are installed register additional counters associated with the application or service being installed. Depending on the software installed and the machine configuration, there can be hundreds of counters registered in Performance Monitor. The counters that you need to monitor in a given scenario depend on the scenario at hand. The counters monitored by default in Performance Monitor are \Memory\Pages/sec, \PhysicalDisk(_Total)\Avg. Disk Queue Length, and \Processor(_Total)\% Processor Time.

Performance Monitor also maintains logs of counters that are actively being monitored, and alerts can be configured to trigger an action based on the status of a performance metric. Performance Monitor is located in Administrative Tools in Control Panel and might be listed as Performance Monitor or simply Performance. Figure 13-1 illustrates Performance Monitor.

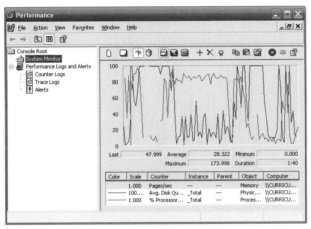

Figure 13-1   Windows Performance Monitor

To add a new counter to those that are being monitored actively by Performance Monitor, right-click anywhere in the graphic detail pane and select Add Counters. The Add Counters dialog box will be displayed and will list all registered counters. At the top of the Add Counters dialog box, the performance metric target computer is selected. Next, select the performance object, which represents an application, service, or primary component of an application or service. Each performance object includes one or more counters displayed in the counters list representing a single performance metric. A performance counter can occur in multiple instances as well, and it can be tracked at the instance level. For example, Figure 13-2 illustrates the Add Counters dialog box with the local computer, the Print Queue performance object, and the Jobs counter selected. So you're monitoring jobs in the print queue, but for which printer? You might have multiple printer instances installed. Hence, the instance of the performance object allows you to monitor performance metrics at the printer level.

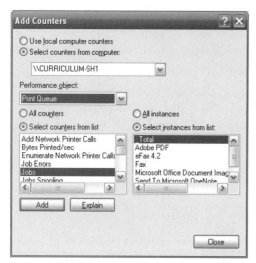

Figure 13-2   The Windows Performance Monitor Add Counters dialog box

When selecting a counter to begin monitoring, the Add Counters dialog box includes an Explain button that you can use to display additional help related to the selected counter.

MORE INFO   About Performance Monitor

For more information about using Windows Performance Monitor, see the help file located in Performance Monitor.

Microsoft Operations Manager   The Microsoft Operations Manager (MOM) was created by Microsoft to facilitate monitoring enterprise environments and applications. However, although the Windows Performance Monitor accommodates monitoring of the operating system, applications, and services, it is primarily intended for local and isolated application use.

The MOM is composed of agent services and a central data repository, management, and analysis service. Each server to be monitored can have a MOM agent installed on it and be configured to monitor as needed. Performance metric data from each agent service is stored in the central data repository that is created by using Microsoft SQL Server. Once the metric data is stored in SQL Server, it can be analyzed for performance information and trends and can be used for troubleshooting and to track bugs.

MORE INFO   Microsoft Operations Manager

For more information about the MOM, visit the Microsoft Operations Manager home page, located at *http://www.microsoft.com/mom/default.mspx*.

Network Monitor   At a lower level, Microsoft Network Monitor was created specifically to capture and monitor network traffic. Network Monitor can be configured to capture, in memory, varying degrees of information about network traffic. The captured information can be saved to physical files that generally bear an .adr extension. Network Monitor must be installed from the Windows installation CD and is started by using the netmon.exe command.

MORE INFO   **Microsoft Network Monitor**

For more information about Microsoft Network Monitor, see the Network Monitor MSDN article, "Description of the Network Monitor Capture Utility," located at *http://support.microsoft.com/kb /310875/EN-US/*.

Profiling Tools

Monitoring tools are designed to render generally high-level views of the performance of an operating system, application, service, or component. Profiling tools are tightly coupled to their source and are designed to render very low-level, specific results. Conversely, because they are tightly coupled, profiling tools are considered to be intrusive because they significantly degrade the performance of the applications being profiled. Application profiling should be performed at length in a test environment only and not in a production environment. Applications are generally profiled in a production environment only if a production security concern must be traced or a production environment bug must be reproduced. Two commonly used profiling tools are CLR Profiler and SQL Server Profiler.

CLR Profiler   CLR Profiler is designed to profile common language runtime (CLR)-managed applications created by using the .NET Framework. The CLR manages .NET applications, and the primary point of concern and area for improvement is memory use. As such, CLR Profiler is used principally to analyze how the application uses memory in the managed heap. CLR Profiler is capable of profiling executable applications, ASP.NET Web applications, and Windows Services applications and is capable of saving the profiler results and passing parameters to applications.

CLR Profiler is not included with the .NET Framework and must be downloaded separately at *http://download.microsoft.com/download/4/4/2/442d67c7-a1c1-4884-9715-803a7b485b82 /clr%20profiler.exe*. The CLR Profiler download includes both the compiled CLR Profiler binary and the source code to extend the profiler. To start the profiler, navigate to the folder in which you extracted the downloaded files and type CLRProfiler.exe. Figure 13-3 shows CLR Profiler in its default state.

Figure 13-3 CLR Profiler

Figure 13-4 illustrates a portion of the CLR Profiler Call Graph for a sample application. CLR Profiler accommodates many graphs and charts to convey profiler coverage of the target application.

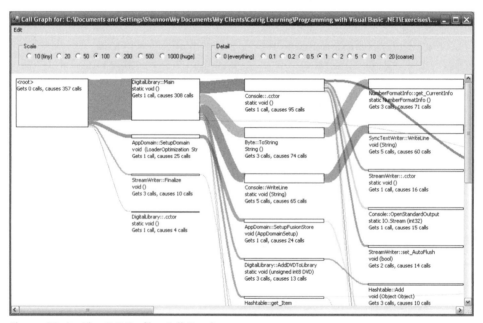

Figure 13-4 The CLR Profiler Call Graph

MORE INFO CLR Profiler

For more information about CLR Profiler, see the MSDN article entitled "How To: Use CLR Profiler," located at *http://msdn.microsoft.com/library/default.asp?url=/library/en-us/dnpag/html /scalenethowto13.asp.*

SQL Server Profiler SQL Server Profiler is similar to CLR Profiler; however, it is designed to profile SQL Server databases. SQL Server Profiler was originally released with SQL Server 7.0 and has been available a little longer than CLR Profiler.

Each profile monitored by SQL Server Profiler is referred to as a trace. A trace can be configured to capture virtually any level of detail and any event initiated by a SQL Server database application, including queries, locks, and transactions. In fact, if a trace is not configured to ignore activity carried out in SQL Server Profiler, you will notice that the actions you are carrying out in the profiler are added to the log as soon as you begin monitoring metrics using the trace.

Trace log information can be saved to a file with a .trc extension, known as a trace file or workload file, or saved to a table in a SQL Server database. The log information captured can be analyzed or used as an input for other tools such as the Index Tuning Wizard or the Database Tuning Wizard. Figure 13-5 displays the SQL Server Profiler.

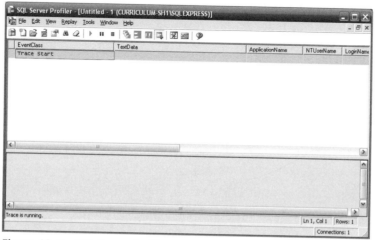

Figure 13-5   SQL Server Profiler

MORE INFO   **SQL Server Profiler**

For more information about SQL Server Profiler, see the MSDN article entitled "Monitoring with SQL Server Profiler," located at *http://msdn.microsoft.com/library/default.asp?url=/library/en-us /adminsql/ad_mon_perf_86ib.asp.*

Visual Studio 2005 Team System Performance Explorer   Visual Studio 2005 Team System includes performance monitoring and profiling tools. If you have Visual Studio Team System, you should be able to access the Performance Explorer by using the View menu. The Performance Explorer includes a Performance Wizard and the ability to create a Performance Session directly. The Performance Wizard simplifies creating a Performance Session, which consists of profiling or *instrumentation* for a .NET application. The Performance Explorer lists multiple performance sessions. Each Performance Session can contain a list of targets and a list of reports. A target is an application to be monitored, and a report displays the performance results.

MORE INFO Using the Visual Studio 2005 Team System Performance Explorer

For more information about using the Visual Studio 2005 Team System Performance Explorer, see the MSDN article entitled "TN_1210: Using the Performance Explorer," located at *http:// msdn.microsoft.com/vstudio/teamsystem/reference/technotes/profiling_windows_apps/perf_explorer.aspx.*

Instrumentation

Monitoring tools and profiling tools are used externally to measure application performance metrics. Instrumentation is the process of adding code to an application internally to initiate events that measure application performance metrics. One of four methods—including Event Tracing for Windows (ETW), Windows Management Instrumentation (WMI), Enterprise Instrumentation Framework (EIF), or the .NET Framework *Trace* and *Debug* classes—are generally used to instrument .NET applications. The most common methods are EIF or the *Trace* and *Debug* classes.

Enterprise Instrumentation Framework   Microsoft developed the EIF to provide a complete instrumentation solution for .NET applications. EIF encapsulates everything found in most monitoring, tracking, and profiling tools as well as WMI does and does so through a single interface. Using EIF, errors, warnings, diagnostic events, and business events can be logged to an event sink such as the Windows Event Log.

To instrument an application by using EIF in Visual Studio 2005, you must:

- Add a reference to the EIF assemblies to your application project.
- Add an empty installer class to your application project.
- Add code to your application to raise EIF events.
- Recompile your application.
- Enable tracing for your application in the TraceSessions.config file.
- Run InstallUtil.exe for your application.
- Bind EIF events to event sinks.

EIF is not included in the .NET Framework and must be downloaded separately from the MSDN link at *http://www.microsoft.com/downloads/details.aspx?FamilyId=80DF04BC-267D-4919-8BB4-1F84B7EB1368&displaylang=en.*

MORE INFO Enterprise Instrumentation Framework

For more information about the Enterprise Instrumentation Framework (EIF), see the MSDN article entitled "How To: Use EIF," located at *http://msdn.microsoft.com/library/default.asp?url=/library/en-us /dnpag/html/scalenethowto14.asp.*

***Debug* and *Trace* Classes**   The .NET Framework provides classes to assist in analyzing and identifying application bugs and performance in the *System.Diagnostics* namespace. These classes focus on using the Windows Event Log and Windows Performance Monitor as well as on custom performance monitoring. The two primary classes available in the *System.Diagnostics* namespace are the *Debug* class and the *Trace* class.

***Debug* Class**   The *Debug* class is intended to be used just as its name implies: for debugging purposes. It contains methods to enable you to write information to a designated listener (output location). Using the *Debug* class is similar to rudimentary debugging techniques that were used prior to the development of advanced debuggers. However, the *Debug* class is useful for logging diagnostic information automatically without the need of breakpoints and stepping through code execution in a debugger. Calls to methods of the *Debug* class do have a somewhat negative impact on performance and are intended for a debug build of an application, not for a production build. Statements that use the *Debug* class will not be compiled into application output when the build configuration for an application is set to *Release*. The following code example illustrates using the *Debug* class to write information to the Output window of the Visual Studio 2005 debugger.

Using the *Debug* Class

```vb
'VB
Imports System
Imports System.Collections.Generic
Imports System.Diagnostics
Imports System.Text

Namespace DebugClass

    Class Program

        Shared Sub Main()

            Debug.AutoFlush = True
            Debug.WriteLine("Starting the Main method...")

            ' Do something that requires iterating...
            For counter As Integer = 0 To 10 Step 1

                Debug.WriteLine(counter.ToString())
            Next

            Debug.WriteLine("Ending the Main method...")
        End Sub
    End Class
End Namespace
```

```csharp
//C#
using System;
using System.Collections.Generic;
```

```
using System.Diagnostics;
using System.Text;

namespace DebugClass
{
    class Program
    {
        static void Main(string[] args)
        {

            Debug.AutoFlush = true;
            Debug.WriteLine("Starting the Main method...");

            // Do something that requires iterating...
            for (int counter = 0; counter <= 10; counter++)
            {

                Debug.WriteLine(counter.ToString());
            }

            Debug.WriteLine("Ending the Main method...");
        }
    }
}
```

Figure 13-6 shows the results in the Visual Studio 2005 debugger Output window.

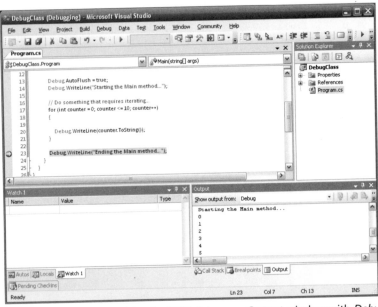

Figure 13-6   The Visual Studio 2005 debugger Output window with *DebugClass* output

---

MORE INFO *Debug* class

For more information about using the *Debug* class, see the MSDN article entitled *"Debug Class,"* located at *http://msdn2.microsoft.com/en-us/library/system.diagnostics.debug.aspx.*

Trace Class   The *Trace* class is also used to capture diagnostic information. However, the *Trace* class is intended for safe use in both debugging environments and production environments. *Trace* class method calls can be placed in code and remain there in production. The behavior of all *Trace* class methods can be controlled externally to the application by using settings in an application configuration file. The methods contained in the *Trace* class are almost identical to those contained in the *Debug* class. The primary difference between the *Trace* class and the *Debug* class is their intended use.

Both the *Debug* class and the *Trace* class can direct output to one or more listeners. A trace listener represents a destination in which output can be stored. Furthermore, performance output generated using the *Trace* class can be filtered by using a trace filter class or a trace switch. A trace switch can be configured to enable or disable trace output or to limit output to errors, warnings, information messages, or all trace information. The following code example illustrates using the *Trace* class to write information to the Output window of the Visual Studio 2005 debugger.

Using the *Trace* Class

```vb
'VB
Imports System
Imports System.Collections.Generic
Imports System.Diagnostics
Imports System.Text

Namespace TraceClass

    Class Program

        Shared Sub Main()

            Trace.AutoFlush = True
            Trace.WriteLine("Starting the Main method...")

            ' Do something that requires iterating...
            For counter As Integer = 0 To 10 Step 1

                Trace.WriteLine(counter.ToString())
            Next

            Trace.WriteLine("Ending the Main method...")
        End Sub
    End Class
End Namespace
```

```csharp
//C#
using System;
```

```csharp
using System.Collections.Generic;
using System.Diagnostics;
using System.Text;

namespace TraceClass
{
    class Program
    {
        static void Main(string[] args)
        {

            Trace.AutoFlush = true;
            Trace.WriteLine("Starting the Main method...");

            // Do something that requires iterating...
            for (int counter = 0; counter <= 10; counter++)
            {

                Trace.WriteLine(counter.ToString());
            }

            Trace.WriteLine("Ending the Main method...");
        }
    }
}
```

Figure 13-7 shows the results in the Visual Studio 2005 debugger Output window.

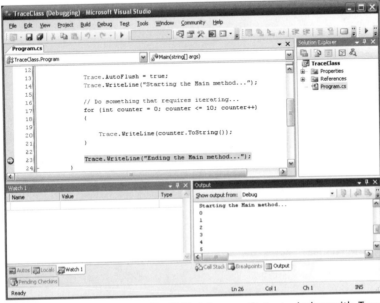

Figure 13-7 The Visual Studio 2005 debugger Output window with *TraceClass* output

MORE INFO *Trace* class

For more information about using the *Trace* class, see the MSDN article entitled *"Trace* Class" located at *http://msdn2.microsoft.com/en-us/library/system.diagnostics.trace.aspx.*

Real World

Shannon Horn

A few years ago, I was working on an ASP.NET Web application. The project was pro bono for a nonprofit client. My goal was to minimize expense while experimenting a little. The site needed to store some data for display to users. The data stored needed to be updated frequently by a single user and would be read-only for all site visitors. I decided to store all of the site data in custom XML files.

The site was working flawlessly and performing well with one puzzling exception. One of the pages on the site was designed to display a list of upcoming events for the organization. All event data was pulled from a custom XML file, and the data included the name, date and time, description, location, photo, and other information about the event. The events page was designed to display all future events and any events no more than three days old. The page worked perfectly on my laptop, but when I deployed it to the host server, the events page did not display any events in the repeater control I was using.

I was mystified, as was the technical support team for the host. The host support team reviewed all of my code and agreed that it should be functioning perfectly. I enabled tracing for the site and used the *Trace* class to perform some production diagnostics. The trace information showed me that everything was working perfectly, but the repeater control was loading zero bytes. This was extremely helpful information because it enabled me to focus precisely on what was happening with the repeater and was more information than the host support team had.

Well, it wasn't an easy issue to spot, but it was an error that I should have never made. In the events custom XML file, I was storing the date and time of the event by using a date and time format that was correct but was not the standardized W3C XML format. My code was comparing the date and time stored in the file to the date and time for the server. The problem was that the date and time format used on the server differed from that stored in the file and, thus, no events were ever matching the date and time on the server. As I mentioned, the code worked perfectly on my laptop, but the issue was a difference in date and time formats between my laptop and the host server. I corrected the problem by using the standard full W3C datetime format. The problem existed in the production environment only, and tracing allowed me to identify it while the application continued to serve users.

Quick Check

1. What performance monitoring tool is free and available with Windows?
2. What is the difference among monitoring, profiling, and instrumentation?
3. What is the difference between the *Debug* class and the *Trace* class?

Quick Check Answers

1. The Windows Performance Monitor is freely available with Windows and is the most commonly used application performance monitoring tool.
2. Monitoring is typically more generic information that is recorded externally and applicable to many applications. Profiling is very specific information and is tightly coupled to a particular application while still being recorded externally to the application. Instrumentation is very specific information and is generated internally to the application programmatically.
3. The *Debug* class is designed to be used in a debug environment whereas the *Trace* class can be used in a debug environment, but its strength lies in being useful in a production environment.

Monitoring Security

Application security is an even more pressing issue to be considered than application performance. Yes, an application must perform well if it is to be well regarded by users. However, if an application is not secure, it will generally be ridiculed in the industry and not considered a viable option for serious scenarios.

Designing a secure application is not an easy task. There are many things to consider and guard against. Depending on the application, such as for most medium-to-large databases, full-time dedicated personnel might even have to manage application security constantly.

Application security must be considered early in the design phase of the application development cycle. All security considerations for an application should be compiled into a *security plan*. As mentioned in Lesson 1, an application performance plan should integrate all other application and business plans, including the security plan, to determine how steps taken to secure an application affect performance.

An application security plan should be created during the design phase of the development cycle and should include security policies for application data confidentiality, integrity, and availability. Furthermore, a security plan should focus on the physical security of the computer on which an application is installed, the security of the data managed by an application, and the security of the network hosting an application. A security plan should also contain multiple security scenarios that outline how to secure an application in the target execution environments. Just as with an application performance plan, a security plan is typically a narrative-style document that can be created by using the editor of choice, the most common of which is Microsoft Office Word.

Just as with a performance plan, once a security plan is in place, it must be thoroughly and continually tested, re-evaluated, and adjusted to guard against new threats that arise. Adjusting for new threats is a constant process that involves using tools, auditing, and event logs.

Tools

Examples of tools that can be used to both monitor security and improve security are SQL Server Profiler, the Microsoft Baseline Security Analyzer (MBSA), and the IP Security Monitor. SQL Server Profiler was discussed in the previous section.

The MBSA is a free download located at *http://www.microsoft.com/technet/security/tools /mbsahome.mspx*. Once installed, the MBSA analyzes your installation of Windows and many other known applications, such as SQL Server and Internet Information Services (IIS), to be sure that all possible updates and patches are applied, and all actions are taken to obtain the highest level of security possible. Figure 13-8 shows the MBSA results page.

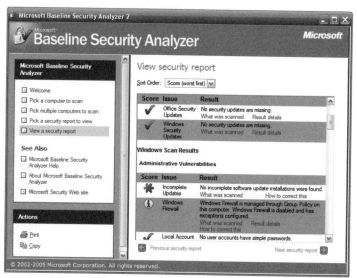

Figure 13-8 The Microsoft Baseline Security Analyzer scan results page

The IP Security Monitor is available by default in Windows XP and Windows Server 2003, using a Microsoft Management Console (MMC) plug-in. The IP Security Monitor manages restrictions and filters placed on IP communications. Figure 13-9 shows the IP Security Monitor.

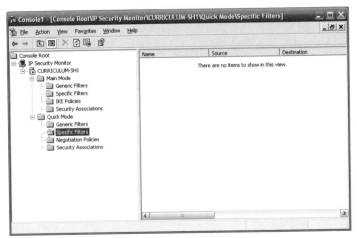

Figure 13-9 The IP Security Monitor

MORE INFO IP Security Monitor

For more information about using the IP Security Monitor, see the MSDN article entitled "How to Configure IPSec Tunneling in Windows Server 2003," located at *http://support.microsoft.com/kb /816514*.

Auditing

Auditing consists of logging events. Windows includes the ability to audit security events, particularly successful and unsuccessful logon attempts. Auditing is disabled by default, but it is simple to enable by the following steps.

1. From Control Panel, double-click Administrative Tools, and then double-click Local Security Policy.

2. In the left pane, under Local Policies, select Audit Policy. In the right pane, all of the audit policy settings will be displayed.

3. Right-click any of the audit policy settings, and select Properties to modify the setting.

Figure 13-10 shows the Local Security Policy plug-in with Audit Policy displayed.

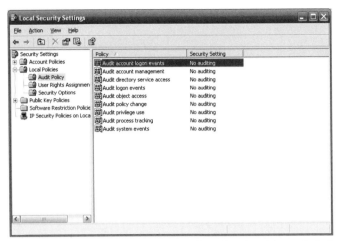

Figure 13-10   The Local Security Policy plug-in with Audit Policy displayed

Event Logs

Once you have enabled auditing, the status of the events that are being audited will be logged in the Windows system event logs. Enabling auditing is really useless unless you continually review the results of the audit process through the event logs. To review the Windows event logs, follow these steps.

1. From Control Panel, double-click Administrative Tools, and then double-click Event Viewer.

2. From the left pane of Event Viewer, select Security. Security audit events will be displayed in the right pane.

3. To view the details of a security event log, right-click the event log in the right pane, and select Properties.

Figure 13-11 shows the Windows Event Viewer with the Security audit category selected.

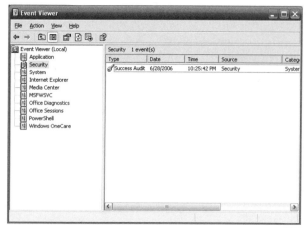

Figure 13-11 The Windows Event Viewer

MORE INFO Monitoring event logs

For more information on monitoring security and the topics discussed here, see the MSDN article entitled "Maintaining Security," located at *http://msdn2.microsoft.com/en-us/library/960f31dx.aspx*.

Real World

Shannon Horn

If you chose to be a software developer or to play a role in software development, bugs are a part of life; they are inevitable. I have taught software development classes for several leading companies for many years. In a recent class, I read some recommended practices from the curriculum out loud to the class. One of the practices simply said, "Don't make coding errors." This, without a doubt, brought a laugh from the class. An application generally includes so much code and so many factors to consider that it is almost impossible to avoid making coding errors, which, in turn, produce bugs. With that in mind, plan ahead to track identified bugs, including the steps involved to produce the bug, the severity of the bug, the priority assigned to fixing the bug, the status of the bug, and a history of all bugs that have been corrected.

Applications are typically developed in phases. Phases after the initial development phase generally include new and improved functionality as well as bugs that have been corrected. For example, Microsoft releases service packs that generally do not include significant changes to the application but comprise bug fixes for applications.

When the developer or team identifies bugs in an application, the goal is to correct the bugs in the least amount of time. Prioritize bugs so that the most critical bugs are attended to first. After a bug is corrected, the developer or team working on the fix must ensure that the fix is thoroughly tested from unit testing to integration and regression testing to be sure that a fix in one piece of code does not adversely affect other parts of the application. Furthermore, it is useful to maintain a history of all corrected bugs, when they were corrected, and who corrected them.

Bug fixes in Web applications are much easier to implement due to the central hosting environment, which normally requires no deployment. However, bug fixes in an enterprise or locally installed application are much more difficult to implement because fixes must be deployed to all installations.

Visual Studio Team System 2005 Work Item Tracking

Bugs could be tracked using any editor; however, an editor designed specifically for the purpose of tracking bugs would make the process much easier. At a minimum, a bug-tracking application should track the status, the severity, and the priority of bugs as well as to which resource the task of fixing the bug was assigned and a complete bug fix history. Many third-party tools are available for tracking bugs, also. In the Microsoft applications camp, bugs can be tracked by using Microsoft Office Excel or Microsoft Office Project. Many administrators manage projects by using Excel. Because Excel is a spreadsheet and is not designed specifically for tracking bugs, using it makes the process slightly cumbersome. Project is designed specifically for managing projects, tracking budgets and timelines, and assigning tasks to developer resources. Managing a project by using Project is, obviously, easier than managing one using Office Excel; however, Project does not include a dedicated bug-tracking feature.

Microsoft has to track bugs in its applications just as any other software development team does and decided several years ago to develop an internal application known as Product Studio to track bugs. The company greatly enhanced the developer package when it released Visual Studio 2005. Product Studio was renamed Work Item Tracking (WIT) and integrated into Visual Studio 2005 Team System (VSTS). You can configure permissions on bugs and tasks stored in WIT as needed. For instance, project managers can be granted access to create and assign items whereas developers can be granted access to only modify particular item data that pertains to the fix on which they are working. WIT bugs, tasks, and items contain more information than standard Visual Studio 2005 tasks.

Bug, task, and item data managed by WIT is accessible by using the VSTS Team Explorer and is stored in a central Team Foundation Server (TFS) database. To access WIT, select Team Explorer from the VSTS View menu. Once the Team Explorer is displayed, bugs, tasks, and other items can be added to the WIT database. Figure 13-12 shows the VSTS Team Explorer.

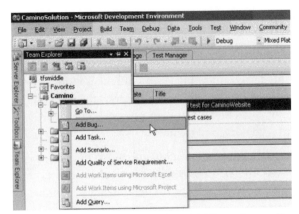

Figure 13-12 The Visual Studio 2005 Team System Team Explorer

Lab 2: Monitoring and Instrumentation

In this lab, you will walk through the steps to monitor the performance of the local operating system. The lab will also instruct you in how to instrument an application. If you encounter a problem completing an exercise, the completed projects can be installed from the Code folder on the companion CD.

▶ Exercise 1: Monitoring Performance

This exercise directs you to monitor the performance of your local installation of Windows, Visual Studio 2005, and a CLR-managed application by using the Windows Performance Monitor.

1. From the Windows Start menu, select Control Panel. Double-click Administrative Tools, and then double-click Performance.

   With a minimal number of applications running, the Performance Monitor should display minimal activity, as shown in Figure 13-13.

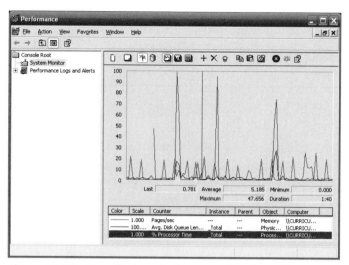

Figure 13-13   The Windows Performance Monitor with minimal activity

2. Add one or more performance counters.

   a. To begin monitoring performance using a performance counter in the Windows Performance Monitor, right-click anywhere in the performance display area, and select Add Counters.

   b. There are many performance counters to choose from. Explore the available counters to determine what they track.

   You can find detailed information for most performance counters by searching online. For instance, you can view a list of CLR performance counters and what information they monitor at *http://msdn.microsoft.com/library/default.asp?url= /library/en-us/cpgenref/html/gngrfRemotingPerformanceCounters.asp*.

   c. To add a counter to track the number of classes loaded by the CLR from the Performance Object drop-down, in the Add Counters dialog box, select the local computer and .NET CLR Loading from the Performance Object drop-down.

   d. Be sure the Select counters from list radio button is selected, and select Current Classes Loaded from the counters list. Select Add and Close.

3. Start Visual Studio 2005, and open the TraceClass (Microsoft Visual Basic or C#) project from the Chapter 13 source files. Run the application.

4. Select Performance Monitor, and observe the performance spikes in the CLR, processor, and memory counters as the application is loaded and executed. Figure 13-14 displays Performance Monitor.

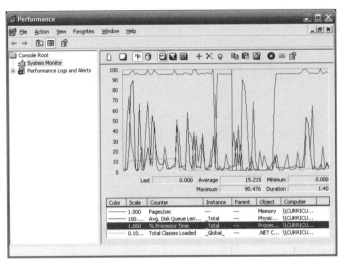

Figure 13-14   Windows Performance Monitor with the CLR counter performance reading

▶ **Exercise 2: Instrument a .NET Application**

This exercise walks you through the process of instrumenting a .NET application. You will use a sample application that mimics printing an invoice. The instrumentation will be used to log printing activities to the Output window of the Visual Studio debugger.

1. Start Visual Studio 2005.

2. Open the InvoicePrinter project.

3. Open Program.cs or Module1.vb.

4. To add instrumentation code to the main method:

   a. Include the *System.Diagnostics* namespace in the code as shown in the following sample.

      ```
      'VB
      Imports System.Diagnostics
      ```

      ```
      //C#
      using System.Diagnostics;
      ```

   b. Using the *Debug.WriteLine* method, add a line of code just before the foreach (For Each) loop that displays the message "Printing invoices . . ." or something similar in the Output window of the debugger.

   c. Using the *Debug.WriteLine* method, add a line of code inside the foreach (For Each) loop that displays details in the Output window of the debugger about the invoice being printed. The following is the modified code.

      ```
      'VB
      Imports System
      Imports System.Collections
      Imports System.Collections.Generic
      ```

```vbnet
Imports System.Text

Imports System.Diagnostics

Module InvoicePrinter

    Sub Main()

        ' Create a collection of invoices that need to be printed.
        Dim invoicesToPrint As ArrayList = New ArrayList()

        ' Create a new invoice.
        Dim newInvoice As Invoice = New Invoice("21556", "Alpine Ski House", 256.1)

        ' Add the invoice to the list.
        invoicesToPrint.Add(newInvoice)

        ' Print invoices.
        Console.WriteLine("Printing invoices...")
        Console.WriteLine("============================")
        Console.WriteLine()

        Debug.WriteLine("Printing invoices...")

        For Each invoiceToPrint As Invoice In invoicesToPrint

            invoiceToPrint.Print()

            Debug.WriteLine(invoiceToPrint.Id + "," + invoiceToPrint.Customer + ","
+ invoiceToPrint.Total.ToString("C"))
        Next
    End Sub
End Module
```

```csharp
//C#
using System;
using System.Collections;
using System.Collections.Generic;
using System.Text;

using System.Diagnostics;

namespace InvoicePrinter
{
    class Program
    {
        static void Main(string[] args)
        {

            // Create a collection of invoices that need to be printed.
            ArrayList invoiceToPrint = new ArrayList();

            // Create a new invoice.
            Invoice newInvoice = new Invoice("21556", "Alpine Ski House", 256.10);
```

```
        // Add the invoice to the list.
        invoiceToPrint.Add(newInvoice);

        // Print invoices.
        Console.WriteLine("Printing invoices...");
        Console.WriteLine("=============================");
        Console.WriteLine();

        Debug.WriteLine("Printing invoices...");

        foreach (Invoice invoice in invoiceToPrint)
        {

            invoice.Print();

            Debug.WriteLine(invoice.Id + "," + invoice.Customer + "," +
invoice.Total.ToString("C"));
        }
    }
  }
}
```

d. Set a breakpoint on the line that instantiates a new ArrayList for storing invoices to print.

e. Run the application in Debug mode by pressing F5. As you step through the code, watch the output displayed in the Output window of the debugger. Figure 13-15 shows the results in the Output window.

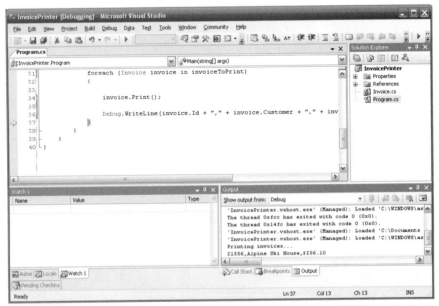

Figure 13-15 The Visual Studio 2005 Debugger Output window with lab results displayed

As mentioned earlier, you can experiment with additional performance counters as well as instrumentation code. Instrumentation coding could be extended to direct diagnostic information to different destinations. Furthermore, if you have Visual Studio 2005 Team System available, you can also experiment using the Team Explorer and Work Item Tracking functionality.

Lesson Summary

- Application performance monitoring is the practice of using loosely coupled tools external to the application to track high-level statistical information about the performance metrics of an application. The most commonly used monitoring tool is Windows Performance Monitor. Microsoft Operations Manager (MOM) is a Microsoft application designed to accommodate enterprise-level application performance monitoring.

- Application performance profiling is the practice of using tools tightly coupled with an application to track low-level information about the performance metrics of an application. Examples of profiling tools are CLR Profiler and SQL Server Profiler.

- Instrumentation is the practice of using code integrated into an application to track user-defined information about the performance of an application. The .NET Framework *System.Diagnostics* namespace includes the *Trace* and *Debug* classes for instrumentation.

- Application security must be considered in the design phase of the application development cycle even before performance. A formal security plan should be created for each application. Application security monitoring practices include auditing and analyzing event logs.

- Bugs identified in application code should be tracked and managed using a dedicated bug-tracking tool. Visual Studio 2005 Team System includes Work Item Tracking (WIT) functionality for tracking bugs, application tasks, and issues.

Lesson Review

You can use the following questions to test your knowledge of the information in Lesson 2, "Analyzing Monitoring Data." The questions are also available on the companion CD if you prefer to review them in electronic form.

NOTE Answers

Answers to these questions and explanations of why each answer choice is right or wrong are located in the "Answers" section at the end of the book.

---

1. What is the difference between the *Trace* class and the *Debug* class used for instrumentation?

    A. The *Trace* class is designed to be used in production code.

    B. The *Trace* class is used only in debug code.

    C. The *Debug* class is designed to be used in production code.

    D. The *Debug* class is obsolete, and the *Trace* class replaces it.

2. Which steps are involved in monitoring application security? (Choose all that apply.)

    A. Analyze server performance logs.

    B. Analyze event logs.

    C. Change user passwords regularly.

    D. Audit security events.

3. What is the recommended tool to use for tracking bugs in a Microsoft environment?

    A. Office Excel

    B. Visual Studio 2005 Professional

    C. Microsoft Project

    D. Visual Studio 2005 Team System

Lesson 3: Evaluating the Deployment Plan

This lesson discusses how to create an application deployment plan and what should be included in a deployment plan, including how to identify component dependencies and how to determine scripting requirements.

After this lesson, you will be able to:
- Use an editor of choice to create an application deployment plan.
- Identify component dependencies.
- Determine application scripting requirements.

Estimated lesson time: 15 minutes

What Is a Deployment Plan?

Application design and development is a complex process, so all aspects of development should be thoroughly planned. An application *deployment plan* should be created in the same manner that a performance plan and a security plan are created. An application deployment plan should be created in the design phase of the application development cycle. However, the deployment plan, as with most of the application development plans, should remain in flux because it will, undoubtedly, need to be modified and updated as the application is developed and tested.

A deployment plan is a single sub-plan of the larger collective project plan. The deployment plan should:

- Briefly restate the purpose of the application. The application should be described in detail in the primary project plan document.
- Determine all proposed target execution environments.
- List all resource requirements, both minimum and recommended, for all target execution environments. This list should also determine if the .NET Framework must be redistributed with the deployed solution.
- List any configuration requirements that must be made to the target execution environment when the solution is deployed.
- Outline expected deployment scenarios, possible issues, and how to resolve them ahead of time based on testing. Every step of a deployment plan should be tested thoroughly to ensure success.
- Identify who will complete the deployment. Will the application be installed on a server or at the client? Will the application be downloaded and installed by users, purchased and installed by users, deployed across an enterprise, or installed by internal staff?

- Integrate information contained in the security plan, the performance plan, the disaster recovery plan, and any other plans to ensure that the target execution environment is configured correctly.

- Identify any preexisting applications with which the deployed solution must integrate and the specifics of how this will occur.

A deployment plan can be created using your editor of choice; however, Office Word, Office Excel, or Project are commonly used to create deployment plans.

MORE INFO   Application deployment plans

For more information about creating an application deployment plan, see the MSDN article entitled ".NET Deployment Guide," located at *http://msdn.microsoft.com/netframework/technologyinfo /infrastructure/deployment/default.aspx#EHAA*.

Visual Studio 2005 Deployment Projects

One type of project that can be created by using Visual Studio is a deployment project. A deployment project is used to compile all deliverables that should be deployed with a solution into a single distributable package. The resulting distributable package can be either a setup.exe executable installation file with an associated setup.ini file or a Microsoft Installer (.msi) file. A deployment project is generally not created independently of a solution but is added to the solution that is to be deployed.

▶ **To create a deployment project using Visual Studio**

1. Open the solution to be deployed.
2. From the File menu, click Add, and select New Project.
3. From the left pane of the Add New Project dialog box, click Other Project Types, and then select Setup and Deployment.
4. From the right pane of the Add New Project dialog box, select one of the six options available.
    - ❑ **Setup Project**   A setup project is used to deploy console applications, Windows Forms applications, Windows Services applications, and other application types that are installed on the client, such as a .NET remoting client.
    - ❑ **Web Setup Project**   A Web setup project is used to deploy an ASP.NET Web Forms application or an ASP.NET Web Service application to a Web server hosted by using IIS.
    - ❑ **Merge Module Project**   A merge module project is used to merge application code, typically in the form of a *.netmodule* assembly, with existing code at the target execution environment.

❑ **CAB Project**   A CAB file is a cabinet file and is a compressed file similar to a ZIP file. A CAB project is used simply to compress files that must be extracted at the target execution environment.

❑ **Smart Device CAB Project**   A smart device CAB project is used to compress files to be deployed to a smart device such as a Smart Phone, a PocketPC, or another type of Microsoft Windows Mobile device.

❑ **Setup Wizard**   The Setup Wizard is used to walk through a set of screens with prompts that help you determine which type of deployment project you need for your application and to pre-configure certain settings.

5. Click OK.

A setup project in Visual Studio is configurable by using six editors.

■ **File System editor**   The File System editor is used to determine which actions the installation program will take to configure the target execution environment. Using the File System editor, you can configure which files are deployed with the solution, the installation folder, any other folders created on the target by the installation program, and shortcuts to the deployed solution.

■ **Registry editor**   The Registry editor is used to determine which actions the installation program will take to modify and configure the registry on the target computer. Using the Registry editor, you can add keys, values, and dwords to the target registry.

■ **File Types editor**   The File Types editor is used to modify file type associations on the target execution environment. Windows associates files with the applications that are used to manage the file by using the file extension. For instance, Windows will attempt to open a file with an extension of .doc by using Office Word. Using the File Types editor, you can create file type associations on the target computer so that Windows will attempt to manage certain files by using your application.

■ **User Interface editor**   The User Interface editor is used to configure the dialog screens displayed by the installation program during installation. You can modify the existing default screens as well as add and remove dialog screens.

■ **Custom Actions editor**   The Custom Actions editor is used to configure any custom actions that the installation program will take during installation. For instance, installation programs commonly instantiate Windows Notepad to display small help files once installation is complete.

■ **Launch Conditions editor**   The Launch Conditions editor is used to configure the installation program to detect configuration settings and conditions on the target computer. Generally, the Launch Conditions editor is used to determine if all minimum requirements have been satisfied prior to beginning installation. For instance, the Launch Conditions editor can be used to determine whether IIS is installed on the target computer prior to beginning installation.

Once the setup project has been configured, you must build it. To build a setup project, right-click Setup Project in Solution Explorer, and select Build. When a setup project is built, the distributable package is created. The distributable package will be located in the bin subdirectory of the setup project directory. You can double-click the distributable package to test the installation program. You can also right-click Setup Project in Solution Explorer and select Install.

When installation completes successfully, the installed application will appear in the Windows Add or Remove Programs list in Control Panel. The application can be uninstalled by selecting it from this list. The application can also be uninstalled by right-clicking Setup Project in Solution Explorer and selecting Uninstall.

MORE INFO   Deployment editors

For more information about the File System editor, Registry editor, File Types editor, User Interface editor, Custom Actions editor, and Launch Conditions editor, follow the appropriate "See Also" link at the bottom of the article "Opening the Deployment Editors," located at *http://msdn.microsoft.com /library/default.asp?url=/library/en-us/vsintro7/html/vbtskopeningpackagedeploymenteditor.asp*.

Identifying Component Dependencies

It is not uncommon for an application to require additional functionality beyond that contained in the .NET Framework. For instance, the user interface in your application might require an advanced text editing control, or your application might need to interface programmatically with another application such as Microsoft SQL Server. There is an abundance of third-party components available, and most applications expose some programmatic functionality.

If you use additional components in your application or interface with another application, your application must maintain a reference to the external component. References to external components that reside in a .NET application are stored in the assembly manifest once the application is built. However, you cannot be certain that the additional components or application will be present in the target execution environment. If any external components that are referenced by your application are missing when you deploy your application, your application might not function correctly.

To remedy the situation, you must deploy external components referenced by your application to the target execution environment or verify that they already exist. When you create a setup project by using Visual Studio 2005, Visual Studio will automatically attempt to detect references to external components or applications when you add an application assembly to the setup project. Visual Studio will not be able to detect references to unmanaged components. However, if your application contains references to external components, you should be aware of what action to take to ensure that your application will function correctly once it is deployed.

If your application contains a reference to an external component that is available only as a part of another application, such as the SQL Server 2005 SMO utility, that component cannot be deployed with your application. The only option you have is to include a launch condition in the setup project to detect whether the component existed prior to installing your application. If your application contains a reference to an unmanaged component that is not an integral part of another application, add the component to the setup project. If the unmanaged component cannot be added to the setup project, you must add a launch condition to the setup project to detect whether the unmanaged component existed in the target execution environment prior to installing your application.

The preferred scenario is that your application includes references to only externally managed components. If Visual Studio detects a reference in your application to an external assembly, it will automatically add the assembly to the setup project for deployment with your application.

There are many tools on the market to detect dependencies your application might have on external components. Microsoft offers a free utility called Depends.exe for this purpose, but it is primarily used with C++ applications.

Identifying Scripting Requirements

Visual Studio 2005 is a powerful Integrated Development Environment (IDE) program that includes functionality, particularly with Visual Studio 2005 Team System, to complete most development tasks. However, despite the massive power and functionality contained in Visual Studio 2005, scenarios can arise in which you need to customize or extend the behavior of Visual Studio through scripting.

There are several reasons you might need to write a script. For instance, a common use of scripts in Visual Studio 2005 is to take custom actions beyond what a setup project offers. Custom actions are defined by using the Visual Studio Setup Project Custom Actions editor. With the Custom Actions editor displayed, if you right-click one of the installation actions such as Install, you can select Add Custom Action from the context menu. The Add Custom Action dialog box allows you to select an executable file or script file by default. A script file would typically be written using VBScript, but the language can vary. When a custom action is added to a setup project, the CustomActionData property can be modified to pass data into a script at run time similar to a parameter.

Another scenario in which a custom script could be required is when customizing the application build process. Visual Studio 2005 introduces a new build framework called MSBuild. MSBuild is an XML-based file format that describes the entire project build process. MSBuild files are composed of projects and tasks that can be customized using scripts. Furthermore, although it is not necessary as often, the version of assemblies and files can be set during deployment by using scripts. Scripts are also useful when deploying smart client applications.

MORE INFO   **MSBuild**

For more information about MSBuild, see the MSDN article entitled "MSBuild," located at *http://msdn2.microsoft.com/en-us/library/wea2sca5.aspx*.

The most common use for scripts in Visual Studio 2005 is to deploy SQL Server 2005 database updates and CLR database objects. SQL Server 2005 was completely redesigned with the .NET Framework 2.0 natively integrated into it, so SQL Server 2005 can work directly with objects created using a .NET Framework language, such as Visual Basic or C#, and managed by using the CLR. Visual Studio 2005 is used to manage SQL Server 2005 database operations that are using SQL Server Management Studio and Business Intelligence Development Studio renditions. Visual Studio 2005 can be used to deploy SQL Server 2005 objects by using a database project.

When you create a database project by using Visual Studio 2005, a target database server is selected. As a best practice for development, projects should always be deployed from a developer to a test environment. Thus, the database server selected as the target when the project is created should be a test server. SQL Server 2005 CLR database objects and projects can be deployed to the selected target database server by using Visual Studio 2005 and selecting the Deploy from the Build menu once the project has been built successfully.

SQL Server 2005 CLR database objects and projects can also be built and deployed by using .NET Framework 2.0 command prompt utilities; however, using command prompt utilities is complex and tedious. Visual Studio 2005 is the recommended and preferred method of deploying SQL Server 2005 CLR database objects and projects.

Assuming that proper development practices were followed, and CLR database objects and projects were initially deployed to a test database server, scripts enter the SQL Server 2005 CLR database object and project deployment picture when the items are ready to deploy to a production server. Visual Studio 2005 offers an option to deploy only to the target database server selected when the database project was created. Scripts must be used to implement database objects and projects in a production environment. Scripts that are used to deploy SQL Server 2005 database objects and projects are written using Transact SQL. Once a database solution has been fully tested, scripts can be generated easily by using the Generate Scripts option in SQL Server Management Studio. A script is implemented on a production server by opening a connection to the production server and executing the script.

NOTE   **Visual Studio 2003 incompatibility**

Visual Studio .NET 2003 cannot use .NET Framework 2.0 functionality; therefore, it also cannot be used to deploy SQL Server 2005 CLR database objects.

Lab 3: Creating a Setup Project

This lab will walk you through the process of using Visual Studio 2005 to create a setup project, configure it, install the application, and execute and uninstall the application. If you encounter a problem completing an exercise, the completed projects can be installed from the Code folder on the companion CD.

▶ **Exercise 1: Create a Setup Project**

This exercise illustrates how to use Visual Studio 2005 to open a solution and add a setup project to the solution.

1. Start Visual Studio 2005, and open the InvoicePrinter solution located in the directory for Lesson 3, "Evaluating the Deployment Plan." Open the solution in the language of your choice, Visual Basic or C#.

2. To add a setup project, perform the following steps.
   a. From the File menu, select New Project from the Add cascading submenu.
   b. From the Add New Project dialog box, select Other Project Types, and then select Setup and Deployment in the Project Types pane.
   c. In the Templates pane, select Setup Project.
   d. Assign the Setup Project a name similar to InvoiceSetup.
   e. Click OK. The setup project should be added to the solution in Solution Explorer, and the File System editor should be displayed.

▶ **Exercise 2: Configure a Setup Project**

This exercise illustrates how to configure a few of the options in a setup project. Note that there are many more configuring options available beyond the few dealt with in this exercise, and the behavior of a setup project can be fully customized by using scripts.

To add the InvoicePrinter project output to the Application Folder, perform the following steps.

1. In the left pane of the File System editor, right-click the Application Folder icon, and select Project Output from the Add options on the context menu.

2. In the Add Project Output Group dialog box, select Primary output.

3. Click OK. Visual Studio 2005 should resemble Figure 13-16.

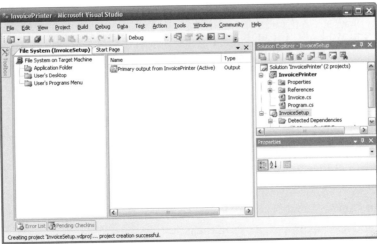

Figure 13-16   The Visual Studio 2005 setup project File System editor with Project Output added

To add an application shortcut to the user's desktop, follow these steps.

1. In the left pane of the File System editor, be sure to select the Application Folder icon. The Primary Output should appear in the right pane.

2. Right-click the Primary Output icon in the right pane, and select Create Shortcut to Primary Output.

3. Assign a name similar to Invoice Printer to the shortcut.

4. Right-click the shortcut, and select Cut.

5. In the left pane of the File System editor, select the User's Desktop icon.

6. In the right pane, right-click anywhere, and select Paste. The Invoice Printer shortcut should appear.

▶ **Exercise 3: Install a Setup Project**

This exercise walks you through the process of installing an application by using a setup project. There are two easy methods to install an application from the developer computer. You can install the application directly from within Visual Studio 2005, or you can navigate to the directory where the setup project output was built and install the application from that location.

To install the application from within Visual Studio 2005, follow these steps.

1. Right-click the InvoiceSetup setup project in Solution Explorer, and select Build to build the setup project. If any build errors occur, correct them.

2. Once the setup project builds successfully, right-click it in Solution Explorer, and select Install.

3. The application installation program will begin. Perform the steps through the installation program to install the application.

▶ **Exercise 4: Execute and Uninstall an Application**

This exercise illustrates how to execute an application that was installed using a Visual Studio 2005 setup project and then uninstall the application.

Executing the application should be easy. A shortcut to the application was installed on the user's desktop. To execute the application, follow these steps.

1. Double-click the shortcut to execute the application.
2. Verify that the application executes successfully.
3. Work with the application, and test it to your liking. Explore the file system to determine which files were deployed and to what locations.

Uninstall the application as you would any other Windows application; follow these steps.

1. In Control Panel, double-click the Add or Remove Programs applet. Follow those steps to uninstall the application.
2. Verify that all files and directories for the application were successfully removed from the system.

Lesson Summary

An application deployment plan that describes the details of deploying an application to target execution environments should be created in the design phase of the application development cycle.

- Visual Studio 2005 includes functionality for creating setup and deployment projects and offers six editors to customize various aspects of the deployment process.
- Applications commonly depend on external components to supply additional functionality. Visual Studio 2005 will attempt to deploy externally referenced components when you create a setup and deployment project. However, there can be scenarios in which you will be forced to deploy external components or customize the setup and deployment project manually.
- You can use scripts to extend and customize the behavior of a setup and deployment project or to manually deploy an application or component such as a SQL Server 2005 CLR-managed component.

Lesson Review

You can use the following questions to test your knowledge of the information in Lesson 3, "Evaluating the Deployment Plan." The questions are also available on the companion CD if you prefer to review them in electronic form.

NOTE **Answers**

Answers to these questions and explanations of why each answer choice is right or wrong are located in the "Answers" section at the end of the book.

---

1. Which of the following editors is available in a Visual Studio 2005 Setup and Deployment project? (Choose all that apply.)

    A. File Types editor

    B. Registry editor

    C. File System editor

    D. User Interface editor

2. How would you deploy an application that includes a reference to an external component that is available only as part of another application?

    A. Include the external component in a Visual Studio 2005 Setup and Deployment project.

    B. Manually copy the external component to the target environment over a remote connection after the application is deployed.

    C. Provide a link to download the component.

    D. Include a launch condition in a Visual Studio 2005 Setup and Deployment project to ensure that the component already exists in the target environment.

3. SQL Server 2005 database projects are deployed to a production server by using scripts written in which language?

    A. C#

    B. VBScript

    C. Visual Basic

    D. Transact-SQL

Lesson 4: Understanding an Application Flow-Logic Diagram

This lesson discusses a little history about diagramming and how diagramming is valuable in the application development process. The particular diagram on which this lesson will focus is the *application flow-logic diagram* that describes component dependencies and application complexity.

After this lesson, you will be able to:
- Create an application flow-logic diagram.
- Identify component dependencies.
- Determine application complexity.

Estimated lesson time: 15 minutes

Software Diagrams

Software development can be a complex process. Most individuals who are not developers consider software development to be beyond their mental capability and are intimidated by the slightest thought of writing code. However, software development projects are generally funded by individuals who are not developers. Administrators, management, and business decision makers are not likely to provide adequate funding for a software development project that they do not understand. Hence, a primary goal in the application development life cycle is to be able to convey the need, purpose, goals, basic structure, and technology involved in a software development project. Diagrams play an integral role in illustrating complex application processes and infrastructure.

Unified Modeling Language

The process of using diagrams to convey or define a complex process such as an application process or database structure is referred to as modeling. Many modeling methods have been created to convey software development processes. Some modeling methods have been adopted as industry standards, including the database entity-relationship diagram (ERD), which is used to document a relational database structure.

The Unified Modeling Language (UML) was introduced as an industry standard method of modeling software processes and infrastructure. UML includes many modeling standards, documents, and diagrams to address every aspect of software development, including use cases, use case diagrams, sequence diagrams, class diagrams, flow charts, and activity diagrams.

There are many tools and editors available to create and manage UML diagrams and documents. Microsoft's premiere UML editor is Microsoft Office Visio. There are several editions of

Visio, and the edition for Enterprise Architects is the most comprehensive. Visual Studio 2005 Team System also includes the ability to create several types of diagrams directly in the IDE. The benefit of creating diagrams in the IDE is that they are natively part of the solution and, in most cases, are active diagrams. An active diagram is one that is tightly coupled to the application with which it is associated. For instance, if a class diagram is created in a Visual Studio 2005 solution, functionality is provided so that the classes conveyed on the diagram can be created automatically by the IDE. Conversely, an active diagram will reflect any changes made to classes illustrated by the diagram. Additionally, Visio for Enterprise Architects integrates with Visual Studio 2005 and is available on the menu.

Application Flow-Logic Diagrams

An application is generally not designed as a monolithic piece of code but usually is a compilation of components that function together to perform a specific set of tasks, particularly in an object-oriented development environment. All developers working on an application must understand the relationships and interactions between the components that comprise an application. UML diagrams are useful in describing component relationships and interactions.

Several types of UML diagrams can be used to describe component interactions and relationships; however, an application flow-logic diagram is very appropriate. An application flow-logic diagram depicts the components that comprise an application and how they relate. Prior to moving on, it will be helpful to have a foundational understanding about the difference between components and classes.

A class is a representation of an entity within a compilation of code that contains data and functionality for working with the contained data. Classes should be designed in accordance with standard object-oriented principles.

A component is a separate compilation of classes and code that works to perform a task. In terms of .NET, the most common form a component will take is as an assembly. Classes are contained within an assembly, or component. In simple applications, a component might be able to function on its own; however, in more complex applications, components generally perform specific tasks and require other components to carry out overall application functionality.

An application flow-logic diagram illustrates three primary entities: components, interfaces, and dependencies. This chapter has already defined components; however, components expose interfaces through the classes contained in them. Functionality contained in a component is externally accessible only through publicly declared interfaces. Note that, although a component may expose multiple interfaces, an application flow-logic diagram should depict only those interfaces that are relevant to the diagram. An interface is depicted using the UML lollipop symbol.

In some cases, a component must be present for other components to function correctly. For example, a data access component must be present for components containing business classes to store data in and retrieve data from a database. A dependency is depicted on an application flow-logic diagram when one component depends on another component to function correctly. A dependency is depicted by using a dashed directional line that includes an arrow on the end of the line pointing in the direction of the dependency.

Figure 13-17 illustrates an application flow-logic diagram depicting an application comprising five components: Security, BusinessBase, Student, Faculty, and Schedule. The Security and BusinessBase components expose interfaces. The Student component is dependent on the *ISecurity* interface, and the Student, Faculty, and Schedule components are dependent on the *IBusinessBase* interface.

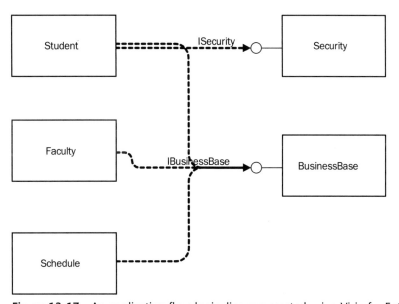

Figure 13-17   An application flow-logic diagram created using Visio for Enterprise Architects

Identifying Component Complexity

The number of components that comprise an application generally increases in direct proportion to the complexity and number of the tasks being performed by the application. There are several algorithms used to measure application and component complexity. This topic will illustrate using *cyclomatic complexity* because the algorithm relates well to application flow-logic diagrams.

Cyclomatic complexity is used to measure the complexity of an application by using the number of independent lines and paths between elements and components that comprise an application. A complexity value is rendered by measuring the connectedness of application components. A lower cyclomatic complexity value generally indicates a less-complex application. In most scenarios, as an application becomes more complex, it also becomes more difficult to maintain and enhance.

Cyclomatic complexity is calculated using the following algorithm:

$$C = E - N + P$$

In this algorithm, when applied to an application flow-logic diagram, C represents the cyclomatic complexity value, E represents the number of edges (dashed lines) depicted in the diagram, N represents the number of nodes (components) depicted in the diagram, and P represents the number of components depicted in the diagram that are dependent on other components. Table 13-1 lists estimated interpretations for the cyclomatic complexity value.

Table 13-1   Cyclomatic Complexity Values

Complexity	Interpretation
1–10	A simple, easy-to-comprehend application.
11–20	A moderately complicated application. Reasonably easy to modify, but some care is required.
21–50	A complex application with many interactions to be considered. Enhancements can be made but with a high risk of unplanned behavior.
>50	A very complex application that makes catching all bugs through initial testing difficult. Enhancements are almost certain to have unexpected side effects.

Lesson Summary

- Diagrams are useful in conveying complex software development processes.
- The Unified Modeling Language (UML) was created as an industry standard method of modeling, diagramming, designing, and describing software development processes.
- An application flow-logic diagram depicts the components that comprise an application and how they relate.
- Cyclomatic complexity is used to measure the complexity of an application by using the number of independent lines and paths between elements and components that comprise an application.

Lesson Review

You can use the following questions to test your knowledge of the information in Lesson 4, "Understanding an Application Flow-Logic Diagram." The questions are also available on the companion CD if you prefer to review them in electronic form.

NOTE Answers

Answers to these questions and explanations of why each answer choice is right or wrong are located in the "Answers" section at the end of the book.

1. Which of the following items are depicted on an application flow-logic diagram? (Choose all that apply.)

    A. Classes

    B. Interfaces

    C. Methods

    D. Components

    E. Dependencies

2. Which of the following items are represented in the cyclomatic complexity algorithm? (Choose all that apply.)

    A. Number of classes in the diagram

    B. Number of edges in the diagram

    C. Number of components with dependencies in the diagram

    D. Number of components in the diagram

    E. Number of interfaces in the diagram

Lesson 5: Validating the Production Configuration Environment

This lesson recaps elements to verify once an application has been deployed. It also introduces a few useful ways to observe an application to ensure that the application and the production environment maintain a performance balance.

After this lesson, you will be able to:

- ■ Verify that an application is configured correctly once deployed.
- ■ Monitor a production application.

Estimated lesson time: 15 minutes

Validate a Deployed Application

Although every application should be thoroughly tested before being deployed to a production environment, post-production deployment testing is also necessary. Testing performed after an application is deployed to production is conducted not for the sake of application functionality and integrity but to determine how the application performs in the production environment. Several points of interest require attention when testing an application that is deployed to production.

Correct application function is an initial point to test when an application is deployed to a production environment. Starting the application and quickly observing all functionality is an easy test to determine whether everything deployed successfully. If you start an application and immediately notice something functioning incorrectly, you will have a reference point from which to begin troubleshooting. Conversely, if you start an application and all appears to be functioning correctly, you should still verify that the production environment is configured correctly, as described in the following section. When an application is developed and deployed, it is rare that only a single person is involved. Typically, as the number of people, stages, and steps involved in the process increases, the more likely it is that an error can occur at some point along the way.

Resources

The lifeblood of an application is the physical resources available to it. If an application does not have adequate resources, it will typically exhibit unpredictable behavior. The primary physical resources are available processor(s) (CPU), available hard disk space, and available memory. Other physical resources, such as video card memory or network bandwidth, can also have an impact on application performance but are generally not as crucial as the processor, hard disk space, and memory.

Verify that a production environment has adequate physical resources available when the production environment is designed and well prior to application deployment. The physical resources necessary to support an application should be determined in the application performance model that is created in the application design phase. Remember that the application performance model is created in the application design phase and might be approximate. Once an application is deployed to a production environment, you might determine that the physical resources necessary to support the deployed application should be adjusted somewhat.

As an example of an application not performing as a result of a lack of physical resources, SQL Server will return a fatal error and no longer allow data to be stored in a database if disk space is no longer available. As a general rule, most Microsoft applications will continue to perform better as the amount of physical resources available to the application increases.

Security

Another configuration element of the production environment that must be verified is the security configuration settings. Prior to deploying an application to a production environment, the environment should be configured in accordance with the application security plan, which will determine which user accounts should exist, which permissions should be granted or denied, which resources should be available, and, possibly, which ports should be open or closed.

A common impediment when initially starting an application is inadequate permissions to a resource. For instance, if an application must read or write to a file or access a physical resource, and permission to access the resource has not been granted to the user account under which the application is running, the application will generally fail at that point. Verifying security settings is also vitally important to the integrity of an application as well as to the performance of an application.

Interoperability

A final area to consider when verifying a production environment prior to and after application deployment is application interoperability. Interoperability might not apply to all applications, but it is critical to applications that depend on it. For example, does the application depend on other applications or components to provide functionality? Does the application require Web access to function or consume Web services? Does the application require database connectivity?

When verifying interoperability in a production environment, ensure that dependent applications and components, and the correct versions, exist and are located where expected. Ensure that database servers are installed and operational, that databases exist, and that connection strings are known and correct. Ensure that required ports are open for accessing the Web and Web services.

Production Monitoring

Monitoring was discussed at length in Lesson 1, but its importance should be restated here because it will typically be most relevant to a production environment. The amount of physical resources necessary to support an application will generally increase as the loads placed on it increase. Therefore, pay close attention to loads being placed on an application and how well the application is performing. Monitoring is the key you will need to determine when to upgrade physical resources to prevent application performance below acceptable levels.

Furthermore, tracing will play a vital role in production applications to determine details about bugs that persist into production. Bugs do slip into production for many reasons. Generally, the larger the scope of an application, the greater the number of bugs that will appear in a production release. Unit testing is performed by the developers who use an application exactly as they envision it needing to be used. Higher levels of testing are performed by test teams and scripts. However, application users and malicious users will, undoubtedly, find ways never conceived by developers to break and exploit even the best tested applications. Tracing will enable you to gather detailed information about bugs as they make themselves known.

Profiling is vital in a production environment, primarily to monitor security issues such as unauthorized application access and attempts.

Lesson Summary

- The configuration of a production environment must be validated prior to and after application deployment.
- Applications deployed to production should be monitored for performance and security issues.

Lesson Review

You can use the following questions to test your knowledge of the information in Lesson 5, "Validating the Production Configuration Environment." The questions are also available on the companion CD if you prefer to review them in electronic form.

NOTE   Answers

Answers to these questions and explanations of why each answer choice is right or wrong are located in the "Answers" section at the end of the book.

---

1. What are the three primary physical resources that must be adequately supplied to support an application? (Choose all that apply.)

   A. Memory

   B. Video card display capability

   C. Processor

   D. Hard disk space

   E. Web connectivity

2. How would you gather detailed information about bugs that appear in an application after it has been deployed to production?

   A. Monitoring

   B. Debugging

   C. Tracing

   D. Profiling

Chapter Review

To further practice and reinforce the skills you learned in this chapter, you can perform the following tasks:

- Review the chapter summary.
- Review the list of key terms introduced in this chapter.
- Complete the case scenarios. These scenarios set up real-world situations involving the topcs of this chapter and ask you to create a solution.
- Complete the suggested practices.
- Take a practice test.

Chapter Summary

- The three most common performance objectives are response time, throughput, and resource use.
- A performance model should be created in the design phase of the application development life cycle. A performance model is used to ensure that the resulting application meets business performance requirements. The output of a performance model is a performance baseline. Using a performance baseline, you can determine whether an application is performing well or poorly in a given execution environment.
- Application performance monitoring is the practice of using loosely coupled tools external to the application to track high-level statistical information about the performance metrics of an application. The most commonly used monitoring tool is Windows Performance Monitor.
- Application performance profiling is the practice of using tools tightly coupled with an application to track low-level information about the performance metrics of an application.
- Instrumentation is the practice of using code integrated into an application to track user-defined information about the performance of an application. The .NET Framework *System.Diagnostics* namespace includes the *Trace* and *Debug* classes for instrumentation.
- Application security must be considered in the design phase of the application development cycle even before performance. A formal security plan should be created for each application. Application security monitoring practices include auditing and analyzing event logs.
- An application deployment plan should be created in the design phase of the application development cycle. An application deployment plan describes the details of deploying an application to target execution environments.
- Visual Studio 2005 includes functionality for creating setup and deployment projects and offers six editors to customize various aspects of the deployment process. You can

use scripts to extend and customize the behavior of a setup and deployment project, or you can manually deploy an application or component.

- Applications commonly depend on external components to supply additional functionality.

- The UML was created as an industry standard method of modeling, diagramming, designing, and describing software development processes. An application flow-logic diagram depicts the components that comprise an application and how they relate.

- Cyclomatic complexity is used to measure the complexity of an application by using the number of independent lines and paths between elements and components that comprise an application.

Key Terms

Do you know what these key terms mean? You can check your answers by looking up the terms in the glossary at the end of the book.

- application flow-logic diagram
- capacity planning
- cyclomatic complexity
- deployment plan
- instrumentation
- performance baseline
- performance modeling
- performance spike
- profiling
- security plan

Case Scenarios

In the following case scenarios, you will apply what you've learned about deploying and supporting an application. You can find answers to these questions in the "Answers" section at the end of the book.

Case Scenario 1: Deploying an Application

You are the lead developer on a sales application that stores individual sales receipts in XML files. The XML sales receipts are imported into a central sales database each night. You verified that the physical resources were in compliance with the deployment plan prior to deploying the application.

The application appears to be installed correctly and lists any XML sales receipts stored in the system when it is started. However, when a new sale is entered into the application, a fatal error occurs, and the application crashes. The error message returned does not give adequate information to identify the source of the problem. When the application was developed, the development team designed the application to assist in identifying bugs encountered after the application was deployed to production.

Questions

Answer the following questions to identify and correct the issue.

1. What step should you take first in identifying the problem?
2. Assuming that you were able to take steps to identify the problem, what is the most likely cause of the problem?
3. How can you attempt to prevent future configuration issues?

Suggested Practices

To help you successfully master the exam objectives presented in this chapter, complete the following tasks.

Deploy and Monitor an Application

- **Practice 1** Validate a production environment by verifying that the environment configuration settings comply with an application performance model, security plan, and deployment plan.
- **Practice 2** Deploy an application to the validated production environment by using a Visual Studio 2005 Setup and Deployment project.
- **Practice 3** Monitor an application that has been deployed by using Performance Monitor to track the allocation of memory. Use the private bytes and allocated bytes/sec counter to determine whether an excessive number of objects is being created.

Take a Practice Test

The practice tests on this book's companion CD offer many options. For example, you can test yourself on just one exam objective, or you can test yourself on all the 70-549 certification exam content. You can set up the test so that it closely simulates the experience of taking a certification exam, or you can set it up in study mode so that you can look at the correct answers and explanations after you answer each question.

MORE INFO Practice tests

For details about all the practice test options available, see the "How to Use the Practice Tests" section in this book's Introduction.

Answers

Chapter 1: Lesson Review Answers

Lesson 1

1. **Correct Answer: B**

    A. **Incorrect:** A business requirement defines an actionable, measurable feature for the system from the business perspective.

    B. **Correct:** This requirement is talking about supportability. That is a quality-of-service requirement.

    C. **Incorrect:** A user requirement defines a task the users need to be able to perform to meet the objectives of their jobs.

    D. **Incorrect:** A functional requirement is a specification for a developer.

2. **Correct Answer: D**

    A. **Incorrect:** The browser communicates with the Web server by using the HTTP protocol.

    B. **Incorrect:** Given the size of the user base, the system is most likely distributed. To improve performance, it is best to use .NET remoting for communication between the application and database servers.

    C. **Incorrect:** .NET remoting is the best communication choice for communication between Windows environments. It is more secure and affords better performance because the data is transferred in binary format (which is much smaller in size than XML).

    D. **Correct:** Web services is the best choice for communication when using multiple platforms and multiple protocols. The data is transferred in XML format, which is generally recognized by non-Windows platforms.

3. **Correct Answer: D**

    A. **Incorrect:** This is a data-entry application. It should be written as a forms-based user interface. There are no requirements that push this toward Office Excel.

    B. **Incorrect:** A standard client is not easy to deploy, cannot be updated easily, and doesn't provide offline access to users.

    C. **Incorrect:** Users must access the application from their corporate computers.

    D. **Correct:** A Smart Client will allow easy deployment through ClickOnce and offline access through Smart Client Offline Application Block (SCOAB). Smart Clients also yield a highly interactive user experience because they are rich Windows clients.

4. **Correct Answer: C**

   A. **Incorrect:** There is no justification for SQL Enterprise in this situation.

   B. **Incorrect:** SQL Express would work. However, it has a larger footprint than SQL Everywhere. In addition, it does not synchronize as easily.

   C. **Correct:** This offers a low-impact installation with the ability to work while disconnected. Users have to get database updates only on a monthly basis.

   D. **Incorrect:** This is too big and too costly to install on each user's computer or device.

5. **Correct Answer: C**

   A. **Incorrect:** Synchronous message processing is supported. This provides a means of communication whereby the application awaits a reply before processing can continue.

   B. **Incorrect:** Asynchronous message processing is supported. This provides a means of communication without forcing the application to await a reply before processing can continue.

   C. **Correct:** MSMQ does not inherently perform data transformation.

   D. **Incorrect:** MSMQ supports connecting to a message queue and examining the contents of the queue, as well as sending and receiving messages. This provides a system with a method of holding messages in the event that there are connectivity issues with the network.

Lesson 2

1. **Correct Answer: A**

   A. **Correct:** A vertical prototype covers a vertical slice of the entire application through the layers. The questions all define how data will be managed between these layers.

   B. **Incorrect:** A horizontal prototype, also called a mockup prototype, fills in the gaps that exist in the understanding of the user interface.

   C. **Incorrect:** A database prototype considers only the database and not the layers of the system.

   D. **Incorrect:** A mockup prototype, also called a horizontal prototype, fills in the gaps that exist in the understanding of the user interface.

2. **Correct Answers: A, B, and C**

   A. **Correct:** You should define the types (or categories) of screens in your system. A type might be data entry or report. All screens in the system should have a type.

   B. **Correct:** To help establish the size of your UI, you need to know all of the screens, their types, and the complexity in terms of read, write, and so on.

C. **Correct:** Creating an instance of each screen type will help you understand the effort that will be required to create similar screens.

D. **Incorrect:** You should not have to mock up each screen at this stage. This could take more time than you have and should not be required, provided you've followed the prior steps.

3. **Correct Answers: A, B, C, and D**

A. **Correct:** You need to confirm your authentication mechanism (forms or Windows).

B. **Correct:** You need to verify your approach to how users will be authorized to access features and data.

C. **Correct:** You should evaluate how key resources, such as files or connection strings, will be secured.

D. **Correct:** You should work with the infrastructure team to understand whether your recommendations are feasible in terms of firewall rules and the like.

4. **Correct Answers: A and C**

A. **Correct:** The intent of a prototype is to uncover gaps. You know you've done your job when you see this happen.

B. **Incorrect:** The uses cases might have been validated, but that does not indicate that the prototype was effective. It might indicate that either the prototype did not go far enough or it was not warranted.

C. **Correct:** Finding areas of the design that need more focus is a good sign. You need to identify areas of high risk and work to reduce this risk.

D. **Incorrect:** New technology working just as expected at the prototype phase rarely happens. You need to make sure the prototype went far enough. If it did, great. However, by itself, that does not indicate effectiveness.

Chapter 1: Case Scenario Answers

Case Scenario: Evaluate Requirements and Propose an Application Design

1. The high-level user requirements of the system might be documented as follows:

   ❑ A system should be created to allow members to view their insurance accounts, claims, and historical records.

   ❑ Healthcare providers should be able to use the system to verify insurance information for a given member. They should be able to look up a member based on the member's ID number.

   ❑ A member should be tracked only once in any system.

❑ A quarterly member data extract should be created for the analysis team. This data should be aggregated and scrubbed of any data that is private to any given member.

❑ Users must be allowed to define and establish security credentials upon initial access.

2. The high-level business requirements of the system might be documented as follows:

❑ We need an application that centralizes storage and access to member data and eliminates duplicate work and duplicate management.

❑ The requirements must follow best practices related to the organization's security policies.

❑ The system should reduce the cost of healthcare provider lookups (which are done by phone today).

3. The high-level QOS requirements of the system might be documented as follows:

❑ The application should respond to user requests in less than five seconds.

❑ The application should have a clean user interface, be easy to use, be approachable, and reduce confusion about what needs to be done.

❑ The application should support up to 1,000 concurrent users.

❑ The application should expect to store the data from over 50,000 members.

❑ The application should be made easily available to users.

4. The following are requirements that are functional in nature from the interviews:

❑ The application should be written as a Web-based user interface that supports standard, DHTML 4.x–compatible browsers.

❑ There are seven systems that need to be updated to work with the centralized member data.

❑ Member data should be retrieved as XML from *http://contoso/members/member-service.asmx*. There are two Web service methods: *GetMembers(searchCriteria)* and *UpdateMember(memberData)*.

❑ The application will be built using .NET Framework 2.0.

❑ The application should provide a scrubbed data extract to the statistical modeling tool. This extract should follow the MemberExtract schema and be in CSV format.

5. All the business requirements are ambiguous and not very actionable. For example, "The application should have a clean user interface, be easy to use, and be approachable" is a general description. These read like goals, not requirements. You might decide to turn these into goals and then track the requirements that realize a goal back to the given request. Or you might rewrite these in an unambiguous manner.

6. You should recommend a standard version of SQL Server. You have a large number of users, a sizable scale, and a lot of information you need to store and protect.

7. You should create a mockup prototype to validate the requirements and define the inter-
    action both a member and a healthcare provider will have with the system. You should
    also work to prototype your user validation system. In addition, your developers are new
    to .NET. Therefore, you should consider creating a reference architecture of key elements
    in the system. This includes screens, business objects, and data access code (a vertical
    implementation).

Chapter 2: Lesson Review Answers

Lesson 1

1. **Correct Answer: C**

    A. **Incorrect:** These items represent only some of the primary objects. The answer
        misses the other logical objects that are important to the ORM.

    B. **Incorrect:** These items represent only some of the primary objects. The answer
        misses the other logical objects that are important to the ORM.

    C. **Correct:** These are all objects from the statements. You can use these objects to
        begin building your ORM.

    D. **Incorrect:** These are not objects. They are actions.

2. **Correct Answer: C**

    A. **Incorrect:** Three objects make up the relationship (corporate user, support
        request, and application access). Unary is a single object relationship to itself.

    B. **Incorrect:** A support request can't exist with just a corporate user or just an appli-
        cation access definition. Therefore, two binary relationships would not really rep-
        resent the relationship.

    C. **Correct:** A ternary relationship exists among support request, corporate user, and
        application access as: support request has a corporate user; support request
        defines application access.

    D. **Incorrect:** A quaternary relationship is among four objects. Only three are defined
        in this question.

3. **Correct Answers: A and C**

    A. **Correct:** This is the left-to-right reading of the relationship fact.

    B. **Incorrect:** This does not model the fact as defined. It assumes a new object,
        Approval.

    C. **Correct:** This is the right-to-left reading of the relationship fact.

    D. **Incorrect:** This does not model the fact. It, too, assumes a new object, Approval.

4.   **Correct Answer: A**

   A.   **Correct:** A shipping slip must have a single ship-to address. Therefore, the ship-ping slip is mandatory to form the relationship. However, a ship-to address does not need a shipping slip. So the inverse part of the relationship is not mandatory (a ship-to address defines zero or more shipping slips). The arrow over the left side (Shipping Slip) indicates a many-to-one relationship. That is, each ship-to address can define many Shipping Slips.

   B.   **Incorrect:** This indicates that the ship-to address is mandatory to form this rela-tionship. However, the relationship does not exist without a Shipping Slip. The arrow on the right indicates a one-to-many relationship. This would be true only if a shipping slip were allowed to ship to multiple locations.

   C.   **Incorrect:** No circle indicates that neither item is required for the relationship. This is not true. Shipping Slip is required to form this relationship. The two arrows indicate a one-to-one relationship. That would be true only if the ship-to address could exist only on a single shipping slip. That is, an address could receive only a single shipment.

   D.   **Incorrect:** The mandatory part of the relationship is correct. However, the single long arrow indicates a many-to-many relationship. This would be true if the ship-ping slip allowed multiple ship-to addresses. However, this would confuse the shipper.

Lesson 2

1.   **Correct Answers: A, B, and D**

   A.   **Correct:** Creating layers can increase reuse. A business logic–only layer, for exam-ple, might allow other systems to access this information. Other applications can take advantage of a database abstraction class or application services code.

   B.   **Correct:** Layers give developers a logical understanding of where their code should be written and what code is accessible (referenced) from that code. Layers provide guidelines and structure to code base.

   C.   **Incorrect:** Layers are logical. They do not dictate the physical packaging or deploy-ment. The layers might influence some of your decisions, but it is not a primary benefit.

   D.   **Correct:** By encapsulating code into layers, you can more easily change individual pieces without affecting other code elements.

2.   **Correct Answers: A and C**

   A.   **Correct:** The presentation layer abstracts the user interface layout code from the code that is used to transact (such as business object and database access code). Therefore, your Windows Forms code would fit the definition of presentation.

B. **Incorrect:** The presentation code would not couple the business processing rules tightly. Rather, it would separate itself from these duties.

C. **Correct:** The use controls of the system are similar to forms. They abstract presentation from the business and transaction code.

D. **Incorrect:** The database access code should not be coupled in the presentation tier. The presentation tier should concern itself only with form layout and responding to user activity.

3. **Correct Answer: C**

A. **Incorrect:** This many layers are excessive, based on the constraints. The application is simple and small. The layers should be few in number.

B. **Incorrect:** Separating the application into even three layers is not warranted, based on the constraints. The simple business layer code can be embedded in the user interface.

C. **Correct:** The application is a throwaway, has a tight timeframe and a small number of users, is simple, and will be deployed on a single server. Therefore, the fastest solution here will be a Windows client-server application.

D. **Incorrect:** Nothing in the constraints indicates the use (or need) for application services.

Lesson 3

1. **Correct Answer: D**

A. **Incorrect:** The component diagram shows the logical grouping of classes into components. It does not show the static structure of objects.

B. **Incorrect:** A collaboration diagram shows how objects work together through message calls. It does not define the static structure for those objects.

C. **Incorrect:** Pseudocode illustrates a complex method, using code-like terms.

D. **Correct:** A class diagram is a static view of your classes and their relationships, properties, and methods. Developers can use this model to implement code. They use the other model to help understand how that code works as a solution.

2. **Correct Answers: B, C, and D**

A. **Incorrect:** Both sequence and collaboration diagrams can show asynchronous messaging.

B. **Correct:** A sequence diagram is read left to right, top to bottom. You must follow the numbers on the messages to read the order in a collaboration diagram.

C. **Correct:** A collaboration diagram does not show when objects are created and destroyed. This is left for interpretation.

    D. **Correct:** A collaboration diagram can be useful when you want to see objects laid out in a different manner.

  3. **Correct Answers: B, C, and D**

    A. **Incorrect:** Class interactions are best defined through sequence diagrams. Class groupings are defined through component diagrams.

    B. **Correct:** An activity diagram is good for modeling the steps inside complex algorithms.

    C. **Correct:** An activity diagram allows you to indicate activities both in sequence and in parallel. It also shows where things fork and where they come back together (or join). Therefore, it is very good at showing workflow. This is not often a physical model, but it can be useful nonetheless.

    D. **Correct:** An activity diagram can show actions in parallel. For this reason, it is often used to model multithreaded methods.

  4. **Correct Answer: D**

    A. **Incorrect**: A sequence diagram is a representation of an object in operation. Objects are shown as rectangles across the top of the diagram.

    B. **Incorrect**: The lines extending from the objects at the top of a sequence diagram are called lifelines. Lifelines can be wrapped in rectangles called activation lines, which indicate the specific time periods when the given object is active. In other words, they indicate when the object is in memory.

    C. **Incorrect**: Messages represent the lines between the object lifelines. Messages translate into functions and subroutine calls.

    D. **Correct**: Branch is part of a UML activity diagram. It specifies alternate paths for an activity.

Chapter 2: Case Scenario Answers

Case Scenario: Evaluate User Inputs and Create Physical Models

  1. The two following illustrations present possible ORM diagrams for this use case. (The ORM diagram is split into two illustrations to fit in this book.) This ORM diagram model was created by defining the objects in the system and their relationships from the use case.

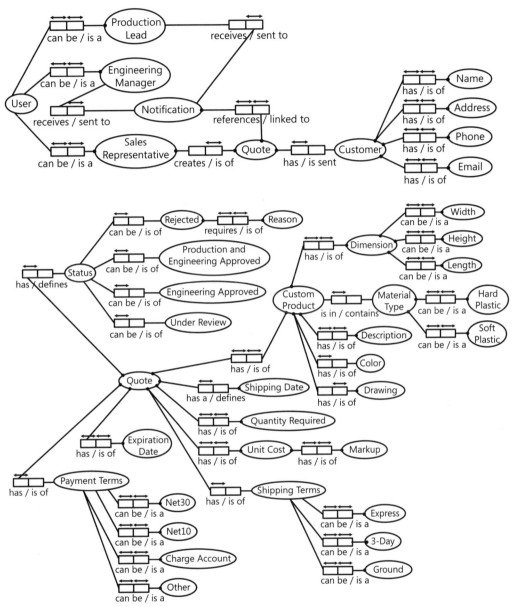

2. The following illustration presents a possible application layers diagram based on the aforementioned design goals. The presentation tier is both a Windows UI and the e-mail client. The business objects should be their own layers, given that the business services will be reused across different user experiences. Each business object also accesses the database directly.

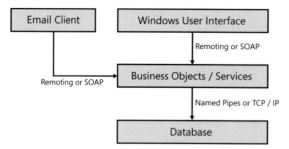

3. The following illustration presents a possible object model for the solution. This model does not show the additional details (properties and methods) not indicated by the use case. It also does not consider the user interface.

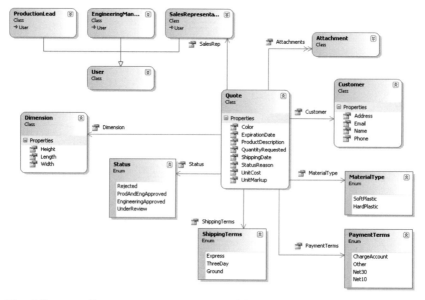

4. The following illustration presents a possible sequence diagram for the use case previously listed. This use case assumes the application layers defined as part of the model. The call to *GetDetails()* is illustrating the calls to return the properties of the quote for display to the user (by means of *ApproveQuoteUI*).

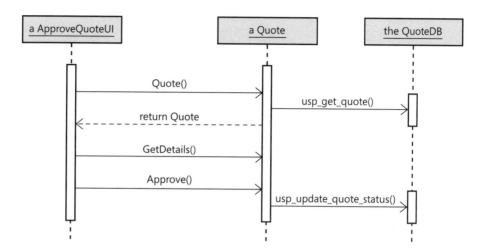

Chapter 3: Lesson Review Answers

Lesson 1

1. **Correct Answer: B**

   A. **Incorrect:** Your application will need to read the configuration file; therefore, using NTFS security will not protect your configuration data.

   B. **Correct:** Yes, using Windows Data Protection will enable you to protect your data without having to compromise the data by keeping shared secrets.

   C. **Incorrect:** Storing the sensitive data inside assemblies does not protect it from unscrupulous users.

   D. **Incorrect:** Protecting your data with the .NET Framework encryption classes can work, but the protection is either weak or requires shared secrets, which can provide unscrupulous users with a way to decrypt the data.

2. **Correct Answer: C**

   A. **Incorrect:** Stored procedures are an implementation detail that can improve performance and security of your application, but they do not have an impact on the logical design's scalability.

   B. **Incorrect:** Reliable transactions can improve data integrity of your application, but they do not have an impact on the logical design's scalability.

   C. **Correct:** Having a distinct data (or middle) tier of your application provides the maximum scalability in the logical design.

   D. **Incorrect:** Database failover can improve the data integrity of your application, but it does not have an impact on the logical design's scalability.

3. **Correct Answer: A**

    A. **Correct:** A component in the logical design should be part of one—and only one—of the logical tiers. This separation ensures that the code is maintainable over the long term.
    B. **Incorrect:** See the explanation for the correct answer.
    C. **Incorrect:** See the explanation for the correct answer.
    D. **Incorrect:** See the explanation for the correct answer.

Lesson 2

1. **Correct Answer: D**

    A. **Incorrect:** Opening ports in the firewall to accommodate specific types of applications will open your network up to Internet-based attacks.
    B. **Incorrect:** Using Web services can reduce your surface area of attack, but any critical data that is exposed through a Web service is a potential point of attack.
    C. **Incorrect:** Although Web applications can be secure, they do not (in themselves) prevent attacks.
    D. **Correct:** Using a VPN can allow users of the network to treat the network as if they are inside without having to design your software specifically for special security situations.

2. **Correct Answer: A**

    A. **Correct:** Enforcing the data integrity outside the database allows you to help the user enter valid data without the overhead of going all the way to the database to find incorrect data.
    B. **Incorrect:** Enforcing the data integrity outside the database allows you to help the user enter valid data without the overhead of going all the way to the database to find incorrect data.

3. **Correct Answer: B**

    A. **Incorrect:** Whether your data tier exists on a separate computer is determined by the performance and security constraints of your design. Deploying the data tier on the same computer as the user interface is an acceptable design choice.
    B. **Correct:** It is unnecessary to force the user interface and data tiers to be segmented into different physical machines.

Chapter 3: Case Scenario Answers

Case Scenario 1: Review the Logical Design of an Enterprise Application

1. By reviewing the original requirements, I will compare them to the logical design to ensure that there are no gaps.
2. By ensuring that the design has kept the user interface and business logic tiers separate, I can ensure that the maintainability of the system is adequate for our needs. By separating the logical designs into logical tiers, changes in one tier will not necessarily cascade into wholesale rewriting of parts of the application.

Case Scenario 2: Review the Physical Design of an Enterprise Application

1. By reviewing the physical design to determine what kind of security is going to be used, we can evaluate the security model of the physical design.
2. The location of shared components and controls needs to be evaluated to ensure that updating individual shared elements will positively affect other projects that are using those same controls.

Chapter 4: Lesson Review Answers

Lesson 1

1. Correct Answers: B and C
   A. **Incorrect:** Entity relationships should be modeled as foreign keys and/or mapping tables, not as primary keys.
   B. **Correct:** Entity relationships should be modeled as foreign keys and/or mapping tables.
   C. **Correct:** Entity relationships should be modeled as foreign keys and/or mapping tables.
   D. **Incorrect:** Entity relationships should be modeled as foreign keys and/or mapping tables, not as tables.
2. Correct Answer: C
   A. **Incorrect:** See the explanation for the correct answer.
   B. **Incorrect:** See the explanation for the correct answer.
   C. **Correct:** Concurrency management ensures that data is not changed by different users mistakenly.

D. **Incorrect:** See the explanation for the correct answer.

3. **Correct Answer: B**

A. **Incorrect:** A primary key, not the primary index, defines uniqueness.

B. **Correct:** The primary index provides a fast way to search for a specific primary key value in a table.

C. **Incorrect:** Foreign keys, not primary indexes, provide consistency across data tables.

D. **Incorrect:** Primary indexes have no relationship to sorting.

Lesson 2

1. **Correct Answer: C**

A. **Incorrect:** See the correct answer explanation.

B. **Incorrect:** See the correct answer explanation.

C. **Correct:** Web site user interfaces should be packaged as an ASP.NET control.

D. **Incorrect:** See the correct answer explanation.

2. **Correct Answer: A**

A. **Correct:** Components that show a user interface belong in the user interface tier.

B. **Incorrect:** Components that show a user interface belong in the user interface tier.

C. **Incorrect:** Components that show a user interface belong in the user interface tier.

Lesson 3

1. **Correct Answer: A**

A. **Correct:** Initialization data should be passed as part of the construction of an object. There is no benefit to using a multi-phase construction.

B. **Incorrect:** Single-phase construction prevents unexpected work flow patterns such as when the initialization method is called multiple times.

Chapter 4: Case Scenario Answers

Case Scenario 1: Design an Employee Component

1. The component will be packaged as a library assembly, so you can use it simply as a library assembly, or you could host it in a middle tier using Web services or remoting as necessary.

2. Because the component will be packaged as a library assembly, it can be referred to from the Web application by simple reference.

Case Scenario 2: Design a Database for the Company Library

1. There will be three tables—an Employee table, a Book table, and a CheckOut table—to store data about which employees have checked out which books.

2. There will be a foreign key from the CheckOut table into the Employee table as well as a foreign key from the CheckOut table to the Book table.

Chapter 5: Lesson Review Answers

Lesson 1

1. **Correct Answer: C**
   A. **Incorrect:** See the explanation for the correct answer.
   B. **Incorrect:** See the explanation for the correct answer.
   C. **Correct:** You need to implement *IDisposable* only if the contained object's lifetime is the same as your component.

2. **Correct Answer: B**
   A. **Incorrect:** Abstract classes are used to share a common implementation through inheritance. To stop instantiation of your class, use a private constructor.
   B. **Correct:** Abstract classes are used to share a common implementation through inheritance.
   C. **Incorrect:** If you need inheritors to conform to a particular interface, use an *Interface* instead.
   D. **Incorrect:** That a class is abstract has no affect on which tier it is used in.

3. **Correct Answers: A, B, and C**
   A. **Correct:** If the cost of development is more important than using the component in a multithreaded environment, avoiding thread safety may be an appropriate choice.
   B. **Correct:** If the overhead is more important than using the component in a multithreaded environment, avoiding thread safety may be an appropriate choice.
   C. **Correct:** If the component will not be used by multithreaded code, there is no need to make it thread safe.
   D. **Incorrect:** Thread safety is not required by all components.

Lesson 2

1. **Correct Answers: B and C**
   A. **Incorrect:** *DataReader*, in combination with *Command*, does not have client-side schema rules.

    B. **Correct:** Datasets support client-side schema.

    C. **Correct:** Typed datasets, because they are still datasets, also have support for client-side schema.

2. **Correct Answer: A**

    A. **Correct:** Using the event model of a *DataSet* is the appropriate way to add business logic to untyped datasets.

    B. **Incorrect:** Container classes are labor intensive to write and can be problematic to maintain.

    C. **Incorrect:** The *DataSet* schema is appropriate for data validation but not for business logic. Using the event model of a *DataSet* is the appropriate way to add business logic to untyped datasets.

    D. **Incorrect:** The *DataSet* schema is appropriate for data validation but not for business logic because *DataSet* schema is not powerful enough to test against business rules. Using the event model of a *DataSet* is the appropriate way to add business logic to untyped datasets.

3. **Correct Answer: C**

    A. **Incorrect:** *DataReader*, in combination with *Command*, is the most labor intensive; therefore, you should be using typed datasets to prototype a project.

    B. **Incorrect:** No, typed datasets will allow you to prototype your project most quickly.

    C. **Correct:** Typed datasets are the quickest way to develop data access and, therefore, should be used for prototyping

Lesson 3

1. **Correct Answers: A, C, and D**

    A. **Correct:** Sending a method an invalid argument is an exceptional case and should result in an exception being thrown.

    B. **Incorrect:** Executing a search and finding no results is not exceptional but is a valid result; therefore, you should not throw an exception.

    C. **Correct:** Running out of memory is exceptional and should result in an exception being thrown.

    D. **Correct:** An unavailable database is exceptional and should result in an exception being thrown.

2. **Correct Answer: B**

    A. **Incorrect:** See correct answer explanation.

    B. **Correct:** You should include contextual information only if it is helpful in correcting exceptional cases. For systemic issues (for instance, for an *OutOfMemoryException*), just allowing exceptions to propagate without context is acceptable.

3. **Correct Answers: B and C**

   A. **Incorrect:** Profiling does not test functional requirements.

   B. **Correct:** Profiling is performed to ensure that a component meets performance requirements and to find resource leaks.

   C. **Correct:** Profiling is performed to ensure that a component meets performance requirements and to find resource leaks.

   D. **Incorrect:** You cannot profile code that does not compile.

Chapter 5: Case Scenario Answers

Case Scenario 1: Choose a Data Access Methodology

1. Because time is the most important factor, we should use typed datasets, even though it might mean that we have to re-engineer part of this project later.

2. Put any business logic in the partial class file that is used in conjunction with the typed dataset. Do not put any code in the generated classes.

Case Scenario 2: Search for Resource Leaks

1. We should profile the system in two phases. First, use CLR Profiler to see which components are consuming the most memory. Second, instrument the targeted components to see why they are consuming the memory.

2. We can isolate the problem by using a variety of profiling tools, although CLR Profiler and the Visual Studio Performance Wizard are probably the best tools for the job.

Chapter 6: Lesson Review Answers

Lesson 1

1. **Correct Answer: D**

   A. **Incorrect:** When objects are serialized for passing across a Web service boundary, only the public properties are sent. The stem requires that the entire state of the object be transmitted.

   B. **Incorrect:** This explanation is the same as A.

   C. **Incorrect:** The XmlMessageFormatter uses *IXmlSerializable*, which, by default, marshals only public properties.

   D. **Correct:** The BinaryMessageFormatter uses the current state of the object in its binary form. When the message is received, a clone of the object is created, complete with all of its public and private state information.

2. **Correct Answer: B**

   A. **Incorrect:** Using SOAP with Attachments doesn't allow for the binary data in the attachment to be secured by using WS-Security.

   B. **Correct:** MTOM will encrypt the binary data payload by using WS-Security.

   C. **Incorrect:** MSMQ has a difficult time working in the Java world, and the ability to use WS-Security on the message would be very challenging.

   D. **Incorrect:** This explanation is the same as C.

3. **Correct Answer: C**

   A. **Incorrect:** Using SOAP with Attachments causes the message to be converted into base64, which increases the message size by at least 1.33 times. Although the message could be buffered to the client, it is not the solution of choice for a minimal impact.

   B. **Incorrect:** DIME shares the same problem as SOAP with Attachments with respect to the base64 requirement and the size of the message.

   C. **Correct:** Serving the content in MTOM optimizes the message size, and streaming the content minimizes the impact on the server's memory usage.

   D. **Incorrect:** Although MTOM optimizes the message size, the fact that the data is served in a single blob means that it needs to be completely constructed on the server. This doesn't bode well for scalability and memory usage concerns.

Lesson 2

1. **Correct Answers: B and D**

   A. **Incorrect:** Increasing the sampling rate increases the amount of data saved for the content, which increases its size, making it more difficult to move across slow connections.

   B. **Correct:** Decreasing the sampling rate reduces the size of the content, something that 56KB modem users will appreciate.

   C. **Incorrect:** The WAV format is uncompressed and, thus, isn't as small as it could be.

   D. **Correct:** The MP3 format uses compression to reduce the size of the content.

Chapter 6: Case Scenario Answer

Case Scenario: Delivering Graphics to Multiple Client Applications

1. The correct answer to this question is difficult to identify with certainty. Ultimately, Windows Services using MSMQ is the right choice for this environment, although most people will probably lean toward a Web service for reasons of familiarity. However, for

performance reasons, Windows Services will provide a higher level of responsiveness to the clients.

The use of MSMQ means that the graphic will be delivered in a binary form with no conversion required. Although MTOM doesn't require conversion into MIME-encoded format, some effort is still required to parse the SOAP message to extract the image. The MSMQ message, when sent using a BinaryMessageFormatter, sends the data in a raw format. It is very fast to re-create the graphic object by using that stream of data.

An objection to this choice is that MSMQ is too slow to act as a communications channel in a high-performance environment. This is rarely an issue. MSMQ is a very fast mechanism, especially if the queue is not set up as transactional. Sending an MSMQ message is close to the same speed as making a Web service call, if not faster.

Chapter 7: Lesson Review Answers

Lesson 1

1. **Correct Answer: C**
   A. **Incorrect:** The Friend (VB) / intern (C#) access modifier prevents your class from being accessible to other assemblies. Friend (VB) / intern (C#) is accessible to the current component and derived components.
   B. **Incorrect:** The Private (VB) / private (C#) access modifier prevents your class from being accessible to other assemblies.
   C. **Correct:** By making the derived class and the overridden method public, you expose the functionality to other assemblies.
   D. **Incorrect:** As shown in the previous answer, a solution is possible.

2. **Correct Answer: C**
   A. **Incorrect:** Visual Basic and C# do not permit multiple inheritances. You can inherit from only one class. You can implement multiple interfaces, but all three of these were components, not interfaces.
   B. **Incorrect:** A class that is declared with the *MustInherit* (VB) / *abstract* (C#) modifier cannot be created; it can be used only as a base class for a derived class.
   C. **Correct:** Classes can inherit from other classes. Classes can also create instances of other classes as long as the appropriate references have been set.
   D. **Incorrect:** A component that has been declared with the *NotInheritable* (VB) / *sealed* (C#) modifier cannot be used as a base class.

3. **Correct Answer: C**
   A. **Incorrect:** Private methods are *Overridable* by default.
   B. **Incorrect:** Public methods are *NotOverridable* by default.

    C. **Correct:** If you are creating *MustOverride* methods or properties, the class must be inherited.

    D. **Incorrect:** *MustOverride* methods contain only the declaration statement for a Sub, Function, or Property. In addition, there is no End Sub or End Function statement for methods.

Chapter 7: Case Scenario Answers

Case Scenario 1: Extending a Reusable Component

1. Recipes might be appropriate. However, because there are multiple custom systems that will use the application, it is more appropriate to create a distributed binary component that provides centralized access to the features in the third-party application.

2. You can create a derived class of the class that calculates the interest and overloads the interest calculating method to provide a method signature that accepts appropriate parameters for computing the interest.

Case Scenario 2: Restricting a Reusable Component

1. You can shadow the methods and properties not supported. In the shadowed versions, you can throw an exception of type *NotImplementedException*.

2. You can create a class that inherits from the third-party class. You can override the members as required but, instead of implementing functionality, you can throw an exception of type *NotImplementedException*.

Case Scenario 3: Restricting a Reusable Component

1. You can extend the components defined in the citizen information system by creating your own components that inherit from the existing components. In this way, you can provide a custom view of the citizen information. Additionally, you can use shadowing to hide and make unavailable restricted information in the base components.

2. You should wrap permitting system components in your own components that expose the limited functionality available. Apply security so that only the wrapper has permission to invoke the permitting system functionality.

Chapter 8: Lesson Review Answers

Lesson 1

1. **Correct Answers: C and D**

    A. **Incorrect:** Agile development requires a lot of interaction between end user and developer, face-to-face interaction being the preferred form of communication, and is, therefore, not suited to outsourcing development to another country.

    B. **Incorrect:** Waterfall development is geared toward delivering products in one phase and handing those over to the next phase. Requirements and design are fixed products, handed to the developer for implementation. Implementation does not require interaction with the user.

    C. **Correct:** The premise of agile development is that the development team needs to create a mindset in which the members welcome change. A change provides the team with an opportunity to deliver better what the end user needs.

    D. **Correct:** Waterfall development is geared toward delivering predetermined products.

2. **Correct Answer: B**

    A. **Incorrect:** The key word in the question is *always*. The world is not black and white, and no solution fits all. There are many scenarios in which the benefits of waterfall outweigh its disadvantages and, by proper risk management, can nullify some disadvantages. At the start of any project, consider alternatives and choose what fits this particular project best.

    B. **Correct:** See answer A.

Lesson 2

1. **Correct Answer: A**

    A. **Correct:** Action driven and state driven are the two styles of interface design.

    B. **Incorrect:** See the explanation for answer A.

2. **Correct Answer: A**

    A. **Correct:** State-driven interfaces have methods that are named very generically. The method will look at the state of the data it receives and choose an appropriate action. In this example, the order could be new or changed, requiring an insert action or a delete action. This is for the application logic to decide.

    B. **Incorrect:** In an action-driven design, there would be multiple methods, for instance, *AddNewOrder* and *UpdateOrder*.

Lesson 3

1. **Correct Answers: C and D**

   A. **Incorrect:** The registry should be considered a read-only data store.

   B. **Incorrect:** The application configuration file should be considered a read-only data store.

   C. **Correct:** Storing data as XML files is an option. Key here is that data is updated by only a few users compared to a large group of users reading the data. Concurrency issues can be managed.

   D. **Correct:** Relational databases are designed to handle large volumes of users and offer excellent options for managing concurrency issues.

2. **Correct Answer: A**

   A. **Correct:** Rather than passing a business object or data transfer object (DTO), a dataset is passed. The dataset will mirror the relational database.

   B. **Incorrect:** See answer A.

3. **Correct Answer: A**

   A. **Correct:** The name of the parameter being passed to the *Save* method indicates an object type that is limited in scope to the interface. It is unlikely that a *RequestSaveOrder* is a business object that will be persisted to the database, nor does the name of the class indicate a typed dataset.

   B. **Incorrect:** See answer A.

Lesson 4

1. **Correct Answer: B**

   A. **Incorrect:** A Web service is stateless by default, but by using session state, you can implement a stateful service.

   B. **Correct:** See answer A.

2. **Correct Answer: B**

   A. **Incorrect:** A SingleCall service is always stateless.

   B. **Correct:** A SingleCall service is always stateless.

Lesson 5

1. **Correct Answer: B**

   A. **Incorrect:** A component does not incur a remoting call penalty, but connection pooling and proximity of logic to database can outweigh the remoting call penalty.

   B. **Correct:** See answer A.

2. **Correct Answer: C**

   A. **Incorrect:** A Java Server Page would not be able to reuse your component.

   B. **Incorrect:** A Java Server Page is not able to implement a .NET remoting call.

   C. **Correct:** A Java Server Page can implement a call to a Web service and reuse the logic.

Lesson 6

1. **Correct Answer: B**

   A. **Incorrect:** The application logic layer has no way of directly interacting with the user. The presentation layer should provide valid credentials to the service. If not, the service will fail.

   B. **Correct:** See answer A.

2. **Correct Answer: C**

   A. **Incorrect:** *ClientChannelSink* objects are used for .NET remoting, not for Web services.

   B. **Incorrect:** This is an option, but answer C is better.

   C. **Correct:** By using Web Services Enhancements (WSE) to add identity information to the SOAP request, the server can re-create the principal on the Web server.

Chapter 8: Case Scenario Answers

Case Scenario 1: Scaling Out

1. The best approach is to design your application in layers. The application logic and data access should be as independent of the user interface as possible. You need to implement this in a separate assembly, increasing the opportunity for reuse. At this point, aim at deploying both Web application and additional assemblies to the Web server. For intranet purposes, this will suffice, and the customer needs it quickly.

2. When the marketing people get their project underway, you'll be able to reuse the application logic and data access and just rewrite the user interface. In this scenario, you might want to deploy your application logic on a server other than your Web server.

Case Scenario 2: Services

1. Your manager wants to have reusable software. The end user wants information about workflow items to be visible in both the custom application and in Office Outlook. You also heard indications that pieces of code should be reused.

2. The application logic layer should be implemented by using Web services. Build the custom application to use these Web services and, with Visual Studio for Office, create an Office Outlook add-in that reuses the same Web service to retrieve the pending workflow items for the current user.

Chapter 9: Lesson Review Answers

Lesson 1

1. **Correct Answers: A and E**

    A. **Correct:** The Error level is intended for critical, application-threatening situations, certainly something that operations should see immediately.

    B. **Incorrect:** The Warning level is not as critical as an error. Although operations might want to see warnings, it won't want to monitor for them because the number of false-positive log entries might obscure serious problems.

    C. **Incorrect:** The Information level is purely for informational messages and should not be directed to the operations monitoring application.

    D. **Incorrect:** Accessing a resource successfully is not something that operations should be alerted to.

    E. **Correct:** If someone attempts to access a resource to which he or she hasn't been given permission, operations should be notified immediately.

2. **Correct Answer: D**

    A. **Incorrect:** The flat file log will be placed on the local (that is, production) computer. This would make it inaccessible to the development staff.

    B. **Incorrect:** The event log is a local mechanism, meaning that the data is stored locally, and although the Event Viewer does enable viewing events on remote computers, permission isn't available to the developers.

    C. **Incorrect:** Tracing runs into the same problems as the event log. It is really intended to be a local-only mechanism and, without any listeners, the information will be of no use to developers.

    D. **Correct:** The database is the only data storage mechanism that works in this environment. That the database is already available fairly clinches the argument.

Lesson 2

1. **Correct Answers: B and D**

    A. **Incorrect:** The normal path taken by a distributed application will include the provision of a valid set of credentials. Because this will be the common event, operations shouldn't be bothered with it; it should not be monitored.

B. **Correct:** Unlike valid credentials, receiving invalid credentials is of more interest to the operations staff. In a Web application, this type of event might not be raised until there have been multiple failed logon attempts from the same source or within a short period of time. However, if this is a distributed application and the client requests are coming from a known source (such as from another part of the application), even a single instance would be unexpected and worthy of attention.

C. **Incorrect:** In a data-driven application, database access will take place on a frequent basis. Operations isn't likely to care unless the database access failed.

D. **Correct:** The logic for whether badly formatted requests should be monitored is the same as for invalid requests. In a distributed application, in which you control both sides of a request, a badly formatted one should never happen. Therefore, if even a single invalid request is received, operations should be notified immediately.

E. **Incorrect:** Although the completion of a request is an event that someone within the company might want to know about, operations isn't that group. Using a monitoring infrastructure to provide business-level functionality is not a good ideThere are too many other options that are better suited for request completion notification.

Chapter 9: Case Scenario Answer

Case Scenario: Instrumenting a Distributed Application

1. The ability to process usage pattern information will hinge on how easy it is to visualize the large volume of data that could be generated. The conversion of data into a visual format (such as a report) is best accomplished by retrieving information from a data store designed for reporting. This means that the usage log messages should be stored in a database.

2. The application status information should be made available through a number of counters in the performance monitor. This mechanism allows for monitoring applications of all types through a common repository. The fact that it's common means that third-party tools designed to hook into the performance counter system will be able to interact with the application you're creating in the same manner as any Windows application.

3. For tracing information, it might seem that a flat file is the most appropriate choice; in many situations, it is. However, an application running on multiple servers makes flat files less practical, and multiple requests from the same user can be processed on different servers, making correlation between them difficult at best. As a result, the tracing information should be stored in a central repository, which, in this case, would be a database.

Chapter 10: Lesson Review Answers

Lesson 1

1. **Correct Answer: B**
   A. **Incorrect:** The functionality of the test was clear, at least as far as the description of the problem goes.
   B. **Correct:** The problem with the unit test was that it was dependent on the correct functionality of the *Customer* class to succeed or fail.
   C. **Incorrect:** Speed of execution does not appear to be the issue with the unit test.
   D. **Incorrect:** Although it might appear that the test isn't limited in scope, that really isn't the case. The test is only testing one piece of functionality within the *Order* class.

2. **Correct Answer: C**
   A. **Incorrect:** A single test case is insufficient because you cannot test both success and parameter validation.
   B. **Incorrect:** Two test cases are insufficient. Although you can now test success and failure, you can't test the validation of both parameters individually.
   C. **Correct:** With three test cases, you can test the successful case, an invalid product number, and a quantity that is less than or equal to zero.
   D. **Incorrect:** You might be able to make a case for four test cases because the tests would be success, invalid product number, invalid quantity, and invalid product number and quantity. However, it is likely that this last test case would not cover any logic paths that the other two failed tests had not.

Lesson 2

1. **Correct Answer: B**
   A. **Incorrect:** Although you might make a case for unit testing, it really isn't. When testing is performed against the interface between multiple components, it is no longer unit testing.
   B. **Correct:** Integration testing exercises how different components interact with one another.
   C. **Incorrect:** This isn't a performance testing situation because the current concern isn't the speed of the component but its integration.
   D. **Incorrect:** As with performance testing, stress testing is not the issue in this situation.

2. **Correct Answer: B**

A. **Incorrect:** There is a problem with this strategy that will be detailed in the description of the correct answer.

B. **Correct:** The test is being performed over the network. This means that any vagaries in the network speed have an impact on the results. To perform a good performance test, it should be run directly against the method invoked by the Web service and not from a remote client. This is true even if the client is on the same piece of hardware.

C. **Incorrect:** Resetting the virtual directory would be incorrect because the normal method for invoking a Web service method doesn't involve starting the virtual directory. A good performance test should perform any ramped up processing before executing the test code, so you could make the case that the testing strategy should include at least one call prior to the five that are timed. However, this is not the worst problem with this strategy.

D. **Incorrect:** This is not the description of a stress test. In a Web service environment, a stress test would invoke multiple simultaneous calls from different client machines, not sequential calls from one client.

Lesson 3

1. **Correct Answer: C**

    A. **Incorrect:** If care has been taken to minimize the differences between the environments, it's fair to exclude this as a possibility.

    B. **Incorrect:** It is highly unlikely that the cause for the different in performance is additional services, especially because the remainder of the application runs acceptably.

    C. **Correct:** Given that most of the environments have been kept the same, it seems most likely that the problem is that the database has been tuned for the data modeled in the test database, but that the production database has a different pattern.

    D. **Incorrect:** If care has been taken to minimize the differences between the environments, it's fair to exclude this as a possibility.

2. **Correct Answer: B**

    A. **Incorrect:** It's certainly possible that a difference between production and testing hardware could be the cause, but it is not a likely culprit.

    B. **Correct:** It is highly likely that the cause for the difference in performances is the presence of additional services, especially because the other factors associated with performance have been eliminated.

    C. **Incorrect:** Given that the test and production database environments have been kept the same, it seems unlikely that data or the database is the cause.

   D.   **Incorrect:** Because effort has been expended (presumably successfully) to keep the production and test environments as similar as possible, it seems unlikely that software versioning is the problem.

Chapter 10: Case Scenario Answers

Case Scenario 1: Choosing the Tests

1.   Unit tests are required on the exposed methods of the business classes. Integration tests might or might not be required. There isn't enough information given in the scenario to be certain. User interface testing with the Windows Forms application is probably not required. Given that the application is time-critical, the business classes should also be performance tested. Stress testing also should be performed to ensure that the application acts appropriately in case of a serious failure. This is because the application is in the line-of-business area.

Case Scenario 2: Choosing the Tests

1.   Unit tests are required on the exposed methods of the business classes. Integration tests are definitely required to ensure that the status information retrieved by the Web method is the correct status. User interface testing is not required because the Web service doesn't have a user interface. Detailed performance testing is not an issue, assuming that the base performance is adequate. Only if there is a problem should performance testing be done. Finally, because no updating is being performed, stress testing is not necessary.

Chapter 11: Lesson Review Answers

Lesson 1

1.   **Correct Answer: A**
   A.   **Correct:** The easiest (and, therefore, the first) place to identify the unit tests is the methods that are part of the class interface.
   B.   **Incorrect:** Although creating test scenarios for a class is useful when trying to ensure that the unit test suite is complete, it is not the first place to look for an existing class. It is more important to focus on the methods in the interface.
   C.   **Incorrect:** Perform code coverage analysis once unit tests have been created, not before.

    D. **Incorrect:** Reading the source code is unnecessary when identifying the unit tests to create. It can be helpful to identify areas worthy of testing, but not for the initial unit tests.

2. **Correct Answers: C and D**

    A. **Incorrect:** Testing that a product is returned successfully is quite a valid test. In fact, it's probably the first one that would be written.

    B. **Incorrect:** Testing for no product to be returned is also a valid test

    C. **Correct:** As a unit test for the *Load* method, testing the success and failure of the constructor is not appropriate.

    D. **Correct:** A unit test that is focusing on the *Load* method should not be concerned with the security exception thrown when the credentials are invalid.

    E. **Incorrect:** Validating that the product number is the correct format is a good test.

Lesson 2

1. **Correct Answer: C**

    A. **Incorrect:** 70 percent is an inadequate coverage level. It should be possible to raise this measure without significant effort.

    B. **Incorrect:** Although 80 percent is reasonable for some applications, it is still a little light for a commercial application.

    C. **Correct:** 90 percent is a reasonable balance between covering all of the easy cases and some of the more difficult ones with the demands of trying to cover 100 percent of the code.

    D. **Incorrect:** Ensuring that every single line is covered by a unit test is onerous, especially if there are cost and time-to-market considerations in play.

2. **Correct Answer: C**

    A. **Incorrect:** The system time is a non-deterministic value, which makes mock objects a good choice. Using mock objects allows for behavior during different times of the day to be emulated at any time.

    B. **Incorrect:** Mock objects are quite useful when trying to emulate network failure errors.

    C. **Correct:** Calculations based on readily available data (that is, data that is not in a database) do not require mock objects to be tested.

    D. **Incorrect:** A Web service method is an external resource in which failures, such as network outages or response time-outs, would be difficult to emulate reliably in a testing environment. Therefore, mock objects are needed.

Chapter 11: Case Scenario Answers

Case Scenario 1: Unit Testing for a Web Application

1. Unit tests should be created for all of the business classes. Because unit testing on the Web user interface is challenging, Web tests should be used to ensure that the user interface is working as expected. Finally, to prepare for the hundreds of Internet users who are going to use your application, load testing should be performed to ensure that scalability is not a problem.

2. Although the interfaces for the business classes are helpful, for a Web application, the real information is in the use case scenarios. Unlike a Windows Forms application, the flow from screen to screen is much easier to document in a Web application. For this reason, looking at the use case scenarios and deriving the test scenarios will help ensure that the classes are given the appropriate coverage.

Case Scenario 2: Identifying External Dependencies

1. There are three external dependencies for the application. The Web service is outside of the control of a test, as is the database used to retrieve information. The third dependency is the configuration file. That the information in the Web service and database are polled every 30 seconds does not make the system clock a dependency.

2. Of the three external dependencies, only the Web service and the database need a mock object to test reliably. For the configuration file, the unit test can change the configuration file the method uses under test prior to the test to simulate error conditions such as a missing element.

Chapter 12: Lesson Review Answers

Lesson 1

1. **Correct Answers: A and C**

   A. **Correct:** The described environment is at the high end of functionality for software. The criticality of the application in the client environment implies that a great deal of effort is required to ensure that quality software is created. Formal inspections ensure consistency across the reviews and produce metrics for improving the process.

   B. **Incorrect:** Although code walkthroughs are valuable, the lack of formality and metrics makes this is a less likely choice for the organization.

   C. **Correct:** Pair programming does not supplant formal inspections in terms of use. However, given that the research on pair programming shows an increase in quality of code with only a minimal impact on productivity, it could be used in conjunction with formal inspections.

   D. **Incorrect:** Over-the-shoulder reviews are not going to provide an adequate level of certainty that quality code is being produced.

2. **Correct Answers: B and D**

   A. **Incorrect:** The weight of the inspection process is too much for a small company to bear, and there aren't enough people with the technical skills to implement the methodology.

   B. **Correct:** Code walkthroughs are certainly a good possibility for this environment.

   C. **Incorrect:** Pair programming requires at least two developers. In this environment, there aren't two available, so pair programming is not an option.

   D. **Correct:** The informality of over-the-shoulder reviews is appropriate for this environment.

Lesson 2

1. **Correct Answer: D**

   A. **Incorrect:** Although the public methods are how other classes will interface with yours, they are not the starting point for testing the integration of your class with its dependent assemblies.

   B. **Incorrect:** The use case document includes information about when a particular class and method will be called; the level of detail is not sufficient to develop an integration test plan.

   C. **Incorrect:** The existing unit tests simply demonstrate how a method is used. They say nothing about how the method interacts with other classes.

   D. **Correct:** The list of dependent assemblies can be used to identify the specific points in the class where external access is performed. This is the area to focus on during the integration testing.

2. **Correct Answer: D**

   A. **Incorrect:** Calling the Web service is definitely part of the integration test because the component needs to be successfully integrated to function properly.

   B. **Incorrect:** The local database is an external resource (that should have been implemented as a mock object during unit testing), so it should be part of the integration test.

   C. **Incorrect:** The passing of credentials across boundaries is part of the scope of an integration test.

   D. **Correct:** Retrieving information from the configuration file should have been covered by the unit tests. As such, it is not needed for integration testing.

Chapter 12: Case Scenario Answers

Case Scenario 1: Determine the Code Review Requirements

1. For the described environment, there is likely a conflict between the desire of the developers to develop and the need to establish legitimate standards. The need for the formality imposed by the Fagan Inspection methodology is not apparent. By the same token, the informality of over-the-shoulder review, combined with the attitude of the team, means that in many cases, the review won't be performed.

   Pair programming might or might not be an option, depending on the personalities of the people involved and the support that management gives the idea. If this isn't possible, then using code walkthroughs would be the best choice, especially if the walkthrough can be done by a limited number of peers (to reduce the time spent by any individual developer).

Case Scenario 2: Integration Testing for a Web Application

1. Integration tests should focus on the parts of the application where interfacing is performed. For the described application, that would be the database and the Web service calls. For the database, the test should ensure that the expected records are being retrieved and that any updates are being performed as expected. For the Web service calls, the test needs to ensure that the retrieved status information matches the actual status and that calling the validation Web service performs as expected.

2. On the database side, you will need connection to an actual database to ensure that the integration is performing as expected. It doesn't need to be a production database, but the schema for this test database needs to match the production schema. On the Web service side, it's a little more challenging. Because the status Web service is all in-house, it should be possible to confirm the returned status in other ways, allowing that test to be validated. The external Web service is also a little more challenging. It is likely that test data can be identified along with the expected result from calling the Web service. This information needs to be made available to the application so that the integration test can be properly verified.

Chapter 13: Lesson Review Answers

Lesson 1

1. **Correct Answers: A and C**

   A. **Correct**: Resource use includes CPU use.

    B. **Incorrect:** Resource use refers to physical computer resources but not to budget use.

    C. **Correct:** Resource use includes memory use.

    D. **Incorrect:** Resource use refers to physical computer resources but not to developer time use.

2. **Correct Answers: A and D**

    A. **Correct**: Identifying key scenarios is normally the first step in creating a performance model.

    B. **Incorrect:** Identifying localized resources is not a key step in creating a performance model.

    C. **Incorrect:** Identifying payloads is not a key step in creating a performance model.

    D. **Correct:** Identifying workloads is normally the second step in creating a performance model.

3. **Correct Answer: D**

    A. **Incorrect**: Idle memory is typically memory not being used and will only serve to improve application performance.

    B. **Incorrect:** Hard disk size typically affects application performance only when the disk becomes full.

    C. **Incorrect:** CPU idle time represents a CPU not being used by an application and should improve application performance.

    D. **Correct:** Memory paging occurs when memory is no longer available for application use, and the contents of memory must be written to and read from the hard drive.

Lesson 2

1. **Correct Answer: A**

    A. **Correct**: The *Trace* class is designed so that you can leave it in production code and simply disable it by using a configuration file when it is not needed.

    B. **Incorrect:** The *Trace* class can be used in both debugging and production code.

    C. **Incorrect:** The *Debug* class is designed to be used only in a debugging environment and not in a production environment.

    D. **Incorrect:** The *Debug* class is not obsolete. It is used primarily to output information to the Output window in the debugger, whereas the *Trace* class is used primarily to redirect output information to other destinations.

2. **Correct Answers: B and D**

    A. **Incorrect:** Server performance logs aren't generally associated with application security monitoring.

    B. **Correct:** Event logs should be analyzed to detect any security events that are a concern.

    C. **Incorrect:** Changing a user's password regularly is a recommended security policy practice, but it is not associated with monitoring application security.

    D. **Correct:** Security events can be automatically audited and logged to the Windows event logs for analysis.

3. **Correct Answer: D**

    A. **Incorrect:** Bugs can be tracked using Office Excel. However, it is not designed for tracking bugs, so it is difficult to use.

    B. **Incorrect:** Visual Studio 2005 Professional does not include a bug-tracking feature. Standard tasks could be used, but they are extremely simple in nature and do not include bug-tracking data.

    C. **Incorrect:** Bugs can be tracked by using Project. However, it is not designed for tracking bugs, so it is difficult to use.

    D. **Correct:** Visual Studio 2005 Team System includes Work Item Tracking (WIT) and is the recommended approach for tracking bugs in a Microsoft environment.

Lesson 3

1. **Correct Answers: A, B, C, and D**

    A. **Correct:** The File Types editor is used to manage file extension associations.

    B. **Correct:** The Registry editor is used to manage registry modifications.

    C. **Correct:** The File System editor is used to manage file system modifications.

    D. **Correct:** The User Interface editor is used to manage the installation application.

2. **Correct Answer: D**

    A. **Incorrect:** A component that is available only as part of another application cannot be deployed by using a Setup and Deployment project.

    B. **Incorrect:** An application should not be deployed without referenced components because it will not function correctly.

    C. **Incorrect:** You cannot guarantee that a user will download the application that includes the component, and the component cannot be downloaded by itself if it is available only as part of another application.

    D. **Correct:** If your application to be deployed includes a reference to a component that is available only as part of another application, you should include a launch condition in the Setup and Deployment project to guarantee that the component exists prior to installation.

3. **Correct Answer: D**

   A. **Incorrect**: SQL Server 2005 database projects are not deployed by using scripts written in C#.

   B. **Incorrect**: SQL Server 2005 database projects are not deployed by using scripts written in VBScript.

   C. **Incorrect**: SQL Server 2005 database projects are not deployed using scripts written in Visual Basic.

   D. **Correct**: SQL Server 2005 database projects are deployed by using scripts written in Transact-SQL.

Lesson 4

1. **Correct Answers: B, D, and E**

   A. **Incorrect**: Classes are not depicted on application flow-logic diagrams.

   B. **Correct**: Relevant interfaces are depicted on application flow-logic diagrams.

   C. **Incorrect**: Methods are not depicted on application flow-logic diagrams.

   D. **Correct**: Components are depicted on application flow-logic diagrams.

   E. **Correct**: Component dependencies are depicted on application flow-logic diagrams.

2. **Correct Answers: B, C, and D**

   A. **Incorrect**: Classes are not represented in the cyclomatic complexity algorithm.

   B. **Correct**: The number of edges (dashed lines) is represented in the cyclomatic complexity algorithm.

   C. **Correct**: The number of components with dependencies is represented in the cyclomatic complexity algorithm.

   D. **Correct**: The total number of components is represented in the cyclomatic complexity algorithm.

   E. **Incorrect**: The number of interfaces is not represented in the cyclomatic complexity algorithm.

Lesson 5

1. **Correct Answers: A, C, and D**

   A. **Correct**: Memory is a primary resource required to support an application.

   B. **Incorrect**: Although video card capabilities can be important in some types of graphic applications and games, in general, it is not considered one of the primary resources required by an application.

    C. **Correct:** Central processing unit power is a primary resource required to support an application.

    D. **Correct:** Hard disk space is a primary resource required to support an application.

    E. **Incorrect:** Although Web connectivity can be important in Web applications, in general, it is not considered one of the primary resources required by an application.

2. **Correct Answer: C**

    A. **Incorrect:** Monitoring is used to record application performance, security, and other metrics.

    B. **Incorrect:** Debugging cannot be conducted in a production environment.

    C. **Correct:** Tracing is used to gather detailed information about bugs that appear in applications already deployed to production.

    D. **Incorrect:** Profiling is used to track performance and security metrics specific to a particular application.

Chapter 13: Case Scenario Answers

Case Scenario 1: Deploying an Application

1. The first step in identifying the problem should be to enable application tracing to gather more information about the issue. Tracing will identify many details about the problem encountered, including the stack trace, the line of code, and the values of locally declared variables.

2. Given the stated scenario, the most likely problem is a file system permissions issue. More than likely, the problem is that the user account under which the application is running has read permission granted to the location of the XML sales receipts but does not have write permission granted.

3. The described problem should have been identified prior to the application deployment by verifying that the production environment complies with all application design plans, including the deployment plan, the disaster recovery plan, and the security plan.

Glossary

abstract class A class that can be used only as a base class for a derived class. An abstract class cannot be created. The *NotInheritable* identifier is used with this type of class.

access rule The combination of a user or role and a permission that is granted or denied.

activity diagram A diagram that is like a UML flow chart. It shows the actions that happen one after another, the decisions that are made to gate those actions, and which actions happen in parallel. An activity diagram is useful for modeling business workflow and complex algorithms.

ADO.NET ADO stands for Active Data Objects, which refers to COM-era technology. ADO.NET is the natural evolution of this technology into managed code. It can be found in the *System.Data* namespace.

aggregation Refers to an object-oriented concept in which members of one object are exposed through a containing object.

application flow-logic diagram A diagram that depicts the components that comprise an application and how they relate.

application library A set of components that you can use in your solution.

application server The server software that runs your server code (typically ASP.NET and the .NET Framework). Internet Information Server (IIS) is an application server.

authentication The process of attempting to verify the identity of the sender of a request to log on. The sender being authenticated might be a computer program or a person using a computer.

authorization The process of allowing those resources to be used only by users who have been granted authority to use them.

base64 encoding A character-set encoding that maps binary data to a 7-bit format suitable for transmission in SMTP and HTTP protocols.

business domain A domain that represents the classes that are derived from your logical model or ORM diagram. These classes solve the primary business functions of the application.

business logic Any functionality added to data access components that aids the business case for a component.

business requirement A requirement that defines the success factors from the perspective of project stakeholders. A business requirement represents what the business believes to be important for the success of the project.

capacity planning Predictive application resource use planning based on a performance baseline and thorough testing.

cascading dependency When an assembly depends on a second assembly, which in turn depends on a third assembly.

class diagram A diagram that is a static representation of the classes, enumerations, structures, and interfaces that make up your code. A class diagram shows associations and inheritance.

client A technology choice about how an application will be presented to the users. Client choices include Windows, console, Office, and Mobile.

codec A piece of software or hardware that is responsible for coding and decoding data from one format to another. Typically, this term is used with audio and video content served on the Internet.

collaboration diagram A diagram that illustrates how objects work together to realize a use case. The order of message interaction is shown by numbered messages.

component   1. In Enterprise Application Design, a group of logically related classes and methods. Components often become .dll files. 2. In the .NET Framework, a class that implements the *System.Component-Model.IComponent* interface or that derives directly or indirectly from a class that implements *IComponent*. In general, a class or object that is reusable and works with other classes and objects.

component diagram   A diagram that shows the components and their relationships (references). It might also show how those components are deployed onto nodes.

consumers   Any piece of code or architecture that will consume a component.

control   A component that provides user interface features. Controls are broken into two classes: Web controls and Microsoft Windows controls.

cyclomatic complexity   A mathematical tool used to measure the complexity of an application by using the number of independent lines and paths between elements and components that comprise an application.

data storage   Storage that represents how your application will store and provide access to its data.

database schema   The layout of related data in a database, including rules about how data is stored, related, and constrained.

dependent assembly   An assembly that another assembly requires to be present to function correctly.

deployment plan   A plan that should be created in the design phase of the application development cycle. An application deployment plan describes the details of deploying an application to a target execution environment.

design pattern   A standard solution to a common but specific problem. By applying one or more design patterns when designing your application, your design will be more readable to someone who does not know the problems in your application domain but who does know about design patterns.

Direct Internet Message Encapsulation (DIME)   A standard message format that is used to send attachments with SOAP messages. It is similar to SOAP with Attachments but has lost momentum and has been supplanted by MTOM.

driver   A piece of code that handles the coordination and flow between two or more components during an integration test.

edge case   A case or a situation that occurs at one of the extremes of parameters for a method or class. In this case, the extreme could be caused by a minimal value, a maximal value, or a null or empty value.

encode   A term that refers to the process of converting from one form to another. The most typical usage in the multimedia world involves converting data from a non-HTTP-compliant format to one that can be sent over HTTP.

entity-relationship diagram   An entity-relationship (ER) diagram is a diagram used to model relational systems such as databases. ER diagrams generally consist of entities and the relationships among them.

exception   Represents an error that occurs during application execution.

extreme programming   A software development discipline that focuses on short-term deliverables and a high level of communication to overcome projects that have incomplete or changing requirements. For more information, visit *http://www.xprogramming.com*.

Fagan Inspection   A formalized code review process that was introduced by Michael Fagan and is based on his extensive research of what works and what doesn't in a code review.

flat file   The name given to a text in which each line in the file is the equivalent of a record in a database.

foreign key A primary key value from a related table that is used to identify a relationship between the two tables.

framework A set of base classes and components that abstract a lot of the architectural plumbing away from the developer.

functional requirement A requirement that defines a feature from the perspective of a developer. A developer should be able to review the specification or requirement and implement to that specification.

functional specification *See* functional requirement.

granularity The level of detail at which information is required or described.

horizontal prototype *See* mockup.

infoset (also XML Information Set) The information contained in a well-formed XML document. To have an infoset, an XML document must be well formed and satisfy namespace constraints.

inheritance The ability to define classes that contain implementations or interfaces that serve as the basis for other classes called derived classes.

instrumentation The process of adding code to an application to initiate events internally that are used to measure application performance metrics.

IMessageFormatter interface The interface that a class must implement to be used as a formatter by the *MessageQueue* class in .NET.

IXmlSerializable interface The interface that a class must implement to provide a custom XML representation.

layers The logical division of code in your application to satisfy design goals such as increased reusability. Layers include user interface, middle tier, and database.

load testing Another name for stress testing.

log level A configuration setting that indicates the minimum severity required for a prospective log entry to be processed.

logging The process of placing information about the status, progress, and problems of an application into a persistent data store.

logical design The separation of individual discrete units of work into logical groups for the purpose of designing a system.

looping In the event flow for a use case, a loop occurs when the case calls for invalid input to be reprompted and then corrected, allowing the flow to continue.

maintainability It actually costs more to modify a block of code over its lifetime than it does to create the code in the first place. For this reason, it is important for the code to be clear and readable so it can be maintained easily in the future.

Message Transmission Optimization Mechanism (MTOM) A format for transmitting binary data in a SOAP message by using a combination of techniques to ensure the ability to compose and optimal data compression.

Microsoft Message Queue (MSMQ) The service built into Windows that provides for reliable and secure messaging between applications.

mock object An object that emulates a real class. It includes not only stub functionality but an emulation of method calls and property values.

mockup A set of user interface screens that help verify the application's navigation, requirements, and use cases; also called a user interface mockup or horizontal prototype.

monitoring The real-time (or near real-time) watching of information about the status, progress, and problems of an application.

multiple condition coverage Another (and more accurate) name for branch coverage. It refers to the fact that the individual conditions within an If statement are included in determining which parts of the code have been addressed by the unit tests.

multiplicity   The definition of the number of objects in a relationship between two objects. These can be one-to-one, one-to-many, or many-to-many.

Multipurpose Internet Mail Extensions (MIME)   An Internet standard that describes the format of e-mail messages. It is also a common term describing how to convert binary data into a format suitable for e-mail and Web site transmission.

node   A UML representation of a place of deployment. It typically represents a piece of hardware (such as a server).

object role modeling (ORM)   A diagram that represents real-world concepts and their relationships. It is a logical model of your software.

pair programming   When two developers work on a single workstation to design and write code. Frequently used as part of extreme programming.

partitioning   The division of a range of input values into groups based on their equivalence with respect to the output of the method.

peer review   The process of involving colleagues in a code review, whether formal or informal.

performance baseline   A performance baseline, or benchmark, that is used to predict how an application will perform with given resources and loads.

performance modeling   The process of prototyping an application to determine what resources your application will require to perform well and continue performing well.

Performance Monitor   The Windows application that is included with the operating system to allow for monitoring various counters about the system and the running applications.

performance spike   A noticeable and dramatic increase in the use of processor time, memory resources, disk activity, or similar resource usage by an application.

physical design   The physical layout of a system, segmenting different layers onto separate computers or data centers.

polymorphism   From the Greek meaning "many forms"; describes the ability to define classes that can be used interchangeably by client code at run time with identically named members having differing implementations.

primary key   A value in a database table that is used to identify a row uniquely.

profiling   Profiling is a means of application metrics monitoring, using tools that are tightly coupled to their sources and designed to render very low-level, specific results.

proof-of-concept prototype   A complete implementation of a feature through the architecture of the system. It examines the application across the entire stack (UI, services, business objects, and database). It is meant to confirm the technology recommendations and high-level design.

pseudocode   Code that shows a complex algorithm as code-like text. This can be useful for those used to writing or reading code (and not models).

quality of service (QOS) requirement   A requirement that defines non-functional requirements for the system concerning considerations such as performance, scalability, and standards.

reference architecture   Provides a reference implementation through the vertical stack of the application for the development team. It gives the developers a model on just how they should implement their code. A reference architecture is like a proof-of-concept prototype.

reliability testing   Another name for stress testing.

security plan   A plan that should be created during the design phase of the development cycle and should include security policies for application data confidentiality, integrity, and availability.

sequence diagram   A diagram that illustrates the sequence of messages that collaborate between objects to realize a use case. A sequence diagram illustrates a message flow from left to right and top-down.

shadowing   Refers to the ability to hide and replace an implementation in a base class with that of a derived class.

SOAP with Attachments (SwA)   A technique of using a combination of MIME and SOAP to transfer files into and out of Web services.

state (or application state)   Represents the data for an application. This state moves between the layers of your system (from the user to the database and back).

stateless   Being able to perform work without storing data at the component level.

stub   A piece of code that mimics the functionality exposed by a component. A stub is used during testing to handle classes that might be implemented or completely tested.

test-driven development   A development methodology that involves writing a test that fails before writing any code. After the test is complete (and fails), code is added to make the test pass. The project is then refactored to improve the design of the class(es) with the new case, ensuring that all of the tests continue to pass.

test case   Code (or a description thereof) that tests a single part of functionality for one method in one class.

test fixture   An artifact, such as an image or a text file, that is used in the execution of the test case but is not itself executable.

test suite   One or more test cases grouped into logical collections to facilitate execution and management.

third-party control   A control that is not created or maintained by the project team. Developers use these controls to decrease the schedule and reduce risk. A third-party control can be something embedded in the Visual Studio Toolbox and used on a form, or it could be an entire application such as BizTalk or Commerce Server.

thread safe   Being able to use data simultaneously from multiple threads without data corruption.

Unified Modeling Language (UML)   An object-modeling and specification language used in software engineering.

unit test suite   A collection of unit tests that are performed on a single logical entity. The logical entity is typically a class.

user requirement   A requirement that defines a task the users must be able to accomplish to meet the objectives of their jobs.

utility modules   In bottom-up integration testing, the lowest level of component, one that forms the basis for higher-level components to use.

vertical prototype   *See* proof-of-concept prototype.

Windows Event Log   The name for the central repository in Windows of log entries as reported by the various system components and applications.

WS-Attachments   The name of a standard that defines how to add attachments to Web service requests.

XML-Binary Optimized Package (XOP)   A standard that describes how to associate binary data with XML documents in an optimized manner that includes not resorting to base64 encoding of the data.

Index

Microsoft®
CERTIFIED
Practice Test Provider

Get Ready. Get Set.
Get Certified.

MeasureUp™ is your one-stop certification destination.

Get to the finish line with MeasureUp! You've experienced a portion of what MeasureUp practice test questions can do to help you get ready for your certification exam. **Take advantage of the full features of the practice test and you'll be ready, guaranteed!**

• Online MCSE hands-on performance-based simulations

• Objectives thoroughly covered in questions similar to the exam

• Study mode gives detailed answer explanations

• Certification mode prepares you for exam taking conditions

Start your race for certification. Purchase your complete practice test at www.measureup.com today!

Test Pass Guarantee:

MeasureUp practice tests are the closest you can get to the actual exam. Use our complete practice test to prepare and you'll pass. **We guarantee it!**

www.measureup.com

MeasureUp is a Dice Company. ©2006 MeasureUp, Inc.

Additional Resources for Web Developers

Published and Forthcoming Titles from Microsoft Press

Microsoft® Visual Web Developer™ 2005 Express Edition: Build a Web Site Now!
Jim Buyens • ISBN 0-7356-2212-4

With this lively, eye-opening, and hands-on book, all you need is a computer and the desire to learn how to create Web pages now using Visual Web Developer Express Edition! Featuring a full working edition of the software, this fun and highly visual guide walks you through a complete Web page project from set-up to launch. You'll get an introduction to the Microsoft Visual Studio® environment and learn how to put the light-weight, easy-to-use tools in Visual Web Developer Express to work right away—building your first, dynamic Web pages with Microsoft ASP.NET 2.0. You'll get expert tips, coaching, and visual examples at each step of the way, along with pointers to additional learning resources.

Microsoft ASP.NET 2.0 Programming
Step by Step
George Shepherd • ISBN 0-7356-2201-9

With dramatic improvements in performance, productivity, and security features, Visual Studio 2005 and ASP.NET 2.0 deliver a simplified, high-performance, and powerful Web development experience. ASP.NET 2.0 features a new set of controls and infrastructure that simplify Web-based data access and include functionality that facilitates code reuse, visual consistency, and aesthetic appeal. Now you can teach yourself the essentials of working with ASP.NET 2.0 in the Visual Studio environment—one step at a time. With *Step by Step*, you work at your own pace through hands-on, learn-by-doing exercises. Whether you're a beginning programmer or new to this version of the technology, you'll understand the core capabilities and fundamental techniques for ASP.NET 2.0. Each chapter puts you to work, showing you how, when, and why to use specific features of the ASP.NET 2.0 rapid application development environment and guiding you as you create actual components and working applications for the Web, including advanced features such as personalization.

Programming Microsoft ASP.NET 2.0
Core Reference
Dino Esposito • ISBN 0-7356-2176-4

Delve into the core topics for ASP.NET 2.0 programming, mastering the essential skills and capabilities needed to build high-performance Web applications successfully. Well-known ASP.NET author Dino Esposito deftly builds your expertise with Web forms, Visual Studio, core controls, master pages, data access, data binding, state management, security services, and other must-know topics—combining definitive reference with practical, hands-on programming instruction. Packed with expert guidance and pragmatic examples, this *Core Reference* delivers the key resources that you need to develop professional-level Web programming skills.

Programming Microsoft ASP.NET 2.0
Applications: *Advanced Topics*
Dino Esposito • ISBN 0-7356-2177-2

Master advanced topics in ASP.NET 2.0 programming—gaining the essential insights and in-depth understanding that you need to build sophisticated, highly functional Web applications successfully. Topics include Web forms, Visual Studio 2005, core controls, master pages, data access, data binding, state management, and security considerations. Developers often discover that the more they use ASP.NET, the more they need to know. With expert guidance from ASP.NET authority Dino Esposito, you get the in-depth, comprehensive information that leads to full mastery of the technology.

Programming Microsoft Windows® Forms
Charles Petzold • ISBN 0-7356-2153-5

Programming Microsoft Web Forms
Douglas J. Reilly • ISBN 0-7356-2179-9

CLR via C++
Jeffrey Richter with Stanley B. Lippman
ISBN 0-7356-2248-5

Debugging, Tuning, and Testing Microsoft .NET 2.0 Applications
John Robbins • ISBN 0-7356-2202-7

CLR via C#, Second Edition
Jeffrey Richter • ISBN 0-7356-2163-2

For more information about Microsoft Press® books and other learning products, visit: **www.microsoft.com/books** *and* **www.microsoft.com/learning**

Additional Resources for Developers: Advanced Topics and Best Practices

Published and Forthcoming Titles from Microsoft Press

Code Complete, Second Edition
Steve McConnell • ISBN 0-7356-1967-0

For more than a decade, Steve McConnell, one of the premier authors and voices in the software community, has helped change the way developers write code—and produce better software. Now his classic book, *Code Complete*, has been fully updated and revised with best practices in the art and science of constructing software. Topics include design, applying good techniques to construction, eliminating errors, planning, managing construction activities, and relating personal character to superior software. This new edition features fully updated information on programming techniques, including the emergence of Web-style programming, and integrated coverage of object-oriented design. You'll also find new code examples—both good and bad—in C++, Microsoft® Visual Basic®, C#, and Java, although the focus is squarely on techniques and practices.

More About Software Requirements: Thorny Issues and Practical Advice
Karl E. Wiegers • ISBN 0-7356-2267-1

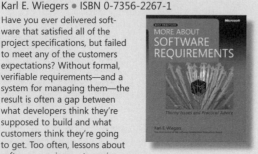

Have you ever delivered software that satisfied all of the project specifications, but failed to meet any of the customers expectations? Without formal, verifiable requirements—and a system for managing them—the result is often a gap between what developers think they're supposed to build and what customers think they're going to get. Too often, lessons about software requirements engineering processes are formal or academic, and not of value to real-world, professional development teams. In this follow-up guide to *Software Requirements*, Second Edition, you will discover even more practical techniques for gathering and managing software requirements that help you deliver software that meets project and customer specifications. Succinct and immediately useful, this book is a must-have for developers and architects.

Software Estimation: Demystifying the Black Art
Steve McConnell • ISBN 0-7356-0535-1

Often referred to as the "black art" because of its complexity and uncertainty, software estimation is not as hard or mysterious as people think. However, the art of how to create effective cost and schedule estimates has not been very well publicized. *Software Estimation* provides a proven set of procedures and heuristics that software developers, technical leads, and project managers can apply to their projects. Instead of arcane treatises and rigid modeling techniques, award-winning author Steve McConnell gives practical guidance to help organizations achieve basic estimation proficiency and lay the groundwork to continue improving project cost estimates. This book does not avoid the more complex mathematical estimation approaches, but the non-mathematical reader will find plenty of useful guidelines without getting bogged down in complex formulas.

Debugging, Tuning, and Testing Microsoft .NET 2.0 Applications
John Robbins • ISBN 0-7356-2202-7

Making an application the best it can be has long been a time-consuming task best accomplished with specialized and costly tools. With Microsoft Visual Studio® 2005, developers have available a new range of built-in functionality that enables them to debug their code quickly and efficiently, tune it to optimum performance, and test applications to ensure compatibility and trouble-free operation. In this accessible and hands-on book, debugging expert John Robbins shows developers how to use the tools and functions in Visual Studio to their full advantage to ensure high-quality applications.

The Security Development Lifecycle
Michael Howard and Steve Lipner • ISBN 0-7356-2214-0

Adapted from Microsoft's standard development process, the Security Development Lifecycle (SDL) is a methodology that helps reduce the number of security defects in code at every stage of the development process, from design to release. This book details each stage of the SDL methodology and discusses its implementation across a range of Microsoft software, including Microsoft Windows Server™ 2003, Microsoft SQL Server™ 2000 Service Pack 3, and Microsoft Exchange Server 2003 Service Pack 1, to help measurably improve security features. You get direct access to insights from Microsoft's security team and lessons that are applicable to software development processes worldwide, whether on a small-scale or a large-scale. This book includes a CD featuring videos of developer training classes.

Software Requirements, Second Edition
Karl E. Wiegers • ISBN 0-7356-1879-8

Writing Secure Code, Second Edition
Michael Howard and David LeBlanc • ISBN 0-7356-1722-8

CLR via C#, Second Edition
Jeffrey Richter • ISBN 0-7356-2163-2

Additional SQL Server Resources for Developers

Published and Forthcoming Titles from Microsoft Press

Microsoft® SQL Server™ 2005 Express Edition
Step by Step
Jackie Goldstein • ISBN 0-7356-2184-5

Teach yourself how to get database projects up and running
quickly with SQL Server Express
Edition—a free, easy-to-use
database product that is based
on SQL Server 2005 technology.
It's designed for building simple,
dynamic applications, with all
the rich functionality of the SQL
Server database engine and
using the same data access APIs,
such as Microsoft ADO.NET, SQL
Native Client, and T-SQL.
Whether you're new to database
programming or new to SQL Server, you'll learn how, when, and
why to use specific features of this simple but powerful database development environment. Each chapter puts you to work,
building your knowledge of core capabilities and guiding you
as you create actual components and working applications.

Microsoft SQL Server 2005 Programming
Step by Step
Fernando Guerrero • ISBN 0-7356-2207-8

SQL Server 2005 is Microsoft's
next-generation data management and analysis solution that
delivers enhanced scalability,
availability, and security features
to enterprise data and analytical
applications while making them
easier to create, deploy, and
manage. Now you can teach
yourself how to design, build, test,
deploy, and maintain SQL Server
databases—one step at a time.
Instead of merely focusing on
describing new features, this book shows new database
programmers and administrators how to use specific features
within typical business scenarios. Each chapter provides a highly
practical learning experience that demonstrates how to build
database solutions to solve common business problems.

Microsoft SQL Server 2005 Analysis Services
Step by Step
Hitachi Consulting Services • ISBN 0-7356-2199-3

One of the key features of SQL Server 2005 is SQL Server Analysis
Services—Microsoft's customizable analysis solution for business
data modeling and interpretation. Just compare SQL Server
Analysis Services to its competition to understand the great
value of its enhanced features. One of the keys to harnessing
the full functionality of SQL Server will be leveraging Analysis
Services for the powerful tool that it is—including creating a cube,
and deploying, customizing, and extending the basic calculations. This step-by-step tutorial discusses how to get started, how
to build scalable analytical applications, and how to use and ad-
minister advanced features. Interactivity (enhanced in SQL Server
2005), data translation, and security are also covered in detail.

Microsoft SQL Server 2005 Reporting Services
Step by Step
Hitachi Consulting Services • ISBN 0-7356-2250-7

SQL Server Reporting Services (SRS) is Microsoft's customizable
reporting solution for business data analysis. It is one of the key
value features of SQL Server 2005: functionality more advanced
and much less expensive than its competition. SRS is powerful,
so an understanding of how to architect a report, as well as how
to install and program SRS, is key to harnessing the full functionality of SQL Server. This procedural tutorial shows how to use the
Report Project Wizard, how to think about and access data, and
how to build queries. It also walks through the creation of charts
and visual layouts for maximum visual understanding of data
analysis. Interactivity (enhanced in SQL Server 2005) and security
are also covered in detail.

Programming Microsoft SQL Server 2005
Andrew J. Brust, Stephen Forte, and William H. Zack
ISBN 0-7356-1923-9

This thorough, hands-on reference for developers and database
administrators teaches the basics of programming custom applications with SQL Server 2005. You will learn the fundamentals
of creating database applications—including coverage of
T-SQL, Microsoft .NET Framework, and Microsoft ADO.NET. In
addition to practical guidance on database architecture and
design, application development, and reporting and data
analysis, this essential reference guide covers performance,
tuning, and availability of SQL Server 2005.

Inside Microsoft SQL Server 2005:
The Storage Engine
Kalen Delaney • ISBN 0-7356-2105-5

Inside Microsoft SQL Server 2005:
T-SQL Programming
Itzik Ben-Gan • ISBN 0-7356-2197-7

Inside Microsoft SQL Server 2005:
Query Processing and Optimization
Kalen Delaney • ISBN 0-7356-2196-9

Programming Microsoft ADO.NET 2.0 Core Reference
David Sceppa • ISBN 0-7356-2206-X

For more information about Microsoft Press® books and other learning products,
visit: **www.microsoft.com/mspress** *and* **www.microsoft.com/learning**

Microsoft® Press

System Requirements

We recommend that you use a computer that is not your primary workstation to do the lab exercises in this book because you will make changes to the operating system and application configuration.

Hardware Requirements

The following hardware is required to complete the lab exercises:

- Computer with a 600-MHz or faster processor (1 GHz recommended)
- 192 MB of RAM or more (512 MB recommended)
- 2 GB of available hard disk space
- DVD-ROM drive
- 1,024 x 768 or higher resolution display with 256 colors
- Keyboard and Microsoft mouse or compatible pointing device

Software Requirements

The following software is required to complete the practice exercises:

- One of the following operating systems:
    - Microsoft Windows 2000 with Service Pack 4
    - Windows XP with Service Pack 2
    - Windows XP Professional, x64 Editions (WOW)
    - Windows Server 2003 with Service Pack 1
    - Windows Server 2003, x64 Editions (WOW)
    - Windows Server 2003 R2
    - Windows Server 2003 R2, x64 Editions (WOW)
    - Windows Vista
- Visual Studio 2005 (A 90-day evaluation edition of Visual Studio 2005 Professional Edition is included on DVD with this book.)

NOTE Windows Vista and Visual Studio

If you are running Windows Vista, it is recommended that you download and install Visual Studio 2005 Service Pack 1 and Visual Studio 2005 Service Pack 1 Update for Windows Vista.

- Visual Studio 2005 Service Pack 1 can be downloaded from *http://www.microsoft.com /downloads/details.aspx?familyid=bb4a75ab-e2d4-4c96-b39d-37baf6b5b1dc&displaylang=en.*

This download is good for the Standard, Professional and Team Editions of Visual Studio 2005.

❑ Visual Studio 2005 Service Pack 1 Update for Windows Vista can be downloaded from *http://www.microsoft.com/downloads/details.aspx?familyid=fb6bb56a-10b7-4c05 -b81c-5863284503cf&displaylang=en*.

■ Microsoft SQL Server 2005 Express Edition running on your computer. (This can be installed as part of Visual Studio.)

■ The Enterprise Library application (January 2006 version) installed on your computer. Enterprise Library can be downloaded from *http://msdn.microsoft.com/library/?url= /library/en-us/dnpag2/html/EntLib2.asp*.

■ NMock installed on your computer. NMock is a free mock object library that can be downloaded from *www.nmock.org*.

■ The Northwind database installed and accessible. To install the Northwind database, follow the instructions found at *http://msdn2.microsoft.com/en-us/library/8b6y4c7s(VS.80) .aspx*.

■ Web Services Enhancements (WSE) 3.0 for Microsoft .NET installed on your computer. WSE 3.0 can be downloaded from *http://www.microsoft.com/downloads/details.aspx ?familyid =018A09FD-3A74-43C5-8EC1-8D789091255D&displaylang=en*

IMPORTANT   Visual Studio Team Suite

To complete the lab exercises for Chapter 10, Lesson 1 and Chapter 11, Lesson 2, you will need to have Microsoft Visual Studio 2005 Team Edition for Software Developers installed on your computer. This is available as part of Visual Studio 2005 Team Suite. You can download a free 180-day trial version of Visual Studio 2005 Team Suite from *http://www.microsoft.com/downloads /details.aspx?FamilyId=5677DDC4-5035-401F-95C3-CC6F46F6D8F7&displaylang=en*. You will need to uninstall Visual Studio 2005 Professional to install Visual Studio Team Suite on the same computer.

To complete the lab exercises for Chapter 10, Lesson 1 and Chapter 11, Lesson 2, you will need:

■ 256 MB of RAM or more

■ 3.3 GB available disk space to download Visual Studio Team Suite

■ 2 GB available disk space to install Visual Studio Team Suite

■ One of the following operating systems:

❑ Microsoft Windows 2000 with Service Pack 4

❑ Windows XP with Service Pack 2

❑ Windows Server 2003 with Service Pack 1

❑ Windows Vista

What do you think of this book? We want to hear from you!

Do you have a few minutes to participate in a brief online survey? Microsoft is interested in hearing your feedback about this publication so that we can continually improve our books and learning resources for you.

To participate in our survey, please visit:

www.microsoft.com/learning/booksurvey

And enter this book's ISBN, 0-7356-2338-4. As a thank-you to survey participants in the United States and Canada, each month we'll randomly select five respondents to win one of five $100 gift certificates from a leading online merchant.* At the conclusion of the survey, you can enter the drawing by providing your e-mail address, which will be used for prize notification *only*.

Thanks in advance for your input. Your opinion counts!

Sincerely,

Microsoft Learning

Learn More. Go Further.